HISTORIES OF
FRENCH SEXUALITY

HISTORIES OF

French Sexuality

FROM *the* ENLIGHTENMENT
to the PRESENT

EDITED BY

Nina Kushner & Andrew Israel Ross

UNIVERSITY OF NEBRASKA PRESS   *Lincoln*

Chapter 11, "Creating Lesbian Community: Sexuality
on the French Minitel in the 1980s," previously
appeared in a different form as "Lesbians Online:
Queer Identity and Community Formation on
the French Minitel," *Journal of the History of
Sexuality* 23, no. 3 (September 2014): 451–72.

The University of Nebraska Press is part of a land-
grant institution with campuses and programs on the
past, present, and future homelands of the Pawnee,
Ponca, Otoe-Missouria, Omaha, Dakota, Lakota, Kaw,
Cheyenne, and Arapaho Peoples, as well as those of the
relocated Ho-Chunk, Sac and Fox, and Iowa Peoples.

∞

Library of Congress Cataloging-in-Publication Data
Names: Kushner, Nina, editor. | Ross,
Andrew Israel, 1983–, editor.
Title: Histories of French Sexuality: from
the Enlightenment to the present / edited
by Nina Kushner, Andrew Israel Ross.
Description: Lincoln: University of Nebraska Press,
[2023] | Includes bibliographical references and index.
Identifiers: LCCN 2022043315
ISBN 9781496214010 (hardback)
ISBN 9781496235497 (paperback)
ISBN 9781496236258 (epub)
ISBN 9781496236265 (pdf)
Subjects: LCSH: Sex customs—France—History. |
Sex—France—History. | BISAC: HISTORY / Europe /
France | SOCIAL SCIENCE / Human Sexuality
(see also PSYCHOLOGY / Human Sexuality)
Classification: LCC HQ18.F8 F74 2023 |
DDC 306.70944—dc23/eng/20220921
LC record available at https://lccn.loc.gov/2022043315

Set and designed in Adobe Jenson Pro
by Mikala R. Kolander.

Dedicated to our families

and to the memory of Michael Sibalis (1949–2019)

CONTENTS

ILLUSTRATIONS

ACKNOWLEDGMENTS

It is always a great pleasure at the end of a project to thank those who helped it come to be. Our thanks, first and foremost, goes to our contributors, without whom there would be no volume. Beyond their willingness to take this journey with us, they readily gave their time and energy to read and comment on each other's drafts. The quality of their work made us think that such a project would be possible in the first place. We would also like to thank the editors at the University of Nebraska Press: Alisa Plant, who encouraged us to develop the project, and Matt Bokovoy, who shepherded it through the various stages of revision and publication. We owe a debt to the anonymous readers at the press, as well as to the production teams. We are enormously grateful to our friends and family for their company and support. Lastly, this volume is built on the scholarship of many historians, including Michael Sibalis. Michael accepted our invitation to write a chapter, but had to withdraw due to health concerns and then, sadly, passed away while we were working on this book. His research, along with that of other scholars, helped develop the field to the point where our intervention became possible. It is to him, and to our families, that we dedicate this work.

HISTORIES OF
FRENCH SEXUALITY

INTRODUCTION

ANDREW ISRAEL ROSS AND NINA KUSHNER

Sexuality has a history. Although this was once a controversial claim, it is by now clear that as both a subject and a category of analysis, sexuality is central to historical inquiry in all times and places. Even a cursory reflection of the field elucidates how sexuality has shaped relations among almost all human beings and has done so in ways that have changed over time. Sexuality has undergirded politics, for example, through dynastic reproduction, as well as through immigration, citizenship, and healthcare policies, not to mention the role of sex scandals in determining who has held power. Sexuality has been central to the development of religion, through moral strictures and the construction of symbolic meaning. Sexuality is an economic issue at a macro level when we consider the management of populations and at a micro one in the context of family economies. A study of sexuality informs our understanding of war, including policies meant to control military forces and the populations they fight and the places they occupy. Sexuality has been a major theme in various forms of cultural production, from ballet and opera to art and film to literature and poetry. Sexuality is also vital to understanding gender through the emergence of specific rules, hierarchies, constraints, and privileges. Given the importance of sexuality to political, social, military, and cultural histories, among others, it is clear that sexuality has moved beyond being a "useful category of historical analysis," in the words of Joan W. Scott.[1] Like gender, class, and race, sexuality is an essential category of historical analysis.

French historians were, paradoxically, both early and slow adopters of this idea. Defining texts in the field, not least of which was Michel Foucault's

History of Sexuality (1976, trans. 1978), emerged from France. Yet the history of sexuality has not been as integrated into French history—on either side of the Atlantic—as it has been into British and American history, for example. In France the field has struggled against cultural and political headwinds, while in the Anglophone world it has not received much attention from the institutions that structure the field, including leading journals.[2] In the past decade, however, this marginalization has begun to lessen. A number of well-established Anglophone historians have turned their attention to sexuality.[3] French journals have published special issues on sexuality while assessing its historiography.[4] Historians working in both French and English have published groundbreaking research on all facets of sexuality, and younger scholars working in both languages have been encouraged to pursue topics in the field.[5] Yet, overall, historians of France have been slow to reckon with the ways that sexuality informs and enhances our understanding of the French past.[6] The history of sexuality in France is thus at an inflection point.

Our goals in producing this volume, then, are twofold. The first is to showcase current work being produced on the French history of sexuality to demonstrate the vibrancy of the field to historians of France and other geographies. The historians featured in this volume explore a wide range of topics, from colonization to the construction of knowledge to the significance of social media. Many of them situate their work in the nexus of other subfields, like the history of medicine, politics, and religion. They thus demonstrate that there are multiple points of entry to the history of sexuality, as it overlaps and complements other forms of historical inquiry. They also show how the history of sexuality often leads us to consider previously overlooked types of sources and to revise how we read more traditional sources, like police archives. In doing so, the contributors demonstrate that French history contains important lessons for historians of other geographies as well.

The second goal is to make explicit what has usually remained implicit in French history: that attention to sexual matters can transform, reshape, and complicate existing historical narratives. In this volume alone, contributors consider the role of sex in promoting and restricting the autonomy of French colonial subjects, use sex to challenge narratives of a liberal Enlightenment, and enrich our understanding of how sex shaped urban geography in Paris and Bordeaux, among other examples. This work deepens our understanding not only of sex and sexuality, but also of French politics, social order, conflict, and culture. It shows that using sexuality as a category of analysis is essential to understanding French historical narratives both within and outside of the hexagon.

This approach is based on a recognition of just how diverse the history of sexuality is. Much to its detriment, the field has long been perceived narrowly, as being dominated by histories of sexual regulation and sexual minorities (especially female prostitutes and gay men).[7] It is not surprising that early histories of sexuality drew on readily available, though infrequently used, archival sources to document these stories. But the history of sexuality is an extremely broad field, including topics as wide-ranging as sexual identity, behavior, and desire; reproduction, marriage, divorce, and the family; race and interracial relations; gender identity; violence; and scandal, to name just some of the more common subjects of scholarly exploration. The field is so capacious that defining it has proved complicated.[8]

For our purposes, we define the history of sexuality through three expansive and interlocking categories of activity in the past. We start with the supposition that the history of sexuality is the history of how bodies become sexed. We include here the processes by which physical bodies became gendered, sexual difference was defined, and bodies were constructed as sexually desiring entities. We also include how these processes intersected with efforts to understand, control, and otherwise deploy those bodies. Next, we argue that the history of sexuality can be investigated through the history of sexual practices and experiences (including emotion), how they relate to the formation and experience of sexual subjectivities and identities, and how these experiences and feelings sometimes serve as the basis of community formation. Last, the history of sexuality is the history of sexual narratives, representations, and discourses.[9] We are particularly interested in the ways in which sexual meanings—how sexual acts, identities, and communities are understood by both individuals and wider societies—are produced, enacted, and lived at different moments. Ultimately, we argue that a history of sexuality is a history of the relationships among all these categories as they change over time.

From *Histoire des mentalités* to Histories of Sexuality

The history of sexuality developed differently in the Anglophone and Francophone spheres. One might understand the competing trajectories of French histories of sexuality in French and English, and how this volume fits within them, in terms of Eve Kosofsky Sedgwick's elaboration of minoritizing and universalizing views of sexuality. Minoritizing views emphasize the existence of a distinct group of people, marked as different by virtue of their deviance from the majority. Universalizing views emphasize the sheer breadth and diversity of sexual identities, desires, and feelings, and that all forms of sexual experience can be informed by others.[10] Both of these understandings, as Sedgwick points out, can be held at the same time. To take the most obvious example, just as historians have traced the emergence of homosexuality as a distinct identity and homosexuals as comprising a distinct subculture, so too have they shown the ways that homosexual practices and desires shape views of the family, of demography, and of health more generally.[11] One might understand ongoing differences between Francophone and Anglophone approaches to the history of sexuality as competing lenses oscillating between minoritizing and universalizing views of the field. More specifically, we can trace an initial French emphasis on universalizing histories and an Anglophone emphasis on minoritizing histories that are now, in a sense, in the process of reversing. This volume seeks, in part, to bridge this shifting divide.

French historians have long been interested in the history of sexuality, even if they did not always name it as such. Scholars produced work on demography and family life, especially, before many spoke of the history of sexuality.[12] During the 1970s and 1980s, French scholars produced important works—many on broad topics in the medieval and early modern world—making clear the viability of sexuality as a serious topic of study. The question of population patterns, contraception, and sexual practices within marriage became important to studies of demographic change generally and of the demographic transition in France specifically.[13] Under the rubric of *histoire des mentalités (history of mentalities)*, French scholars explored how sexual norms shaped everyday life.[14]

In the United Kingdom and North America, meanwhile, the history of sexuality was emerging as a self-aware field. The gay rights movement turned the attention of activist-scholars to the archives to excavate a gay past. In doing so, they built on the work of women's historians who, inspired by the women's movement, researched heterosexual practices, often as they related to reproduction, marriage, family, and birth.[15] These scholars explored the ways in which the heterosexual matrix could function as a site of female oppression in order to understand the experience of women's lives in the past. Meanwhile feminist and what we would now call queer theorists worked to break down sexual categories to develop epistemologies central to a cultural approach to the history of sexuality.[16] As Laura Lee Downs argues, while Francophone historians combined an analysis of social structures and cultural systems or mentalities, Anglophone historians often debated the extent to which one could integrate the two in the first place. These different emphases frequently led Anglophone historians to pay greater attention to specific marginalized groups at the expense of the larger structures emphasized by their Francophone colleagues.[17]

As these endeavors continued apace, the publication of Michel Foucault's first volume of *The History of Sexuality* reshaped how historians addressed the relationship between social structures, the constitution of sexual identities, and sexual experiences, among other topics. Foucault argued that sexuality is constituted historically as an effect of "power" exercised by various institutions, practices, and discourses. In making this claim, Foucault consolidated a new approach, one that emphasized the social construction of sexual identities. His work not only encouraged historians to pay attention to sexual identities once considered marginal (particularly homosexuality), but also laid the groundwork for the historicization of sexuality itself.[18] Historians of sexuality in the Anglophone world, especially, began to incorporate Foucault into their work in the 1980s and 1990s, but they often did so narrowly. They followed Foucault's apparent emphasis on sexual minorities, regulation, and classification, rather than situating sexuality in the broader streams of history, as Foucault himself strove to do and as many in the French-speaking world were already doing, even if the latter did not take on an explicitly Foucauldian approach or claim to be participating in the history of sexuality.[19]

Over time, the influence of Foucault's work became impossible to ignore, and it reshaped the field in ways that had been foreshadowed by developments in histories of women and gender. The emergence of women's history and gender history as fully realized fields, especially in the Anglophone world, led historians to think about women's and then men's sexual bodies in the context of their daily lives and, later, as essential components in the construction of gender; gender included elements of sexuality but was separate from it. Indeed, in the Anglophone world, the growth of gender history out of women's history both informed and paralleled the ways that historians of sexuality were increasingly attuned to and debated the relationships between histories of specific groups of people and the relationship between sexuality and other historical phenomena.[20] Also in this period queer theorists such as Gayle Rubin and Eve Kosofsky Sedgwick began insisting that sexuality required its own set of methodological and theoretical apparatuses.[21] Sexuality studies became a distinct field in the United Kingdom and North America, one that was grounded in but also distinct from women's and gender studies.

The 1980s and 1990s saw the publication of some groundbreaking surveys of the history of sexuality, especially on the United Kingdom and United States, but also on France.[22] By 1990 enough work existed in English (mainly on the United States and the United Kingdom) to launch a journal, the *Journal of the History of Sexuality*. The articles in the first volume were largely on prostitution and homosexuality, but the reviews covered books on menstruation, attitudes toward child rearing, the role of Eve in the Bible, sexology, the politics of free-love radicals, sexuality in women's lives in the nineteenth century, cross-dressing, and cannon law of the medieval church, thereby making the argument that these books, some of which did not have "sexuality" in their titles, were histories of sexuality. At this moment the definition of the field was deliberately stretched. Around the same time, historians of sexuality were able to develop institutional footholds in American and British women's and gender studies programs, some of which had existed for over a decade. Some elite universities began to offer classes on the history of sexuality while housing interdisciplinary gay and lesbian or sexuality studies programs.[23] Despite the continuing influence of French historians and theorists like Alain Corbin and Michel Foucault, the most influential work during this period remained focused on the United Kingdom and the United States.[24]

Scholars in France, however, did produce a large number of works in the field during the 1990s and 2000s. At that time the concept of gender started to influence some French scholars, and major political and public debates erupted on topics ranging from gay rights to prostitution. In the wake of these discussions, new work on the history of homosexuality, prostitution, youth sexuality, and sexual knowledge flourished in France.[25] But French scholars of sexuality still do not have the kinds of institutional support enjoyed by their peers in the United Kingdom and North America. This difficulty may, in part, be attributed to the historiography's turn to a more minoritizing point of view than was previously the case in France, leaving the field open to accusations that it is too particularist or identity-based.[26] Indeed, just as French scholars of race recently found themselves attacked by the president of the republic for importing what he deemed to be American theoretical approaches that threaten the universalizing promise of the republic, French scholars using queer theory have been similarly criticized—despite the fact that much of it came from France in the first place.[27]

Anglophone historians of sexuality in France, entrenched in both traditions, are in an interesting position. Some have been highly influential in the development of the larger field of the history of sexuality.[28] And their work, like that of their counterparts in British and American history, has shifted its focus from sexual minorities and regulation to a wide range of topics, some of which are not obviously related to sexuality, yielding the sorts of rich analyses common in other historiographic traditions. At the same time, this body of work has demonstrated the broader significance of the more traditional topics of homosexuality and prostitution.[29] These historians have drawn on the best of the Anglophone and Francophone traditions, seeking to show not simply the importance of marginalized lives but also the ways in which sexuality is inscribed in areas of traditional historical interest, such as politics, urbanization, and social life.

Nevertheless, the field of the history of sexuality of France is still struggling to break through. Many historians of France—in both the Anglophone and Francophone worlds—remain skeptical of its relevance. In our experience, attendance at conference panels on sexuality is low. English-language French history journals have published almost no assessments of the field, while French-language journals have only shown slightly more interest. French historians of sexuality continue to find it difficult to locate institutional support in France. Meanwhile, with a few notable exceptions, historians of sexuality across the board have paid less attention to work produced by French historians of sexuality than they have to scholarship published by historians of the United States, the United Kingdom, and even Germany. Unlike foundational work on gender by historians of France, the history of French sexuality remains peripheral to larger conversations. This volume, by bridging the divide between the universalizing and minoritizing approaches that have, at different moments, shaped French and Anglophone approaches to the field, seeks to make clear the importance of sexuality to French history and of French history to the history of sexuality.

Sexing the History of France

This volume is organized chronologically. Each author was tasked with taking up a question or theme of major significance within their period of expertise and showing how attention to sexuality changes what we thought we knew about that period. Read back to back, these chapters do not to produce a singular history of sexuality in France, nor are they meant to provide a new narrative of French history to replace the older ones.[30] Their collective lens is at once too wide and too narrow for that. Unfortunately, as in any collection, some topics and periods are not addressed here. These lacunae are in part a function of the fact that the research is still progressing, and some topics, subfields, and periods have not yet been systematically explored by historians of sexuality.[31] We are not arguing that some topics in the history of sexuality are more significant to the history of France than others. Instead, we argue that historians can take any number of topics in the history of sexuality and show how they add nuance to, enhance, or challenge larger narratives in the history of France. The chapters in this volume thus represent a range of topics and approaches central to the history of sexuality that intersect with other areas of inquiry within French history. The volume consequently supports the argument that the historical study of sexuality in France is central to the field of French history as a whole. This collection is only one part of ongoing work in the field.

As important as the range of topics are the range of methodologies the volume deploys, in particular novel approaches to sources old and new alike. In some instances—such as Lisa Jane Graham's reading of Enlightenment documents or Cathy McClive's reading of judicial *mémoires (legal briefs*), for example—attention to sexuality illustrates that even well-mined sources can still yield new and important interpretations. In others—such as Andrew Israel Ross's and Jennifer Anne Boittin's use of police and colonial documents—studying the history of sexuality requires new approaches that rethink the core logic underpinning state archives: the binaries between police and policed and between agency and resistance. Other contributors' scholarship relies on new kinds of sources—for instance, Tamara Chaplin's use of ephemeral Mintel message boards.

The chapters in this volume address a number of key topics in French history. The first is the Enlightenment. Both Jennifer J. Davis and Lisa Jane Graham see contests between claims of individual sexual liberty and of state control as fundamental to our understanding of the Enlightenment. For Davis, the tension was at the heart of imperial dictates governing interracial sexuality and of colonial responses to those dictates, whereas for Graham, the tension was at the center of considerations of the value of pleasure. In exploring this tension, Davis and Graham challenge arguments about the Enlightenment as a liberalizing force and show how some of the forms of policing we often associate with the nineteenth and twentieth centuries were born in the eighteenth.

A second major theme is the relationship of law to society. In her chapter Nina Kushner examines the ways in which the law treated women thought to have had sex outside of marriage as a legal category. Focusing mainly on adultery cases, Kushner argues that there was a recursive relationship between the writings of legal scholars and the construction of reputation, as represented in the stories that plaintiffs and defendants told to policing and judicial bodies. The result was the construction of a broad identity category of "unchaste woman," which was informed by and found its reflection in other discourses and which shaped one component of women's legal existence in the Old Regime. Like Kushner's chapter, Cathy McClive's is situated at the nexus of the law, legal strategy, and public engagement. For McClive the question of whether the novitiate Marie-Catherine Cadière had manifested stigmata was tied up with her sexual relationship with her confessor, a relationship prohibited by both canon and criminal law. As McClive shows, lawyers for both sides relied on popular understandings of menstruation and procreation to make their clients' cases. McClive thus demonstrates the depth of public knowledge about sexual processes and how the law relied on that knowledge for its own legitimacy. Both McClive and Kushner show how the sexual and sexualized female body was at the center of these processes of legal interpretation and manipulation.

Our third topic concerns urbanization during the nineteenth century. Andrew Israel Ross takes up the consequences of Haussmannization: when the city of Paris was radically redeveloped to ensure the proper functioning of a well-ordered consumer society. Part of this process entailed the enhancement of police power over those who used the streets, including men who sought sex with other men in public. Ross shows how the interactions between the police, men seeking sex with each other, and spectators led to the development of a queer space that implicated anyone who entered, including the police themselves. This approach emphasizes the blurriness of social categories and allows us to see nineteenth-century Paris not as the site of discrete subcultures or of an all-powerful and repressive police but rather as a dynamic and integrated social space. Michelle K. Rhoades, meanwhile, takes up the urban history of the port city of Bordeaux. Whereas much urban history of the nineteenth century has emphasized the desire of municipal authorities to sweep away evidence of illicit behavior, a process that entailed regulating female prostitution, Rhoades uses the lens of sexuality to invert the story. She explores how shopkeepers, landlords, musicians, and others living in the red-light district of Bordeaux's Mériadeck *quartier* (neighborhood) who were dependent on profits that the sex trade brought to the area successfully pushed back against municipal efforts to police brothels in the early twentieth century. Ultimately, she argues, urban change was a response to sex work, not the other way around.

The relationship between gender and citizenship in the *fin-de-siècle* is our fourth and largest topic. Historians of feminism continue to debate whether French republicanism enabled or prevented the enjoyment of greater equality and political rights by women.[32] Expanding the framework to more explicitly include sexuality—whether as identity, practice, or desire—shows that this binary does not adequately capture women's experiences of negotiating the constraints to which they were subject in the effort to gain greater political and social freedom during the Third Republic. In Jessie Hewitt's chapter prevailing gender norms allowed men to have sex outside of marriage, yet their honor and hence their masculinity required that both their sexual activities and, especially, any resulting sexually transmitted infections be kept secret from their wives or fiancées, who were considered too innocent and delicate to bear such news. But another discourse emerged at the same time that posited that the nation itself required the revelation of any such medical secrets to ensure healthy progeny and hence a healthy, robust population. Women's sexuality thus became a key tool with which doctors debated the relative needs of the individual versus those of the nation.

Jennifer Anne Boittin also focuses on the effort to restrict sexual rights, though in a different context. In her chapter she argues that, in a slightly later period than is the subject of Hewitt's chapter, colonial practice was predicated partly on restricting the sexual rights—sexual practice and sexual reputation—of colonists, particularly white women. Yet, in chronicling the life of one woman, named Gabrielle, Boittin challenges narratives of colonial power's ability to realize one of its central missions. A member of the Parisian bourgeoisie, Gabrielle left her family in France to go to Senegal to marry a man of her choosing, worked in his brothel, and left her fiancé to live with another man also of her choosing (whom she eventually married). Along the way, Gabrielle shrugged off the efforts of her family and the state to repatriate her. In Boittin's telling Gabrielle's desire for sexual autonomy drove her efforts to control her life.

Finally, for Sarah Horowitz, the relationship between gender and citizenship concerned a conflict between the government and its citizens that was predicated on a contest within each person for sexual self-mastery. Telling the story of the Steinheil Affair, a 1908 scandal that found an infamous courtesan accused of the murder of her husband, Horowitz shows the ways that discussions of the scandal placed elite sexual behavior in a new light. The self-control associated with the right of the bourgeoisie to rule was called into question, as the press revealed how the elite were, in fact, opting for sexual liberty. Ironically, Horowitz argues, the revelation of this sexual affair democratized the republic by showing its citizens what was going on behind the curtain.

Moving further into the twentieth century, our final topic is consumer culture and mass media. The argument that mass media was nothing more than a vehicle for social control has been amply challenged in other fields, but an emphasis on sexuality reveals new ways in which it was deployed in the service of marginalized groups and served as a form of resistance to dominant norms. The young women writing to magazines for advice in the 1950s—the subject of Sarah Fishman's chapter—were engaged in a collective effort to refine what constituted licit sexual behavior before marriage. Fishman's focus on sex helps us to understand how magazines became a public discursive space for working out the meaning of modernization for young women, a full decade before the Sexual Revolution. Tamara Chaplin, in her chapter, shows how a group of lesbian activists seized on the Minitel (an internet prototype) in the 1980s to develop a community but how ultimately their politics rendered their business model unsustainable. Chaplin's chapter is an exploration of the formation of a sexual community, a traditional topic in the history of sexuality. But it is also a model of how to study the relationship of technology to community formation, regardless of what shared traits united the members of any particular group. Chaplin shows how new media could be deployed in unexpected ways.

Building on these themes, we offer one final thought. Histories of sexuality in France have something to offer to the field of the history of sexuality more broadly. Historians of France have long been drawn to the country because France has a great deal to tell us about the world beyond the hexagon. Historians have shown repeatedly that France witnessed and participated in the formation of what are now considered characteristically modern forms of politics, urban life, the family, work, citizenship, gender, and empire. The relevance of France to these themes has often made the country an important point of reference for historians working on other geographic locations. The same conditions make the study of sexuality in France essential to our understanding of the key categories that define social relationships, political formations, and cultural production in the past and today, in France, its empire, and elsewhere.

Notes

1. Joan W. Scott, "Gender: A Useful Category of Historical Analysis," *American Historical Review* 91, no. 5 (December 1986): 1053–75. Although many historians have borrowed Scott's formula to make the explicit case for sexuality as a category of historical analysis, the larger argument can be dated back at least to

Foucault's *History of Sexuality*. Michel Foucault, *L'histoire de la sexualité*, tome 1, *La volonté de savoir* (Paris: Gallimard, 1976); Michel Foucault, *The History of Sexuality*, vol. 1, *An Introduction*, trans. Robert Hurley (New York: Pantheon, 1978).

2. Publication rates for articles on the history of sexuality have ranged from 2 to 5 percent annually of the total articles published from 2000 to 2019 in *French Historical Studies* and *French History*. This includes a single review essay: Lenard R. Berlanstein, "The French in Love and Lust," *French Historical Studies* 27, no. 2 (Spring 2004): 465–79. Neither journal has yet devoted a special issue to the history of sexuality.

3. See, for example, Julian Jackson, *Living in Arcadia: Homosexuality, Politics, and Morality in France from the Liberation to AIDS* (Chicago: University of Chicago Press, 2009); Mary Louise Roberts, *What Soldiers Do: Sex and the American GI in World War II France* (Chicago: University of Chicago Press, 2013); Todd Shepard, *Sex, France, and Arab Men, 1962–1979* (Chicago: University of Chicago Press, 2017); and Julie Hardwick, *Sex in an Old Regime City: Young Workers and Intimacy in France, 1660–1789* (New York: Oxford University Press, 2020). Also see Laura Doan, *Disturbing Practices: History, Sexuality, and Women's Experience of Modern War* (Chicago: University of Chicago Press, 2013), 12.

4. Assessments of the field in French include Sylvie Chaperon, "L'histoire contemporaine des sexualités en France," *Vingtième siècle. Revue d'histoire*, no. 75 (2002): 47–59; Anne-Claire Rebreyend, "Comment écrire l'histoire des sexualités au XXe siècle? Bilan historiographique comparé français/anglo-américain," *Clio. Femmes, Genre, Histoire* 22 (2005): 185–209; Régis Revenin, "Les études et recherches lesbiennes et gays en France (1970–2006)," *Genre & Histoire* no. 1 (2007), https://journals.openedition.org/genrehistoire/219. Special issues include, for example, Sylvie Chaperon and Agnès Fine, eds., "Utopies sexuelles," *Clio. Femmes, Genre, Histoire* 22 (2005); and Lola Gonzalez-Quijano and Agathe Roby, eds., "Prostitutions urbaines du XIVe au XXIe siècles," *Histoire urbaine* 49, no. 2 (2017): 5–135.

5. See, for example, Romain Jaouen, *L'inspecteur et "l'inverti": La police face aux sexualités masculines à Paris, 1919–1940* (Rennes, France: Presses universitaires de Rennes, 2018); Caroline Séquin, "Prostitution and the Policing of Race in the French Atlantic, 1848–1947" (PhD diss., University of Chicago, 2019); Hannah Clare Frydman, "Classified Commerce: Gender, Labor, and Print Capitalism in Paris, 1881–1940" (PhD diss., Rutgers University, 2020).

6. We found only four reviews on the state of the field in French history (both Francophone and Anglophone). In addition to those in French cited above, see Berlanstein, "The French in Love and Lust." Compare this to the dozens

of reviews, including books on historiography, on the state of the field in the United Kingdom, the United States, and Germany. See, for example, Edward R. Dickinson and Richard F. Wetzell, "The Historiography of Sexuality in Modern Germany," *German History* 23, no. 3 (July 2005): 291–305; Brian Lewis, *British Queer History: New Approaches and Perspectives* (Manchester, UK: Manchester University Press, 2013); Jeffrey Weeks, *What Is Sexual History?* (Cambridge: Polity, 2016); and Regina Kunzel, "The Power of Queer History," *American Historical Review* 123, no. 5 (December 2018): 1560–82.

7. This perception has been a barrier in attracting the attention of other historians. Doan, *Disturbing Practices*, 13–14.

8. An important recent attempt, by a founder of the field, is Weeks, *What Is Sexual History?*

9. This division is fairly typical of attempts to categorize the field. See, for example, Anna Clark, *Desire: A History of European Sexuality*, 2nd ed. (Abingdon, UK: Routledge, 2019), 4–8.

10. Eve Kosofsky Sedgwick, *Epistemology of the Closet* (Berkeley: University of California Press, 1990), 83–90.

11. For a recent assessment of the ways that queer historians have integrated an understanding of queer life with other historical themes, see esp. Kunzel, "The Power of Queer History."

12. See, for example, the work by Étienne Gautier and Louis Henry on France in the 1950s and 1960s: Gautier and Henry, *La population de Crulai, paroisse normande* (Paris: Presses universitaires de France, 1958). For an overview of the impact of this work, see Pierre Goubert, "Historical Demography and the Reinterpretation of Early Modern French History: A Research Review," *Journal of Interdisciplinary History* 1, no. 1 (October 1970): 37–48.

13. See, for example, Jacques Dupâquier, *La population française aux XVIIe et XVIIIe siècles* (Paris: Presses universitaries de France, 1979); and Jean-Louis Flandrin, *Familles: Parenté, maison, sexualité dans l'ancienne société* (Paris: Hachette, 1976.)

14. See, for example, foundational work such as Georges Duby, *Le chevalier, la femme et le prêtre: Le mariage dans la France féodale* (Paris: Hachette, 1981); Jean-Louis Flandrin, *Les amours paysannes: Amour et sexualité dans les campagnes de l'ancienne France (XVIe–XIXe siècle)* (Paris: Gallimard, 1975); Jean-Louis Flandrin, *Familles*; and Alain Corbin, *Les filles de noce: Misère sexuelle et prostitution au XIXe siècle* (Paris: Aubier Montaigne, 1978). Corbin's study of prostitution in the nineteenth century has been widely read and remains influential outside the field of French history. For a sample of the range of topics considered by well-established historians in this period, see Philippe Ariès and André Béjin, eds., *Sexualités occidentales* (Paris: Seuil, 1984).

15. The most important of the early historical work emerging from this activist milieu remains Jonathan Katz, ed., *Gay American History: Lesbians and Gay Men in the U.S.A.* (New York: Thomas Y. Crowell, 1976). For an example of women's history along these lines, see esp. Olwen Hufton, "Women and the Family Economy in Eighteenth-Century France," *French Historical Studies* 9, no. 1 (1975): 1–22.

16. Gayle Rubin lays out the need for a distinct paradigm for theorizing sexuality in Gayle Rubin, "Thinking Sex: Notes for a Radical Theory of the Politics of Sexuality," in *Pleasure and Danger: Exploring Female Sexuality*, ed. Carole S. Vance (Boston: Routledge, 1984), 267–319. Robert A. Padgug called for historicizing sexuality in "Sexual Matters: On Conceptualizing Sexuality in History," *Radical History Review* 1979, no. 20 (Spring/Summer 1979): 3–23. John D'Emilio, another founder of the field, describes some of this history in "The History of Sexuality: An Assessment of State of the Field," *History and Theory* 58, no. 1 (2019): 126–34.

17. Laura Lee Downs, *Writing Gender History*, 2nd ed. (London: Bloomsbury, 2010), 77–78. For an example of these two different approaches to the same topic, see, for instance, Corbin, *Les filles de noce*; and Jill Harsin, *Policing Prostitution in Nineteenth-Century Paris* (Princeton NJ: Princeton University Press, 1985). Of course, there are always exceptions to these trends. See, for instance, the work of Michel Rey on eighteenth-century sodomitical subcultures in Paris. Michel Rey, "Police et sodomie à Paris au XVIIIe siècle: Du péché au désordre," *Revue d'histoire moderne et contemporaine* 29, no. 1 (1982): 113–24.

18. Foucault, *L'histoire de la sexualité*.

19. For a critique of these approaches, see David M. Halperin, *How to Do the History of Homosexuality* (Chicago: University of Chicago Press, 2002), chap. 3.

20. This is also the origin point of the essentialist vs. constructionist debates that would reach their height in the 1990s. See, for example, Edward Stein, *Forms of Desire: Sexual Orientation and the Social Constructionist Controversy* (New York: Routledge, 1992).

21. Rubin, "Thinking Sex"; and Sedgwick, *Epistemology of the Closet*, 27–35.

22. For the United Kingdom, see Jeffrey Weeks, *Sex, Politics and Society: The Regulation of Sexuality since 1800* (London: Longman, 1981); for the United States, see John D'Emilio and Estelle B. Freedman, *Intimate Matters: A History of Sexuality in America* (New York: Harper & Row, 1988); for France, see Jean-Louis Flandrin, *Le sexe et l'Occident: Évolution des attitudes et des comportements* (Paris: du Seuil, 1981). Much of the methodological debate concerned the nature and historicism of homosexuality. See, for example, Stein, *Forms of Desire*; and David M. Halperin, John J. Winkler, and Froma I. Zeitlin, eds., *Before Sexuality:*

The Construction of Erotic Experience in the Ancient Greek World (Princeton NJ: Princeton University Press, 1990).

23. The City University of New York launched the first program in the United States in 1986. The City College of San Francisco followed a few years later with the establishment of its Gay and Lesbian Studies Department. The University of Sussex in the United Kingdom launched a master's degree program in queer studies (Sexual Dissidence) in 1991.

24. During its first decade of publication (comprising eight volumes), the *Journal of the History of Sexuality* only published 5 articles that explicitly dealt with France out of a total of 140. This does not count articles that may have addressed France to some extent, which is especially plausible for those dealing with medieval and early modern Europe.

25. Just a few representative examples from the past decade: Sylvie Chaperon, *Les origines de la sexologie: 1850–1900* (Paris: Audibert, 2007); Alain Corbin, *L'harmonie des plaisirs: Les manières de jouir du siècle des Lumières à l'avènement de la sexologie* (Paris: Perrin, 2007); Benoît Garnot, *On n'est point pendu pour être amoureux: La liberté amoureuse au XVIIIe siècle* (Paris: Belin, 2008); Véronique Blanchard, Régis Revenin, and Jean-Jacques Yvorel, eds., *Les jeunes et la sexualité: Initiations, interdits, identités (XIXe–XXIe siècle)* (Paris: Autrement, 2010); Anne-Claire Rebreyend, *Dire et faire l'amour: Écrits intimes et confidences de 1910 à 2010* (Paris: Textuel, 2011); Massimo Prearo, *Le moment politique de l'homosexualité: Mouvements, identités et communautés en France* (Lyon, France: Presses universitaires de Lyon, 2014); Régis Revenin, *Une histoire des garçons et des filles: Amour, genre, sexualité dans la France d'après-guerre* (Paris: Vendémiaire, 2015); Clyde Plumauzille, *Prostitution et révolution: Les femmes publiques dans la cité républicaine, 1789–1804* (Ceyzérieu, France: Champ Vallon, 2016); Jaouen, *L'Inspecteur et "l'inverti."*

26. Scott Gunther, *The Elastic Closet: A History of Homosexuality in France, 1942–Present* (New York: Palgrave Macmillan, 2009), 84–85. On this period of gay politics in France, see also Frédéric Martel, *Le rose et le noir: Les homosexuels en France depuis 1968*, rev. ed. (Paris: du Seuil, 2008); and Jackson, *Living in Arcadia.*

27. One of the first lesbian and gay studies conferences to be held in France—organized by queer theorist and Foucault biographer Didier Eribon in 1997 at the Centre Georges Pompidou and featuring several Anglophone participants, including the historians David Halperin and George Chauncey, as well as the legendary French sociologist Pierre Bourdieu—erupted into controversy over precisely this issue. On the relationship between French anxiety over

communitarianism and sexuality specifically, see Bruno Perreau, *Queer Theory: The French Response* (Stanford CA: Stanford University Press, 2016).

28. See, for example, the work of Lynn Hunt, Robert A. Nye, and Judith Surkis. In particular: Lynn Hunt, ed., *Eroticism and the Body Politic* (Baltimore: Johns Hopkins University Press, 1991); Lynn Hunt, ed., *The Invention of Pornography: Obscenity and the Origins of Modernity, 1500–1800* (New York: Zone, 1993); Robert A. Nye, ed., *Sexuality* (Oxford: Oxford University Press, 1999); Judith Surkis, *Sexing the Citizen: Morality and Masculinity in France, 1870–1920* (Ithaca NY: Cornell University Press, 2006).

29. For some recent examples in French history, see Surkis, *Sexing the Citizen*; Katherine Crawford, *The Sexual Culture of the French Renaissance* (New York: Cambridge University Press, 2010); Roberts, *What Soldiers Do*; Cathy McClive, *Menstruation and Procreation in Early Modern France* (Farnham, UK: Ashgate, 2015); Valerie Traub, *Thinking Sex with the Early Moderns* (Philadelphia: University of Pennsylvania Press, 2016); and Shepard, *Sex, France, and Arab Men*. On newer approaches to the study of prostitution and homosexuality, see Jackson, *Living in Arcadia*; Nina Kushner, *Erotic Exchanges: The World of Elite Prostitution in Eighteenth-Century Paris* (Ithaca NY: Cornell University Press, 2013); Andrew Israel Ross, *Public City / Public Sex: Homosexuality, Prostitution, and Urban Culture in Nineteenth-Century Paris* (Philadelphia: Temple University Press, 2019).

30. For an effort to create such a narrative, see Sylvie Steinberg, ed., *Une histoire des sexualités* (Paris: Presses universitaires de France, 2018).

31. These include, but are not limited to, youth sexuality in the Old Regime, the politics and sexuality of the early nineteenth century, sexology, feminism, translives, pornography, warfare, friendship, abortion, and contraception. See, for example, Roberts, *What Soldiers Do*; Carolyn J. Dean, *The Frail Social Body: Pornography, Homosexuality, and Other Fantasies in Interwar France* (Berkeley CA: University of California Press, 2000); Jean DeJean, *The Reinvention of Obscenity: Sex, Lies, and Tabloids in Early Modern France* (Chicago: University of Chicago Press, 2002); Maxime Foerster, *Histoire des transsexuels en France* (Béziers, France: H&O, 2006); Chaperon, *Les origines de la sexologie*; Brian Joseph Martin, *Napoleonic Friendship: Military Fraternity, Intimacy, and Sexuality in Nineteenth-Century France* (Durham NH: University of New Hampshire Press, 2011); Andrew J. Counter, *The Amorous Restoration: Love, Sex, and Politics in Early Nineteenth-Century France* (Oxford: Oxford University Press, 2016); Judith G. Coffin, *Sex, Love, and Letters: Writing Simone de Beauvoir* (Ithaca NY: Cornell University Press, 2020); Rachel Mesch, *Before Trans: Three Gender Stories from Nineteenth-Century France* (Stanford CA: Stanford University Press, 2020); Françoise Vergès,

The Wombs of Women: Race, Capital and Feminism, trans. Kaiama L. Glover (Durham NC: Duke University Press, 2020); and Hardwick, *Sex in an Old Regime City*.

32. See, for instance, Karen Offen, *Debating the Woman Question in the French Third Republic, 1870–1920* (Cambridge: Cambridge University Press, 2018).

I

COLONIAL LIBERTIES

Sex, Race, and the Law in the
French Atlantic, 1603–1791

JENNIFER J. DAVIS

In 1603 Samuel Champlain assured leaders of the Ottawa and Huron-Wyandot nations inhabiting the Saint Lawrence River valley that French settlers in North America sought long-term communities and peace. He envisioned a future in which French "young men will marry your daughters and we shall be one people."[1] Cross-cultural sex anchored colonial policy in the Americas, and the ideal of forging "one people" animated both royal directives and treaties negotiated between European settlers and Indigenous residents.[2] Make no mistake, Champlain expected that this new people would speak French, worship on Sundays, and submit to the authority of their European fathers. Intimate relations between French settlers and Indigenous Catholic converts were intended to secure French territorial ambitions and cultivate Christianity across the North American continent.[3] Meanwhile, in the French Caribbean, colonial authorities anticipated that rape, sexual assault, and coerced relationships would occur between free European men and enslaved African women. They wrote laws to regulate such unions and determine the legal status of any resulting children.[4] In both spheres authorities determined that French global ambitions depended upon sexual relations to facilitate the exchange of goods, guarantee future generations of workers, and establish durable communities organized by reliable family bonds. In this manner, French men's sexual domination of American and African women constituted a state-sanctioned "colonial liberty" throughout the seventeenth and eighteenth centuries.[5]

And so, tens of thousands of people took up residence in territories around the world to hunt, plant, and mine wealth to the benefit of France.[6]

They built households. They raised children in the woods of Canada, the swamps of Louisiana, the hills of Caribbean islands, and the bustling ports of West Africa and eastern India. In the fractious realities of multilingual unions, caught between competing customs and fraying alliances, French settlers and colonial officials soon began to recognize the limitations of their own assumptions regarding sex, gender, families, and social order. After a surge of confidence that through patriarchy, the French language, and the Catholic faith France would change the world, by the eighteenth century most administrators yielded to the pragmatic assessment that colonial subjects would also change France. The harvest of empire arrived daily in French ports in the form of goods but also in new practices, ideas, networks, and people.[7] Resulting anxieties spurred efforts to limit this founding "colonial liberty" by prohibiting sex across emergent racial lines. I concur with Ann Laura Stoler, who argues that "Europe's eighteenth-century discourses on sexuality can—indeed must—be traced along a more *circuitous imperial* route" in order to recover key sites, ideals and practices that shaped this history.[8]

The historian Saliha Belmessous contends that "racial prejudice in colonial Canada emerged only after an assimilationist approach had been tried for almost a century and had failed."[9] But how are we to measure failure? Champlain's vision of "one people" resulting from unions between French and Indigenous people had, in fact, borne fruit, resulting in generations of individuals raised with the linguistic and cultural skills to mediate between the colonial officials in Quebec, Kaskaskia, Mobile, or New Orleans and the leaders of neighboring Indigenous nations.[10] Catholic missions dotted the river valleys of the Saint Lawrence, the Ohio, the Illinois, and the Mississippi. By several metrics, the French had not been failing at assimilation when they abandoned a century of policies predicated on cross-cultural sex.[11] In Africa and in the French Caribbean islands, the children of European men and African women constituted a substantial part of the ruling elite.[12] They had some advantages over European migrants: disease resistance, multiple language skills, and local family support, to name just a few. The problem—as royal and colonial administrators understood it—was not that assimilation had failed but that it had succeeded too well. French men's descendants belonged to multicultural communities across the Americas and the Caribbean, and their families also belonged to France. Settlers' demands for economic autonomy threatened to disrupt colonial dependency on France.[13] In this environment French colonial race laws of the 1710s appear to have been designed to rupture the local networks and family alliances that supported the developing independence of settlers of European, Indigenous, and African descent.[14]

In highlighting the French state's efforts to prohibit interracial sex in the French Atlantic, this chapter examines links between regions often examined in isolation. I juxtapose legal and literary sources to assess the broader cultural consequences of such legislation and thereby demonstrate how colonial debates transformed the metropole.[15] Furthermore, this research refutes one of the central tropes of studies of the European Enlightenment. The era has been identified as a turning point in the moral codes governing sexuality, with one recent author even portraying it as the "first Sexual Revolution" centuries before the sexual revolution of the 1960s, fueled by chemical birth control.[16] According to this thesis, during the Enlightenment intellectuals overtly questioned religious dogma and authorities, particularly regarding sexual conduct. Some of Europe's most influential authors contended that sex constituted the most important of natural rights, an essential appetite that, alongside hunger and thirst, sustained and reproduced life.[17]

In France, the argument goes, this process led to the secularization of legal institutions as ecclesiastical courts ceded matters of sexual and moral conduct to civil authorities.[18] Penal reforms strove to distinguish crimes— requiring state supervision and punishment—from sins, which were better addressed by religious authorities.[19] As a result of these changes, historians, including Roy Porter, contend, there was a "liberation of the libido" across western Europe in the eighteenth century.[20] In his classic two-volume opus on the Enlightenment, Peter Gay observes that the "demand for the toleration of religious minorities, philosophical dissenters, and sexual deviants was the practical correlative of these propositions about man and society, reinforced by the *philosophes'* characteristic view of philosophy—skeptical, empiricist, a little cynical, and heavily concentrated on social ethics."[21] This rationale concludes that religious skepticism and affective individualism gradually resulted in the decriminalization of adultery, sodomy, and sex outside of marriage.[22]

But upon closer inspection, the story of a general Enlightenment-era sexual liberation fractures.[23] As Julie Hardwick writes, "[The] concept of an eighteenth-century sexual revolution seems to pertain at best to a small group of elite, white, straight men. It ignores the multiplicity of sexual cultures that existed before the second half of the eighteenth century, and the long histories of persistent patterns of intimacy."[24] And when Europeans imagined sexual liberty, their fantasies resulted as much from cross-cultural comparisons as from religious skepticism. Most French readers would have concluded that societies outside of Europe already enjoyed sexual liberty. Indigenous peoples in North America, Caribbean islanders, Africans, and even Euro-American Creoles were all perceived as more sexually expressive than Europeans.[25] But within European societies, interlocking religious, state, and family codes limited all sorts of sexual behavior.[26] To be sure, the policing of some sex acts had waned for some people; punishments declined for most men found guilty of extramarital sex or clandestine marriage during the eighteenth century.[27] But that did not constitute a general liberation of the libido. A woman who committed adultery continued to face steep criminal charges and imprisonment.[28] Young men who engaged in public sodomy continued to attract police surveillance.[29] And the state still enforced laws of celibacy among France's priests, monks, and nuns.[30] What is more, even as ecclesiastical courts ceded authority over sexual conduct to the state, a host of new laws emerged to regulate sexuality in Europe and its American colonies.[31] The surveillance of interracial sex constituted one of these new disciplines.

This chapter makes clear that the history of early modern France and its empire requires the methodological tools and insights provided by histories of sex. So integrated was sex into practices, policies, and imaginings about empire that we cannot fully understand the early modern French empire without it. I examine how the changing significance of cross-cultural relationships kindled anxieties reflected in the laws and literature that bound France and its Atlantic colonies from 1685 to 1791. The first two sections analyze key laws governing cross-cultural sexual relations, first in Quebec and then in Louisiana. I document how race developed as a category intended to limit sexual liberty and inheritance rights. Administrative correspondence and subsequent legislation demonstrate that the perception of cross-cultural sex as a colonial problem took shape in the 1710s. During this decade colonial officials implemented a flurry of new policies designed to criminalize sexual relations previously considered a colonial liberty. But such efforts met resistance. Many members of the clergy rejected radical racialist logic and refused to uphold new prohibitions against sex across the color lines. Lawyers representing mixed-race individuals emphasized the sanctity of property rights and inheritance law, irrespective of race.[32] Abundant evidence documents the political prominence and economic prosperity of mixed-race families in Quebec, Louisiana, Senegal, and the Caribbean.[33] As colonial populations grew, members of these families acquired property and played crucial roles as mediators between increasingly segregated communities. Nor were these negotiations limited to distant colonial courts, dusty legal volumes, or arcane ministerial correspondence. Within France the questions raised by incorporating colonial families into the body politic occupied the highest civil courts, the most popular novels, and leading theatrical performances.

In the final section I provide a close reading of Voltaire's novel *L'Ingénu, A True Story from the Manuscripts of Father Quesnel* (1767) to consider some of the ways that this vigorous debate reverberated in France, and I conclude by considering how such conversations carried into the expansionist revolutionary republic. In novels, plays, and public spectacles, authors and audiences could simultaneously reject racialized repressive regimes and reclaim colonial sexual liberty for all French men, moving these conversations out of the kingdom's courts and into the public sphere. By depicting sexual liberty as a defining feature of American and African societies, French authors participated in a robust colonial fantasia that exoticized the subjects of France's global empire.[34] But these authors also deployed cultural comparison to condemn any government's attempts at sexual surveillance as unjust and hypocritical. If sex constituted the first, the most powerful, and the most ingrained of natural rights, any institution that arbitrarily restricted that right lost legitimacy. Representations of colonial liberties continued to shape French ideals of sex and the rights of man into the revolutionary era.[35]

Race and Sexual Liberty

Not everyone agreed that cross-cultural sex should be a liberty enjoyed by European settlers. Missionaries and travelers depicted the American and

Caribbean colonies as sites of sexual license dominated by lawlessness, and they argued that Indigenous sexual practices threatened the colonists' souls and undermined social stability. Their accounts reveal how Champlain's fantasy fractured. In graphic terms, French missionaries lamented both settlers' sexual license and Indigenous peoples' resistance to sexual mores rooted in European custom and Catholic doctrine. Monogamy within marriage, heterosexuality, and clerical chastity appeared ridiculous, impossible, even wasteful in the estimation of American interlocutors.[36] Men of the cloth particularly denounced Indigenous customs that valued female sexual autonomy, condoned short-term sexual relationships, and recognized two-spirit individuals who defied binary gender conventions and engaged in sexual relations with both men and women.[37] But it was not only Indigenous people who differed from the French in these New World environs. Catholic clerics decried the influence of Protestants—English, Dutch, even French—in neighboring colonies whose alternate readings of biblical texts led them to approve of divorce and clerical marriage.[38] Worst of all, these witnesses warned, French colonists took advantage of the absence of state and church authorities to engage in a wide range of sexual behaviors deemed transgressive back home. In North America and the Caribbean, missionaries bemoaned the fact that French men made their own law and bore no legal or moral restraints on their sexual appetites. Women suffered rape and sexual assault as a result.[39] Indeed, European men's abusive behavior toward their wives constituted one of the most common complaints that Indigenous leaders brought before colonial officials.[40] France had sent its criminals, libertines, and prostitutes to people the colonies, intoned European moralists in travel writings and economic treatises. But, some maintained, with the proper legislation and spiritual guidance, France could turn this past of sexual license to a moral and productive future.[41]

What would turn the colonies around? By 1710 most colonial officials—especially those born in the colonies—agreed on segregation as the only way to curtail the sexual liberties that had come to define European men's existence in the French Atlantic colonies. In 1706 the governor of the Mississippi colony contended that unions between Europeans and Americans threatened good social order. He focused specifically on the liminal figures of the *coureurs de bois*, men of European descent employed as guides and hunters in the continental fur trade. The governor reported that one of the territory's priests, in presiding over interracial marriages, was "authorizing the coureurs de bois to live 'as libertines and under no authority, dispersed among the savage villages, under the pretext that they [had] married among the savages.'"[42] Generations of European men had formed unions with Indigenous women with predictable results; the men and their children became independent of the colonial state, which stood to lose control of their labor and their provisions. The economic consequences of these population losses threatened the French colonial project, argued the officers charged with administering this vast endeavor.

The governor of New France ostensibly directed the territory that stretched from Quebec into the heart of the continent, particularly the fertile river valleys of the Mississippi and Illinois. In 1709 he agreed with his colleague to the south, condemning unions between Europeans and Americans, but for a different reason. He asserted, "Bad blood shouldn't mix with good, our experience in this country is that all the Frenchmen who have married Native women became do-nothing libertines, and of an intolerable independence, and their children are also as worthless as the Natives themselves and should keep us from permitting these types of marriages. . . . It seems that all children born of these unions seek to give the greatest possible pains to the French."[43]

As the historian Guillaume Aubert notes, the concept of blood links this emergent form of racial prejudice with European social hierarchies based on noble versus common blood. Aubert contends that by 1720, "the language of race previously confined to the preservation of the purity of blood of the highest ranks of French society was being extended to the French colonial population at large."[44] Imagine the surprise of a baker's son from Auvergne, or a lowly Indies Company clerk, newly arrived with only the clothes on his back and the debt for his passage fare, who discovered that in Louisiana he possessed valuable blood, a treasure worth protecting against *mésalliance*, a marriage deemed socially beneath him.

In 1715 Jean-Baptiste Dubois Duclos, the chief colonial financial officer in Mississippi, objected to the appointment of a seminarian who supported interracial marriages. Duclos insisted that these unions had failed to establish French dominion over the Indigenous populations of Canada;

instead, they had resulted in French men who "became almost Indian."[45] He articulated a theory of racial difference in this argument, equating skin color with adherence to shared ethical standards and social codes. Such qualities were heritable, he insisted, and he announced that his central objective in limiting marriages between French and Indigenous peoples was to preserve the "whiteness and purity of blood in the children."[46] He lamented that if it went unchecked, interracial sex would transform Louisiana into "a colony of mulattoes who [were] naturally idlers, libertines and even more rascals as those of Peru, Mexico and the other Spanish colonies [gave] evidence."[47] For all their insistence on increasingly stringent racial categories, French colonial officials proved remarkably lax in settling on terminology for interracial combinations, as compared to the specificity of Spanish American *castas*.[48] The French usually used *métis* for individuals with both European and Indigenous relatives, but they also used *mulatto*, though this term served more often to describe individuals with both European and African ancestry.[49] To those officials who had been born in the colonies, the Spanish colonies to the south served as a negative example regarding the consequences of cross-cultural unions, as did the perceived failures of the assimilationist policies of seventeenth-century New France to convert a continent to Catholicism.[50]

The French Crown registered and responded to these critiques from colonial officials. Instructions for the governor of the province of Louisiana in 1716 identified as his primary objective the protection of existing alliances between France and all resident Indigenous peoples, particularly against the English. The governor should ensure that the troops of Louisiana lived in good discipline and should encourage the cultivation of tobacco. Finally, the royal guidelines concluded, "His Majesty is informed that most of the officers and settlers of Louisiana have in their homes enslaved Native women with whom they live in libertinage and debauchery . . . remedy these disorders."[51] But the instructions remained vague on specific mechanisms by which to remedy the perceived problem of cross-cultural relationships. Was the governor to encourage French colonists to marry their Indigenous sexual partners? Break off these relations entirely? On the ground in Louisiana, officials increasingly resolved upon the latter, promulgating a handful of measures intended to separate European and Indigenous communities.[52]

Segregationist policies met resistance, however. As curate of Louisiana, Henri Roulleaux de La Vente continued to celebrate marriages between French men and Illinois women. He pushed back against the racial and cultural prejudices of colonial officials, insisting that Catholic Indigenous women were the key to advancing the goals of French empire: Catholicization, expansion, and French access to Indigenous people's trade networks. He adopted racialized logic, insisting that the women of the "Kaskaskias, Tamaroas, Illinois, and all those of the Missouri" were "whiter, more laborious, cleverer, neater in the household work and more docile than those of the South."[53] The curate relied on the racialist language that bundled epidermal tones into critical factors shaping French-Indigenous alliances, including the women's own family bonds, social status, and property. And the bishop of Quebec contended that not interracial unions but concubinage posed the true threat to colonial social order. In a pastoral letter circulated in 1721, he asserted that the products of illegitimate relationships could "only become bad subjects."[54] The financial health of these congregations, the future growth of faith communities, and the eternal souls of parishioners all figured in clerics' evaluation of these relationships. A handful of missionaries perceived that those policies based on emergent legal categories of race threatened evangelical Catholicism and limited the reach of global France.[55] But many more proved amenable to racial discrimination, quickly adopting terms that quantified degrees of African or Indigenous parentage in parish records of births, deaths, and marriages, with consequences for legal status and inheritance rights.[56]

Race and Sex in the Law of Slavery

In patchwork fashion, colonial officials in North America strove to limit sex between European and Indigenous people in the late seventeenth and early eighteenth centuries. Meanwhile, laws designed to regulate slavery in France's Atlantic colonies moved from conditional acceptance of sex between enslavers and enslaved people to strict prohibition.[57] Promulgated in March 1685 for the French Caribbean islands of Martinique, Guadeloupe, and Saint-Domingue, the Code Noir is best understood as an attempt to promote a distinctly French Catholic form of slavery, reforming the worst abuses associated with over a century of Iberian hegemony over the Atlantic slave trade, as cataloged in the critiques penned from 1677 to 1685.[58]

The Code Noir of 1685 explicitly addressed sexual relations between free men and enslaved women. The law made no mention of race, only legal status, in explaining how such unions were to be discouraged by the colonial state. Articles 12 and 13 established a matrilineal principle for legal status. Children born to enslaved parents would remain enslaved and property of the mother's owner, while children born to one free and one enslaved parent would follow the legal status of their mother. Article 9 stated that any free man who had children with an enslaved woman would be condemned to pay a fine of two thousand pounds of sugar. If he owned the woman, both she and the children would be confiscated by the state, and they would be permanently enslaved to the colonial hospital.[59] However, if a French man should free an enslaved concubine and marry her in the church, their children would be free and recognized as legitimate by the Crown. As historian David Garrigus notes, in practice the "male colonists considered sex with female slaves a perquisite of their status."[60] But these men also may have found in this code a powerful ideal that encouraged them to manumit the enslaved women who had borne their children, the better to retain control of their labor through family bonds.[61] This ideal contributed to the substantial and growing population of free people of color in the French Caribbean, the descendants of European male planters and enslaved African women.[62] As a result, by 1789 in Saint-Domingue, twenty-eight thousand free people of color and emancipated slaves accounted for 46 percent of the free population of the colony; they owned one-quarter of the colony's land and one-third of the slaves.

The Code Noir of 1685, which outlined the legal provisions of slavery in the French Caribbean, also promised equal treatment under the law to all freeborn and freed persons, regardless of race or rank. It is for this reason that the historian Malick Ghachem sees in the law of slavery an "important source of human rights law and ideology."[63] According to article 59 manumitted slaves were recognized as "natural subjects" of the king, following Roman legal precedent. Freed people figured prominently in extensive policy discussions that considered their status in the French empire. According to the law, freed or free people could own property, seek education, hold public office, and marry regardless of race, subject only to their families' interests.

By the eighteenth century colonial administrators in Louisiana and royal officials in France concluded that provisions of the Code Noir risked the collapse of the plantocracy by providing too many paths out of slavery. They sought to remedy perceived problems in the governance of both Canada and the Caribbean by radically changing the laws governing slavery, and they did so by inventing a legal category of race.[64] Officials applied these conclusions to the new colony in the Louisiana territory and to the law code forged to regulate slavery of both Africans and Indigenous peoples.[65]

The Code Noir of Louisiana, enacted in 1724, identified people by color rather than by status as free or enslaved. The category of "white" erased powerful linguistic and confessional divisions, promising that recent German-speaking Protestant migrants would be considered equal to French-speaking Catholic settlers. And the category of "Black" conflated all enslaved people, regardless of their skin color or geographic origin. Brett Rushforth explains that "census records that once recorded 'mulatto, Negro, and Indian slaves' by 1719 collapsed those categories into a single group, sometimes labeled 'negro' or 'negress,' other times merely 'slaves.'"[66] This code prohibited marriages between the white and Black residents of the colony, regardless of their legal status, and outlawed interracial sex by defining concubinage in terms that profoundly discriminated against the offspring of these informal unions.[67] Guillaume Aubert contends that "the 1724 Code Noir thus constituted the most racially exclusive colonial law of the French Empire."[68] But resistance to this code's policies was widespread. Sex across the emergent color lines continued. Parish priests often declined to report race in marriage and birth registries, effectively whitening populations in the historical record.[69]

Manumission was made much more difficult to secure than it had been in the earlier code so as to more effectively create a population of perpetually enslaved people. In this manner, the French colonial state sought to make race—informed by skin color and geographic origin—a category in family law and the law of slavery. By prohibiting marriages and sex between people of these emergent races, the French state risked invalidating existing unions in the eyes of the law. The consequences were profound for those who found themselves defined as "mixed-race" in France and in the American colonies. Threats to property, inheritance, and social status resulted.[70] At precisely the moment in which historians of the Enlightenment see evidence of the first sexual revolution and the withering of laws regulating Catholic sexual morality, new laws sprouted across the empire to segregate French subjects by race, prohibit marriage and sex across those categories, and lay a secular, racialist foundation for sexual unions in the colonies with implications for families back in France.

Voltaire's Empire Strikes Back

What sense did French men and women make of their government's efforts to limit the sexual liberty of settlers in the American colonies by criminalizing interracial relationships? We might assume that such affairs posed little concern in the workshops and cafés of the metropole. But in fact, characters including settlers, Indigenous and enslaved people refused to remain consigned to court transcripts. They animated the pages of contemporary novels and stalked the stages of the kingdom's theaters. Readers and spectators cheered for the triumph of true love over barriers set by class, age, and race, even as these barriers gained durability and force in colonial and metropolitan law codes. These sources provide an avenue to assess how colonial liberties reverberated in France. In 1767 Voltaire published the satirical novel *L'Ingénu*, in which a Huron character voices sharp critiques of the Catholic church, religious intolerance, and sexual mores in France.[71] The novel was popularly acclaimed, widely reviewed, and adapted for the stage within the year.[72] In both the novel and the stage adaptation, the narrative contrasts an idealized American sexual liberty with the multiple social and religious barriers that regulated sexual relations in France.[73] Within a year English translations printed in London, Dublin, Glasgow, and Amsterdam circulated the Atlantic.

Set in 1689, this text takes as its hero a fictional son of French parents who emigrated to Canada and died during the son's infancy. Raised by a Huron community before returning to France, this child grows to be a young man who represents the ideal union of the old and new worlds. He arrives in France with a group of British smugglers on the coast of Brittany and there makes the acquaintance of his uncle and aunt, a prior and the prior's middle-aged sister, at the precise moment when they have been lamenting the disappearance of their long-departed brother and his wife to serve in Canada. Leaping over the side of the boat, the young man is "bare-headed, bare-legged, feet in little sandals" and his chief ornament is his long, braided hair. He wears a little *pourpoint* vest of a fine and loose style; his demeanor conveys a "martial and gentle air."[74] He is a self-possessed man, an innocent called L'Ingénu because, as he himself puts it, "I always say what I think, just as I do what I want."[75]

In Voltaire's telling, L'Ingénu's climate of origin and his American upbringing take precedence over blood—for everyone he meets, he is Huron rather than French. And in this manner, Voltaire undercut developing categories of race rooted in skin color or parentage. Voltaire's characters take note of L'Ingénu's light skin tone and they marvel at his excellent memory and gift for languages. The narrator attributes these gifts to his "low Breton organs fortified by the climate of Canada," which gave him a vigorous intellect.[76] The passage reminds us of the enduring influence of climate on eighteenth-century concepts of race and national character.[77] Such references to the young man's Breton ancestry or "organs" are rare, however. According to all the characters in this novel, L'Ingénu is Huron because he was nursed by a Huron woman and raised within a Huron community, speaking the language, following the customs, and observing the traditions of this nation wracked by the disease and warfare that attended European colonial expansion in Canada.[78]

In an evocative scene, L'Ingénu translates between Huron and French for the assembled neighbors, and his uncle perceives this as a proof of the young man's identity. After several translations his uncle goes to the library, and he returns with the Huron grammar published by Gabriel Sagard-Théodat, a Récollet friar who had lived among the Huron nation and published a dictionary in 1632. With the evidence provided by this text—created by a French missionary for use by other French missionaries—the uncle is prepared to agree that the newcomer is "a real Huron."[79] Voltaire's reference to Sagard reminds his readers that relations between France and America extended back over a century. But in this moment, taking the child of European parents seriously as a Huron because he was raised within Huron language and culture, Voltaire also effectively countered the epidermal discourse of race that had gained traction in the years after 1710.

Furthermore, the novelist rejected segregationist sexuality. From the moment L'Ingénu arrives in France, he attracts the attention of every woman he meets, thanks to his physical grace and sexual confidence. And the author consistently emphasized that although sexual appetites were universal to humanity, some societies accepted and celebrated those appetites, whereas others criminalized them. But because only pornographers and foreigners could address sexual desire frankly in eighteenth-century France, Voltaire adopted a foreigner's voice. L'Ingénu describes his first love affair with a beautiful Huron woman, Abacaba, in terms that stress mutual attraction, like polyamory and a prohibition on jealousy, as central to Indigenous sexual ethics. She was older, a friend of the woman who had nursed him after his parents' death. He proudly proclaims that she preferred him to her other lovers—that is, until she was eaten by a bear. In relating their affair, L'Ingénu subverts European ideals of sexual relations that valorized monogamy, female virginity, and men's possession of women as wives or daughters. And still, L'Ingénu's French interlocutors are charmed by his memories.

When asked, "How do they make love in the land of the Hurons?" L'Ingénu responds, "In doing beautiful things to please the people you love."[80] Spontaneous applause breaks out, and such scenes insist on the profound universality of sexual desire and romantic attachment. It is tempting in this scene to perceive Champlain's vision to have succeeded, but in Voltaire's telling, the resulting "one people" are not French, but American. France's sons have been absorbed into American customs and sexual ethics. In this manner, Voltaire's Huron strikes back at the empire, holding a mirror up to France to make it consider itself in comparison to those it presumes to govern.

Upon his arrival in Europe, L'Ingénu discovers that some European individuals express desire without any intention of initiating sex. Indeed, the entire story revolves around the countless theological and social impediments L'Ingénu encounters in his desire to bed a young French maiden, Mlle de St.-Yves. He wants her. She wants him. Why should they not love each other? he asks. She protests and counsels him to seek permission to marry her from his aunt, his uncle, and her brother. He declines, observing, "I don't consult anyone when I want to eat or hunt, or sleep; I know that in love it is not bad to have the consent of the person that you want; but since it's neither my uncle nor my aunt that I want, I need not address them in this matter."[81] L'Ingénu professes confusion and then anger at the seemingly arbitrary barriers to sexual relationships in Europe set out by families, church authorities, and social hierarchies.

Although the Huron character repeatedly proclaims that sexual desire is natural, he has landed in a society in which individuals' expressions of desire are highly regulated. Just because an appetite is natural does not make it socially acceptable, nor is it always responsible to pursue that desire regardless of the circumstances. In a code of sexual conduct that required women to dissemble their desires and that penalized the victims rather than the perpetrators of rape and extortion, sexual assault had been written into the hierarchies of French society. Rape was the predictable result of men's monopoly on political power and the value placed on women's chastity. Toward the end of the novel, the Huron's Mlle de St.-Yves receives an offer; she can secure L'Ingénu's release from prison if she succumbs to the sexual advances of a powerful courtier. Her friends counsel her to give in. "Do you think all of those in charge of provinces or armies earned their honors and fortunes just by their services? They owe it all to Mesdames their wives. The dignities of war were solicited by love, and the place given to the husband of the prettiest."[82] In these exchanges readers should realize that the sexual favors demanded of Mlle de St.-Yves are neither shocking nor rare in this society that ostensibly prizes abstinence and monogamy. Women's sexuality is a currency regularly spent by men of political influence and wealth, even those who have sworn oaths of chastity. Perhaps, Voltaire suggested, the true threat to French sexual mores lay in this corrupt system of two-faced courtiers and hypocritical clerics rather than in the sexual liberties attributed to the American colonies. Mlle de St.-Yves ultimately agrees to these terms and wins her lover's release, but she dies soon after their reunion. "Her soul killed her body. The crowd of thoughts carried into her veins a poison more dangerous than the most forceful fever," which the author linked to the shame of sexual transgression.[83]

Throughout the tragic tale of love between L'Ingénu and Mlle de St.-Yves, Voltaire neutered race as a meaningful social category.[84] Within this narrative, geography, climate, and upbringing all play more significant roles in forging an individual's identity than do ancestors' origins or skin color. Even as segregationists gained influence at the French court and in colonial office, the author rejected racialist arguments to offer a searing indictment of the hypocrisy of sexual ideals in eighteenth-century France.[85] Voltaire offered no direct comment on the laws that sought to codify racial categories and criminalize interracial sex, but his satire provides ample ammunition against these forms of injustice.

The character of L'Ingénu provides a glimpse into contemporaneous conversations about what might happen if colonial liberties—those sexual, economic, and political freedoms purportedly practiced by French settlers across the empire—boomeranged back to Europe. As Lisa Jane Graham observes in her contribution to this volume, the "domestication" of sexual pleasure proved to be one of the central themes concerning Enlightenment authors.

France's flirtation with American liberties did not end with the Treaty of Paris of 1763, nor the one of 1783. But these treaties and the decades-long fallout of France's imperial wars exposed the hidden costs of colonial liberties. In 1763 thousands of refugees fled their homes in Acadia ahead of the advancing British army.[86] Acadians learned at this moment that they were both French subjects and fundamentally foreign, just as the colonies were simultaneously part of and apart from France.[87] In 1777, in a series of laws referred to as the *Police des Noirs*, the French kingdom required all Blacks resident in France to register with the Admiralty, regardless of their legal status, wealth, or kinship. The end goal of this legislation? Removal.[88] In both cases the French monarch's actions took aim at the basic political compact between ruler and ruled. What did those born in the colonies owe the French king, and what protections did he owe them? When the French king failed to protect imperial subjects, did he lose the right to their loyalty? In the years after France's extensive losses of populations and territories in the Seven Years' War, colonial residents of European, African, and American descent posed these questions with persistence. Across the Atlantic, in French-language enclaves ceded to imperial rivals and in the retained possessions, metropolitan authorities developed arguments to resist a social order based on settlers' claimed colonial liberties.[89] Simultaneously, settlers regularly subordinated imperial authority to European-descended men's colonial liberties as the foundation for a new political contract.[90] These demands, united with those formulated within Europe, proposed a dramatic challenge to imperial monarchies and inaugurated an age of revolutions that transformed the political systems around the Atlantic.[91]

But not everyone fell for this sleight-of-hand. Even as European settlers sought to protect their own privileges by using the language of liberty and equality, this discourse highlighted the racial and sexual inequalities that structured colonial societies. In this context the ideal of sexual liberty smacked of predation, prompting the question: Whose liberty? In 1791, in the pages of the *Marriage Gazette*, a new weekly paper dedicated to uniting couples in republican matrimony, a young deputy advertised for a spouse. He described himself: "[An] American who has the honor of sitting in the National Assembly, as a deputy from our colonies, who has never abused his rights as master to subject his black or mulatto women to his desires, who has focused solely on making his lands prosper, would like to share his fortune with a young citizen of Paris, even if she has no dowry beyond a good education, a gentle character, and an agreeable figure."[92] That a Caribbean landowner felt the need to insist he had taken no sexual liberties with enslaved women—those so-called rights as master—as preface to his matrimonial aspirations paradoxically reiterated the claim that the colonies were a site of unrestrained predation. He was the exception to the rule, announced this advertisement, but he omitted that enslaved people's labor built his own prosperity.

Two weeks later, the American's advertisement earned a response from a young French novitiate who had been confined to a convent against her will. Since the National Assembly had closed the convents and released her from her vows, she sought a husband and specified her preferences to the editor of the *Gazette*. Fortune mattered not at all, she had money enough for both. She described her ideal match: "Someone not as young as myself, nor old, well-born and moral. I prefer someone who, like me, has long been a victim of injustice and blind predilection." And here, the lady's letter took a distinctly political turn. She recalled the American deputy's letter from the previous month, declaring, "I don't want an American though he were an impartial deputy, even if he alone had the 660,000 unfortunates who pay with their liberty and blood for the pleasures and the opulence of 40,000 Europeans. I hate tyrants and executioners."[93] The young American deputy's concern for his land's "prosperity" obscured the people who made that wealth, but this reader was not fooled. She asserted common cause with any "victim of injustice." But she also erroneously envisioned a stricter barrier between colonial and metropolitan economies than existed in fact. For although the work of enslaved men, women, and children created the opulence enjoyed by the European settlers in Saint-Domingue, their labors also funneled goods and wealth into the port towns and the commercial hubs of France, enriching, for example, the grocers who sold sugar, coffee, and rum, along with the textile merchants who purveyed indigos and calicos.[94] Within the pages of novels like *L'Ingénu* and on the stage of the Comédie-Française, colonial characters and settings invited the French public to imagine colonial liberties for themselves, meaning a society unconstrained by canon law; royal writ; and hierarchies of rank, wealth, or family. But the fiction dissolved in the light of revolutionary political scrutiny. Cross-cultural sexual relations, once presumed to be the foundation for peaceful French imperial authority, instead connoted its worst abuses: rape, slavery, and genocide.

Notes

1. Reuben Gold Thwaites, ed., *The Jesuit Relations and Allied Documents: Travels and Explorations of the Jesuit Missionaries in New France, 1610–1791*, 73 vols. (1896–1901; repr. New York: Pageant, 1959), 5: 211.

2. Saliha Belmessous, *Assimilation and Empire: Uniformity in French and British Colonies, 1541–1954* (Oxford: Oxford University Press, 2013), 25–28; Olive Patricia Dickason, "From 'One Nation' in the Northeast to 'New Nation' in the Northwest: A Look at the Emergence of the Métis," in *The New Peoples: Being and Becoming Métis in North America*, ed. Jacqueline Peterson and Jennifer S. H. Brown (St. Paul: Minnesota Historical Association, 2001), 25–27.

3. Jennifer M. Spear, *Race, Sex, and Social Order in Early New Orleans* (Baltimore: Johns Hopkins University Press, 2009), 18.

4. Jennifer L. Palmer, *Intimate Bonds: Family and Slavery in the French Atlantic* (Philadelphia: University of Pennsylvania Press, 2016).

5. Colonial liberties, or "libertés des colonies," became a keyword in the French press and foreign ministry in the 1770s, particularly referencing British North American settlers' revolt against the British Crown, as in Pierre Augustin Caron de Beaumarchais, *Observations sur le mémoire justicatif de la Cour de Londres* (Londres, Philadelphie [Paris], 1779), 14. This chapter adapts that political term to consider the gendered and racialized dynamics of sexual relationships among European settlers, Indigenous, and enslaved peoples in the colonies. Evidence of interracial sex as de facto policy is addressed in Jennifer M. Spear, "They Need Wives: Métissage and the Regulation of Sexuality in French Louisiana,

1699–1730," in *Sex, Love, Race: Crossing Boundaries in North American History*, ed. Martha Hodes (New York: New York University Press, 1999), 41; Susan Sleeper-Smith, *Indian Women and French Men: Rethinking Cultural Encounter in the Western Great Lakes* (Amherst: University of Massachusetts Press, 2001); John D. Garrigus, *Before Haiti: Race and Citizenship in French Saint-Domingue* (London: Palgrave Macmillan, 2010), 40; and Sara Melzer, *Colonizer or Colonized: The Hidden Stories of Early Modern French Culture* (Philadelphia: University of Pennsylvania Press, 2012), 91–122.

6. Despite ministerial assumptions that French men would dominate colonial settlement, women typically constituted 20 to 30 percent of the European migrant populations. Stanley L. Engerman, "France, Britain and the Economic Growth of Colonial North America," in *The Early Modern Atlantic Economy*, ed. John J. McCusker and Kenneth Morgan (Cambridge: Cambridge University Press, 2000), 247. By 1763 the French colonies of North America comprised 65,000 individuals, while 80,000 settled on the Caribbean island of Guadeloupe. Trevor Burnard and John Garrigus estimate populations of 500,000 in Saint-Domingue and 7,500 in Guiana, including Indigenous and enslaved people. Burnard and Garrigus, *The Plantation Machine: Atlantic Capitalism in French Saint-Domingue and British Jamaica* (Philadelphia: University of Pennsylvania Press, 2016), 97.

7. See Pernille Røge's persuasive analysis of empire's impact on French economic and political theory: Røge, *Economistes and the Reinvention of Empire: France in the Americas and Africa, 1750–1802* (Cambridge: Cambridge University Press, 2019). Elizabeth Heath adopts quantitative methods to document the economic and cultural impact of the early modern French empire in metropolitan commerce. See initial research reports published on Heath's website: https://blogs .baruch.cuny.edu/elizabethheath/?page_id=36.

8. Ann Laura Stoler, *Race and the Education of Desire: Foucault's "History of Sexuality" and the Colonial Order of Things* (Durham NC: Duke University Press, 1995), 7.

9. Saliha Belmessous, "Assimilation and Racialism in Seventeenth- and Eighteenth-Century French Colonial Policy," *American Historical Review* 110, no. 2 (April 2005): 323.

10. Richard White, *The Middle Ground: Indians, Empires, and Republics in the Great Lakes Region, 1650–1815*, twentieth anniversary ed. (1991; Cambridge: Cambridge University Press, 2011).

11. As evidenced in Sophie White's analysis of the Franco-American population, for whom textiles, clothing styles, architectural elements, and Catholicism became the essential signs of French identity: White, *Wild Frenchmen and Frenchified*

Indians: Material Culture and Race in Colonial Louisiana (Philadelphia: University of Pennsylvania Press, 2012).

12. Lorelle Semley, *To Be Free and French: Citizenship in France's Atlantic Empire* (Cambridge: Cambridge University Press, 2017), 3–20; and Stewart R. King, *Blue Coat or Powdered Wig: Free People of Color in Pre-Revolutionary Saint Domingue* (Athens: University of Georgia Press, 2001).

13. See Shannon Lee Dawdy, *Building the Devil's Empire: French Colonial New Orleans* (Chicago: University of Chicago Press, 2008), 15–16, 67–69, 228, 241–45.

14. Kathleen DuVal characterizes these alliances in DuVal, *The Native Ground: Indians and Colonists in the Heart of the Continent* (Philadelphia: University of Pennsylvania Press, 2006), and highlights the colonists' continued dependence on Indigenous trade and diplomatic alliances in the vast Mississippi Territory into the nineteenth century.

15. Sue Peabody, *"There Are No Slaves in France": The Political Culture of Race and Slavery in the Ancien Régime* (New York: Oxford University Press, 2002), documents how the racialization of slavery across France's early modern empire resulted in the set of racial exclusionary laws passed in 1776–77 known as the *Police des Noirs*.

16. Faramerz Dabhoiwala, *The Origins of Sex: A History of the First Sexual Revolution* (Oxford: Oxford University Press, 2012), 3–4. Dabhoiwala builds on the insights of a generation of social historians who identified secularization, affective individualism, and demographic patterns indicating extensive use of birth control among social elites by the eighteenth century. See Lawrence Stone, *Family, Sex, and Marriage in England, 1500–1800* (New York: Penguin, 1977); and Jean-Louis Flandrin, *Families in Former Times: Kinship, Household and Sexuality*, trans. Richard Southern (Cambridge: Cambridge University Press, 1979), 214–16.

17. Expressed by Jonathan I. Israel, *Radical Enlightenment: Philosophy and the Making of Modernity 1650–1750* (Oxford: Oxford University Press, 2002), chap. 4. Hugo Grotius was one of the most influential theorists of natural law who addressed sex, marriage, and family formation. See John Witte, "Hugo Grotius and the Natural Law of Marriage: A Case Study of Harmonizing Confessional Differences in Early Modern Europe," in *Studies in Canon Law and Common Law in Honor of R. H. Helmholz*, ed. Troy L. Harris (Berkeley: Robbins Collection, 2015), 231–49.

18. Benoît Garnot, *Crime et justice aux XVIIe et XVIIIe siècles* (Paris: Imago, 2000).

19. Cesare Beccaria, *On Crimes and Punishments and Other Writings*, ed. Jeremy Parzen, trans. Aaron Thomas (Toronto: University of Toronto Press, 2008), 105.

20. This quote refers to eighteenth-century Britain, but many French historians would concur. Roy Porter, "Mixed Feelings: The Enlightenment and Sexuality

in Eighteenth-Century Britain," in *Sexuality in Eighteenth-Century Britain*, ed. Paul-Gabriel Boucé (Manchester, UK: Manchester University Press, 1982), 5.

21. Peter Gay, *The Enlightenment: An Interpretation*, vol. 2, *The Science of Freedom* (1977; repr., New York: W. W. Norton, 1996), 399.

22. Bryant T. Ragan Jr., "The Enlightenment Confronts Homosexuality," in *Homosexuality in Modern France*, ed. Jeffrey Merrick and Bryant T. Ragan Jr. (New York: Oxford University Press, 1996), 8–29.

23. Michel Foucault contends that contrary to conventional wisdom, which would assume that prudish Victorians denied sexuality and prohibited discussions of diverse sexual behaviors, modern societies "dedicated themselves to speaking of it *ad infinitum*, while exploiting it as *the* secret." *The History of Sexuality*, vol. 1, *An Introduction*, trans. Robert Hurley (New York: Vintage, 1980), 35. Foucault abandons the binary of liberation versus repression to determine what powers are gained, and by whom, as discourses proliferate about sexual repression.

24. Julie Hardwick, "A Sexual Revolution in the Eighteenth Century?," *Age of Revolutions*, March 15, 2021. https://ageofrevolutions.com/2021/03/15/a-sexual -revolution-in-the-eighteenth-century/.

25. Among the most influential novels that assert sexual liberty as defined by locales outside of Europe are Abbé Prévot, *Manon Lescaut* (1731); [Claude Propser Jolyot de] Crébillon fils, *Le sopha: Conte moral* (1742); and Denis Diderot, *Supplement au voyage de Bougainville* (written in 1772, published in 1796).

26. See Lisa Jane Graham's contribution to this volume. In response to such strictures, Enlightenment-era philosophers engaged in a rehabilitation of pleasure, including sexual pleasure. See also Alain Corbin, *L'harmonie des plaisirs: Les manières de jouir du siècle des Lumières à l'avènement de la sexologie* (Paris: Perrin, 2008). On norms governing sexual practices depending on gender, age, and class, see Julie Hardwick, *Sex in an Old Regime City: Young Workers and Intimacy in France, 1660–1789* (Oxford: Oxford University Press, 2020), 43–77.

27. Benoît Garnot, *On n'est point pendu pour être amoureux: Liberté amoureuse au XVIIIe siècle* (Paris: Belin, 2008). Even heterosexual adult men found themselves subject to family expectations regarding licit sexuality, as evident in the cases profiled in Arlette Farge and Michel Foucault, *Le désordre des familles: Lettres de cachet des Archives de la Bastille au XVIIIe siècle* (Paris: Gallimard, 1982).

28. See Nina Kushner's contribution to this volume.

29. Jeffrey Merrick, "New Sources and Questions for Research on Sexual Relations between Men in Eighteenth-Century France," *Gender & History* 30, no. 1 (March 2018): 9–29.

30. Myriam Deniel-Ternant, *Ecclésiastiques en débauche (1700–1790)* (Ceyzérieu, France: Champ Vallon, 2017).

31. Thomas Laqueur emphasizes the role of scientific and medical discourse in this transition in Laqueur, *Making Sex: Body and Gender from the Greeks to Freud* (Cambridge MA: Harvard University Press, 1992).

32. Matthew Gerber, "Bastardy, Race, and the Law in the Eighteenth-Century French Atlantic: The Evidence of Litigation," *French Historical Studies* 36, no. 4 (Fall 2013): 571–600. See also the contributions to Nancy Christie, Michael Gauvreau, and Matthew Gerber, eds., *Voices in the Archives in the French Colonial World: "The King Is Listening"* (New York: Routledge, 2021).

33. Brenda Macdougall, Carolyn Podruchny, and Nicole St-Onge, eds., *Contours of a People: Métis Family, Mobility, and History* (Norman: University of Oklahoma Press, 2014); and Jessica Marie Johnson, *Wicked Flesh: Black Women, Intimacy and Freedom in the Atlantic World* (Philadelphia: University of Pennsylvania Press, 2020).

34. Following the insights of Stoler, *Race and the Education of Desire*; and Doris Garraway, *The Libertine Colony: Creolization in the Early French Empire* (Durham NC: Duke University Press, 2005).

35. Political caricatures regularly used the phallus to represent the "rights of man" in revolutionary discourse. See Antoine de Baeque, *The Body Politic: Corporeal Metaphor in Revolutionary France, 1770–1800*, trans. Charlotte Mandell (Stanford CA: Stanford University Press, 1997), 131–56, ill. 10.

36. Jesuit missionaries reported that Indigenous men responded with incredulity to Catholic doctrine regarding premarital and clerical celibacy as a "very heavy and galling yoke for carnal men." Thwaites, *Jesuit Relations*, vol. 53, chap. 12, 148–49.

37. Karen Anderson, *Chain Her by One Foot: The Subjugation of Native Women in Seventeenth-Century New France* (New York: Routledge, 1993).

38. Merry Wiesner-Hanks, *Christianity and Sexuality in the Early Modern World: Regulating Desire, Reforming Practice* (New York: Routledge, 1999).

39. Lisa Ze Winters, *The Mulatta Concubine: Terror, Intimacy, Freedom and Desire in the Black Transatlantic* (Athens: University of Georgia Press, 2018); DuVal, *The Native Ground*.

40. White, *Wild Frenchmen*, 89–90.

41. Belmessous, "Assimilation and Racialism," 322–49.

42. As cited in Spear, *Race, Sex, and Social Order*, 26.

43. Saliha Belmessous, "Être français en Nouvelle France: Identité française et identité coloniale aux dix-septième et dix-huitième siècles," *French Historical Studies* 27, no. 3 (Summer 2004): 507–40, quote at 527.

44. Guillaume Aubert, "'The Blood of France': Race and Purity of Blood in the French Atlantic," *William and Mary Quarterly* 61, no. 3 (June 2004): 439–78, quote on 442.

45. Jean-Baptiste Dubois Duclos to Pontchartrain, December 25, 1715, *Mississippi Provincial Archives, French Dominion*, trans. and ed. Dunbar Rowland, A. G. Sanders, and Patricia Galloway (Jackson: Mississippi Provincial Archives, 1926–1984), 2: 205, cited in White, *Wild Frenchmen*, 23.

46. Duclos, as cited in White, *Wild Frenchmen*, 24.

47. Duclos, as cited in White, *Wild Frenchmen*, 24.

48. Magali Carrera, *Imagining Identity in New Spain: Race, Lineage, and the Colonial Body in Portraiture and Casta Paintings* (Austin: University of Texas Press, 2010).

49. These words and concepts retain the painful associations of the racial hierarchy that resulted from these policies, with consequences to the present day. See the discussion in Semley, *To Be Free and French*, 7–9.

50. Aubert, "'The Blood of France.'"

51. Mémoire du Roy pour server d'instruction au S. de l'Epinay, October 20, 1716, 4DFC/9, Archives Nationales d'Outre-Mer, Aix-en-Provence, France.

52. Duval, *The Native Ground*, 76–96.

53. Henri Roulleaux de La Vente, 1716, as cited by Robert Michael Morrissey, *Empire by Collaboration: Indians, Colonists and Governments in Colonial Illinois Country* (Philadelphia: University of Pennsylvania Press, 2015), 99.

54. Spear, *Race, Sex, and Social Order*, 34.

55. Sue Peabody, "'A Nation Born to Slavery': Missionaries and Racial Discourse in Seventeenth-Century French Antilles," *Journal of Social History* 38, no. 1 (Fall 2004): 113–26, quote at 121.

56. Cécile Vidal, *Caribbean New Orleans: Empire, Race, and the Making of a Slave Society* (Chapel Hill: University of North Carolina Press, 2019), 376–78.

57. Aubert, "'The Blood of France.'"

58. Guillaume Aubert, "'To Establish One Law and Definite Rules': Race, Religion, and the Transatlantic Origins of the Louisiana Code Noir," in *Louisiana: Crossroads of the Atlantic World*, ed. Cécile Vidal (Philadelphia: University of Pennsylvania Press, 2014), 21–43.

59. Code Noir, 1685, article 9.

60. Garrigus, *Before Haiti*, 56.

61. Perceptively analyzed in Palmer, *Intimate Bonds*, 40–44.

62. Simon Henochsberg, "Public Debt and Slavery: The Case of Haiti (1765–1915)" (Master's thesis, École d'Économie de Paris, 2016), 9.

63. Malick Ghachem, *The Old Regime and the Haitian Revolution* (Cambridge: Cambridge University Press, 2012), 210.

64. Aubert, "'To Establish One Law'"; and Cécile Vidal, "Caribbean Louisiana: Church, *Métissage*, and the Language of Race in the Mississippi Colony during the French Period," in Vidal, *Louisiana*, 21–43, 125–46.

65. On this interaction, see Brett Rushforth, *Bonds of Alliance: Indigenous and Atlantic Slaveries in New France* (Chapel Hill: University of North Carolina Press and the Omohundro Institute, 2013).

66. Rushforth, *Bonds of Alliance*, 355.

67. Aubert, "'To Establish One Law,'" 41.

68. Aubert, "'To Establish One Law,'" 23.

69. Vidal, "Caribbean Louisiana," 125–46.

70. See Johnson, *Wicked Flesh*, 121–60.

71. The title references the renowned Jansenist priest Pasquier Quesnel (1634–1719), exiled from France for his reformist beliefs and one of the leading voices of religious dissent, in Quesnel, *Le Nouveau Testament en françois, avec des Réflexions morales sur chaque verset* (Paris: Pralard, 1699). With this subtitle Voltaire signaled his support for the Jansenists reformers against the Jesuit Order, as explored at length by Catherine M. Northeast, *The Parisian Jesuits and the Enlightenment, 1700–1762* (Oxford: SVEC, 1991). Literary scholars' treatments of this novel have focused on its social critique, as in Nicole Masson, *L'Ingénu de Voltaire et la critique de la société à la veille de la Révolution* (Paris: Bordas, 1989); irony, as in David Lévy, "L'ironie de Voltaire dans le chapitre 16 de L'Ingénu," *Studies on Voltaire and the Eighteenth Century* 341 (1996): 127; or the narrative stranger, as in Sylvain Menant, "L'étranger dans le conte voltairien: Le cas de L'Ingénu," in *À l'ombre des Lumières: Littérature et pensée françaises du XVIIIe siècle*, ed. Trude Kolderup and Svein-Eirik Fauskevåg (Paris: L'Harmattan, 2008). The following interpretation departs from these studies by attending to Voltaire's analysis of colonial power dynamics in sexual relationships.

72. André Grétry and Jean-François Marmontel, *Le Huron* (1768), performed at the Comédie-Italienne, Hôtel de Bourgogne, rue Mauconseil, Paris, in August 1768 and in the Théâtre des Jésuites in Liège, 1769; John Warrack and Ewan West, eds., *Oxford Dictionary of Opera* (Oxford: Oxford University Press, 1992), 302.

73. Richard A. Francis, ed., *L'Ingénu*, vol. 63c of *Oeuvres complètes de Voltaire* (Oxford: Voltaire Foundation, 2006). In addition to Francis's fine scholarly edition of the novel, the analysis that follows builds on scholarship by Jean Goldzink, Kathryn Fredericks, and Véronique Bartoli-Anglard. See *L'Ingénu. Edition et dossier de Jean Goldzink* (Paris: Flammarion, 2017); Kathryn E. Fredericks, "Leaving Home: Geography in Voltaire's Philosophical Tales: 'Zadig,' 'Micromegas,' 'Candide,' and 'l'Ingénu'" (PhD diss., University of Florida, 2012); and Véronique Bartoli-Anglard, *Etude sur Voltaire, "L'Ingénu"* (Paris: Ellipses, 2019).

74. Francis, ed., Voltaire, *L'Ingénu*, 6.

75. Francis, ed., Voltaire, *L'Ingénu*, 11.

76. Francis, ed., Voltaire, *L'Ingénu*, 37.

77. Notably in Montesquieu's discussions of the relationship between climate, national character, and government in *The Spirit of the Laws* (1748).

78. On the contemporary debates regarding breastfeeding, see Londa Schiebinger, "Why Mammals Are Called Mammals: Gender Politics in Eighteenth-Century Natural History," *American Historical Review* 98, no. 2 (April 1993): 382–411. Waves of epidemic disease and warfare with both neighboring nations and European colonists devastated the Huron-Wyandot nation after the 1630s. See Gary Warrick, *A Population History of the Huron-Petun, A.D. 500–1650* (Cambridge: Cambridge University Press, 2008). The devastation of the Huron nation was widely noted in eighteenth-century France and provided a rare example of self-recrimination in French letters. See Pierre Charlevoix, *Histoire et description générale de la Nouvelle France* (Paris: chez Pierre-François Giffart, 1744), 3:200.

79. Francis, ed., Voltaire, *L'Ingénu*, 16.

80. Francis, ed., Voltaire, *L'Ingénu*, 17.

81. Francis, ed., Voltaire, *L'Ingénu*, 58–9.

82. Francis, ed., Voltaire, *L'Ingénu*, 178–79.

83. Francis, ed., Voltaire, *L'Ingénu*, 217.

84. Where does this fit in the larger *oeuvre* of Voltaire's work? Voltaire opposed slavery and the slave trade but embraced contemporary theories for polygenism, the independent origins of fundamentally distinct human races. Voltaire, *Traité de métaphysique* (1734), in *Oeuvres complètes* (Paris: Garnier Frères, 1879), *Mélanges*, 1: 181–93.

85. In the wake of the 1759 Parlement of Paris decision that established the "freedom principle" in French territory. See Sue Peabody's analysis of this decision and subsequent suits brought by enslaved people to secure their freedom in Peabody, *There Are No Slaves in France*, 57–71.

86. Surveyed in Christopher Hodson, *The Acadian Diaspora: An Eighteenth-Century History* (Oxford: Oxford University Press, 2012).

87. This paradox is most developed in the historiography of French imperial law and economic theory. See Laurie M. Wood, *Archipelago of Justice: Law in France's Early Modern Empire* (New Haven CT: Yale University Press, 2020); and Røge, *Economistes and the Reinvention of Empire*.

88. Peabody, *There Are No Slaves in France*, 106–20.

89. Garrigus, *Before Haiti*, 109–40.

90. Ghachem, *The Old Regime and the Haitian Revolution*, 112–13, 250–52.

91. Alan Forrest dramatically terms these processes "the death of the French Atlantic." See Forrest, *The Death of the French Atlantic: Trade, War, and Slavery in the Age of Revolution* (Oxford: Oxford University Press, 2020). The death of French empire has been announced for centuries, but it continues to this day, as evidenced in the

French response to the devastating 2017 hurricane season that caused 2 billion euros in damages to Saint-Martin, Guadeloupe, Saint-Barthelemy, Barbuda, and Martinique, all French overseas departments or territories.

92. *Le courier de l'hymen, ou Journal des dames*, no. 1, February 20, 1791, 1. This exchange is also noted in Suzanne Desan, *The Family on Trial in Revolutionary France* (Berkeley: University of California Press, 2004), 47; and in Siobhán McIlvenney, *Figurations of the Feminine in the Early French Women's Press, 1758–1848* (Liverpool, UK: Liverpool University Press, 2019), 175.

93. *Le courier de l'hymen, ou Journal des dames*, no. 4, March 3, 1791, 14–15.

94. See Forrest, *The Death of the French Atlantic*. On the social composition and economic capacity of Saint-Domingue prior to 1789, see Garrigus, *Before Haiti*, 2–3, 171–94.

Suggested Reading

Johnson, Jessica Marie. *Wicked Flesh: Black Women, Intimacy and Freedom in the Atlantic World*. Philadelphia: University of Pennsylvania Press, 2020.

Morgan, Jennifer L. *Laboring Women: Reproduction and Gender in New World Slavery*. Philadelphia: University of Pennsylvania Press, 2004.

Palmer, Jennifer L. *Intimate Bonds: Family and Slavery in the French Atlantic*. Philadelphia: University of Pennsylvania Press, 2016.

Peakman, Julie. *Licentious Worlds: Sex and Exploitation in Global Empires*. London: Reaktion, 2019.

Rushforth, Brett. *Bonds of Alliance: Indigenous and Atlantic Slaveries in New France*. Chapel Hill: University of North Carolina Press and the Omohundro Institute, 2013.

Spear, Jennifer M. *Race, Sex, and Social Order in Early New Orleans*. Baltimore: Johns Hopkins University Press, 2009.

Stoler, Ann Laura. *Race and the Education of Desire: Foucault's "History of Sexuality" and the Colonial Order of Things*. Durham NC: Duke University Press, 1995.

Tuttle, Leslie. *Conceiving the Old Regime: Pronatalism and the Politics of Reproduction in Early Modern France*. New York: Oxford University Press, 2010.

Vidal, Cecile, ed., *Louisiana: Crossroads of the Atlantic World*. Philadelphia: University of Pennsylvania Press, 2014.

White, Sophie. *Voices of the Enslaved: Love, Labor, and Longing in French Louisiana*. Chapel Hill: University of North Carolina Press, 2019.

2

BLOOD, RAPE, AND STIGMATA

Revisiting the Cadière-Girard Affair of 1730

CATHY MCCLIVE

In November 1730 fifty-year-old Jesuit priest Jean-Baptiste Girard accused his penitent, eighteen-year-old Marie-Catherine Cadière of "spiritual imposture," faking the stigmata using her menstrual blood. Cadière retaliated the same day, denouncing Girard for "spiritual incest": fornication between a penitent and the penitent's spiritual director, which violated their spiritual kinship.[1] She also accused him of bewitching her, sexually assaulting her during her religious ecstasies, impregnating her, and procuring an abortion. The high-profile ecclesiastical and secular trials that ensued divided French and European public opinion.[2] After much political, religious, and legal wrangling, an initial death sentence for Cadière on September 11, 1731, was commuted into an acquittal a month later, with a requirement for Cadière to pay all court costs. Girard was never convicted. He died two years later and Cadière disappeared from the historical record.[3]

This exceptional affair is a staple of the history of religious politics in eighteenth-century France. But its sexual dimensions have been silenced. The scandal is usually analyzed against the backdrop of profound religious strife following the Unigenitus Bull of 1713, the deepening schism between Jesuits and Jansenists, and the development of public opinion.[4] Although existing studies acknowledge the sexual elements of the affair, they approach Cadière's body primarily as a vehicle for anti-Jesuit politics.[5] I argue that analysis of how lawyers portrayed Cadière's sexual, stigmatic, and reproductive body is central to the history of the affair.[6] Three main questions emerge from this approach to an example of what Edoardo Grendi calls the "exceptional normal" in eighteenth-century French history.[7] What was the nature of Cadière and Girard's sexual relationship? Was Cadière's stigmata natural or supernatural? And did she have and lose a pregnancy? The lawyers for each party, Jean-Baptiste Chaudon and Claude-François Pazery de Thorame, presented Cadière's body as evidence in their answers to all three questions and interpreted it as violated or deceptive. Specifically, in their arguments Cadière embodied shared understandings of three elements of the reproductive and bleeding body: menstrual periodicity, the connection between menstruation and procreation, and distinctions between stigmatic, menstrual, and abortive blood. Lawyers weaponized each of these differently for professional gain.

The available sources regarding the Cadière-Girard affair are the myriad uncensored sensationalized legal briefs, called *mémoires* or factums, mostly written by Chaudon and Thorame.[8] The lawyers constructed written narratives to suit their legal strategies, ranging from short four-page pamphlets to longer, repetitive accounts that run into hundreds of pages. They include material from apparent interrogation transcripts, witness depositions, correspondence between the parties, and Cadière's controversial Lent diary, as well as the lawyers' pleas.[9] In the Cadière case, as in many others, a factum war ran alongside and fed into the trial. Factums were printed rapidly as lawyers reacted to their adversary's latest missive and were later reissued as multivolume compilations. Factums were distributed within legal and social circles in France and abroad, significantly preempting the politicization and sexualization of private matters and bodies later in the eighteenth century.[10] The actual trial documents have not survived; they were destroyed as part of the sentence. Therefore, we cannot test the apparent authenticity of the parts of the trial reproduced in these briefs. Historians must unpack the lawyers' ventriloquizing not only of Cadière's voice but also Girard's to access the cultural work that constructions of Cadière's bleeding, violated body were doing.

The repetitive and partisan nature of the factums makes it hard to pin down a precise timeline of what happened. They do agree on certain points, however. When Cadière and Girard met in 1728, she was eighteen and he was fifty. She had aspirations to saintliness, and he had an ambiguous reputation for inducing corporeal manifestations of piety in young penitents. Following Girard's advice, Cadière began to fast and, weakened from ensuing illness and convulsions, confined herself to her room in her mother's house in Toulon from November 1729 to June 1730, during which time Girard made frequent unchaperoned visits behind locked doors. During Holy Week, April 1730, Cadière suffered the five wounds of the stigmata for the first time, an experience that repeated in May, June, and July. After Easter she filled her chamber pot with a clotted mass of blood. In June Girard transferred her to a convent at Ollioules, where she remained until September. Accounts of what happened next vary, but apparently the bishop of Toulon, desiring proof of Cadière's miracles, sent her home, assigned her a new confessor, and exorcised her. At this point either Cadière, Girard, or both panicked.[11]

The factums provide a unique vantage point from which to study the case. They contain particular legal arguments and strategies meant to help the judges interpret the evidence and to mobilize public opinion. The ways in which lawyers crafted their narratives about what happened to Cadière's body and the tropes they deployed show what arguments they anticipated their readers would respond to. Cadière's and Girard's narratives and bodies were on trial. Both parties mobilized common presumptions about when, where, and how menstruating bodies should bleed and about the stereotypically deceptive female sexual and reproductive body in order to make different arguments about whether Cadière's body and blood were evidence of sexual violence, pregnancy and abortion, or of faked stigmata.[12] To do this they drew on a range of sources, including medical and theological texts, judicial precedents, and the expertise that ordinary people routinely put into practice to interrupt unwanted reproduction.[13] The scandal aired these arguments in judicial, theological, and public arenas, and the lawyers' sexualization of Cadière's body added to her public and private violations.

Historians of France have long been interested in what ordinary people knew about the world and how they gained this knowledge. Traditionally this has focused on reading, book ownership and circulation, and education.[14] Others have examined how a wider, broadly educated public, exactly the kind of people who would have read Chaudon's and Thorame's factums, interpreted legal briefs.[15] Historians of science and medicine increasingly focus on collaboration and shared knowledge. The central role of early modern and Enlightenment households, families, networks, and salons in the production and circulation of medical and scientific knowledge is well established.[16] Analyses of patient-practitioner correspondence, casebooks, consultation records, ego-documents, and legal records reveal the extent of shared understandings of embodiment and reproduction between patients from different backgrounds and their medical practitioners.[17] Attention to the ways in which the lawyers in the Cadière-Girard case deployed and manipulated medical tropes about pregnancy, menstruation, and the female body underscores the extent to which these widely circulated understandings were shared with their readers. Constant references in the factums to sexual violence and menstruation were fundamental to the ways that the legal dispute played out. Therefore, attention to sexuality—here, the portrayal of sexual violence and reproductive processes—highlights the ways in which the production of knowledge was always in some ways embodied in those represented. It also brings into focus how legal and medical discourses intertwined, supported, and undermined one another, and thus the ways in which the law and its practitioners constructed, shared, and negotiated with their readership what we might think of as "common knowledge" about sexual violence and female reproductive and sexual bodies.[18]

There is another critical component in centering bodies and blood here. In an earlier reflection on this case, I wrote that I was not seeking the truth about what happened and that, because it is largely a case of Cadière's word against Girard's, we shall probably never know.[19] But in the light of Amy Stanley's reflections on writing about historical sexual assault in the context of #MeToo, that conclusion seems inadequate.[20] If we leave the history of sexual assault out of analyses of cases such as the Cadière-Girard affair, we distort the history of women, of gender, and of social relations more broadly, and we are ultimately silencing narratives about sexual violence done to female bodies because of our own discomfort.[21] This affair was fundamentally about sexual violence and its unwanted reproductive consequences. Therefore, even when we have little to no direct access to women's voices, as with Cadière, we must pay attention to the full range of possibilities of what happened to their bodies.[22] Behind the exaggerated and sensationalized textual and visual depictions of Cadière and Girard's sexual encounters were two real bodies, one of which probably violated the other. So, before we examine the lawyers' weaponization of Cadière's stigmatic and reproductive body, we must address Cadière and Girard's sexual relationship.

Locked Doors, Sorcery, and Renegade Priests

Jean-Baptiste Chaudon, Cadière's lawyer, did not need to attest rape to prove pregnancy and abortion, only that sex had taken place.[23] Nevertheless, drawing on strategies that signaled illicit, nonconsensual, and violent sex underscored the extent of Girard's spiritual and physical violations and Cadière's victimhood, paving the way for discussions of when and why she bled. Cadière's accusation of spiritual incest was an obvious and not uncommon strategy to attack Girard's credibility, playing into fears surrounding the intimacy of the confessional relationship.[24] It also cleverly connected the longstanding gendering of witchcraft as masculine in France with fears of "renegade priests" and the *affaire des poisons* of the previous century, to anti-Jesuit sentiment.[25] Explicitly comparing Girard to the priests Gaufridy and Grandier, associated with the infamous possession cases of the convents of Louviers and Loudun, Chaudon weaponized sorcery, indicating to his readers that Girard's violation of the bewitched Cadière extended beyond the priestly crime of fornicating with a penitent; it was also rape.[26] Although Girard could not be formally charged with witchcraft, a crime that was repealed in 1682, Chaudon repeatedly accused Girard of magic, enchantment, devilish pacts, and taking advantage of Cadière when she was in religious trances, having bewitched her with his breath.[27] The inference his readers would have understood was that, bewitched by magic and stripped of her agency, Cadière could not have consented to sex.[28] Recent controversy surrounding the "saint of Marseilles," Anne-Madeleine Rémusat (1696–1730), and her Jesuit confessor's predatory examinations of her pious wounds provided a local and contemporary blueprint for Chaudon's presentation of Girard as a powerful priestly predator bewitching and violating a younger, innocent victim who had little knowledge of the realities of sexual encounters.[29]

Chaudon used discussions of locked doors—synonymous with sexual violence—as a clear signal to his readers that Girard had violated Cadière during his repeated unchaperoned visits.[30] Dismissing Girard's lawyer's claims that the priest only briefly locked doors to inspect Cadière's stigmata, Chaudon cited Cadière's own statements and witness depositions, including that of Claire Bernarde, the Cadière family servant, to demonstrate the frequency of Girard's visits, the timing of the locked doors since Carnival in February 1730, that Girard's visits often lasted three to four hours, and that Cadière had frequently come to her senses to find herself in compromising positions on the bed with Girard, half dressed and with her corset unlaced.[31] Chaudon asked why Girard had played physician and surgeon, instead of calling an expert to authenticate Cadière's corporeal signs, as the law required, and why her mother was not present if his intentions had been anything other than predatory.[32]

Girard's lawyer, Claude-François Pazery de Thorame, responded by casting doubt on the timing of the locked doors, and hence of sex, to dismiss the possibility of pregnancy and abortion. He argued that Girard had only admitted to locking the doors during Holy Week (April 1730), when Cadière first experienced the stigmata, thus eliminating the possibility that she had been pregnant and had an abortion that same week. He noted that Cadière confessed under interrogation that she had had sex with Girard when he "disciplined" her on May 22–23, 1730, meaning there could have been no pregnancy or abortion in April.[33]

Chaudon was not defeated. His language escalated in response to Girard's second factum as he detailed "the unequivocal marks of a violated girl," and "violation," "rape," and "jouissance" replaced "spiritual incest."[34] Prior to May 23, 1730, he argued, Cadière had always been in a religious ecstasy when Girard abused her, and only with hindsight had she understood what had happened. But on May 23, he argued, Girard had sworn Cadière to secrecy, not because it was his first violation of her, but because it was the first time she had been aware of what was happening during the assault.[35] Sex on May 23 did not rule out earlier sexual violence, or, more significantly, pregnancy and abortion in April. Moreover, Chaudon implied that this act had been sodomitical—one of "those sexual encounters the law punishes by fire"— adding to the charges against Girard and offering a second interpretation for Cadière's loss of sexual innocence on May 23, 1730.[36]

Stigmata: Blood and Sex

While Chaudon used familiar tropes of locked doors, renegade priests, and sorcery to make his case, both lawyers based much of their arguments on discussions of "spiritual incest," "spiritual imposture," and blood, all of which were powerful cultural signifiers in the early eighteenth century and potent vehicles for the assaults that Cadière and Girard's lawyers fired at one another. Here, the lawyers drew on a rich and widely accepted set of understandings about the role of blood in stigmata and of the stereotypically deceitful female reproductive body.[37] By the time of the trial, there was no longer any question of authenticating Cadière's stigmata. Rather, it had become a case of understanding what and who had caused them, and how. To make a case for "spiritual imposture," Thorame drew on two common anxieties that would have resonated with his audience: that stigmata could be falsified, and that women could use their menstrual blood to fake the signs of violence and crime, even to the extent that they might collect their menses and secret them about their person until an opportunity to use them arose.[38] He was helped in this by the fact that Cadière's story did not follow the blueprint for stigmatic spirituality in 1730. Chaudon defended Cadière on multiple levels, arguing that Girard had believed in the authenticity of the marks and renewing charges of bewitching and sexual abuse. The arguments both lawyers made, given the purpose of the factums, underscore how widely understood and processed ideas of blood and stigmata were.

The history of stigmatic wounds is complex and multivalent. What it meant to bear the stigmata—whether they should be visible, invisible, bloody, internal, or external—changed across the centuries, as did the nature of proof required to authenticate miracles.[39] Bleeding Franciscan stigmata are the most familiar corporeal mark of piety, but Saint Catherine of Siena, who provided the model for later French stigmatics, suffered internal, invisible stigmata, which did not bleed. As Xenia von Tippelskirch notes, the myth that stigmatics always bleed is a nineteenth-century invention.[40] Cadière's extravagant, bloody transfigurations were, to use Mary Douglas's concept, "matter out of place" in 1730.[41]

Increasingly, early modern medical experts tested corporeal manifestations of piety as the Catholic church pursued proof and imposture more rigorously. Once commonly accepted beliefs that the imagination could imprint corporeal marks onto flesh during contemplation of spiritual models were met with increasing skepticism.[42] Accordingly, very few eighteenth-century cases were interpreted as stigmata.[43] Accusations of spiritual imposture were frequent, and many female stigmatics admitted to pricking or cutting themselves, or using paint or red dye and hot wax or ash to burn marks into themselves.[44] Yet, there is surprisingly little evidence of women accused of faking Christ's Passion with menses.[45] Thorame's accusation is thus even more striking.

In this context, Chaudon quickly recognized the limited usefulness of maintaining that Cadière's daily bleeding through Lent had been the pious corporeal impression of the pain of her sins, but continued to argue that the stigmata were supernatural.[46] Girard's iniquities, he maintained, indicated a demonic rather than divine origin for Cadière's stigmatic bleeding, connecting her stigmata to Girard's bewitching and, by implication, sexual abuse.[47] In making the case for a demonic cause, Chaudon drew his readers' attention to the multiple exorcisms Cadière underwent in October and November 1730 to end her violent transfigurations.[48] Girard denied his part, but he too blamed malefic spirits for Cadière's physical symptoms, with Thorame arguing that the stigmata had closed up immediately in response to exorcism, proving malign supernatural origins.[49]

Chaudon worked hard to counter Thorame's accusation that Cadière had faked the stigmata with menstrual blood. He cited numerous witnesses testifying to having seen Cadière's stigmata actively bleeding to refute Thorame's claim that no one had seen the commencement of her stigmatic transfigurations.[50] Girard himself had been with Cadière from 9 a.m. to midday on Good Friday of April 1730 when she first experienced the full stigmata, he protested.[51] Moreover, on July 7, 1730, when the full stigmata appeared a fourth time, Dame de Reimbaud testified to having been with Cadière all day, apart from fifteen minutes, which was not long enough, Chaudon reasoned, for her to have painted herself with menstrual blood. How, he asked, "would this blood which was dry at the start of the transfiguration have become suddenly liquid and flowed, not only from the crown and her forehead, but also her hands," if it were dried menstrual blood?[52] Indeed, Chaudon argued that Girard had been the first to use the term *stigmata* to describe Cadière's wounds, testifying under interrogation that they were sometimes closed and sometimes bleeding copiously.[53]

Chaudon drew on anxieties about predatory priests abusing their power over their penitents to argue that Girard had crossed the line between appropriate and inappropriate knowledge of a penitent's corporeality. Spiritual directors walked a fine line; they had to act as guarantors of their penitents' saintliness and credibility in order to protect them from allegations of fraud and imposture, while avoiding accusations of impropriety. Confessors regularly testified to the authenticity of their penitents' extreme fasting, physical marks of piety, and lack of menstruation or excretion.[54] But, Chaudon argued, Girard had gone too far. He had failed to secure official medical examinations of the transfigurations and had used them as a pretext for sexual abuse. Hearkening back to the scandal surrounding Rémusat, Chaudon argued that Girard had used Cadière's bleeding marks as a pretext to assault her, neatly linking the blood of stigmata to their sexual relationship in the minds of his readers.[55] A spiritual director did not need to lock doors to examine a penitent's blood-soaked linen or stigmata, Chaudon reminded his readers.[56] Girard offered "a seductive description" of a wound four fingers away from Cadière's left nipple that was always bleeding, thereby demonstrating, Chaudon asserted, unholy knowledge of Cadière's corporeality and narrative, far beyond the expectations of a confessor's role.[57]

Chaudon repeatedly called out Girard for acting as physician and theologian. Chaudon did so because both the public and the judges would have known that external, impartial verification of Cadière's claims to stigmata was necessary and that Girard knew that it was his duty as confessor to ensure that this was done.[58] The only medical evaluation noted before the trial began is that of an anonymous physician who examined Cadière at Ollioules in July 1730.[59] Tellingly, the most detailed descriptions of Cadière's wounds in the briefs were given not by medical experts, but by Girard during his interrogation.[60]

Chaudon's deliberate eroticization of the bloodied and sexual exchanges between Girard and Cadière heightened the impression of Girard's inequities, while exacerbating the violation of Cadière's body and narrative. For example, Chaudon reported that on one occasion, Girard and Cadière drank the water used to wash her bloodied face, ingesting the blood of their shared spiritual and sexual passion.[61] On another, Girard reproached Cadière for putting plasters on her wounds, kissing them better himself.[62] "She often sweated blood," Chaudon quoted Girard as having said, "and her wounds changed their color and figure."[63] Girard also allegedly cut Cadière's hair so that the "drops of blood which fell in a crown around her head" might be more visible—an act he denied.[64] Chaudon even eroticized Girard's own bodily fluids. Once Girard reportedly left Cadière to lick lumps of phlegm he had coughed up in her cell, representing another level of corporeal violation and submission and the power Girard had over his penitent.[65]

Chaudon's and Thorame's inscriptions of this scandal in and on Cadière's sexual body show how the affair connects to issues of knowledge and stereotypes of the female sexual and stigmatic body, as well as the predatory priestly body. Girard, Chaudon argued, had transgressed boundaries he should have upheld, boundaries his readers would have recognized. Chaudon's overt sexualization of Cadière and her bleeding wounds emphasized Girard's transgressions while rendering the lawyer complicit in the public violation of Cadière's sexual body and its bloody periodicity.

Periodicity: What Kind of Blood?

Legal and public perceptions of Cadière's saintliness or trickery and her pregnancy and abortion depended largely on estimations of how and when she bled, and why. Chaudon and Thorame publicly mapped their arguments about the provenance, nature, and meaning of Cadière's blood onto contemporary medical norms of menstruation and reproduction. They did so because the normative model of regular monthly periodicity suited the different arguments they were making about Cadière's sexual body and Girard's relationship to it, and understanding of this model was widespread. Speculation in medical and jurisprudential literature and wider society about the practical application of normative models in ambiguous cases might have been helpful to some aspects of Chaudon and Thorame's arguments. But both lawyers ignored debates that destabilized any straightforward connection between menstruation and reproduction, in which women menstruated without ever conceiving, conceived without ever menstruating, or menstruated throughout pregnancy.[66] That they did so, using the same models to make opposite arguments about the origin and type of bloody flows Cadière emitted, whether they were stigmatic, menstrual, or abortive depending on the timing and periodicity of their appearances, suggests that these are the arguments they decided would be most effective and far-reaching because they were based on common knowledge.

In constructing their arguments, Chaudon and Thorame also recognized and deliberately appealed to broad cultural anxieties about menstrual blood, the stereotypically deceptive capacities of the female sexual and reproductive body, and the ambiguities of blood-related substances.[67] Thorame's task was easier here, as discussed below. He simply had to tap into these anxieties, suggesting that Cadière had misinterpreted her corporeal periodicity willfully or through ignorance, or that she had taken advantage of the ambivalence of blood and the difficulty of telling one blood-related substance from another in practical terms, to pass off her menses as the blood of stigmata. For Chaudon, mapping Cadière's menstrual periodicity onto recognizable and regular norms meant he could argue that it was disciplined, ordered and moral, and that the rhythms of her menstrual and stigmatic bleeding were separate and distinct, subverting tropes of women's bodies as "leaky vessels."[68] Once Chaudon had established distinct periodicities, he could insist on this as evidence that she had not faked the stigmata with menses and that the pregnancy and abortion had indeed occurred.

In the trial, both sides used Cadière's Lent journal and correspondence with Girard to determine whether she could have used menses to fake the stigmata. Thorame attacked the credibility of these sources, suggesting that Cadière's brothers had written them *a postiori*, thereby introducing a third charge of fraud and imposture to those of spiritual imposture and spiritual incest that sparked the judicial proceedings. Still, both sides cited these sources to underscore their dating of Cadière's bleeding and their interpretation of the type of blood emitted, suggesting that even if the sources had been falsified, it suited both parties to use them to reconstruct Cadière's menstrual and stigmatic periodicity along normative lines.[69] Winning the argument clearly seemed more important to both lawyers than the messy, bloody, corporeal truth.

Each lawyer put together a calendar of bleeding with dates and type of bloody emissions taken from the letters and diary, which they interpreted differently. On March 8, 1730 (the fourteenth day of Cadière's Lent diary), contemplation of the pain of the sin of men sent Cadière to bed with heavy spitting and discharging of blood. On April 7, Good Friday, she experienced her first stigmata with smearing of blood on her face. The stigmata and smeared blood repeated on May 8, June 11, July 7, and July 20. Cadière wrote to Girard on June 11 that she had a "lot of spitting of blood and heavy blood loss." On August 8 she wrote to Girard that her medicine had caused her to cough a lot of blood and that she was bedridden. On September 9 her diary noted that her hands and feet were covered in blood.[70]

Based on this calendar, Thorame insisted that Cadière's menstrual and stigmatic bleeding had coincided around the seventh to the eleventh of each month from February to October of 1730. Hence, he contended, there had been no pregnancy or abortion, and she could have easily faked her stigmatic transfigurations.[71] Chaudon argued the opposite. He claimed that Cadière's menstrual and stigmatic emissions were entirely distinct, her periods occurring at the end of the month and her transfigurations continuously. Here, Chaudon cited Girard's letter of July 30, indicating that Cadière had her periods on the twenty-ninth or thirtieth of each month, to refute the possibility that the transfigurations that had occurred around the seventh and eighth of the month could have been faked using menses.[72] Emphasizing the normative monthly model of menstruation, he argued that "periodic bleeding does not come twice a month," and so the stigmata could not have been menses.[73] Moreover, whereas menstrual blood was evacuated through the genitals, during her transfigurations, Cadière emitted the blood of stigmata from all over her body, like a sweating of blood.[74] Here, Chaudon was playing physician, interpreting evidence about Cadière's sexual and reproductive body, much as he accused Girard of doing.

Thorame's claim that Cadière's blood was menstrual rather than stigmatic was designed to resonate with elite medieval pseudoscientific anxieties concerning the nature of menses, arouse repugnance, play to fears of artful women who used menses to fake the blood of crimes, and discredit Cadière further.[75] Ingeniously, Chaudon turned this argument back onto Girard. Chaudon asserted that Girard would not have told the nuns who had gathered to watch Cadière's transfiguration on July 7 to "conserve the water used to wash her face which was mixed with her blood because it would produce miraculous effects," nor would he himself have drunk from that water, had he regarded "these transfigurations as a daubing of periodic blood." Girard would not have wanted contact with menstrual blood, let alone to ingest it.[76] Nor would he have kissed Cadière's wounds if he had believed them to be scrofula or menstrual rather than stigmatic blood.[77] Chaudon also manipulated Levitical interdictions on sex during menstruation, arguing that "Girard would have been the first to complain" if the daily

Lenten transfigurations and bleeding had been menstruation, inferring that Girard would not have been able to or would not have wanted to have sex with Cadière.[78]

Abortion?

Proving pregnancy and abortion was crucial to disproving spiritual imposture; Cadière could not have smeared herself with menses during Holy Week if she miscarried a few days later. Chaudon and Thorame used medical norms about the cessation of menstruation during pregnancy, focusing on Cadière's bloody chamber pot. Both ultimately drew yet again on the stereotype of the deceitful female reproductive body and narrative, arguing that they were better placed than Cadière to interpret her corporeality.

Chaudon used the bloody chamber pot to drive home his argument about "incest," connecting the blood and sexual abuse. First, Chaudon argued that Girard's regular assaults from Carnival in February onward resulted in a "suppression of those marks (menstruation) which pregnancy excludes for three months."[79] Next, Chaudon claimed that Girard, afraid of pregnancy, prepared an abortifacient beverage, which he gave to Cadière to "cool her blood" over eight days following Lent in 1730. Cadière complained of the taste and reddish color.[80] Bernarde situated the resulting abortion two or three days after Easter, in April, when Cadière asked her to dispose of a bloody chamber pot.[81] Chaudon described "a great hemorrhage" that Cadière suffered, "which lasted several days and made her pass a small mass of flesh of clotted blood."[82] Girard admitted under interrogation that Cadière had shown him a chamber pot full of "a blackish liquid" a few days after Easter, but denied that this contained a fetus, claiming he had only given her water to drink.[83] Chaudon accused him of playing physician again.[84] Witness depositions confirmed Cadière's heavy blood loss after Easter, Girard's preparation of her drinks, and his refusal to let her be seen by anyone else.[85] Chaudon asked, "How many women would take the same pains to show such a pot of blood to their husbands?" He was alluding to the viscerality of the chamber pot's contents, while intimating that the pot and its contents incarnated Cadière and Girard's transgressive unholy intimacy.[86]

Refuting the charge of abortion, Thorame disputed the contents of the chamber pot. He claimed that Cadière had not interpreted the blood in her chamber pot as a fetus straight away. She had initially spoken of blood, he argued, changing that description to a "mass of flesh" during the trial, suggesting confusion and coaching.[87] In response Chaudon played physician again, arguing here not for common knowledge of the materials of interrupted reproduction, but instead for inexperience born of innocence in such matters. He contended that neither Cadière nor the witnesses would have been able to differentiate between a pot full of blood from an early miscarriage and menstrual blood and that no one (meaning no surgeon or physician) "took the trouble of dissecting it to see if it was flesh stained by the blood it was in, or all blood." Here he again argued that Girard had not sought impartial medical advice at this point because a surgeon or physician would have perceived the truth of the situation: that the pot contained the blood and flesh of an abortion.[88] Chaudon drew at great length on classical and contemporary medical and legal examples (including the 1682 *affaire des poisons*) to demonstrate the wide availability of abortifacients and to show that Cadière's symptoms fit with an abortion. Thus he countered claims by a physician who had examined Cadière at Ollioules months after the alleged abortion that nonfatal, effective abortions were impossible.[89]

Having argued that the heavy blood loss after Easter was the result of an abortion, Chaudon then posited that Cadière could not have been menstruating over Easter weekend, because she was pregnant; therefore, her Holy Week transfigurations were not faked using menses. Chaudon could make this argument because he knew that he shared with his audience knowledge of normative models of female reproductive functions. His readers knew that if the heavy blood loss in the chamber pot had been an abortion, menstruation would not have occurred so soon afterward, and that conversely, if the heavy blood loss had been a period, menstruation would not have occurred twice in eight days. Either way, it was impossible for Cadière to have faked her transfigurations on those days with menses.[90] Neither lawyer mentioned the possibility of the blood of pregnancy loss being used to fake stigmatic bleeding; presumably that was a step too far for their readers.

Chaudon demonstrated that when Girard sent Cadière to Ollioules in June 1730, he had taken precautions to ensure that the abortion had been successful and that Cadière had not become pregnant again from subsequent abuse. Cadière entered the convent on the condition that Girard could visit her secretly and that their correspondence would not be censored.[91] Girard later enquired whether Cadière had suffered any "blood losses," explaining that she had recently "lost twenty *livres* of blood" and asking the abbess whether Cadière's menstrual cycle had resumed.[92]

Neither party openly considered the possibility that Cadière's—real or contrived—individual humoral temperament might not have conformed exactly to medical norms of menstrual periodicity, because drawing on norms better suited their arguments. The strong cultural and etymological connection between calendar months and menstrual time made this an obvious argument for Chaudon to push. Moreover, it allowed him to argue that Cadière's stigmatic bleeding was temporally distinct from her menstrual bleeding and that because menstruation ceases during pregnancy, she could not have faked the first stigmata in April with menses. Strikingly, although Thorame drew less on medical knowledge than did Chaudon, he also claimed that Cadière's body followed constructed menstrual and reproductive norms, rather than pushing back against Chaudon's use of these models. Thorame could plausibly have argued that the uncertain timing of individual menstrual cycles meant that Cadière could have faked her stigmata with menses twice in one month, or that if she had continued to menstruate during pregnancy, as some women did, she would have had ample matter to fake her Lenten transfigurations. To argue the latter, however, meant conceding pregnancy, which, obviously, Thorame was disputing.[93] Both lawyers seem to have calculated that it would be easier for the public and the judges to follow arguments based on accepted norms rather than more complex, and potentially confusing, medical arguments about possible exceptions to these rules. Chaudon may have had an additional reason to rely on medical norms. Doing so disallowed the possibility that Cadière's body was uncontainable, instead allowing him to assert control over his interpretation of an otherwise potentially unstable signifier.

Having seemingly lost the medical argument about menstrual and stigmatic periodicity, Thorame turned to another set of female stereotypes, accusing Cadière of confusion. Cadière, he argued, was confused about the dates of her transfigurations and her alleged pregnancy and abortion; her body and her narrative were deceitful. As discussed above, in a second round of legal briefs, Girard's lawyer used Cadière's admission that sex had occurred on May 23, 1730, to rule out pregnancy and abortion in April. Given that Cadière had entered the convent on June 6, it was highly unlikely, if not impossible, that Girard could have suspected pregnancy and induced abortion in the intervening ten days.[94] Thorame drew on the anonymous physician's interpretation of Cadière's bleeding and stomach cramps in July as periodic and menstrual, rather than stigmatic, and the result of purgatives given to her at the convent, rather than ongoing symptoms of an April abortion, to rule out any suggestion of pregnancy and abortion resulting from the May 23 sexual encounter.[95] Thorame then used Bernarde's testimony to undermine Cadière's timeline. The servant, the only witness to Cadière and Girard having been alone in Cadière's bedchamber (although Girard himself admitted this, as stated above), claimed that she had first noticed the locked door during Carnival in February 1730, not in December 1729 as Cadière had said.[96] Sexual intercourse in February could have resulted in pregnancy and thus an abortion in April, but Thorame meant to emphasize Cadière's slippery narrative as well as her deceitful body.

Chaudon reiterated the cultural stereotype that Thorame had introduced, but he did so to show that he knew the truth. It was imperative for Chaudon to prove that Cadière had been pregnant during Lent and hence could not have faked her stigmata with menstrual blood. To do so, he applied the norm of the cessation of menstruation during pregnancy, arguing that Cadière had simply been mistaken about her bodily time, misinterpreting her menstrual cycle as women were wont to do. In so doing, Chaudon drew on medical observations that women were often mistaken about the timing of conception and pregnancy length because they misinterpreted their own corporeal signs.[97] A three-month suppression of menstrual bleeding meant that Cadière was two, not three, months pregnant, Chaudon argued. In order to have been two months pregnant in early April, pregnancy must have begun during Carnival (February 12–15, 1730), which was consistent with Bernarde's account of when the door to Cadière's chamber was first locked during Girard's visits.[98] Having established that Cadière's pregnancy was possible, Chaudon then cycled back to infer the normative absence of menstrual blood with which to fake stigmata during this time. Drawing further on medical norms about the symptoms of pregnancy and the relationship between pregnancy and menstruation, Chaudon argued that fetuses needed only menstrual blood as nourishment, rather than external substances, countering Girard's attack that pregnancy during fasting was impossible.[99] Given that Cadière's menses were retained during pregnancy, she could not have faked her stigmata with them. Chaudon also argued that the vomiting Cadière experienced throughout Lent was a normal sign of pregnancy and proved "spiritual incest."[100] In short, much of Chaudon's argument rested on the interlayering of tropes about women's inability to understand what was happening with their own bodies and larger normative conceptions about menstruation and pregnancy that he knew his readers would recognize.

So what does centering the sexual, stigmatic, and reproductive body add to our understanding of the Cadière-Girard affair and to the history of sexuality? Religious politics explain why the Cadière-Girard sexual scandal became such a high-profile *cause célèbre*, but they alone do not explain how and why the lawyers constructed such lengthy and detailed arguments based on commonly held ideas around blood, menstruation, pregnancy, and stigmata. The meanings of Cadière's blood—whether from her stigmata or from her reproductive body—reverberated around France and Europe largely because Chaudon and Thorame deliberately and overtly sexualized and publicized it in their factums. In the lawyers' narratives Cadière's bloodied and bleeding body literally and metaphorically incarnated accusations of misuse of clerical power, questions of Gallican identity in a Catholic war of miracles, and wider anxieties about blood, procreation, and unstable female bodies and narratives in a patriarchal and pronatalist society.

The Cadière-Girard affair marks a significant point in the history of sexuality, stigmata, and reproduction in early eighteenth-century France precisely because Chaudon and Thorame centered Cadière's blood and body in the case, knowing that was an effective strategy. Many of the tropes that the factums drew on were familiar from the long history of priestly sexual abuse, and rape cases: locked doors; sorcery; older predators and young, innocent victims; and abuse of clerical authority to gain intimate access to and knowledge about the penitent's sexual reproductive bodies. Chaudon and Thorame tapped into medical and bodily common knowledge that they knew their readers would understand. This common knowledge underpinned their complex, layered arguments about the source of Cadière's stigmatic bleeding; her possible pregnancy and abortion; the connection between sex, pregnancy, and the cessation of menstruation; and the resonance of blood, stigmatic or otherwise, and of stereotypes about the deceptive female narrative and body. But the fact they cited this body of knowledge at such length, discussing the materiality of the unwanted and interrupted reproduction resulting from sexual violence in lurid detail in the judicial arena, was extraordinary. For the lawyers, Cadière was a vehicle for their personal success. Their weaponizing of her sexual and reproductive body, through their deliberate focus on and sexualization of blood in the factums, embodied and compounded Girard's sexual violations, while allowing them to frame and contain Cadière's slippery, messy, and potentially deceitful corporeality. That they could do this in such a way, and on such a scale tells us about the appetite in France at this point for control of women's narratives, embodiment, and role in procreation.

In 1730 Cadière's stigmatic blood was clearly "matter out of place". Via the new and striking accusation that she faked her stigmata with menses, her blood tied the unstable and potentially deceitful female sexual and reproductive body to acute anxieties about imposture and levels of proof in medico-legal and theological circles. The factums from this case manifest in new ways negative politicization and sexualization of women's bodies by religious, political, medical, and legal actors, and they do so on a scale more generally associated with the last decades of the *ancien régime*. The lawyers depicted as problematic "matter out of place" not only Cadière's stigmatic blood but the female reproductive and sexual body in general. Repeatedly, Thorame and Chaudon demonstrated that they, Girard, and potentially their readers could possess greater knowledge of the meanings of blood than Cadière herself. Girard used that understanding to violate Cadière, Chaudon argued, but the lawyer also played at being a medical expert. Chaudon, in particular, constructed and interpreted Cadière's body as evidence of Girard's crimes and as evidence that the opaque, mysterious sexual and reproductive female body could be controlled by men like him and them, through the application of medical norms.

Historians Mita Choudhury and Stéphane Lamotte interpret the court's striking volte-face in October 1731 to deliver a split verdict as the result of local and national religious, political, and crowd pressure.[101] Undoubtedly this was so. But we should also consider the part that Chaudon and Thorame's map of how to contain and explain Cadière's blood may have played in the judges' decision. To condemn Cadière, as the September verdict did, was to admit fully the dangers and opacity of the female sexual and reproductive body and its capacity for deception. To condemn Girard was to acknowledge the possibility of violent sexual assault and abortion, accepting that the dangers of the confessional were real. The split verdict reduced Cadière's body and narrative to a confused, ignorant young girl who had misinterpreted her corporeal signs. It silenced and repressed the threats contained in the supposedly deceitful sexual and reproductive female body with the reassurance that in the judicial arena, lawyers could use medical norms to correctly read and stabilize Cadière's verbal and corporeal truth. In other words, the verdict followed the map that Chaudon and Thorame had laid out to contain the female sexual and reproductive body, a map that transcended the particulars of the Cadière-Girard affair, providing a blueprint for the rest of the old regime and beyond. In so doing, the lawyers supported larger arguments about female sexual identity discussed by Nina Kushner in this volume.

But we must not forget that before Cadière became a vehicle in the scandal, she experienced sexual assault, ambiguous bleeding, unwanted pregnancy, and a coerced abortion. She was then subject to a long, public, humiliating trial and risked the death penalty. We cannot know the impact of this trauma on Cadière herself, because we do not have access to her version of what she experienced. But we can refuse to accept the documents' silencing of her voice. And, in the context of the history of sexuality and sexual violence, we can examine the affair for what it was: the (extra)ordinary, violent policing of an already violated, exceptional woman's body by theologians, politicians, jurists, medical practitioners, and the wider public seeking to quiet anxieties that her bloodied and bleeding body sparked.

Acknowledgments

Thanks to Nina Kushner, Andrew Israel Ross, Jennifer J. Davis, Julie Hardwick, and the anonymous reviewers for their feedback on this chapter.

Notes

1. Stephen Haliczer, *Sexuality in the Confessional: A Sacrament Profaned* (New York: Oxford University Press, 1996); and Andrew Keit, "The Miraculous Body of Evidence: Visionary Experience, Medical Discourse and the Inquisition in Seventeenth-Century Spain," *Sixteenth Century Journal* 36, no. 1 (Spring, 2005): 77.

2. Stéphane Lamotte, *L'affaire Girard-Cadière: Justice, satire et religion au XVIIIe siècle* (Aix, France: Presses universitaires de Provence, 2016).

3. *Conclusions de Monsieur le Procureur Général du Roy au parlement d'Aix le 11 septembre 1731; au sujet du procès entre le P. Girard, Jésuite et Catherine Cadière* (Aix, France: n.p., 1731), 2.

4. Mita Choudhury, *The Wanton Jesuit and the Wayward Saint: A Tale of Sex, Religion, and Politics in Eighteenth-Century France* (University Park: Pennsylvania State University Press, 2015); Mita Choudhury, "Female Mysticism and the Public Sphere in Eighteenth-Century France," in *Under the Veil*, ed. Katherine Quinsey (Newcastle, UK: Cambridge Scholars, 2012), 145–71; Mita Choudhury, "'Carnal Quietism': Embodying Anti-Jesuit Politics in the Catherine Cadière Affair, 1731," *Eighteenth-Century Studies* 39, no. 2 (Winter 2006): 173–86; Jason Kuznicki, "Sorcery and Publicity: The Cadière-Girard Scandal of 1730–1731," *French History* 21, no. 3 (September 2007): 289–312; Lamotte, *L'affaire Girard-Cadière*; and Colin Haydon, "Anti-Catholicism and Obscene Literature: The Case of Mrs. Mary Catherine Cadière and Its Context," in *The Church and Literature*, ed. Peter Clarke and Charlotte Methuen, Studies in Church History 48 (Woodbridge, UK: Boydell and Brewer, 2012), 208–18.

5. Mita Choudhury interrogates her own silencing of sexual abuse in the affair in a piece published just before this volume went to press. Mita Choudhury, "Tears and Empathy: Possible Methodologies for Studying Sexual Violence," in *On Being Adjacent to Historical Violence*, ed. Irene Kacandes (Berlin: De Gruyter, 2022), 465–84.

6. On the importance of reading bodies as well as texts, see Lyndal Roper, "Beyond Discourse Theory," *Women's History Review* 19, no. 2 (April 2010): 307–19; Cathy McClive and Nicole Pellegrin, eds., *Femmes en fleurs, femmes en corps. Sang, santé et sexualités du Moyen Âge aux Lumières* (Saint-Étienne, France: Presses universitaires de Saint-Étienne, 2010); Cathy McClive, *Menstruation and Procreation in Early Modern France* (Aldershot, UK: Ashgate, 2015).

7. Cited in Carlo Ginzburg, "Microhistory: Two or Three Things That I Know about It," *Critical Inquiry* 20, no. 1 (Autumn 1993): 10–35, citation at 33.

8. Other interested parties wrote pamphlets also, but here I investigate Thorame's and Chaudon's legal wrangling.

9. On factums, see Sarah Maza, *Private Lives and Public Affairs: The Causes Célèbres of Prerevolutionary France* (Berkeley: University of California Press, 1995), 34–37; and *Une histoire de la mémoire judiciaire de l'Antiquité à nos jours* [actes d'un colloque international organisé par l'Institut d'histoire du droit et l'École nationale des chartes, les 12, 13, et 14 mars 2008], ed. Olivier Poncet and Isabelle Storez-Brancourt (Paris: Écoles de Chartres, 2008).

10. Kuznicki, "Sorcery and Publicity"; Maza, *Private Lives and Public Affairs*; and Dena Goodman, ed., *Marie-Antoinette: Writings on the Body of a Queen* (New York: Routledge, 2003).

11. The Bibliothèque Nationale catalogue contains 140 factums relating to this case. I draw on a seven-volume compilation of the lawyers' arguments printed by Joseph David in Aix in 1731 and I reference the volume number and factum number, unless otherwise stated. Claude-François Pazery de Thorame, *Memoire instructif pour le Père Jean-Baptiste Girard, Jesuite, Recteur du College Royal de la Marine de la Ville de Toulon contre Marie Catherine Cadiere; et encore Monsieur le Procureur General du Roy Querellant*, factum 3 in *Recueil general des pieces concernant le procès entre la Dem. Cadiere et le P. Girard, Jésuite*, 7 vols. (Joseph David: Aix, 1731), 1: 5. See also *Histoire du procès entre Demoiselle Cadière et Père Cadière, d'une part et le père Girard* (La Haye, The Netherlands: Swart, 1731), 4; J-B Boyer d'Argens, *Mémoires de Monsieur le Marquis d'Argens* (Paris: Desjonqueres, 1993), 120.

12. J. Andrew Mendelsohn and Annemarie Kinzelbach, "Common Knowledge: Bodies, Evidence, and Expertise in Early Modern Germany," *Isis* 108, no. 2 (June 2017): 259–79.

13. Julie Hardwick, *Sex in an Old Regime City: Young Workers and Intimacy in France, 1660–1789* (New York: Oxford University Press, 2020), 110–39; McClive, *Menstruation and Procreation*, 126–28; John Christoupoulos, *Abortion in Early Modern Italy* (Cambridge MA: Harvard University Press, 2021).

14. For the French context, see Roger Chartier, *Lectures et lecteurs dans la France d'Ancien Régime* (Paris: Seuil, 1987); Roger Chartier, *Cultural Origins of the French Revolution*, trans. Lydia G. Cochrane (Durham NC: Duke University Press, 1991); Robert Darnton, *A Literary Tour de France: The World of Books on the Eve of the French Revolution* (New York: Oxford University Press, 2018); Simon Burrows, *The French Book Trade in Enlightenment Europe II: Enlightenment Bestsellers* (London: Bloomsbury, 2018); and Elizabeth Andrews Bond, *The Writing Public: Participatory Knowledge Production in Enlightenment and Revolutionary France* (Ithaca NY: Cornell University Press, 2021). On sex education, see Shane Agin, ed., *Sex Education in Eighteenth-Century France* (Oxford: SVEC, 2011); and Suellen Diaconoff, *Through the Reading Glass: Women, Books, and*

Sex in the French Enlightenment (Albany: State University of New York Press, 2005).

15. Maza, *Private Lives and Public Affairs*; Pascal Bastien, "Les arrêts criminels et leurs enjeux sur l'opinion publique à Paris au XVIIIe siècle," *Revue d'histoire moderne et contemporaine* 53, no. 1 (2006): 34–57.

16. For France, see Meghan K. Roberts, *Sentimental Savants: Philosophical Families in Enlightenment France* (Chicago: University of Chicago Press, 2016); Nina Gelbart, *Minerva's French Sisters: Women of Science in Enlightenment France* (New Haven CT: Yale University Press, 2021); Jean-François Viaud, "Recettes et remèdes recueillis par les particuliers aux XVIIe et XVIIIe siècles. Origine et Usage," *Histoire, médecine et santé* 2 (Autumn 2012): 61–74; and Marie Baudoin, *The Art of Childbirth: A Seventeenth-Century Midwife's Epistolary Treatise to Dr. Vallant*, ed. and trans. Cathy McClive (Toronto: Iter, 2022).

17. See the influential work by Barbara Duden, *The Woman beneath the Skin: A Doctor's Patients in Eighteenth-Century Germany* (Cambridge MA: Harvard University Press, 1998); and Mendelsohn and Kinzelbach, "Common Knowledge." For the French context, see Séverine Pilloud, "Mettre les maux en mots, médiations dans la consultation épistolaire au XVIIIe siècle: Les malades du Dr. Tissot," *Canadian Bulletin of Medical History* 16, no. 2 (Fall 1999): 215–45; Lisa W. Smith, "'An Account of an Unaccountable Distemper': The Experience of Pain in Early Eighteenth-Century England and France," *Eighteenth-Century Studies* 41, no. 4 (2008): 459–80; Nahema Hanafi, *Le frisson et le baume: Expériences féminines du corps au siècle des lumières* (Rennes, France: Presses universitaires de Rennes, 2017); and McClive, *Menstruation and Procreation*, chaps. 3–5.

18. On law and medicine in eighteenth-century France, see Lindsay Wilson, *Women and Medicine in Enlightenment France: The Debate over Maladies des Femmes* (Baltimore: Johns Hopkins University Press, 1993); and McClive, *Menstruation and Procreation*, chaps. 5–6.

19. McClive, *Menstruation and Procreation*, chap. 3.

20. Amy Stanley, "Writing the History of Sexual Assault in the Age of #MeToo," *Perspectives on History: The Newsmagazine of the American Historical Association*, September 24, 2018, https://www.historians.org/publications-and-directories/perspectives-on-history/november-2018/writing-the-history-of-sexual-assault-in-the-age-of-metoo. For a similar reflection in the French context, see Didier Lett et al., "Éditorial: Les Violences sexuelles au coeur de l'intime," *Clio. Femmes, Genre, Histoire* 2, no. 52 (2020): 7–19.

21. Julie Hardwick, "Sexual Violence and Domesticity," in *The Routledge History of the Domestic Sphere in Europe, Sixteenth to Nineteenth Centuries*, ed. Joachim Eibach and Margareth Lanziger (Abingdon, UK: Routledge, 2021), 239.

22. On the difficulties of working with judicial documents for rape cases, see Sylvie Steinberg, "Lire et interpreter les récits de viol dans les archives judiciaires (Europe, époque moderne)," *Clio. Femmes, Genre, Histoire* 2, no. 52 (2020): 163–93.

23. Lynn Mollenauer Wood, *Strange Revelations: Magic, Poison, and Sacrilege in Louis XIV's France* (University Park: Pennsylvania State University Press, 2007), chap. 4.

24. Choudhury, *Wanton Jesuit.*

25. McClive, *Menstruation and Procreation*, 134–35; William Monter, "Witchcraft Trials in France," in *Oxford Handbook of Witchcraft in Early Modern Europe and America*, ed. Brian Levack (Oxford: Oxford University Press, 2013), 217–31; Wood, *Strange Revelations.*

26. Jean-Baptiste Chaudon, *Reponse à la premiere partie du second memoire instructif du Pere Girard, Jesuite, pour Delle Catherine Cadiere*, factum 2 in *Recueil General*, 7: 77; Jean-Baptiste Chaudon, *Memoire instructif pour Delle Cadière, de la ville de Toulon . . . contre le Père Jean-Baptiste Girard*, factum 2 in *Recueil Général*, 1: 32

27. Jean-Baptiste Chaudon, *Justification de Delle Cadière contenant un recit fidele de tout ce qui s'est passe entre le Père Jean-Baptiste Girard et elle*, factum 3 in *Recueil Général*, 1: 3; Jean-Baptiste Chaudon, *Reponse de ladite Demoiselle Cadiere à la seconde partie du second memoire dudit Pere Girard*, factum 3 in *Recueil Général*, 7: 10–14; Chaudon, *Memoire instructif pour Delle Cadière*, factum 2 in *Recueil Général*, 1: 3, 26–34.

28. Frances Timber, "Liminal Language: Boundaries of Magic and Honor in Early Modern Essex," *Magic, Ritual, and Witchcraft* 2, no. 2 (Winter 2007): 178–79.

29. Xenia von Tippelskirch, "'Ma fille, je te la donne en modèle,' Sainte Catherine de Sienne et les stigmatisées du XVIIe siècle," *Archivio Italiano per la storia della pietà* 26 (2013): 259–78, quote on 278; Choudhury, *Wanton Jesuit*, 41.

30. The "locked door" was a frequent metaphor in rape narratives. Hardwick, *Sex in an Old Regime City*, 45–46; Hardwick, "Sexual Violence"; Garthine Walker, "Rereading Rape and Sexual Violence in Early Modern England," *Gender & History* 10, no. 1 (April 1998): 15–16; Jean-Baptiste Chaudon, *Reponse au memoire instructif du Pere Girard pour Delle Cadière, contre ledit Père Girard*, factum 5 in *Recueil général*, 1: 62; Hardwick, *Sex in an Old Regime City*, 65; Chaudon, *Memoire instructif pour Delle Cadière*, factum 2 in *Recueil Général*, 1: 4, 45–47.

31. Thorame, *Memoire instructif pour le Père Jean-Baptiste Girard*, factum 3 in *Recueil Général*, 1: 6, 31–32; Chaudon, *Reponse au memoire instructif du Pere Girard*, factum 5 in *Recueil Général*, 1: 67, 76; Chaudon, *Memoire instructif pour Delle Cadière*, factum 2 in *Recueil Général*, 1: 3, 26–33, 38, 44–46.

32. Chaudon, *Reponse de ladite Delle Cadière*, factum 3 in *Recueil Général*, 7: 21, 62, 122.

33. Thorame, *Memoire instructif pour le Père Jean-Baptiste Girard*, factum 3 in *Recueil Général*, 1: 5, 6, 31–32; Claude-François Pazery de Thorame, *Second memoire pour le Pere Girard, Jesuite, servant de reponse au nouveau memoire de la Cadière et de ses freres*, factum 4 in *Recueil Général*, 4: 264; Chaudon, *Memoire instructif pour Delle Cadière*, factum 2 in *Recueil Général*, 1: 5, 33, 45; Chaudon, *Reponse au memoire instructif du Pere Girard*, factum 5 in *Recueil Général*, 1: 66–67; Jean-Baptiste Chaudon, *Reponse au second memoire instructif du P. Girard pour Delle Cadière, Iere partie*, factum 5 in *Recueil Général*, 4: 354–56; Chaudon, *Reponse de ladite Delle Cadiere*, factum 3 in *Recueil Général*, 7: 68.

34. Chaudon, *Reponse au second memoire*, factum 5 in *Recueil Général*, 4: 354–56. On the language of rape, see Stéphanie Cautela Gaudillat, "Questions de mot. Le 'viol' au XVIe siècle, un crime contre les femmes?," *Clio. Histoire, Femmes et Sociétés* 24 (2006): 57–74.

35. Chaudon, *Reponse au second memoire*, factum 5 in *Recueil Général*, 4: 354–56; Chaudon, *Reponse de ladite Delle Cadière*, factum 3 in *Recueil Général*, 7: 69.

36. Chaudon, *Reponse au second memoire*, factum 5 in *Recueil Général*, 4: 356.

37. Ian MacInnes, "Stigmata on Trial: The Nun of Portugal and the Politics of the Body," *Viator* 31 (January 2000): 381.

38. Cathy McClive, "Blood and Expertise: The Trials of Female Medical Practitioners in the Ancien-Règime Courtroom," *Bulletin of the History of Medicine* 82, no. 1 (Spring 2008): 93–96.

39. Nicole Pellegrin, "Fleurs Saintes: L'écriture des stigmates (XVIe–XVIIIe siècles)," in McClive and Pellegrin, *Femmes en fleurs*, 101–22; Cordelia Warr, "Proving Stigmata: Antonio Daza, Saint Francis of Assisi and Juana de la Cruz," *Studies in Church History* 52 (June 2016): 283–97; Gianna Pomata, "Malpighi and the Holy Body: Medical Experts and Miraculous Evidence in Seventeenth-Century Italy," *Renaissance Studies* 21, no. 4 (September 2007): 569.

40. von Tippelskirch, "'Ma fille,'" 271.

41. Mary Douglas, *Purity and Danger: An Analysis of Concepts of Pollution and Taboo* (London: Routledge, 1966), 41.

42. Tamar Herzig, "Genuine and Fraudulent Stigmatics in the Sixteenth Century," in *Dissimulation and Deceit in Early Modern Europe*, ed. Miriam Eliav-Feldon and Tamar Herzig (Houndmills, UK: Palgrave Macmillan, 2015), 142–64; von Tippelskirch, "'Ma fille,'" 274–77.

43. von Tippelskirch, "'Ma fille,'" 276.

44. Stephen Haliczer, *Between Exaltation and Infamy: Female Mystics in the Golden Age of Spain* (Oxford: Oxford University Press, 2002), 135, 218; Frans Ciappara, "Simulated Sanctity in Seventeenth- and Eighteenth-Century Malta," *Studies in Church History* 47 (2011): 284.

45. For a nineteenth-century Mexican example, see Nora E. Jaffary, *False Mystics: Deviant Orthodoxy in Colonial Mexico* (Lincoln: University of Nebraska Press, 2004).

46. Chaudon, *Reponse au memoire instructif du Pere Girard*, factum 5 in *Recueil Général*, 1: 69; Chauduon, *Mémoire instructif pour Delle Cadière*, factum 2 in *Recueil Général*, 1: 3, 34. Thorame also argued that the stigmata were supernatural See Thorame, *Memoire instructif pour le Pere Jean-Baptiste Girard*, factum 3 in *Recueil Général*, 1: 3, 20.

47. Chaudon, *Memoire instructif pour Delle Cadière*, factum 2 in *Recueil Général*, 1: 33–34.

48. Chaudon, *Reponse au second memoire*, factum 5 in *Recueil Général*, 4: 348; Chaudon, *Reponse au memoire instrucif du pere Girard*, factum 5 in *Recueil Général*, 1: 3–4.

49. Thorame, *Memoire instructif pour le Pere Jean-Baptiste Girard*, factum 3 in *Recueil Général*, 1: 12–17, 20.

50. Thorame, *Second memoire pour le Père Girard*, factum 4 in *Recueil Général*, 4: 17, 54–55, 164; Chaudon, *Reponse au second memoire*, factum 5 in *Recueil Général*, 4: 372–74, 375; Chaudon, *Memoire instructif pour Delle Cadière*, factum 2 in *Recueil Général*, 1: 33; Chaudon, *Reponse de ladite Delle Cadière*, factum 3 in *Recueil Général*, 7: 63.

51. Chaudon, *Reponse au memoire instructif du Pere Girard*, factum 5 in *Recueil Général*, 1: 62.

52. Chaudon, *Reponse au second memoire*, factum 5 in *Recueil Général*, 4: 373.

53. Chaudon, *Memoire instructif pour Delle Cadière*, factum 2 in *Recueil Général*, 1: 5, 33.

54. Jodi Bilinkoff, *Related Lives: Confessors and Their Female Penitents, 1450–1750* (Ithaca NY: Cornell University Press, 2005), chap. 1.

55. Chaudon, *Reponse au memoire instructif du Pere Girard*, factum 5 in *Recueil Général*, 1: 54–55.

56. Chaudon, *Memoire instructif pour Delle Cadière*, factum 2 in *Recueil Général*, 1: 33–34, 63–64.

57. Chaudon, *Reponse au memoire instructif du Pere Girard*, factum 5 in *Recueil Général*, 1: 54–55.

58. Pomata, "Malpighi and the Holy Body"; McClive, "Blood and Expertise."

59. *Procedure sur laquelle le Père Jean-Baptiste Girard, Catherine Cadière ont été jugez par arrest du 10 octobre 1731* (Aix, France: Joseph David, 1733), 129.

60. Chaudon, *Reponse au memoire instructif du Pere Girard*, factum 5 in *Recueil Général*, 1: 9–10, 54–56.

61. Chaudon, *Reponse au second mémoire*, factum 5 in *Recueil Général*, 4: 75.

62. Chaudon, *Reponse au memoire instructif du Pere Girard*, factum 5 in *Recueil Général*, 1: 5, 45; Thorame, *Memoire instructif pour le Père Girard*, factum 3 in *Recueil Général*, 1: 6, 31–32.

63. Chaudon, *Reponse au memoire instructif du Pere Girard*, factum 5 in *Recueil Général*, 1: 7, 69.

64. Chaudon, *Reponse au memoire instructif du Pere Girard*, factum 5 in *Recueil Général*, 1: 10.

65. *Procedure sur laquelle le Père Jean-Baptiste Girard*, 69.

66. McClive, *Menstruation and Procreation*, chaps. 3–4.

67. Cathy McClive, "The Hidden Truths of the Belly: The Uncertainties of Pregnancy in Early Modern Europe," *Social History of Medicine* 15, no. 2 (August 2002): 209–27; McClive, "Blood and Expertise."

68. McClive, *Menstruation and Procreation*, 135.

69. Thorame, *Second memoire pour le Père Girard*, factum 4 in *Recueil Général*, 4: 11, 165; Choudhury, *Wanton Jesuit*, 100–1.

70. Thorame, *Memoire instructif pour le Pere Jean-Baptiste Girard*, factum 3 in *Recueil Général*, 1: 8, 38–41; Chaudon, *Reponse au memoire instructif du Pere Girard*, factum 5 in *Recueil Général*, 1: 68–69; Thorame, *Second memoire pour le Père Girard*, factum 4 in *Recueil Général*, 4: 266–69.

71. Thorame, *Memoire instructif pour le Pere Jean-Baptiste Girard*, factum 3 in *Recueil Général*, 1: 41–42; Chaudon, *Reponse au mémoire instructif du Pere Girard*, factum 5 in *Recueil Général*, 1: 68.

72. Chaudon, *Reponse au second memoire*, factum 5 in *Recueil Général*, 4: 370.

73. Chaudon, *Reponse au memoire instructif du Pere Girard*, factum 5 in *Recueil Général*, 1: 69.

74. Chaudon, *Reponse au memoire instructif du Pere Girard*, factum 5 in *Recueil Général*, 1: 7–8, 69.

75. See McClive, *Menstruation and Procreation*, chaps. 1–2.

76. Chaudon, *Reponse au second memoire*, factum 5 in *Recueil Général*, 4: 375; Chaudon, *Reponse au memoire instructif du Père Girard*, factum 5 in *Recueil Général*, 1: 8, 37.

77. Chaudon, *Reponse au memoire instructif du Pere Girard*, factum 5 in *Recueil Général*, 1: 37.

78. Chaudon, *Reponse au memoire instructif du Pere Girard*, factum 5 in *Recueil Général*, 1: 69.

79. Chaudon, *Memoire instructif pour Delle Cadière*, factum 2 in *Recueil Général*, 1: 48.

80. Chaudon, *Memoire instructif pour Delle Cadière*, factum 2 in *Recueil Général*, 1: 6, 48–49.

81. Chaudon, *Memoire instructif pour Delle Cadière*, factum 2 in *Recueil Général*, 1: 48–49; Chaudon, *Justification de Delle Cadière*, factum 1 in *Recueil Général*, 1: 2–4.

82. Chaudon, *Memoire instructif pour Delle Cadière*, factum 2 in *Recueil Général*, 1: 9, 48; Chaudon, *Reponse au memoire instructif du Pere Girard*, factum 5 in *Recueil Général*, 1: 69. Chaudon, *Justification de Delle Cadière*, factum 1 in *Recueil Général*, 1: 4.

83. Chaudon, *Reponse au memoire instructif du Père Girard*, factum 5 in *Recueil Général*, 1: 72; Chaudon, *Memoire instructif pour Delle Cadière*, factum 2 in *Recueil Général*, 1: 49; Thorame, *Memoire instructif pour le Pere Jean-Baptiste Girard*, factum 3 in *Recueil Général*, 1: 5, 38–39.

84. Chaudon, *Reponse à la premiere partie*, factum 2 in *Recueil Général*, 7: 21, 122, 159.

85. Chaudon, *Memoire instructif pour Delle Cadière*, factum 2 in *Recueil Général*, 1: 48–50; Thorame, *Memoire instructif pour le Pere Jean-Baptiste Girard*, factum 3 in *Recueil Général*, 1: 40.

86. Chaudon, *Memoire instructif pour Delle Cadière*, factum 2 in *Recueil Général*, 1: 46; Chaudon, *Reponse au memoire instructif du Pere Girard*, factum 5 in *Recueil Général*, 1: 72.

87. Thorame, *Second mémoire pour le Père Girard*, factum 4 in *Recueil Général*, 4: 269.

88. Chaudon, *Reponse de ladite Delle Cadière*, factum 3 in *Recueil Général*, 7: 72–74.

89. Chaudon, *Reponse de ladite Delle Cadière*, factum 3 in *Recueil Général*, 7: 77–85.

90. Chaudon, *Reponse au memoire instructif du Pere Girard*, factum 5 in *Recueil Général*, 1: 69.

91. Chaudon, *Justification de Delle Cadière*, factum 1 in *Recueil Général*, 1: 4.

92. Chaudon, *Memoire instructif pour Delle Cadière*, factum 2 in *Recueil Général*, 1: 7–8; Anonymous, *Précis des charges pour Demoiselle Catherine Cadière* (Aix, France: Imprimerie de la Veuve de Joseph Senz, 1731), 21; Chaudon, *Reponse au memoire instructif du Pere Girard*, factum 5 in *Recueil Général*, 1: 74; Thorame, *Memoire instructif pour le Père Girard*, factum 3 in *Recueil Général*, 1: 7.

93. McClive, *Menstruation and Procreation*, chap. 4.

94. Thorame, *Memoire instructif pour le Pere Jean-Baptiste Girard*, factum 3 in *Recueil Général*, 1: 39–41.

95. Chaudon, *Reponse de ladite Delle Cadière*, factum 3 in *Recueil Général*, 7: 74–75; Thorame, *Memoire instructif pour le Pere Jean-Baptiste Girard*, factum 3 in *Recueil Général*, 1: 3 9–41.

96. Thorame, *Memoire instructif du Pere Girard*, factum 3 in *Recueil Général*, 1: 39. Chaudon refuted this argument in *Reponse de ladite Delle Cadière*, factum 3 in *Recueil Général*, 7: 70.

97. McClive, *Menstruation and Procreation*, chap. 5.

98. Chaudon, *Reponse de ladite Delle Cadière*, factum 3 in *Recueil Général*, 7: 69–70.

99. Chaudon, *Reponse au second memoire*, factum 5 in *Recueil Général*, 4: 368.

100. Chaudon, *Reponse au second memoire*, factum 5 in *Recueil Général*, 4: 368.

101. Choudhury, *Wanton Jesuit*, 153–69; Lamotte, *L'affaire Girard-Cadière*, 88–98.

Suggested Reading

Choudhury, Mita. "Tears and Empathy: Possible Methodologies for Studying Sexual Violence." In *On Being Adjacent to Historical Violence*, edited by Irene Kacandes, 465–84. Berlin: De Gruyter, 2022.

———. *The Wanton Jesuit and the Wayward Saint: A Tale of Sex, Religion and Politics in Eighteenth-Century France*. University Park: Pennsylvania State University Press, 2015.

Duden, Barbara. *The Woman beneath the Skin: A Doctor's Patients in Eighteenth-Century Germany*. Cambridge MA: Harvard University Press, 1998.

Hanafi, Nahema. *Le frisson et le baume: Expériences féminines du corps au siècle des Lumières.* Rennes, France: Presses universitaires de Rennes, 2017.

Mara, Sarah. *Private Lives and Public Affairs: The Causes Célèbres of Prerevolutionary France*. Berkeley: University of California Press, 1995.

McClive, Cathy. "Masculinity on Trial: Penises, Hermaphrodites and the Uncertain Male Body in Early Modern France." *History Workshop Journal* 68, no. 1. (Autumn 2009): 45–68.

———. *Menstruation and Procreation in Early Modern France*. Aldershot, UK: Ashgate, 2015.

McClive, Cathy, and Nicole Pellegrin, eds. *Femmes en fleurs, femmes en corps. Sang, santé, sexualités du Moyen Âge aux Lumières*. Saint-Étienne, France: Presses universitaires de Saint-Étienne.

Mendelsohn, J. Andrew, and Annemarie Kinzelbach. "Common Knowledge: Bodies, Evidence, and Expertise in Early Modern Germany." *Isis* 108, no. 2 (June 2017): 259–79.

Roper, Lyndal. "Beyond Discourse Theory." *Women's History Review* 19, no. 2 (2010): 307–19.

Stanley, Amy. "Writing the History of Sexual Assault in the Age of #MeToo." *Perspectives on History: The Newsmagazine of the American Historical Association*, September 24, 2018, https://www.historians.org/publications-and-directories

/perspectives-on-history/november-2018/writing-the-history-of-sexual-assault
-in-the-age-of-metoo.

Vigarello, Georges. *A History of Rape: Sexual Violence in France from the 16th to the 20th Century*. Translated by Jean Birrell. Malden MA: Polity, 2001.

von Tippelskirch, Xenia. "'Ma fille, je te la donne en modèle,' Sainte Catherine de Sienne et les stigmatisées du XVIIe siècle." *Archivio Italiano per la storia della pietà* 26 (2013): 259–78.

3

UNCHASTE WOMEN

Sexuality and Identity in the Eighteenth Century

NINA KUSHNER

In the fall of 1718, Magdelaine Le Moyne, daughter of a cavalry captain, wrote the first of what would be a number of complaints that she and her family sent to the police of Paris. She was protesting the long-standing affair between her husband, a man named Guevin, a clerk for the Duc de Noailles, and his lover, a woman named Louise Le Cœur. A rather complicated story emerges from the file, the central fact of which was that Guevin had a second family with Louise. Although he was legally married to Magdelaine and saw her and their children from time to time, he lived with Louise and their children. The two often passed as a married couple, having taken the surname Rademont. The affair likely predated the marriage, and it certainly continued for years before Magdelaine finally turned to the police. She asked for Louise's arrest and incarceration, anticipating that her husband would then return to her. The police agent charged with the case summarized it as follows: Louise was "known as a prostitute with married men and is at the point of giving birth to her sixth child."[1] Louise was arrested and then disappeared from the historical record.

Many elements of this case might catch an historian's attention. But when thinking about the relationship of sexuality to identity—the subject of this chapter—the most conspicuous is the police agent's use of the word "prostitute" (*prostituée*). Why did he call Louise a prostitute and what was a "prostitute with married men"? Louise certainly did not seem to be a prostitute in any modern sense of the word. There was no record of her having had sex with anyone but Guevin, with whom she was in a long-term relationship. Yet, Louise and thousands of women like her were labeled prostitutes by the police, other judicial agents, and people writing to complain about their sexual behavior. The police practice of labeling such women prostitutes—and the shift in the meaning of the word over the course of the century—was both constitutive and emblematic of a larger one: the construction of a sexual identity category, which I am calling the "unchaste woman." "Unchaste" has no direct equivalent in French and the police did not use the term *chasteté* (chastity). Chastity, however, was one of the underlying conceptual frameworks supporting various categories of heterosexual sexual deviance, and hence my decision to use the term "unchaste."

Another element of the case that catches the historian's attention is just how long the affair continued before Magdelaine and her family started to complain to the police. At least three years had elapsed since Magdelaine's marriage to Guevin, during which time she suspected her husband and Louise. What triggered the first complaint and what other steps the family might have taken to remedy the situation in the interim were not noted in the police file. Whatever the facts, that Guevin and Louise had lived together openly, though in a different city than Magdelaine, brings up a second set of questions. Were Guevin and Louise simply excellent dissimulators, as the complainants insisted, fooling those around them into believing they were legally wed? Or was their status as an adulterous couple not particularly problematic for the community in which they were living? The latter possibility raises a question: To what extent was the identity category of unchaste woman contingent, given that it rested on the violation of the rules of sexual decorum, which were themselves not set in stone?[2] It suggests that the sexual identity category of unchaste woman functioned differently in different registers and differently over time. This chapter attempts to make sense of the ways in which the construct of the unchaste woman developed across a wide range of discourses, but especially in law, and how the construct mattered in the lives of people as it was manipulated and deployed by lawyers, agents of the police, and Parisians wanting state intervention in family issues, particularly marriages. The relationship between the construct in discourse and its use in practice supports the argument that "unchaste woman" was a sexual identity category.

In considering the unchaste woman, this chapter makes the larger argument that sexual behavior was a core component of identity in the eighteenth century. This claim builds on existing scholarship on sexual identity, but it also deviates from it in important ways. Definitions of sexual identity are usually linked to Michel Foucault's work on the topic from the late 1970s. In his first volume of *The History of Sexuality*, Foucault posits that sexual orientation only emerged in the late eighteenth and early nineteenth centuries. In this period, and in conjunction with the rise of biopower, inner psychology and outer sexual behavior came to align. As a result, to use Foucault's example, the sodomite—a man who had sex with other men but was not differentiated on the basis of identity—now became a new type of person, the homosexual, and understood himself to be different as such.[3] For historians, especially those studying the modern period, sexual identity (and ultimately sexuality itself) came to be defined by desire on the one hand and subjectivity on the other. One's desires came to reveal a fundamental truth about who a person was. The construction of what we might call modern sexual identity was considered both a product and a characteristic of modernity.[4]

Scholars of earlier periods have since pushed back against this definition. Many have, in the words of historian Katherine Crawford, brought into question "the distinction between modern sexual 'identity' and premodern sexual 'acts', which at once located modernity in self-consciously sexual terms and privileged a teleological scheme with modern subjectivity as its end point."[5] These historians and literary scholars were joined by queer theorists who made much the same point, arguing that sexuality in the earlier periods must be understood in its context and hence on its own terms.[6] I lean on this research in a number of ways, as it allows for a definition of sexual identity that encompasses a range of relationships between sexual acts and sexual subjectivity. In this chapter I argue that sexual identities in the eighteenth century did not necessarily include their interiorization, or that, if they did, such subjectivity remains inaccessible to the historian. Thus, the question of sexual desire has to be treated very carefully. Whereas prospective sources have a great deal to say about female lust, sources generated from cases and ego documents are much quieter on the subject.

I deviate from this scholarship, however, in one critical way. I do not focus on sexual identity as it related to sex between men, or even between women, which is far less studied. The array of policing mechanisms—from family, to church, to the state—devoted to the control of same-sex sexual relations, even in the eighteenth century, was dwarfed by an order of magnitude by those focused on controlling sexual relations between men and women. These mechanisms were so pervasive, embedded in almost every power structure, that they are sometimes difficult to see. Whether or not some men and women understood themselves to be part of a group and different from others on the basis of their sexual desire for others of their sex, most sexual boundaries defining licit and illicit sexuality did not concern them.[7] Rather, those boundaries served to differentiate men and women who limited their sexual activity to stable heterosexual relationships (ideally, but not always, sanctified by or heading toward marriage) from those who did not. Those boundaries, which were socially and culturally specific, generated particular sexual identities, of which the unchaste woman was one.[8]

I am not the first scholar of the early modern period to develop the general idea that sexual identity could be based on something other than same-sex sexual acts or desire. In a 1999 article, Ruth Mazo Karras uses Eve Kosofsky Sedgwick's concept of the relationship between universalizing and minoritizing discourses to argue that in medieval Europe "prostitute" constituted a sexual identity.[9] In a more recent book, Anna Clark summarizes the field and pushes it a bit further: "It is important to point out that premodern societies *did* have a concept of sexual identities, not just acts. . . . After all, the celibate priest, the procreative married couple, the prostitute or the virgin spinster all had social identities defined by their sexual behavior or lack thereof."[10] This chapter builds on Karras's and Clark's work, analyzing the ways in which the unchaste woman was defined through religious and philosophical discourses, as well as through law, policing, and judicial practices. This argument may, at first, seem obvious. Since the 1970s feminist scholars have considered the relationship between sexual behavior and constructions of gender, and hence the origins and operations of sex-gender systems.[11] More generally, chaste and unchaste woman are lived identities. We are still dismantling structures that divide women into "good girls" and "bad girls." Scholars of the early modern period, however, have generally treated and explored these as gender constructs, rather than as sexual identities. This approach has been enormously productive. Yet, I argue that we should treat them as identity categories because this is how they functioned—marking individuals in a way that shaped how they were treated and perceived by institutions and neighbors.

The practice of linking sexual behavior to gender but not directly to identity more broadly is challenged by some of the work on identity in the early modern period. For whatever reason, the scholarship on identity as a general category and that specifically on sexual identity in the premodern period seem to be mutually exclusive fields. The former rarely considers sexuality, perhaps because of its association with subjectivity and modernity.[12] Works that focus more generally on how people were recognized or labeled, and on how they categorized themselves, provide templates for understanding the ways in which identity can be based on sexual activity. Here I follow Vincent Denis in his exploration of how various state actors developed bureaucratic practices to fix identification over the course of the long eighteenth century by coopting and codifying a set of social data that reflected social and cultural norms. Specifically, they categorized a subject's name, profession, and origin, and included a description of each subject. Each of these categories contained implicit judgments and associations; profession, for example, was "synonymous with status and condition, and considered consubstantial with the individual and his life."[13] Thus, identity was not about the self—defined as the unique psychological core of one's being that differentiates one person from another—but was built upon deeply interiorized and widely shared concepts of how people defined themselves in the world. Sexual identity, in the form of the unchaste woman, followed suit.

A focus on sexuality in this context thus does much more than add to the literature challenging definitions of sexual identity and hence the temporal boundaries around when, exactly, sexuality came to be constitutive of subjectivity. If nothing else, it forces us to think about the impact of sexual behavior both in conjunction with and beyond the operations of gender so that we deepen our understanding of the meaning and production of identity more generally, specifically in its relationship to the law. The law, however, was just one component of the construction of the category of unchaste woman. It was simultaneously a legal category, a moral prescription, and a pattern of behavior that coalesced into the definition of a particular kind of person, as well as a set of community norms that varyingly accepted this definition or ignored it. Identity was constructed through a series of dialectical relationships. Sex, along with gender, class, and religion, was thus a fundamental component of how people understood themselves in this period.

Ideas of the Unchaste Woman

As the philosopher Lisabeth During demonstrates in her book *The Chastity Plot*, chastity is a complicated concept, and one with a rich history. During identifies two variations on the quest for and meanings of sexual renunciation. In the eunuch's plot, individuals seek full sexual renunciation (virginity). In the maiden's plot, which concerns mainly women, "the married are expected to conduct their lives with propriety, and the unmarried, especially the female unmarried, are expected to abstain."[14] Those questing after the former, she notes, hope to "flee the body," whereas those in the maiden plot are emmeshed in the "sexed and problematic body."[15] During shows that the roots of ideas about chastity lay in Christian writings (which in turn pulled from the Greeks). Even with the diminished power of the Church in the eighteenth century, ideas of chastity (and hence unchastity) were still based in part on religious conceptualizations. These bled into and informed legal codes and other discourses.

The Christian case for radical sexual renunciation, and its tie to moral perfection, took centuries to build. This case was institutionalized and reenforced many times in the requirement that priests, monks, and nuns be celibate. Running alongside the debates about the merits of sexual abstinence was the concomitant evolution of understandings of marriage, from marriage's position as a backup plan for those too weak to remain celibate, to its acceptance as coequal with the states of virginity and celibacy in the rulings of the Council of Trent, to its position as a realization of spiritual potential by Protestant reformers in the sixteenth century.[16]

Understandably, the value of sex and sexual pleasure varied enormously in these constructs of marriage. At one end was open hostility to marital sex, the claim that it was for reproduction only and that couples should take care to avoid anything that would enhance their pleasure.[17] In contrast, many Protestant reformers understood marital sex as being at the center of marriage, something that "expressed and increased a couple's love for one another," while some post-Tridentine Catholic writers came to approve of sexual pleasure that accompanied the sexual act.[18] In all quarters, as represented by the catechisms taught in French churches in the eighteenth century, marriage was seen, at the very least, as a remedy to the problem of lust.[19] Through the eighteenth century, women were usually considered the more lustful of the two sexes. Following in the footsteps of Eve, they posed a threat to both their own salvation and to that of the men around them.[20] The idea of the unchaste woman was thus linked with the development of religious ideas about women, from early Jewish and Christian writings through the Middle Ages and into the early modern period. That particular story has been explored extensively and is well documented.[21]

As Olwen Hufton reminds us, the unchaste woman was developed more fully through injunctions than in the Bible.[22] The good woman, from Paul through the Counter-Reformation, was obedient, silent, humble, and modest. Most importantly, she was chaste. A woman's virtue and hence her honor were linked to her chastity, which carried a double meaning: limiting sexual intercourse to the marital bed and maintaining the appearance of having done so. Problematic behavior imperiled not only a woman's reputation but also her family's honor. From the Reformation and Counter-Reformation onward, sermons and advice books explained to women and girls how exactly to achieve the lofty goals of obedience, silence, humility, modesty, and chastity. Such texts articulated a relationship of chastity to modesty on the one hand, and of chastity to the avoidance of excess—particularly in speech, dress, and consumption—on the other. Many reminded the girls and women who were their intended audience to suppress the sexual desires they would feel after the age of thirteen and gave them advice on how to do so. Nadine Berenguier's survey of girls' conduct books that were published in the late seventeenth and eighteenth centuries found that many authors used the concepts of modesty (*pudeur*) and virtue (*vertu*) interchangeably.[23] Popular pamphlets and plays brought home much the same message by focusing on another trope, that of the disorderly or unruly woman. She was characterized in part by her lust and her lack of chastity as she searched for sexual gratification. The message of these varied texts was clear. Only through careful self-control could a woman keep herself in line, and she would most likely be unable to do so without male oversight, through the institution of marriage.

Various early modern medical writers supported religious and popular notions that women experienced sexual desire more strongly than did men. Greek ideas about the body, even as they were revised in numerous paradigm shifts through the seventeenth century, often blamed the uterus. Women deprived of sexual intercourse could become victims of *furor uterinus* (uterine fury). The uterus was hungry for sperm in some tellings, orgasm in others.[24] Teens who reached sexual maturity without having had sex were susceptible to "green sickness," while older, sexually experienced women going through a dry spell ran the risk of various neurological and circulatory impairments.[25] Doctors and medical writers started to pay more attention to the issue of uterine fury in the sixteenth and seventeenth centuries, producing a number of treatises on the topic.[26] One of the most important was Jacques Ferrand's *Traité de l'essence et guérison de l'amour ou de la melancolie érotique* (1612), which summarized Renaissance knowledge on the subject. Ferrand argued that women were "more furious and manic in love" than were men, in part because they did not have sufficient "reason to master [their passions]," but also because of their particular physiology.[27] Female lust was thus both urgent and naturalized.[28] Furor uterinus was considered possible for all women, and medical texts did not differentiate women according to the severity of their furor uterinus. That had to wait until J. D. T. Bienville's 1771 publication *La nymphomanie*, which is most commonly interpreted as arguing, according to scholar Mary Peace, that "excessive female desire is a pathology and not a natural attribute of femininity."[29] In pushing against the dominant paradigm, Bienville laid the groundwork for the construction of the sexually deviant nymphomaniac. But through the eighteenth century, medical writing on women and sexual differences underscored the difficulties women faced in remaining chaste. In ancient Greece, Hippocrates had recommended marriage as a cure for furor uterinus. In the eighteenth century most medical writers also saw marriage as a prophylactic.[30]

The major shift in the eighteenth century came less in the content of these discourses than in their place within larger conversations about chastity and, indeed, womanhood, as Enlightenment thinkers shifted their parameters.[31] Philosophes considered the nature of woman on a new basis, through the lens of sexual difference, or what distinguished men and women from each other. To do so, they turned to medicine and to the emerging fields of education and psychology. Historian Marta Vicente notes that the eighteenth century saw the rise of the anatomist movement, in which all that could be known about the body was thought to be in evidence in its various parts, and which competed with the galenic-humoral school of medicine for prominence. Anatomists and their supporters, in search for what she calls the "legitimate body" on which the state could legislate, fully divided and differentiated men and women on the basis of their sexual organs. (Vicente argues persuasively that this very taxonomy was challenged by the existence of what we understand to be transgender or intersex bodies.)[32]

In the eighteenth century, authors including Julien-Joseph Virey worked these general ideas into texts written for wider audiences. Woman came to be consubstantial with her sexual organs—less those linked to sexual pleasure than those that established her reproductive function. Diderot summarized a commonly held definition of the uterus: "An organ subject to terrible spasms, which rules [woman] and rouses up in her phantoms of every sort."[33] Woman's character, disposition, and intellectual and moral capacity were increasingly naturalized, based as they were on the defining element of her biology. As such, where men were thought to be endowed with the capacity for rational, abstract thought, women were not.[34] Pierre Roussel argued in his *Système physique et moral de la femme* (1775) that women had "a difficult time retaining a single idea or attaining high conceptions or philosophical abstraction."[35] Instead, he believed women were governed more by instinct and passion; they possessed an enhanced moral faculty, which best suited them for the home and for domination by men. Rousseau laid out this conception of woman almost completely in the fifth book of his educational treatise *Émile* (1762).[36]

Some philosophes who considered the issue of female sexual desire still asserted that women experienced it more strongly and more continuously than did men. But that desire was now thought to be curbed by women's naturally endowed sense of modesty or shame. Pornographers and libertine writers, in contrast, often bequeathed their female characters with limitless sexual curiosity and drive; toward the end of the century, female sexual drive in these texts even came to be equated with political excess. Moreover, older ideas certainly persisted, particularly in religious and popular circles. But these developments were situated in a wider dispersion in the second half of the century of the idea of companionate marriage, in which it was woman's role to please and submit to her husband, stay home, breastfeed her babies, educate her children, and thus find true contentment, if not actual happiness in doing so. This life was most famously depicted by Rousseau in his novel *La Nouvelle Héloïse* (1761).

As marriage now was supposed to be the site not just of sexual intimacy but also of emotional intimacy, the significance of marital chastity shifted. In *Émile*, Rousseau argued that a wife's infidelity, the prospect of giving her husband children not his own, did not just steal an inheritance. It was an emotional crime, striking at the heart of the family. Adultery "destroys the family and breaks the bonds of nature." A wife's infidelity transforms a family from a loving unit into "little more than a group of secret enemies, armed against each other by a guilty woman, who compels them to pretend to love one another." Rousseau asserted: "Her crime is not infidelity but treason." Infusing an old refrain with a new sensibility, Rousseau emphasized the importance of female marital chastity: "It is not enough that a wife should be faithful." All should believe her so as she should be "modest, devoted, retiring. . . . In a word, if the father must love his children, he must be able to respect their mother. For these reasons it is not enough that the woman should be chaste, she must preserve her reputation and her good name."[37] Rousseau thereby established a countermodel to the perfect wife: the unchaste woman.

Models of the unchaste woman were in view everywhere in Enlightenment writings, including the *Encyclopédie*, Denis Diderot's and Jean le Rond d'Alembert's thirty-two volume project that aimed to summarize Enlightenment thinking on every conceivable topic.[38] In the third of its four articles devoted to the topic of *femme* (woman), author Joseph-François-Édouard de Corsembleu de Desmahis focused on defining woman as a moral creature. He quickly divided women into the virtuous and the vicious. He made his point by contrasting a fictional character named Chloé with the unnamed securely happy virtuous woman, "the submissive wife, gentle mother, and kind household mistress," who reigns over a single place, the home.[39] This nameless wife is happy because she ignores worldly pleasures, argued Desmahis: "Her glory is to live in obscurity. Caught up in the duties of wife and mother, she devotes her days to the practice of unobtrusive virtues." As a result, "her house is the abode of religious sentiment, filial piety, conjugal love, maternal tenderness, order, interior peace, gentle sleep and of health." She is happy and well respected. Chloé, by contrast, is a coquette turned courtesan, practiced in artifice. She teases men, "running always after vain pleasures," and finally finds love, only to be betrayed. She marries "a pompous fool," only to later be rejected by her social crowd—the demimonde—when she ages, at which point she turns desperately to religion.[40] For Desmahis, chastity was not a religious category; it was a moral one. Thus, chaste women were virtuous, and, given that virtue was connected to an integrated worldview, these women contributed to the greater good by creating happy families. But—and this is important—the unnamed chaste wife is happier than the wanton Chloé. Chastity had been interiorized. Living chastely (or not) determined one's mood, and these characters seem to be aware of this. We see similar themes run through literature, especially prostitute fiction.

Other deliberate efforts to define chastity, however, were less obvious about what constituted its inverse. In the seventeenth and eighteenth centuries, the *Dictionnaire de l'Académie française* defined "chasteté" (chastity) as "a complete abstinence of pleasures of the flesh" and "*chaste*" (chaste) as characterizing one "who abstains from the pleasures of the flesh, or who engages in it only in accordance with the law of God." "Pleasures of the flesh" referred to sexual pleasure but could also refer to eating or drinking. Yet, as "chasteté" was also defined as a core characteristic of "honesté" (honesty), "pudeur" (decency or modesty), and "sagesse" (wisdom), it was tied to the secular foundations of what it meant to be an honorable person, especially for women.[41] Denis Diderot similarly defined "chasteté" in his article on the subject for the *Encyclopédie* as "a moral virtue, one by which one moderates the unregulated desires of the flesh," namely sex. Diderot did identify chastity's opposite, arguing that "enjoying the pleasure that comes with propagating the species" without actually doing so was "the essence of impurity." He thus situated chastity at the intersection of what he considered natural sexual urges and socially constructed restraint, identifying the requirements of chastity within and outside of marriage. In marriage chastity involved "satisfying all that nature demands of us, and that religion and the laws of the state have authorized." In the unmarried state, it involved "resisting the impulse of nature which urges us without regard for times, places, circumstances, customs, worship, customs, laws, [and] would lead us to proscribed actions."[42] These definitions did not allow for a spectrum. They established clear lines between what was chastity and what was not.

Unchaste Woman and the Law

French law did not specifically criminalize all sex outside of marriage. Forms that were criminalized included adultery, sodomy, prostitution, rape (of various forms), incest, and bigamy. Some crimes were gender specific. Tying directly into chastity discourses that emphasized the need to guarantee the licit transfer of property and the husbandly possession of a wife's sexual labor, women could be found guilty of adultery, whereas men could not. Men could be found guilty of rape, but women could not.[43] Most consensual premarital and extramarital heterosex between those who had reached the legal age of majority, however, was, when it was prosecuted at all, subsumed under the large and poorly defined categories of libertinage and debauchery, the latter discussed by Lisa Jane Graham in her chapter in this volume.[44] The state did very little to crack down on extramarital sex that qualified as libertinage or debauchery unless someone complained. Yet, it was exactly in this space that Louise and many like her found themselves moving from being an example of an ideological construct to inhabiting a sexual identity category.

Although the idea that women fell into two categories—chaste and unchaste—developed across a wide range of prescriptive literature, legal commentaries classified unchaste women as a group, one that had fewer rights under the law. For example, Daniel Jousse, whose 1771 *Traité de la justice criminelle de France* is considered the most complete Old Regime law synthesis, laid out a number of circumstances that could diminish punishment for any man found guilty of *rapt de seduction*, a capital offense that usually involved kidnapping a woman with the assumption that the kidnapper would rape or seduce his victim.[45] They included when the kidnapper was a minor or when the victim's parents favored the union. These circumstances also included when the "girl who had been kidnapped, even if she was a minor, *est de mauvais conduit*," meaning that she had a history of improper conduct, specifically sexually inappropriate behavior. (In principle, the minor status of a victim "aggravated" the crime of rapt, making the rapist-kidnapper liable to a worse punishment.) Jousse then elaborated: "This misconduct is usually presumed with regard to women and maids working in cabarets, and this is why such people cannot bring charges of *rapt*." In judicial proceedings, a woman would be believed only if she had a spotless reputation. The logic here is *not* that a woman or girl with a history of improper conduct had already lost her virginity and as such that it could no longer be stolen through rape; wives and widows could be victims of rapt.[46]

The logic might become clearer when we examine instances in which *femmes de mauvaise vie* (women who engaged in loose living) were not allowed to bring charges for other categories of rape. For example, when a jailer sexually abused a female prisoner, he was to be sentenced to the galleys, unless she was a femme de mauvaise vie, in which case the punishment was to be less severe.[47] Muyart de Vouglans, in his widely read *Instruction criminelle suivant les loix et ordonnances du royaume* (1752), made a similar distinction. In section 28 of his first volume of this legal commentary, de Vouglans examined the conditions under which certain crimes could not be prosecuted because they had not happened. It was a short list and included bringing a murder charge when the victim was found alive, bringing a charge of theft when the accused could prove he had bought the item in question, and bringing the charge of rapt de seduction when the accuser was a girl or woman "who was a debauched person."[48] Debauched, in this context, referred to sexual misbehavior. Rousseau de la Combe concurred in his *Traité des matières criminelles* (1670): There was no crime as "there [was] no violation of modesty with a prostitute."[49] These legal commentators separated femmes et filles de mauvaise vie into a group whose members did not receive the same legal protections against sex crimes as did others. They made this separation on the grounds that femme et filles de mauvaise vie had already violated the rules of sexual decorum by allowing those other than their husbands sexual access to their bodies—or by behaving in a way that implied that they would be likely to do so—suggesting that these women and girls would be less resistant to allowing others that access. Consequently, all sex they had was classified as consensual.[50] In other words, the femme or fille de mauvaise vie was legally differentiated because, based on her sexual behavior, she was a different kind of person.

For several legal commentators, the unchaste woman constituted a sexual identity category to the point that her past actions could be used as predictors of future behavior. For most crimes in this period, the proof standard was either two witnesses or a voluntary confession. For sex crimes, this was often impossible. Because the accused rarely confessed, the burden of proof generally lay on witnesses. What with doors left ajar, large keyholes, cracks in walls, crowded accommodations, and ever-present servants, all embedded in a culture in which people actively minded one another's business, one might wonder how difficult finding two witnesses might have been. But complicating matters, according to the legal theorists, was the problem that witnesses were supposed to be of unimpeachable character, a qualification that, at least theoretically, disqualified entire categories of people, such as actors and criminals, because they were considered dishonorable or had incurred *infamia* (infamy). Members of some categories (women, children, and servants, among others) might be disqualified because they were considered too easily swayed by others, or because they (servants again) owed loyalty to their masters.[51] So prosecution, in theory, often rested on what were called indices and presumptions. We can define a presumption as a finding that, though unproven, can be assumed to follow from certain facts that are proven.[52] To give an example, the best-known presumption regards paternity. In French law, stemming from Roman law, a child born to a cohabitating married couple is presumed to be legitimate. The established facts are the marriage and the cohabitation. The actual paternity of a child born under these circumstances is unknown. But that child is considered, or presumed, legitimate until proven otherwise.

Presumptions and indices functioned as legal work-arounds, or in modern-day parlance, hacks. At its heart a presumption is a probability statement. If A happened, B is almost sure to have happened (strong likelihood). Or, if A happened, B is most likely to have happened (moderate likelihood). But what are A and B? Which actions and behaviors constitute evidence of other actions and behaviors? The answer reveals a social and cultural logic underpinning the legal one and, ultimately, the assumption that the unchaste woman constituted a sexual identity category. Many presumptions, like the one concerning paternity, stemmed from Roman law. But French jurisprudence had shed a great deal of Roman law by the eighteenth century. Jousse and other jurists recognized and wrote about the ways in which French jurisprudence had evolved to fit the French state and French society.

So, the presumptions allowed for sex crimes reflected a long evolution in French judicial thinking about human nature; they also reflected a series of correlations between one kind of behavior and another. Presumptions pointed to behaviors that suggested the accused was the kind of person who might commit other sexual crimes.

This logic pervades evidentiary standards. In his *Dictionnaire de droit et de pratique* (1771), Claude-Joseph Ferrière explained that how much weight presumptions carried depended on the "good or bad conduct" (*bonne ou mauvaise conduite*) of the accused.[53] In the context of sex crimes, "bad conduct" referred to a set of behaviors that cast suspicion on a woman's sexual probity. Jousse provided a list: a woman's "indecent" and "immodest" dress, the habit of walking alone at night in "suspect places," being seen to welcome young or "otherwise suspect" people to her home, throwing parties, being poor or in financial distress, and working at a bar or other public place. As discussed above, such mauvaise conduite could nullify or seriously lessen various charges of rape brought by a woman or her male relatives. Even charges for raping a minor, something the French took fairly seriously, would be lessened if the girl had a history of such "bad behavior."[54] The assumption was that women who dressed immodestly, for example, had lose sexual morals and hence were likely engaging in consensual sex. Presumptions in this case are not so much predictive as descriptive. They suggest a worldview of female sexual behavior firmly emmeshed in the binary. Those believed to be good girls behaved in certain ways, and a woman or girl could not be just a little bit bad. Any deviation from the ideal suggested that a woman or girl was not good at all.

Presumptions and indices that helped construct the unchaste woman as a sexual identity category were not just dry legal concepts discussed by lawyers among themselves. They shaped larger public legal discourse around sex crimes. In cases of adultery, for example, the parties often released *mémoires*, or factums. These were legal briefs written and published by lawyers for both parties to convince judges and others of the merits of their party's case, as Cathy McClive shows in her chapter in this volume. Mémoires were discursive spaces in which the parties had greater control over the narrative they wished to create than they did in the judicial chambers. Hence the mémoires were part narrative—"this is what happened and why

I am right"—and part legal treatise. Published and released to the public, mémoires were among the bestsellers of the latter half of the century.[55] Some mémoires were then redacted and reprinted in the various *causes célèbres*, compendiums of juicy cases of interest to the public.[56] In many of the factums produced for adultery cases, for example, lawyers used indices and presumptions as a narrative logic. A husband's lawyer often worked to show how the wife had led a mauvaise vie and hence was guilty of adultery, even without direct proof. The wife's defense always centered around her probity and chastity. These factums embodied a character war over whether the wife was, by the definitions of the time, unchaste. Therefore, what lawyers wrote in legal treatises and the ways in which they implicated sexuality could have a significant impact on court cases and their outcomes.

Between Discourse and Practice—Mind the Gap

If we look at other ways in which these ideas were put into practice, specifically around the use of *lettres de cachet*, we see how "unchaste woman" functioned as a sexual identity. A lettre de cachet was a royal order for extrajudicial, secret, and indefinite incarceration. In the initial demand, the *placet*, which was usually processed by the police, the complainant(s) had to explain why the state should take action on their behalf. In doing so, these individuals tended to appeal to concerns of shared importance. Hence, placets often represent moments of interface between local sexual culture and discursive norms of the state.[57]

Those who wished to have wives, daughters, or sisters incarcerated for extramarital or premarital sexuality often called these women "prostituées" (as was the case with Louise), "libertine," "debauched," or some combination of these terms. Yet, as with Louise, the women under suspicion were not necessarily accused of having each had multiple sexual partners. To take one example, in March of 1720, Philippe Joly, who had held a prestigious position at the Hôtel de Ville, started submitting requests to the police asking to have his wife, Marie Genevieve Remy, incarcerated because she had been living with another man. That Joly submitted his request six to seven years after he claimed his wife had first started the affair suggests that it was not the affair but something else that triggered him to take this action. Yet, Joly called his wife a prostituée. The police officer who summarized the case explained that Joly "revealed that his wife had abandoned herself to an outrageous debauchery and prostitution, not wanting to listen to any reprimand."[58]

"Prostitute" had two meanings in this period, the second eliding the first.[59] First, it was a criminal category. Though poorly defined in legal writing, it tended to refer to what we would think of as a sex worker: that is, a woman who had sex outside of marriage habitually, with multiple partners, and for some sort of remuneration. Second, the word referred to women—like Louise—who simply had had sex outside of marriage, usually habitually, though not necessarily with numerous partners and not for money. The difference was not always evident in the juridical literature, where the common phrase was simply *filles ou femmes du monde*, with no further clarification. Du monde meant "public" and hence that the woman or girl in question belonged not her husband but to all. None of the major dictionaries offered any more precision. Jousse, however, made an effort to distinguish a prostitute from a fille ou femme de mauvaise vie. Hence, he gave a better sense of both constructs: "The woman or girl who abandons herself only to one or two persons, even for money, should not be regarded as a public prostitute, even if she was *une fille ou femme de mauvaise conduite*."[60] For Jousse, it seemed to be a matter of numbers. The *Encyclopédie* defined prostitution as being an exchange: "A prostitute is one who abandons herself to the lust of a man for a vile or mercenary motive."[61] From the late seventeenth century onward, judicial and policing practices began to differentiate the two groups, at least partially.[62] Royal ordinances required that women arrested for streetwalking or working in brothels (i.e., sex workers) be housed apart from those arrested for having had sex outside of marriage, for fear the former would corrupt the latter. The differentiation was just one example of at least some conceptual space for women to be sexually active outside of marriage without being considered sex workers.[63] When the police called Louise a prostitute, however, they collapsed that space, and brought the shame and criminal penalties of the first definition to bear on the second. They did so deliberately. There is ample evidence that many men and women had sex with each other—either in short relationships or in long-term free unions—without coming under police scrutiny, living in their communities without arousing concern. The women in these partnerships may have been behaving unchastely, but they were not unchaste women.

Despite the great consternation of abandoned husbands and wives, we should not assume that all adulterous couples were the subject of community policing or even concern. In some instances the police noted that such couples were causing public scandal. But in most, they said nothing, suggesting there was none. Some adulterous couples passed as husband and wife, sometimes taking a new last name. Others did not. In either case, neighbors might very well have been cognizant of the couple's true marital status. David Garrioch and Arlette Farge both show how residents of Parisian quarters were well aware of who their neighbors were and what they were doing.[64] Community conventions around adultery and extramarital and premarital sexuality more generally differed from those of elite discourse. Julie Hardwick shows that this was certainly the case in late seventeenth- and eighteenth-century Lyon. Young working people who were in intimate, serious relationships headed toward marriage were not penalized by the church, the courts, or their communities for having babies out of wedlock, as long as they were responsible about planning for the infant. When pregnant and new mothers were abandoned by their intimate partners, courts usually sided with the women, policed male sexuality, and ordered remedies to support the child and restore female honor. Women who had sex with partners they reasonably expected to marry were not unchaste by community or judicial standards.[65] Unchastity was defined differently in different segments of the Parisian population, though not wildly so. We can see a spectrum in how chastity was understood, from limiting sex to marriage to limiting sex to a stable, monogamous relationship, one that was ideally financially self-sustaining.

We have no idea if Louise and Marie considered themselves unchaste women. That they were living with men married to other women for so long, however, raises a number of issues, especially when we consider certain characteristics of cases like these. In placets requesting state intervention in adultery cases in 1720, the average time between the onset of the adulterous affair and the turn to the police was about four years. We should not assume that nothing was being done over the course of those years to break up these relationships and bring the errant spouses back to their duty. Beleaguered husbands and wives often used informal mechanisms to get their spouses to come home. For example, in 1787 Antoine Baumé, the famous chemist, a *maître de pharmacie* (master pharmacist), and a member of the Académie de sciences, engaged at least two friends to help him reconcile with his wife, Marie Louise Matis, who had been having an affair. Both friends reported that Matis vehemently resisted all such entreaties, claimed to hate her husband, and wanted to push him to separate from her, stating that she would rather live with the devil.[66] Other spouses asked trusted clergy to help mediate the split. What pushed spouses to turn from informal mediation to official intervention varied. As with Baumé, a few went to the police because of spousal violence (or threats thereof) and fear for their lives. Others, like Magdelaine, were driven by financial precarity, the adulterous spouse's use of marital funds to support their extramarital relationships. Arlette Farge and Michel Foucault, in their analysis of lettres de cachet generated by family members' attempts to incarcerate each other for a range of problems, including adultery, find other triggers to include the birth of a child and the move of the couple back to their original neighborhood.[67]

Magdelaine did not call Louise a prostitute, but the police did and in so doing made it clear they intervened because they decided that she fit the identity category of unchaste woman. Joly did call his wife a prostitute, and his rhetoric fit a familiar pattern in which husbands attempted to paint their wives as prostitutes to compel the state to take action, though such ploys were not always successful.[68] The state investigated all complaints requesting a lettre de cachet. Claiming a woman was a prostitute made the argument that her sexual behavior was a form of scandal and violated community conventions of chaste and therefore licit sexual behavior. The possibility of scandal (along with violence and a threat to the family's financial stability) often compelled the police to act.[69] Whatever the players in these domestic dramas thought about themselves and their spouses, the existence of the identity category of unchaste woman enabled Magdelaine and Joly get help from the state in stabilizing their marriages. The state intervened not because of a need to police women's bodies, but rather to maintain the tranquility and *bon ordre* of the quarter—to avoid scandal. For the king, on whose behalf the police administered lettres de cachet, granting a request for a lettre de cachet was a question of the need to support the institution of marriage.

Farge and Foucault argue, "The confrontation between husband and wife had the same status as a treason against the king or an affront to religion."[70]

As the term "prostitute" came to be associated with sex work more often in the latter half of the century, its use in lettres de cachet to refer to sex outside of marriage generally declined. It was used by the police in sixteen adultery cases in 1720, but by complainants in only five of those cases. In 1745 the police used the term in five cases, among which only one complainant used the term. The term does not appear in any cases from 1745 or 1770. Over the same period, the use of a lettre de cachet as a way to incarcerate family members for adultery and other wayward sexuality decreased.[71] In other words, use of the term "prostituée" in placets and police responses to them started to decline as the term's definition sharpened and as families turned to the courts to deal with sexually problematic behavior. Around the same time, we see a shift in elite discourse on the role of women in marriage, on the construction of women's sexuality, and thus on the meanings of chastity. More research is required to determine the relationship of these developments to each other.

I have argued that unchaste woman was an ideological construct that existed in slightly different, though related, forms across a number of different discourses and that it further developed through use in legal suits and policing. Unchaste woman was a sexual identity category not just for these reasons but also because it was a social identity defined by sexual behavior, and as such, was very similar to other forms of identity; it reflected social practices rooted in deeply held beliefs. Like other social identities, the sexual identity of unchaste woman helped set the paramaters of women's capacity and ability to maneuver within the family and the community, ultimately shaping the relationship of women with their husbands, other family members, neighbors, coworkers, and political authorities, among others. In so doing, the sexual identity of unchaste woman helped to police the boundaries of the sex-gender system that we can define as premodern heterosexuality. Sexuality was consequently essential to understanding women's identities in eighteenth-century France. My argument thus complements Cathy McClive's and Lisa Jane Graham's in this volume. While McClive emphasizes the need to take into account the sexual meaning of religious scandal in the same time period, Graham argues that sex and pleasure were fundamental to Enlightenment thinking around freedom itself.

These findings challenge how historians have considered identity in this period. The idea that people were differentiated and differentiated themselves from each other not just on the basis of gender, religion, social status, and geographic region, but also on the basis of their sexuality, asks us to consider how sexuality was refracted through and informed these other identity categories. This is an especially complicated endeavor in the face of the fact that multiple sexual cultures existed simultaneously in the eighteenth century. While Louise was arrested, there were many others who had sex with married men, or who lived other kinds of irregular sexual lives without it being a problem. That these women were not just among the very poor or the aristocracy—as most scholarship assumes—suggests that sexual identity, like class or religion, was at once hardened in law and discourse and differentiated in life in the context other identity categories.

Notes

1. Dossier of Louise Le Cœur, October 8, 1720, ms. 10703, Bibliothèque de l'Arsenal, Paris.
2. As Julie Hardwick shows in her study of young working adults in early modern Lyon, those rules were sometimes defined differently in elite discourses than they were by community convention. Julie Hardwick, *Sex in an Old Regime City: Young Workers and Intimacy in France, 1660–1789* (New York: Oxford University Press, 2020).
3. Michel Foucault, *The History of Sexuality*, vol. 1, *An Introduction*, trans. Robert Hurley (New York: Vintage, 1980), 42–43.
4. For a discussion of how this has played out across a number of different studies, see H. G. Cocks, "Modernity and the Self in the History of Sexuality," *Historical Journal* 49, no. 4 (December 2006): 1211–27.
5. Katherine Crawford, "Privilege, Possibility, and Perversion: Rethinking the Study of Early Modern Sexuality," *Journal of Modern History* 78, no. 2 (June 2006): 413. There is a large body of work exploring this subject, much of which Crawford cites in her review essay. For a good example, see Cristian Berco, *Sexual Hierarchies, Public Status: Men, Sodomy, and Society in Spain's Golden Age* (Toronto: University of Toronto Press, 2007).
6. For a good overview of this literature, see Barry Reay, "Writing the Modern Histories of Homosexual England," *Historical Journal* 52, no. 1 (Mar. 2009):

213–33. Important works include Eve Kosofsky Sedgwick, *Epistemology of the Closet* (Berkeley: University of California Press, 1990); David M. Halperin, *How to Do the History of Homosexuality* (Chicago: University of Chicago Press, 2002); Judith M. Bennet, *History Matters: Patriarchy and the Challenge of Feminism* (Philadelphia: University of Pennsylvania Press, 2006); Susan S. Lanser, *The Sexuality of History: Modernity and the Sapphic, 1565–1830* (Chicago: University of Chicago Press, 2014); and Valerie Traub, *Thinking Sex with the Early Moderns* (Philadelphia: University of Pennsylvania Press, 2016).

7. The most thorough investigation of male same-sex sexual relations in eighteenth-century France can be found in the work of Jeffrey Merrick, including Merrick, *Sodomites, Pederasts, and Tribades in Eighteenth-Century France: A Documentary History* (University Park: Pennsylvania State University Press, 2019); and Merrick, *Sodomy in Eighteenth-Century France* (Newcastle, UK: Cambridge Scholars Publishing, 2020).

8. Another important sexual identity, which I do not explore in this chapter, is that of the eunuch. See Katherine Crawford, *Eunuchs and Castrati: Disability and Normativity in Early Modern Europe* (New York: Routledge, 2019).

9. Ruth Mazo Karras, "Prostitution and the Question of Sexual Identity in Medieval Europe," *Journal of Women's History* 11, no. 2 (Summer 1999): 159–77; Sedgwick, *Epistemology of the Closet*, 82–86.

10. Anna Clark, *Desire: A History of European Sexuality* (New York: Routledge, 2008), 6. See also Clark, *Alternative Histories of the Self: A Cultural History of Sexuality and Secrets, 1762–1917* (London: Bloomsbury, 2017).

11. See, for example, Gayle Rubin, "The Traffic in Women: Notes on the 'Political Economy' of Sex," in *Toward an Anthropology of Women*, ed. Rayna R. Reiter (New York: Monthly Review Press, 1975), 157–210.

12. Many of these works do place identity in the context of the emergence of the self. See Clark, *Alternative Histories of the Self*; and Lynn Hunt, "The Self and Its History," *American Historical Review* 119, no. 5 (December 2014): 1576–86. For considerations of the self in the prerevolutionary French context, see, among others, Jan Goldstein, *The Post-Revolutionary Self: Politics and Psyche in France, 1750–1850* (Cambridge MA: Harvard University Press, 2008); Howard G. Brown, *Mass Violence and the Self: From the French Wars of Religion to the Paris Commune* (Ithaca NY: Cornell University Press, 2018). On the relation of the self to identity, see Dror Wahrman, *The Making of the Modern Self: Identity and Culture in Eighteenth-Century England* (New Haven CT: Yale University Press, 2004).

13. Vincent Denis, *Une histoire de l'identité: France 1715–1815* (Seyssel, France: Champ Vallon, 2008), 22.

14. Lisabeth During, *The Chastity Plot* (Chicago: University of Chicago Press, 2021), 14.

15. During, *Chastity Plot*, 28

16. For an overview, see James Brundage, *Law, Sex, and Christian Society in Medieval Europe* (Chicago: University of Chicago Press, 1987).

17. See, for example, the writings of Clement of Alexandria (ca. 150–215 CE) and, most famously, Jerome (ca. 342–420 CE). Brundage, *Law, Sex, and Christian Society*, 90; During, *Chastity Plot*, 171.

18. Brundage, *Law, Sex, and Christian Society*, 555–56.

19. Marcel Bernos, "Le concile de Trente et la sexualité: La doctrine et sa postérité," in *Sexualité et religions*, ed. Marcel Bernos (Paris: Cerf, 1988), 222–28.

20. John McManners, *Church and Society in Eighteenth-Century France*, vol. 2, *The Religion of the People and the Politics of Religion* (Oxford: Clarendon, 1998), 19.

21. Find excellent summaries that cover the construction of women within the Christian tradition in the first chapters of the following works: Olwen Hufton, *The Prospect before Her: A History of Women in Western Europe, 1500–1800* (New York: Random House, 1996); Merry E. Wiesner-Hanks, *Women and Gender in Early Modern Europe*, third ed. (Cambridge: Cambridge University Press, 2008); Dominique Godineau, *Les femmes dans la France moderne, XVIe–XVIIIe siècle* (Paris: Armand Colin, 2015). My own rendering is necessarily smoothed out. There were contrary discourses and even ambiguities with the dominant ones.

22. Hufton, *The Prospect before Her*, 30–32.

23. Nadine Berenguier, *Conduct Books for Girls in Enlightenment France* (Farnham, UK: Ashgate, 2011), 88.

24. For a summary of the medical literature please see Hufton, *The Prospect before Her*, 44; Ian Maclean, *The Renaissance Notion of Woman: A Study in the Fortunes of Scholasticism and Medical Science in European Intellectual Life* (Cambridge: Cambridge University Press, 1980), 40–43; Évelyne Berriot-Salvadore, "The Discourse of Medicine and Science," trans. Arthur Goldhammer, in *A History of Women in the West*, vol. 3, *Renaissance and Enlightenment Paradoxes*, ed. Natalie Zemon Davis and Arlette Farge (Cambridge, MA: Belknap, 1994), 348–88.

25. Katherine Crawford, *European Sexualities: 1400–1800* (Cambridge: Cambridge University Press, 2007), 122–23; Helen King, *The Disease of Virgins: Green Sickness, Chlorosis and the Problems of Puberty* (Abingdon, UK: Routledge, 2004), 29–52.

26. Carol Groneman, "Nymphomania: The Historical Construction of Female Sexuality," *Signs* 19, no. 2 (Winter 1994): 343.

27. Jacques Ferrand, *Traité de l'essence et guérison de l'amour ou de la melancolie érotique* (Tolose: Par la Vefue de Jacques Colonmiez, 1612), 114–17. Also see the lengthy introduction to the annotated edition of Jacques Ferrand, *De la maladie*

d'amour ou mélancholie érotique, ed. Donald Beecher and Massimo Ciavolella (Paris: Éditions Classiques Garnier, 2010); and D. A. Beecher, "Erotic Love and the Inquisition: Jacques Ferrand and the Tribunal of Toulouse, 1620," *Sixteenth Century Journal* 20, no. 1 (Spring 1989): 41–53.

28. Berriot-Salvadore, "The Discourse of Medicine and Science," 358–59.

29. Peace complicates this reading in the context of sentimental values. Mary Peace, "The Economy of Nymphomania: Luxury, Virtue, Sentiment and Desire in Mid Eighteenth Century Medical Discourse," in *At the Borders of the Human: Beasts, Bodies and Natural Philosophy*, ed. Erica Fudge, Ruth Gilbert, and Susan Wiseman (New York: St. Martin's, 1999), 245; J. D. T. de Bienville, *La Nymphomanie, ou Traité de la fureur utérine* (Amsterdam: Chez Marc-Michel Rey, 1771).

30. Berriot-Salvadore, "The Discourse of Medicine and Science," 371.

31. There is extensive scholarship on this subject, including studies of works by women themselves. Classic texts include Samia I. Spencer, *French Women in the Age of Enlightenment* (Bloomington: Indiana University Press, 1984); Lieselotte Steinbrügge, *The Moral Sex: Women's Nature in the French Enlightenment*, trans. Pamela E. Selwyn (New York: Oxford University Press, 1995); Hans Erich Böedeker and Lieselotte Steinbrügge, eds., *Conceptualising Woman in Enlightenment Thought* (Berlin: Berlin Verlag Arno Spitz, 2001); and Sarah Knott and Barbara Taylor, eds., *Women, Gender, and Enlightenment* (New York: Palgrave Macmillan, 2005). Also see James McMillan, *France and Women 1789–1914: Gender, Politics and Society* (London: Routledge, 2002), 5.

32. Marta V. Vicente, *Debating Sex and Gender in Eighteenth-Century Spain* (Cambridge: Cambridge University Press, 2017).

33. Denis Diderot, "On Women," in *Dialogues* (1772; London: George Routledge and Sons, 1827), quoted in McMillan, *France and Women*, 5.

34. For a good overview of views of women produced by male philosophes, see Michèle Crampe-Casnabet, "A Sampling of Eighteenth-Century Philosophy," trans. Arthur Goldhammer, in Davis and Farge, *A History of Women in the West*, vol. 3, 315–48.

35. Pierre Roussel, *Système physique et moral de la femme . . .* (Paris, 1775), paraphrased in Kathleen Wellman, "Physicians and Philosophes: Physiology and Sexual Morality in the French Enlightenment," *Eighteenth-Century Studies* 35, no. 2 (Winter 2002): 269.

36. These ideas are fully developed in both in Jean-Jacques Rousseau, *Émile*, trans. Babara Foxley (La Haye, The Netherlands, 1762; New York: Everyman, 1993); and Charles-Louis Montesquieu, *De l'esprit des lois* (Geneve: Chez Barrillot et fils, 1748), book 14, chap. 2. See Crampe-Casnabet, "A Sampling," 327; Godineau,

Les Femmes, 186; Joel Schwartz, *The Sexual Politics of Jean-Jacques Rousseau* (Chicago: University of Chicago Press, 1984), 35–40.

37. Jean-Jacques Rousseau, *Émile*, 388;

38. Denis Diderot and Jean le Rond d'Alembert, eds., *Encyclopédie ou dictionnaire raisonné des sciences, des arts et des métiers* (Paris, 1751–77). I used an online version for the original French: Denis Diderot and Jean le Rond d'Alembert, eds., *Encyclopédie, ou dictionnaire raisonné des sciences, des arts et des métiers, etc.*, ed. Robert Morrissey and Glenn Roe (Chicago: University of Chicago, ARTFL Encyclopédie Project, Autumn 2017), http://encyclopedie.uchicago.edu/. Some translations in this chapter come from the University of Michigan translation project: *The Encyclopedia of Diderot and d'Alembert Collaborative Translation Project* (Ann Arbor: Michigan Publishing, University of Michigan Library), https://quod.lib.umich.edu/d/did/.

39. Quote from Crampe-Casnabet, "A Sampling," 323; Joseph-François-Édouard de Corsembleu de Desmahis, "Woman," trans. Naomi J. Andrews, in *The Encyclopedia of Diderot and d'Alembert Collaborative Translation Project*, http://hdl.handle.net/2027/spo.did2222.0000.287, accessed July 27, 2020; originally published as "Femme," in Diderot and d'Alembert, *Encyclopédie ou dictionnaire raisonné des sciences, des arts et des métiers* (Paris, 1756), 6: 472–75.

40. Desmahis, "Woman".

41. *Le Dictionnaire de l'Académie française* (1694; 1762), s.v. "Chaste," https://artflsrv03.uchicago.edu/philologic4/publicdicos/query?report=bibliography&head=chaste; and s.v. "Chasteté," https://artflsrv03.uchicago.edu/philologic4/publicdicos/query?report=bibliography&head=chasteté.

42. Denis Diderot, "Chasteté," in Diderot and d'Alembert, *Encyclopédie, ou dictionnaire raisonné des sciences, des arts et des métiers, etc.*, http://encyclopedie.uchicago.edu/.

43. Muyart de Vouglans, *Institutes au droit criminel ou principes generaux sur les matieres* (Paris: Chez LeBreton, 1752), 497. Cited by Georges Vigarello, *A History of Rape: Sexual Violence in France from the 16th to the 20th Century*, trans. Jean Birrell (Cambridge: Polity, 2001), 17.

44. See Benoît Garnot, *On n'est point pendu pour être amoureux: La liberté amoureuse au XVIIIe siècle* (Paris: Belin, 2008); Arlette Farge and Michel Foucault, *Le désordre des familles: Lettres de cachet des Archives de la Bastille* (Paris: Gallimard, 1982).

45. On the status of Jousse, see Vigarello, *History of Rape*, 52.

46. Daniel Jousse, *Traité de la justice criminelle de France, où l'on examine tout ce qui concerne les Crimes & les Peines en général & en particulier* (Paris: Chez Debure Pere, 1771), 3: 738.

47. Jousse, *Traité de la justice criminelle*, 3: 718.

48. Muyart de Vouglans, *Les loix de France dans leur ordre natural* (Paris: Mergot, 1780), 867–68.

49. N. Guy du Rousseau de la Combe, *Traité des matières criminelles suivant l'ordonnance du mois d'août 1670* (Paris: Chez Theodore Le Gras, 1756), 30. Quoted in Vigarello, *History of Rape*, 47.

50. In his analysis of the crime of rape, Vigarello argues that the seriousness of sexual violence depended on two factors: the relative social positions of the attacker and victim, and position of the woman as property. Crimes in which attackers were considered lower ranking than their victims were taken more seriously than when the attacker was thought to hold an equal or superior social position. Rapes in which husbands and fathers suffered an assault on their property (the virginity of daughters and chastity of wives) were also taken seriously by the state. Vigarello, *History of Rape*, 17–23, 45–49. Prostitutes were at the bottom of most social hierarchies and were often unmarried.

51. Jousse, *Traité de la justice criminelle*, 1: 694–734.

52. Claude-Joseph Ferrière, *Dictionnaire de droit et de pratique, nouvelle édition* (Paris: Bauche, 1771), 2: 394–95.

53. Ferrière, *Dictionnaire de droit et de pratique*, 1: 394–95.

54. Jousse, *Traité de la justice criminelle*, 3: 727, 738, 745.

55. On the history of factums, see Sarah Maza, *Private Lives and Public Affairs: The Causes Célèbres of Prerevolutionary France* (Berkeley: University of California Press, 1993), 34–37; and *Une histoire de la mémoire judiciaire de l'Antiquité à nos jours*, ed. Olivier Poncet and Isabelle Storez-Brancourt (Paris: École nationale de Chartres, 2009).

56. See, for example, Nicolas Toussaint le Moyne Des Essarts, *Les causes célèbres, curieuses et intéressantes de toutes les cours souveraines du Royaume avec les jugemens qui les ont décidées*, 179 vols. (Paris: Lacombe, 1773–89).

57. Farge and Foucault, *Le désordre des familles*, 9–17.

58. Dossier of Marie Genevieve Remy, March 1720, prisoner dossiers, ms. 10704, Bibliothèque de l'Arsenal, Paris.

59. For the laws and definitions, see Erica-Marie Benabou, *La prostitution et la police des mœurs au XVIIIe siècle* (Paris: Librairie académique Perrin, 1987), 20–38.

60. Jousse, *Traité de la justice criminelle*, 3: 273.

61. [Denis Diderot], "Prostituée," in Diderot and d'Alembert, *Encyclopédie, ou dictionnaire raisonné des sciences, des arts et des métiers, etc.*, https://artflsrv03.uchicago.edu/philologic4/encyclopedie0521/navigate/13/1929/?byte=5282966, accessed September 25, 2022.

62. Benabou, *Prostitution*, 23.

63. Such was not the case in earlier periods. Ruth Mazo Karras notes that in the medieval period, "there was no conceptual space in the medieval scheme of things for a sexually active single woman who was not a prostitute." *Sexuality in Medieval Europe: Doing unto Others*, third ed. (Abingdon, UK: Routledge, 2017), 141.

64. David Garrioch, *Neighborhood and Community in Paris, 1740–1790* (Cambridge: Cambridge University Press, 1986); Arlette Farge, *Fragile Lives: Violence, Power and Solidarity in Eighteenth-Century Paris*, trans. Carol Shelton (Cambridge MA: Harvard University Press, 1993).

65. Hardwick, *Sex in an Old Regime City*. Police did not always support community conventions, but they did in some surprising cases. In my own work on kept women (mistresses who provided amatory and companionate services to members of the financial, social, and political elites for remuneration), I found that the police mostly supported the rules internal to the demimonde. Nina Kushner, *Erotic Exchanges: The World of Elite Prostitution in Eighteenth-Century Paris* (Ithaca NY: Cornell University Press, 2013).

66. August 18 and 20, 1787, Y 9976, Archives Nationales, Paris.

67. Farge and Foucault, *Le désordre des familles*, 163.

68. Farge and Foucault, *Le désordre des familles*, 30–35.

69. Farge and Foucault, *Le désordre des familles*, 30–35.

70. Quote from the English translation of *Le désordre des familles*. Arlette Farge and Michel Foucault, *Disorderly Families: Infamous Letters from the Bastille Archives*, trans. Thomas Scott-Railton (Minneapolis: University of Minnesota Press, 2016), 48.

71. A sample survey of lettres de cachet reveals thirty-three cases of adultery in 1720, nine in 1745, and none in 1770 and 1785. Farge and Foucault find very few demands for the incarceration of family members by lettre de cachet after 1760. Farge and Foucault, *Le désordre des familles*, 17.

Suggested Reading

Berenguier, Nadine. *Conduct Books for Girls in Enlightenment France*. Farnham, UK: Ashgate, 2011.

Berriot-Salvadore, Évelyne. "The Discourse of Medicine and Science." Translated by Arthur Goldhammer. In *A History of Women in the West*, vol. 3, *Renaissance and Enlightenment Paradoxes*. Edited by Natalie Zemon Davis and Arlette Farge, 348–88. Cambridge, MA: Belknap, 1994.

Crampe-Casnabet, Michèle. "A Sampling of Eighteenth-Century Philosophy." Translated by Arthur Goldhammer. In *A History of Women in the West*, vol. 3, *Renaissance and Enlightenment Paradoxes*. Edited by Natalie Zemon Davis and Arlette Farge, 315–47. Cambridge, MA: Belknap, 1993.

Denis, Vincent. *Une histoire de l'identité: France 1715–1815*. Seyssel, France: Champ Vallon, 2008.

During, Lisabeth. *The Chastity Plot*. Chicago: University of Chicago Press, 2021.

Farge, Arlette, and Michel Foucault. *Disorderly Families: Infamous Letters from the Bastille Archives*. Translated by Thomas Scott-Railton. Minneapolis: University of Minnesota Press, 2016.

Hardwick, Julie. *Sex in an Old Regime City: Young Workers and Intimacy in France, 1660–1789*. New York: Oxford University Press, 2020.

Karras, Ruth Mazo. "Prostitution and the Question of Sexual Identity in Medieval Europe." *Journal of Women's History* 11, no. 2 (Summer 1999): 159–77.

Kushner, Nina. *Erotic Exchanges: The World of Elite Prostitution in Eighteenth-Century Paris*. Ithaca NY: Cornell University Press, 2013.

Steinbrügge, Lieselotte. *The Moral Sex: Women's Nature in the French Enlightenment*. Translated by Pamela E. Selwyn. New York: Oxford University Press, 1995.

Wahrman, Dror. *The Making of the Modern Self: Identity and Culture in Eighteenth-Century England*. New Haven CT: Yale University Press, 2004.

4

DOMESTICATING PLEASURE

The Sexual Politics of the French Enlightenment

LISA JANE GRAHAM

In the summer and early fall of 2018, the Boston Museum of Fine Arts hosted an exhibition titled *Casanova's Europe: Art, Pleasure, and Power in the 18th Century* that devoted a room to eighteenth-century French erotica. The curators placed one set of pornographic prints from the revolutionary period behind red velvet curtains with trigger warnings that heightened the voyeuristic thrill for viewers. Similar to Hollywood films like *Dangerous Liaisons* (Stephen Frears, 1988) or *Marie Antoinette* (Sofia Coppola, 2006), this exhibition catered to the licentious nostalgia that the French Enlightenment conjures in popular imagination. Casanova not only seduced his way through European courts and capitals but also boasted of his adventures for posterity. The celebrated lover stands for an era.

It is significant that this native Venetian, the child of actors, chose to write his memoirs in French, for France was renowned for having an elite society and a philosophical movement that extolled the pursuit of pleasure. Given this reputation, it is strange that general histories of the period ignore sex and desire in their accounts of what distinguished the Century of Lights.[1] In fact, this marginalization of sex does not square with the evidence and raises the question: Why do scholars treat sex as a distraction from the Enlightenment and its legacy? In the following pages, I argue that sex is problematic because it confounds linear narratives that align progressive politics with moral liberation. Sex reminds us that the Enlightenment was and remains a contested site for defining the place of desire and the role of discipline in democratic societies today.

Although scholars have studied happiness in eighteenth-century culture, there is little historical work on pleasure and its ramifications in Enlightenment discourse.[2] Yet, the two concepts emerged in relation to one another as seen, for example, in the *Encyclopédie* article on "Happiness." The author, Abbé Jean Pestre, contrasted the fleeting nature of pleasure to the enduring condition of happiness. He warned readers: "Pleasures cannot accompany every moment of our life [since] our most perfect happiness in this life is nothing but a state of tranquility strewn here and there with passing pleasures."[3] Pleasure was integral to happiness, but in moderate doses, as the writer and collaborator with Diderot, Madeleine d'Arsant de Puisieux, insisted: "The habit of pleasure engenders boredom: hence pleasure requires economy because in repeating it too often, one wears out the senses and reaches the point where one cannot enjoy anything [*ne plus rien goûter*]."[4] Both authors recommended restraint to sustain pleasure, understood as a source of well-being and delight. Their remarks alert us to the wariness about pleasure that persisted even in progressive circles that exalted its benefits. This unease was a legacy of Christian doctrines, most recently spearheaded by Jansenism, that had shaped French attitudes toward sex, sin, and sensuality for centuries.[5] The secularization of sex did not eliminate the need for moral guidelines but reconfigured them. Otherwise, as the historian Carl Becker asked in 1932, "why would any man deny himself?"[6]

Given this ambivalence, it is not surprising that over the course of two decades, this cautious embrace of pleasure exemplified by Pestre and Puisieux hardened into moral condemnation. Rousseau exemplified this stance when he warned his fictional pupil Emile in his educational treatise *Emile, or On Education* (1762), "You do not know the fury with which the senses, by the lure of pleasure, drag young men like you into the abyss of vices."[7] Much of book 4 of *Emile* focuses on teaching Emile to avoid "the horrors of debauchery" through lessons that show how "the taste for chastity is connected with health, strength, courage, the virtues, love itself, and all the true goods of man."[8] By chastity, Rousseau meant sexual continence, not abstinence. He praised one father who curbed his son's promiscuity by taking him to a hospital for syphilitics. This "hideous sight" left an indelible mark on the young soldier, who avoided the libertine lifestyle of his military comrades throughout his career.[9] Rousseau cautioned readers that the senses could not be trusted; they were instruments of corruption in a fallen world. How do we explain this dramatic shift in attitudes toward sex and pleasure in the second half of the century?

To answer this question, we need to understand the challenges posed by sex to those men and women committed to destigmatizing it. Unlike the equable concept of happiness, the impulsive nature of pleasure threatened liberal models of society predicated on rational self-government. The erosion of religious and material constraints had emancipated desire from the shackles of scarcity and sin. This newfound sexual freedom was simultaneously exhilarating and disorienting in an era of commercial expansion, urbanization, and rising literacy. It required a response that coalesced in the category of debauchery, a term used to restrain desire. In the hands of philosophes, physicians, police officers and moralists, debauchery provided an argument for domesticating pleasure. These efforts converged in the campaign to promote marriage as a safeguard against uncontrolled sexuality.

This chapter shows that the question of sexual pleasure was central to the French Enlightenment. Medical and moral qualifications of the philosophes' rehabilitation of pleasure identified marriage as the institution uniquely suited to the task of managing desire in a society of individuals. The shift from arranged to affectionate marriage has been well documented for eighteenth-century France.[10] This story aligns marriage with progressive currents in philosophy, natural law, and politics. Until recently, however, this triumphal tale overlooked the impact of the new model on gender and female desire. A closer look reveals that the effort to domesticate pleasure redefined female sexuality as passive, monogamous, and maternal. In the process, philosophes and doctors classified other expressions as pathological, criminal, or dangerous.

My argument about the use of debauchery to stigmatize extramarital sex and female desire complements Nina Kushner's analysis of the "unchaste woman" in the preceding chapter. The policing of women's sexuality involved both carceral techniques and cultural norms as expressed through medical treatises, urban chronicles, and fiction. These forces converged in the trial of Marie-Antoinette to consolidate the exclusion of women from politics and their legal subjugation to men. These views of female sexuality established a gender regime that linked the First French Republic to the First Empire and persisted into the twentieth century.

The Rehabilitation of Pleasure

The Enlightenment marked a rupture with traditional morality and religion. The Counter-Reformation in France emphasized the emotions as tools for educating the laity and reinforcing faith. These same passions, however, could also foment violence, as seen during the sixteenth-century Wars of Religion and the mid-seventeenth-century political uprising known as the Fronde.[11] This mistrust of the passions nurtured neo-Stoic and Cartesian philosophies that privileged reason as an essential feature of masculine and aristocratic identity. During the reign of Louis XIV (1643–1715), it guided the Crown's policing of morality in the name of public order. Just as the king applied reason to statecraft, so, too, individuals should use reason to manage their desires.[12] This wariness of pleasure was reinforced by the spread of Jansenism in the last decades of the seventeenth century. Armed with an Augustinian theology that emphasized man's sinful nature and his struggle for salvation, the Jansenists denounced the moral laxity of Versailles under the Sun King. These rigorist circles were active at court and attacked the king directly.[13] Worried by their growing appeal, Louis XIV secured a papal bull, *Unigenitus*, in 1713 condemning Jansenism as heresy. Designed to silence his critics, many of whom were entrenched in the magistracy, the encyclical set the stage for a century of politicoreligious conflicts.[14]

The revocation of the Edict of Nantes in 1685 created a Protestant diaspora of opposition centered in England and Holland that subverted the Crown's efforts to censor information. Drawing on Newtonian science, Lockean sensationalism, and Bayle's skepticism, critics of the Sun King denounced religious persecution and royal despotism. These radical ideas found a more receptive climate during the Regency (1715–22) after Louis XIV died. This interlude of political experimentation included an epistemological shift to rescue pleasure from the grip of moral rigorism and political absolutism. The Abbé Prévost crystallized this early Enlightenment pleasure principle in his bestselling tale of thwarted passions and mismatched lovers, *Manon Lescaut* (1731). When the noble protagonist, the Chevalier des Grieux, is detained at his father's request in the Saint-Lazare prison, he refuses to renounce his "fatal passion" for the mercenary courtesan, Manon, who has captured his heart. Instead, he protests, "Being made as we are, it is indisputable that our felicity is found in pleasure, and I challenge anyone to define it in any other way."[15]

With this declaration, des Grieux captures the profound shift in attitudes toward pleasure that distinguished the first half of the eighteenth century. Prévost's novel extolled the pursuit of pleasure, specifically erotic pleasure, as a natural source of well-being without invoking God as arbiter of human destiny. This hedonistic ethos flourished in art and literature until the 1760s, when Jean-Jacques Rousseau railed against pleasure for enslaving men and distracting them from their civic duties. Rousseau discredited pleasure by linking it to a decadent aristocracy and a corrupt society in which women reversed the natural sexual hierarchy to control men.[16] Thus, the view of pleasure evolved over the century from celebrating its benefits to decrying it as a threat to republican virtue.

This reevaluation of pleasure coincided with the emergence of vitalism, a school of medical thought centered on the Montpellier Academy of Sciences. The Montpellier physicians replaced the mechanical view of the human body with a network of fibers that transmitted sensory information to the brain for processing and reaction. The stimulation of fibers corresponded to irritability, a property that was both universal and variable within the human species. According to vitalists, pleasure and pain were physiological responses to stimuli that guided humans in making decisions and understanding their world. Like the encyclopedists with whom they collaborated, the vitalists emphasized the impact of sensory information on health and development. Convinced that irritability varied between bodies, the vitalists designed therapeutic regimens that reinforced social and sexual distinctions.

Many of the medical articles in the *Encyclopédie* were written by the Montpellier-trained physician Jean-Joseph Menuret de Chambaud, who applied vitalist theories to study erotic attraction. Sex and desire were no longer condemned as sources of sin but praised as natural impulses that procured happiness and the survival of the species.[17] For example, in his *Encyclopédie* article "Impotence," Menuret de Chambaud rejected popular superstitions and theological explanations in favor of empathy and expertise: "This malady is not ordinarily accompanied by any kind of danger; it does not generate anything other than inconvenience; it deprives man of a function that is very important to society, & very pleasurable to himself; which makes him sad and plunges him into melancholy."[18] His assessment illustrated the sexual science of the *Encyclopédie* and the *philosophes'* conviction: "The propagation of beings is the greatest goal of Nature. She solicits the two sexes imperiously to this aim [by instilling desire that culminates in] exquisite pleasure."[19] Natural law revealed the absurdity of Christian morality, as Montesquieu reminded readers of his popular novel *The Persian Letters* (1721) when Usbek asks, "How can something that produces nothing be a virtue?"[20]

This medical paradigm identified sexual desire as one of many appetites that procured benefits but also required management. Given this tenet, it made sense that the prevailing advice identified both promiscuity and abstinence as triggers for pathological conditions. We often forget that sexual deprivation was considered as dangerous as excess in the eighteenth century. Unlike excess, however, which was difficult to define, abstinence had a visible target in the French clergy. This assumption explained the pervasive themes of clerical depravity in Enlightenment pornography and libertine literature, as well as in celebrated trials like the Cadière-Girard affair.[21] Wherever French readers looked, they learned that desire was natural and that repression led to debauchery or insanity. Diderot illustrated these consequences in his unfinished novel, *The Nun*, about a girl, Suzanne Simonin, forced into the convent against her will. Suzanne's innocence makes her a perfect foil for the perversions of cloistered men and women. Among the abusers is the Mother Superior at the convent of Arpajon, who "went mad," as Diderot characterized it, after Suzanne rejected her amorous advances. The story was inspired by the real case of a young woman, Marguerite Delamarre, who hired a lawyer to help her revoke her vows.[22] The erotic episodes titillated readers but also demonstrated that the human need for freedom included authority over one's own body and sexual satisfaction.

The rehabilitation of desire as natural and beneficial coincided with a new conception of sexual difference in medicine and culture. Before the eighteenth century, as Thomas Laqueur argues, sex was not a stable category of distinction, because anatomists viewed men and women as versions of the same body with parts arranged differently. Women were considered inferior (inverted genitals, less heat) versions of men but they were not ontologically different.[23] This emphasis on similarity receded in the second half of the century. Although scholars debate the causes of the shift, they agree that the Enlightenment promoted a view of the sexes grounded in natural and incommensurate difference.[24] Within this model doctors recognized that the sex drive was natural for both sexes but warned that in girls "puberty is more precocious, the desires are usually more violent and their constraint more dangerous."[25] They cautioned parents that forced or delayed marriages led to infertility or disease. Sexual science thus converged with an emerging domestic ideology that promoted marriage and maternity as female destiny. These assumptions were codified by Jean-Jacques Rousseau in his educational treatise *Emile, or On Education* (1762) and in popular medical manuals like Pierre Roussel's *Système physique et moral de la femme* (Physical and moral system of women), first published in 1775.[26]

The insistence on difference had important consequences for attitudes toward gender and female pleasure. Drawing on the vitalist principle that girls had more elastic fibers than boys, doctors urged parents to limit intellectual activities and education for their daughters.[27] They singled out novel reading as an especially dangerous activity that inflamed the imagination and destroyed fertility.[28] Reading triggered masturbation, they said, by substituting solitary and fictional pleasures for the real ones provided by marriage and maternity. These worries coincided with the changing view of the role of the female orgasm in conception. If orgasm was not required to fertilize an egg, then female desire had no medical justification. Instead, it became symptomatic of diseases like "nymphomania," invented by the Swiss physician J. D. T. de Bienville in 1771.[29] Female sexual passivity emerged as the norm, an assumption that informed republican arguments to restrict women's political activity as well. By the 1790s, as Elizabeth Colwill concludes from her analysis of the revolutionary journal *La Décade philosophique* (The philosophical decade), "desire was a masculine noun" and women's strength resided in maternity.[30]

The preceding discussion demonstrates that the rehabilitation of pleasure was qualified from its inception during the Regency. Philosophes and physicians fretted about the destructive role of passion and the human proclivity for excess. These anxieties converged on the female body and mounted in response to the disruptive forces of urbanization and commercialization on French society. To counter the challenge, moralists used the category of debauchery to delineate the dangers of excess and the loss of self-control over one's sexual appetites and body. When demographers like Jean-Baptiste Moheau compared birth rates across cultures and over time, they concluded that debauchery reduced fertility and engendered "feeble" offspring.[31] To prescribe behavior, they contrasted the "sterile pleasures" of lovers with the fertile couplings of spouses. In their search for an antidote to debauchery, the philosophes and their allies landed on marriage as a site for domesticating desire. Thus, the Enlightenment confronted the challenge of aligning sexual gratification with conjugal duty as part of its blueprint for progress.

Sex, Pleasure, and Marriage

Historically in the West, sexual pleasure and passion were located outside of marriage. In classical culture marriage secured lineage and property transmission through reproduction, but for erotic gratification, men looked to other partners and practices. Procreation and pleasure were distinct activities that resided in separate spheres. The spread of Christianity added the stigma of sin to sex and condoned marriage as the only licit site for indulging the stirrings of the flesh. Yet even marriage carried risks of inflaming desire when spouses pursued pleasure, not procreation, according to canon law and early Christian thinkers like Saint Augustine.[32] The flowering of medieval romance reinforced this bifurcation of pleasure and marriage by identifying erotic yearning with adulterous relations between wandering knights and neglected or trapped wives. This principle guided religious teachings and confessional techniques that emerged in the wake of the Council of Trent (1545–63). Theologians confirmed the sacramental quality of marriage and clarified sexual injunctions for spouses. Christian doctrine remained ambivalent; people could marry and have sex but they should not enjoy it too much.[33] In these same decades, the French Crown wrested control of marriage from the church and used laws to reinforce patriarchy and hierarchy in the family. From the perspective of the Crown and the community, the family was an institution for controlling property and securing public order.[34] Thus, marriage in France involved everything but pleasure before the eighteenth century, and it required considerable effort to return it to the marriage bed.

As noted above, starting in the eighteenth century, physicians and philosophes rehabilitated erotic attraction as a natural, and therefore beneficial, appetite. Among its many virtues, sex procured health, happiness, and offspring. Doctors prescribed regular sex, or "therapeutic coitus," for husbands and wives, and medical manuals offered advice to foster pleasurable and fertile coupling.[35] Their promotion of sex, however, was not a call for free love, given that "pleasure remained grounded in reproduction."[36] This assumption guided the various articles in the *Encyclopédie* that addressed human sexuality. For example, in his entry "Adultery," François-Vincent Toussaint reminded readers: "The pleasures that God willed attached to the conjugal union tend to make the human race grow; and this result follows from the Providential institution, when these pleasures are subject to law: but the ruin of fertility and the opprobrium of society are infallible results of irregular unions."[37] In other words, the pursuit of sexual pleasure outside marriage diminished fertility and destroyed community.

It helps to recall that since the reign of Louis XIV, discussions of marriage reflected a natalist agenda designed to correct a perceived population decline.[38] Even though the French population doubled in the eighteenth century, prominent philosophes and political economists were convinced of a fertility crisis. They found evidence of this crisis everywhere, from the sex ratio at birth to unhappy marriages. All appetites, including love, as Nicolas de Venette reminded readers of his popular sex manual, needed regulation: "Love which causes so many problems when we abuse it, procures many benefits when reason or necessity incline us to follow its directives."[39] Citing evidence from books and patients, doctors recommended marriage to safeguard against the dangers of deprivation and debauchery.[40]

Thus, unlike earlier Christian reforms, enlightened efforts to improve marriage reflected positive, not negative, views of sex and desire. For example, in *The Persian Letters*, Montesquieu mocked the irrational tenets of Christian morality, observing, "Marriage to them [Christians] does not consist in sensual pleasure; on the contrary, . . . it seems they wish to banish that element from it as much as possible."[41] This skeptical attitude toward religion reinforced the medical views of sexuality as a natural and beneficial drive. Physicians promoted marriage as a mechanism for managing desire and criticized the practice of delayed and arranged marriages. Some voices even called for the legalization of divorce as part of the campaign to improve marriage.[42] The notorious libertine and celebrated warrior Maurice de Saxe believed that society could augment fertility and eliminate debauchery through "wise laws" that rewarded procreation and terminated sterile marriages. He insisted, "The more children a woman has, the happier she is with her situation in life."[43] Saxe captured the philosophes' vision of a happy marriage that posited maternity as destiny for women. In the following decades this assumption grounded a domestic ideology reinforced by materialism and natural law.

Sensing that the stakes were high for women in these debates, some writers questioned the emphasis on female submission. Was marriage, even in its reformed guise, compatible with human nature and the quest for pleasure? A brief glance at literature reveals some skepticism. In 1752 Madeleine d'Arsant de Puisieux, friend and lover of Diderot, published an allegorical tale entitled *Le plaisir et la volupté* (Pleasure and voluptuousness, hereafter referred to as PV).[44] This text considers the physical and emotional sources of desire and their impact on relations between men and women. Puisieux represented the two types of attraction as the twin sons of Venus: Love (Amour) and Pleasure (Plaisir). The tale unfolds in episodes that use the mischievous deities to illustrate the conflicting drives of the human heart. The text opens with a short poem mocking the French: "There is one god who is cherished in France, whom we catch but rarely hold, Pleasure is his name, but he is by nature inconstant." Puisieux's text cautions readers: "Such was the order of fate: Love could not replace Pleasure once Pleasure had lodged himself in a heart without him" (PV 33–34).

The text argues that humans confused desire for intimacy and in the process lost the capacity to love. Puisieux's advice echoed the abbé Jean Pestre, who wrote in the *Encyclopédie* entry "Happiness" that pleasure without love produced "an immense void in the soul."[45] In Puisieux's central anecdote, Pleasure falls in love with the goddess Volupté (Voluptuousness). The two lovers become so absorbed in one another that they neglect their human charges, whose libido plummets to moribund levels. The situation is so dire that Venus intervenes. She decrees that the two gods must marry in order to quell their passion. Volupté is distraught when she learns of her fate: "What . . . the gods want to take away my lover! And for what reason do they deprive me of my happiness?" (PV 80). Puisieux's joke captured contemporary assumptions that marriage signaled the death of desire.

Once married, Volupté's fears are confirmed. Puisieux wrote: "Pleasure was impetuous by nature, his passion could not endure for long. When he felt constrained, boredom overtook him: the duties of a spouse did not suit him at all" (PV 82–83). Puisieux insisted that he did not find his wife less attractive but that possession ("once she had become his property") turned desire into indifference. Pleasure takes up with shady characters like Libertinage, Excess, and Disgust while Volupté languishes from neglect. She implores Venus to revive her husband's affections: "Your son is no longer that agreeable Pleasure who assured my happiness: he is a maniac who cannot stop attracting new victims to Libertinage. He is ruining his empire in order to build up that of his unworthy brother. I look for him in vain; he shows himself from time to time; but then he disappears and fails to return. Ah, Venus, punish my unfaithful spouse, I beg of you" (PV 89–90). Volupté lashes out at Hymen: "Ah, cruel Hymen, you made me lose the heart of my lover" (PV 93). Marriage has transformed her passionate lover into a philandering husband. Moved by her daughter-in-law's plight, Venus decides to teach her son a lesson.

As punishment, Venus gives Pleasure a list of Parisian libertines and orders that he visit each one in order to revive their flagging libido. Everyone he meets is physically and emotionally ravaged from a lifetime of excessive indulgence. Puisieux delivers her moral message with humor, describing Pleasure's heroic efforts to resuscitate men and women whose capacity for desire has been extinguished. He literally wears himself out. When her haggard son returns to her court, Venus takes pity on him and lifts the sentence. She understands that his magic was essential to the happiness of both gods and mortals.

She nurses him through recovery and sends him back to his lovely wife: "He saw Volupté again with all the graces that she had before he became her spouse. A long absence and the sight of all those decrepit women made his spouse even more charming. Love rekindled their flames and accomplished his Oracle" (PV 118–19). The experiment works; by experiencing the wages of libertinage, of indulgence without attachment, Pleasure discovers conjugal bliss. At this point the two brothers (Pleasure and Love) agree to join forces in ministering to married couples. The tale ends, however, on a skeptical note: "How happy the person who can capture just one of these Divinities! How many people have never known them, and don't realize what they are missing! Have they lived as men? I doubt it!" (P V 120).

Puisieux insisted that pleasure and love, desire and affection, were natural and necessary pursuits for men and women. At the same time, she recognized the challenge of coordinating these impulses and fixing them in marriage. She illustrated the prevailing assumptions that marriage killed pleasure but also that pleasure without love was fleeting. Puisieux's skepticism about monogamy found echoes in other texts from the period, including Diderot's tale *Madame de La Carlière*.[46] Both authors suggested that women paid the heavier price for the companionate model, which consigned them to passivity, frustration, or indifference. The emphasis on choice and affection in marriage put more pressure on wives to deliver physical and emotional satisfaction. Yet, as many writers insisted, the human heart was unpredictable and inconstant. Neither vitalist medicine nor sensationalist philosophy had unlocked its secrets.

Puisieux designed her story as a scientific experiment that allowed Pleasure to test the evidence from both sides while Volupté suffered from his neglect. Pleasure learned to appreciate his wife after encountering the ravages of debauchery. Thus, Puisieux used debauchery to steer Pleasure back to his wife and fix his desire on her. This tale questioned the enlightened conviction that choice secured happiness, given the capricious workings of desire. Moreover, as Dena Goodman argues, the promotion of choice never included the option for women not to marry, but only the right to select among potential suitors.[47] In fact, the affectionate model raised expectations about the purpose of marriage compared to the arranged unions of the past. By recasting the household as the couple, an economic unit as an emotional one, reformers made spouses, but especially women, responsible for the success or failure of a marriage. Puisieux worried that this model might well erase female desire *tout court*, and she was not wrong.

Sexual Regulation and Republican Politics

The publication in 1762 of *Emile*, Rousseau's bestselling education treatise, cemented the links between marriage and gender roles in republican discourse when France headed into revolution two decades later. After spending four books on preparing Emile for citizenship, Rousseau devoted book 5 to Sophie, Emile's intended companion, and her duties as wife and mother. Rousseau's lessons shaped emerging definitions of gender, virtue, and citizenship. We glimpse this impact in Alexandre-Balthazar-Laurent Grimod de La Reynière's 1783 essay *Réflexions philosophiques sur le plaisir; par un célibataire* (Philosophical reflections on pleasure; by a bachelor, hereafter RPP).[48] Inspired by a popular play performed at the Comédie Française in 1775 called *Le Célibataire* (The bachelor), La Reynière entered a heated debate about the failure of modern marriage and the rising number of bachelors. His text reflected the distrust of pleasure that fueled the late eighteenth-century attacks on luxury, celibacy, actresses, and prostitutes.[49] The text struck a nerve with readers and went through three editions in two years.

La Reynière is remembered for the *Almanach des Gourmands* (The gourmets' almanac), which appeared annually from 1803 through 1812. Along with Jean Anthelme Brillat-Savarin, he is considered a founder of modern gastronomy and restaurant criticism.[50] The son of a wealthy tax farmer and a noble mother, he studied law and was admitted to the bar in 1780. He was known in enlightened circles as a theater critic and man of letters, but also for the scandalous dinner parties that he hosted. His extravagant lifestyle and the publication of a satirical memoir led his parents to request a *lettre de cachet*, an extrajudicial order of incarceration, in 1786. La Reynière was detained in a monastery near Nancy for two years and struck from the bar. Upon his release, his parents forced him to settle in Lyon, where he survived the Terror and pursued an illustrious career in gastronomy.

In his preface to the *Réflexions philosophiques*, La Reynière introduced himself to readers as a die-hard bachelor and social chronicler. His unmarried status served as a gauge of objectivity for his considerations of women and marriage. His essay denounced rapacious wives, selfish bachelors, tyrannical fathers, and hypocritical abbés for the current crisis. He blamed promiscuity and rampant individualism for the decline of marriage and called for reforms to make women virtuous and men wise (RPP 13). Similar to Puisieux, he approached the problem by distinguishing true from false pleasures, identified as Friendship (*Amitié*) and Love (*Amour*) (RPP 20). Friendship was the only foundation for enduring relationships that satisfied both partners.

As he explained, in order to restore faith in marriage, he had to attack pleasure: "[It is] the product of passions, it flatters and nourishes them" (RPP 17). He warned readers about the dangers of excess, insisting that "men who chased pleasure were hurtling toward death" (RPP 17). He cited greed, ambition, and lust as examples of the false pleasures that led to disappointment. He described love as a "blind and tumultuous passion" that plunged the victim into a crisis from which he could not escape (RPP 19). Unable to control their emotions, men lost their capacity for reason and fell into delirium. This language recalled the medical discussions of debauchery discussed earlier in this chapter. In contrast to lust, Friendship offered "a sweet and tranquil sentiment that filled the soul . . . and consoled man in his misfortune. The joys of Friendship were real and enduring" (RPP 20). Unfortunately, society failed to prepare the young for their future roles as spouses and parents. While boys fell into libertinage, girls were cloistered— neither sex learned how to manage the onset of puberty and awakening desire.

La Reynière incorporated medical and moral assumptions about human sexuality into his redesign of marriage. Marriage allowed young men and women to yield to "the call of Nature" and "by the reciprocal exchange of their sensations, meld their existence in order to increase its duration" (RPP 48). Once the initial ardor subsided, the arrival of children reinforced the bond between husband and wife because "the preservation of these interesting creatures [drew] them even closer together and combin[ed] two wills in one sensation" (RPP 48). To achieve this domestic idyll, however, individuals had to invest in it and make prudent choices.

Much of La Reynière's analysis converged with eighteenth-century efforts to develop a science of marriage that promoted partner choice and compatibility.[51] Like the physicians, La Reynière criticized arranged marriages, decrying parents who "see in the establishment of their children a means to satisfy their own ambition. Little inclined to ensure their happiness, they think only about making them rich, because Fortune is, according to them, the basis of all Happiness" (RPP 57). For La Reynière, marriage negotiations suffered from the materialism that plagued a commercial society.

Echoing the misogynist strains of the debates about luxury that surged in the 1780s, La Reynière blamed women for male aversion to marriages.[52] Observing that "the youth of today dread marriage more than ever," he denounced the "ruinous taste for gambling" that led women to stay up all night and squander their fortunes (RPP 40–41). How could any husband keep up with such debts and hope to maintain his rank and reputation? Writing two years before the Diamond Necklace Affair (1785) exploded in the French news, La Reynière exposed the wages of female extravagance through a trail of broken husbands and ruined families.[53] Drawing on Rousseau's vision of domestic harmony in *Julie, or the New Heloise* (1761), La Reynière insisted that the rehabilitation of marriage depended on grooming men and women for their respective roles in the household.

The *Réflexions philosophiques* cited the large number of single men and women in Paris as evidence of "the degree to which love of liberty carries away the individual" (RPP 65). Both sexes postponed marriage in order to maximize their capacity for indulgence and diversion. Rather than punishing bachelors, society celebrated them (RPP 67). There were no incentives to marry and no penalties for opting out. In addition, the swelling ranks of bachelors increased demand for sex workers who could satisfy their needs. Recalling Diderot's essay in the *Encyclopédie*, La Reynière insisted that marriage reform would simultaneously augment population and improve civic morality by reducing the need for prostitutes. In this vision women were responsible for "making their husbands happy at home" to prevent them from "seeking pleasure elsewhere" (RPP 67).

Like the philosophes and demographers, La Reynière classified celibacy as a social crime: "The general interest of society [is], without doubt, that each individual works to augment the number of members who compose it" (RPP 60). The unmarried were dangerous because they rejected the reproductive labor of the sexual economy.[54] La Reynière condemned the search for sexual satisfaction outside of marriage as selfish and costly. He concluded by citing the example of the first Roman emperor, Augustus, to demand that the monarchy impose penalties on bachelors and outlaw celibacy.[55]

The *Réflexions philosophiques* fanned fears that accompanied the liberation of human desire in the context of a commercial society. As noted above, men of letters relied on marriage to contain desire and channel it toward procreation. Unregulated desire led to debauchery, sterility, and isolation. Initially, La Reynière blamed women for pushing their husbands into the arms of prostitutes: "They seem to study, by contrast, how to render domestic life intolerable, and drive them to search elsewhere for the tranquility missing from their own homes" (RPP 31). To check the recourse to prostitutes, wives should cater to their husbands' needs (RPP 68). At the same time, men were responsible for training their wives: "We have tried to make it clear, on the contrary, that the man is responsible for happiness in a marriage; that he must himself form the character of the woman associated with his existence; and if this work is more difficult in the upper ranks of society compared to the middling ones, we must acknowledge as well that, by a just compensation, the chains are also lighter and that the business, the pleasures and the incessant tumult of life provide distractions from these worries" (RPP 74). The case for marriage had eliminated Puisieux's exploration of reciprocal desire and replaced it with references to "light chains," "work," and "worries." Given this language, the dwindling appeal of marriage hardly seems surprising.

In a twist on the affectionate model, La Reynière argued that, when misguided, free choice led to as much unhappiness as parental constraint. In particular, he insisted that friendship was a superior basis for marriage than love. Love inevitably degenerated into indifference, but esteem blossomed into "a tender friendship, more solid and capable of securing happiness than a passing spark" (RPP 57). Ultimately, spouses would find enduring joy through mutual investment in their offspring.

In the conclusion, Grimaud de La Reynière distilled his argument:

> One fears less the ties of marriage than one searches to avoid it; and the lure of inconstancy, the glimpse of easy pleasures and egotism create more than half of the bachelors. We recognize that there is merit today in bearing the chains of Hymen: they weigh more heavily than ever; but the greater the devotion, so, too, the glory to be attained. We are not put on earth simply to search for pleasures; and since everyone must pay his debt to society, it is glorious to sacrifice oneself for it, and to immolate the pleasures of the fickle man for the duties of the citizen. (RPP 73–74)

This passage defined a secular creed that sacrificed pleasure on the altar of social obligation to transform the selfish man into a virtuous citizen. The basis of this distinction rested on the place and purpose of sex. Marriage prepared citizens and mothers; it was not a site for carnal pleasures, now condemned as unpatriotic.

The mid-century experiment to reform marriage as a home for cultivating mutual pleasures had passed. At best, the chains of marriage allowed humans to subsume sexual desire in procreation for the state. The *Réflexions philosophiques* justified this model through the language of civic republicanism and gender hierarchy. If a husband allowed his wife to dominate in the household, he lost his claim to authority in the polity. The ideal wife was a docile pet, not a plucky partner. There was no place in this equation for female pleasure or autonomy. Women should find fulfillment in catering to their husbands and rearing children. Lest a careless reader miss the point, the text offered a succinct directive, "the only happy marriages are those in which the husband commands" (RPP 52).

Sex, Politics, and the French Revolution

The preceding discussion of efforts to domesticate pleasure capture the ambivalence that distinguished enlightened views of sex and desire. These debates suggest that sex was central to the general debate about how to reform society and align it with principles of individual liberty and natural rights. Ambivalence about female pleasure and its consequences played a central role in discrediting the Old Regime and shaping the institutions that replaced it. The pornographic attacks against Marie-Antoinette acquire new significance when viewed in light of the medical and philosophical prescriptions regarding sexual hygiene and marriage. The efforts to circumscribe female sexuality and harness it to reproduction gained traction decades before the first shot was fired at the Bastille.

Starting with her arrival in France in 1770 to marry Louis XVI, the fourteen-year-old Marie-Antoinette was subject to a barrage of scrutiny, gossip, and criticism.[56] Courtiers blamed her for the couple's failure to consummate the marriage over the course of seven years, even though, by all accounts, Louis XVI had a medical impediment. Once the king's condition was diagnosed and corrected, the marriage was consummated and the queen conceived, giving birth to their first child, a daughter, in 1778. During this first decade of her life in France, Marie-Antoinette was simultaneously denounced for being too masculine, sexually frigid, sexually frustrated, and promiscuous. There was no logic to this litany of attacks unless we read them through the lens of medical assumptions about female desire and sexual science.

The police tracked gossip about the queen from her arrival at the French court and continued their efforts until the revolution erupted. Even though few pamphlets circulated before 1789, we know that letters and manuscripts spread gossip between Versailles and Paris, tarnishing the queen's reputation and fueling scandals like the Diamond Necklace Affair. As Sarah Maza argues, public opinion lacerated the queen for her corruption and greed even though she had no involvement in this elaborate hoax.[57] In addition, the Crown sent agents to London to suppress scurrilous texts produced by an expatriate community of banished authors.[58] Most of the early pamphlets were written by disgruntled courtiers at Versailles and smuggled to Paris for publishing and distribution.[59] The floodgates opened in 1789 when censorship collapsed after the fall of the Bastille. The vilification campaign escalated during the revolution and culminated in the queen's trial and execution in October 1793. A selective glance at these texts demonstrates how they deployed contemporary views of sex and marriage to attack the queen and delineate women's role in the new republic.

One of the most popular texts, the *Essais historiques sur la vie de Marie-Antoinette* (Historical essays on the life of Marie-Antoinette), was written in the 1780s, with later editions furnishing new evidence of the queen's crimes. The word "debauchery" recurs like a refrain to describe both the queen and the French court that welcomed her in 1770. The anonymous author drew an analogy between Marie-Antoinette and the detested former mistress of Louis XV, Madame du Barry, denouncing "the same debauchery, . . the same tumultuous passions," as well as their shared ability "to deceive and degrade the men for whom they should have instilled respect." Just as "Louis XV was the most complete dupe of du Barry . . . Louis XVI was similarly deceived and demeaned by his wife."[60] Unlike du Barry, however, who used sex to propel her social ascension into the royal bed, Marie-Antoinette indulges herself in response to deprivation. The pamphlet invokes the medical arguments about female sexuality to explain the queen's fall into debauchery. Denied satisfaction by her impotent husband, the adolescent princess is vulnerable to the stirrings of desire. The author emphasized the king's impotency ("The King [Louis XVI] is a total loser both physically and morally") and its impact on the queen.[61] Even her attraction to women is explained as a safe (no risk of sullying the royal line) compensation for her "husband's useless caresses."[62] Underneath the licentious attacks, the pamphlet conveys sympathy for the queen's sexual frustration.

Similar sentiments guide the satirical poem *Les Amours de Charlot et Toinette* (*The Love Life of Charlie and Toinette*), which opens with a discussion of the moribund sex life of the royal couple. Because Louis XVI is unable to satisfy his nubile wife, she turns to masturbation as an outlet for her frustration. The poem describes these erotic interludes in lyrical terms that evoke sympathy for the girl who seeks relief while dreaming of her husband:

> Sometimes, dying of boredom in the middle of a lovely day,
> She writhed all alone in her bed:
> Her throbbing tits, her lovely eyes, and her mouth
> half parted, softly panting,
> Seemed to invite the challenge of a good fuck.
>
> In these Lustful positions,
> Antoinette would rather not have
> Remained at foreplay,
> And that L[ouis] had fucked her better.[63]

The king's impotence clears a path for his scatterbrained brother, the Comte d'Artois, who seizes the occasion to offer his services to the languishing queen. After mounting a feeble resistance to protect her honor, Marie-Antoinette succumbs at the sight of the count's erection, and she "feels at last how sweet it is to be well and truly fucked."[64] The text oscillates between celebrating the joys of sex and condemning the adulterous liaison, capturing the ambivalent view of pleasure in the late eighteenth century. The royal couple illustrates the failure of the arranged marriage model to produce either happiness or offspring. Marie-Antoinette represents the physiological and moral risks of female desire unfulfilled by motherhood and marriage.

Even after the birth of her children, Marie-Antoinette suffered attacks for her voracious sexual appetites and her lack of maternal instincts. Her sexuality offered a prism that refracted struggles against despotism, now coded as debauchery. Political opponents and underground journalists regaled readers with graphic descriptions of her frenzied search for new partners and pleasures. The pornographic pamphlets that circulated after 1789 decried "the Austrian woman on the rampage" who consumed men and women indiscriminately for her pleasure, only to discard them after coupling. In *Le Cadran des plaisirs* (The dial of pleasures) she seduces Chérubin, the precocious page from Beaumarchais's play *The Marriage of Figaro*, who recoils before her monstrosity: "In her delirium and voluptuousness, she became a bacchante who sought pleasure in all possible manners, frenzied and furious, no longer respecting any conventions or constraints on her lust."[65] The charges against the queen escalated as the revolution shifted in more radical directions after the royal family's failed flight to Varennes in 1791.

The *Essais historiques* was republished after 1789 and included a second part written as a confession with unsparing candor and lack of remorse. Here, the queen admits her transgressions and relishes the gory details. This reflexive voice removes any doubt about the queen's motives and reinforces the charges circulating in pamphlets and caricatures. The fictive voice in this pseudo-testament guarantees transparency and authenticity.[66] Marie-Antoinette proclaims her hatred of the French and her desire to harm them. In her opening monologue she describes herself as "a monster execrated by all of nature" and admits to being "sullied in crimes and debaucheries" fueled by her insatiable lust. The text links sexual voracity to violence. The most disturbing of her "confessions" involves her admission of poisoning her son, the Dauphin, "this royal embryo" who stood in the way of her plot to place her brother, the emperor of Austria, on the French throne. She describes her crime in calculating language, noting that the boy's frail constitution facilitated the task and shielded her from suspicion. The public speculated about his illness, but nobody questioned the queen, who "laughed to herself about the conjectures people might draw."[67] She indicates that she is already preparing to kill her second son, who is next in line for the throne. This confession confirmed her monstrosity as a mother, a modern Medea who devoured her own offspring.[68] It also found its way into the Revolutionary Tribunal's trial and condemnation of her.

Possibly the most shocking moment of the queen's brief trial occurred when the radical editor Jacques-René Hébert accused her of corrupting her eight-and-a-half-year-old son, Louis Charles Capet. This allegation was repeated in *Testament de Marie-Antoinette, Veuve Capet* (*Testament of Marie-Antoinette, Widow Capet*), a short text appended to the *Essais historiques* after her execution on October 16, 1793: "Simon, to whom her son had been entrusted, when called as a witness, reproached her with the impure habits she has imparted to her son, habits that tended only to sew [*sic*] in him the seeds of debauchery and to make his morals as loose as those of his mother. *This is too far beneath my contempt for me to reply*, she answered."[69] It is significant that Hébert used the word "debauchery" to describe Marie-Antoinette's crimes against her child and the republic. The queen represented an erotic as well as a political regime of nonmaternal and destructive desire. She stood as a warning to the revolutionary leaders of the need to circumscribe female desire through marriage.

The French queen offers one highly visible example of how the Enlightenment wariness of pleasure shaped revolutionary views of gender roles and sexual policing. The queen, along with women across the social and political spectrum, symbolized the threat of debauchery to the survival of the new republic.[70] Pleasure was gendered female and denounced as counterrevolutionary. This suspicion extended to all those who sought erotic satisfaction outside of marriage. Here, we see the continuity with Kushner's analysis of the unchaste woman as a problematic sexual identity before 1789. This marginalization of sex continues, as I have argued, to shape the historical accounts of the period.

"The Enlightenment" refers to an epistemological shift in attitudes toward human nature that emancipated desire from the shackles of material scarcity and Christian sin. Eighteenth-century France was remarkable for having a high society that celebrated pleasure in its various iterations: sensual, intellectual, aesthetic. Even today, the Enlightenment evokes a hedonistic era exemplified by notorious libertines like Casanova and Sade.[71] This image, however, ignores the fears that accompanied the rehabilitation of pleasure. Unlike the stable and rational sentiment of happiness, pleasure threatened to derail liberal models of self and society predicated on disciplined husbands and docile wives. This anxiety about pleasure haunted the philosophes and their followers, who used the category of debauchery to consolidate a sexual and gender order grounded in marriage. Attending to the sexual debates that propelled the Enlightenment explains the restrictive moral policies and laws that guided the First French Republic and the Napoleonic Empire. Jennifer J. Davis, in her chapter on sex in the colonies in this volume, identifies a parallel set of concerns that led the state to police sexual relations, though in that case it was limited to interracial sex. For the metropole, one sees this pattern most clearly in the regulation of sex work by police officers, physicians, and urban administrators in the nineteenth century.[72]

The preceding discussion suggests that the eighteenth-century rehabilitation of pleasure did not entail a rejection of Christian metaphysics so much as the secularization and medicalization of sin. Enlightened thinkers replaced God with Nature to harness sex to reproduction and prescribe rules for sexual hygiene.[73] The emerging field of political economy used debauchery to designate the dangers of unrestrained hedonism for the individual and society. Jessie Hewitt explores one aspect of this legacy in her chapter on sexual secrets in this volume. She identifies the importance of sexual probity (i.e., not being labeled debauched) to the reputation of bourgeois men. Doctors risked the health of wives and fiancées by failing to reveal their exposure, or certain future exposure, to sexually transmitted infections. Extending the argument both spatially and chronologically, Jennifer Anne Boittin explores how the assumption of female sexual passivity shaped the state's reaction to white women who escaped family and sought independence in the French colonies.

The warnings in the Enlightenment about debauchery did not reflect hostility toward sexuality. On the contrary, doctors and demographers were responding to the promotion of pleasure as a source of personal fulfillment and natural morality. Herein lies the legacy of enlightened sexual science and the challenge for democracy in the modern era. Like the concurrent debates about free markets, sex offered a testing ground for the compatibility of political and moral liberty. Marriage emerged as the antidote for destructive individualism, and this premise informed the laws and policies regarding family, gender, and sex work of successive French regimes down to the Fifth Republic.

1. To cite one example of new directions for research that exclude sex or sexuality, see Daniel Brewer, ed., *The Cambridge Companion to the French Enlightenment* (Cambridge: Cambridge University Press, 2015).

2. Robert Mauzi, *L'idée du bonheur dans la littérature et la pensée françaises au XVIIIe* (Paris: Armand Colin, 1960); Darrin M. McMahon, *Happiness: A History* (New York: Grove, 2006); Richie Robertson, *The Enlightenment: The Pursuit of Happiness, 1680–1790* (New York: Harper Collins, 2021). Recent studies of pleasure in eighteenth-century France come from scholars in literature, philosophy, and music. See Georgia J. Cowart, *The Triumph of Pleasure: Louis XIV and the Politics of Spectacle* (Chicago: University of Chicago Press, 2008); Michel Delon, *Le savoir-vivre libertin* (Paris: Hachette, 2000); Colas Duflo, *Philosophie des pornographes: Les ambitions philosophiques du roman libertin* (Paris: Seuil, 2019); and Thomas M. Kavanagh, *Enlightened Pleasures: Eighteenth-Century France and the New Epicureanism* (New Haven CT: Yale University Press, 2010).

3. Abbé Jean Pestre, "Happiness," trans. Nelly S. Hoyt and Thomas Cassirer, in *The Encyclopedia of Diderot and d'Alembert Collaborative Translation Project* (Ann Arbor: University of Michigan Library), https://quod.lib.umich.edu/d/did/. Originally published as "Bonheur," in *Encyclopédie ou Dictionnaire raisonné des sciences, des arts et des métiers*, ed. Denis Diderot and Jean le Rond d'Alembert (Paris, 1752), 2: 322–23.

4. Madeleine d'Arsant de Puisieux, *Réflexions et avis sur les défauts et ridicules à la mode* (Paris, 1761), 212.

5. For background on Christian views, see Katherine Crawford, *European Sexualities, 1400–1800* (New York: Cambridge University Press, 2007), 55–99.

6. Carl Becker, *The Heavenly City of the Eighteenth-Century Philosophes* (New Haven CT: Yale University Press, 1966), 149.

7. Jean-Jacques Rousseau, *Emile, or On Education*, trans. Allan Bloom (New York: Basic, 1979), 326.

8. Rousseau, *Emile*, 324.

9. Rousseau, *Emile*, 230–31.

10. Two classic studies include James F. Traer, *Marriage and the Family in Eighteenth-Century France* (Ithaca NY: Cornell University Press, 1982); and Jean-Louis Flandrin, *Families in Former Times: Kinship, Household and Sexuality*, trans. Richard Southern (New York: Cambridge University Press, 1979). More recently, see Maurice Daumas, *Le mariage amoureux: Histoire du lien conjugal sous l'Ancien Régime* (Paris: Armand Colin, 2004); Suzanne Desan, "Making and Breaking Marriage: An Overview of Old Regime Marriage as a Social Practice," in *Family, Gender, and Law in Early Modern France*, ed. Suzanne Desan and Jeffrey

Merrick (University Park: Pennsylvania State University Press, 2009); and Dena Goodman, "Marriage Choice and Marital Success: Reasoning about Marriage, Love, and Happiness," in *Family, Gender, and Law in Early Modern France*, ed. Suzanne Desan and Jeffrey Merrick (University Park: Pennsylvania State University Press, 2009).

11. Yann Rodier, *Les raisons de la haine: Histoire d'une passion dans la France du premier XVIIe siècle, 1610–1659* (Ceyzérieu, France: Champ Vallon, 2020).

12. James R. Farr, *Authority and Sexuality in Early Modern Burgundy, 1550–1730* (New York: Oxford University Press, 1995), esp. 22–26, 157–61.

13. Damien Tricoire, "Attacking the Monarchy's Sacrality in Late Seventeenth-Century France: The Underground Literature against Louis XIV, Jansenism and the Dauphin's Court Faction," *French History* 31, no. 2 (June 2017): esp. 163–64.

14. Dale K. Van Kley, *The Religious Origins of the French Revolution: From Calvin to the Civil Constitution, 1560–1791* (New Haven CT: Yale University Press, 1999), 58–74.

15. Abbé Prévost, *Manon Lescaut*, ed. Jean Sgard, trans. Leonard Tancock (1731; New York: Penguin, 2004), 67.

16. Kavanagh, *Enlightened Pleasures*, 103–27.

17. Carol Blum, *Strength in Numbers: Population, Reproduction, and Power in Eighteenth-Century France* (Baltimore: Johns Hopkins University Press, 2002); and Alain Corbin, *L'harmonie des plaisirs: Les manières de jouir du siècle des Lumières à l'avènement de la sexologie* (Paris: Perrin, 2008). See also Joan Scott, *Sex and Secularism* (Princeton NJ: Princeton University Press, 2018).

18. Jean-Joseph Menuret de Chambaud, "Impuissance," in Denis Diderot and Jean le Rond d'Alembert, eds., *Encyclopédie, ou dictionnaire raisonné des sciences, des arts et des métiers, etc.*, ed. Robert Morrissey and Glenn Roe (Chicago: University of Chicago, ARTFL Encyclopédie Project, Autumn 2017), http://encyclopedie .uchicago.edu/.

19. Denis Diderot (attributed), "Enjoyment," trans. Anoush Terjanian, in *The Encyclopedia of Diderot and d'Alembert Collaborative Translation Project*. Originally published as "Jouissance," in Diderot and d'Alembert, *Encyclopédie ou Dictionnaire raisonné des sciences, des arts et des métiers* (Paris, 1765), 8: 889. On Menuret de Chambaud, see Roselyne Rey, *Naissance et développement du vitalisme en France de la deuxième moitié du XVIIIe siècle à la fin du Premier Empire* (Oxford: SVEC, 2000), 268.

20. Montesquieu, "Letter CXVII," in *The Persian Letters*, trans. George R. Healy (Indianapolis: Hackett, 1999), 196.

21. See Mita Choudhury's recent analysis of the Cadière-Girard affair, Choudhury, *The Wanton Jesuit and the Wayward Saint: A Tale of Sex, Religion, and Politics in*

Eighteenth-Century France (University Park: Pennsylvania State University Press, 2015); Myriam Deniel-Ternant, Ecclésiastiques en débauche, 1700–1790 (Ceyzérieu, France: Champ Vallon, 2017); and Cathy McClive's chapter in this volume.

22. Georges May, Diderot et "La religieuse": Étude historique et littéraire (New Haven CT: Yale University Press, 1954).

23. Thomas Laqueur, Making Sex: Body and Gender from the Greeks to Freud (Cambridge MA: Harvard University Press, 1990), 122–49.

24. Corbin argues that the "assumption of difference created coherence in the period from 1760 to 1840 despite evidence that might have challenged it." See Corbin, L'harmonie des plaisirs, 19. Also see Robert A. Nye, introduction to "Forum: Biology, Sexuality, and Morality in Eighteenth-Century France," Eighteenth-Century Studies 35, no. 2 (Winter 2002): 236.

25. [Jean-Joseph Menuret de Chambord], "Manstupration," in Encyclopédie (ARTFL Encyclopédie Project, Autumn 2017), https://artflsrv03.uchicago.edu/philologic4/encyclopedie0521/navigate/10/262/, accessed April 15, 2022.

26. Rousseau, Emile; and Pierre Roussel, Système physique et moral de la femme, ou tableau philosophique de la Constitution, de l'État organique, du Tempérament, des Mœurs, & des Fonctions propres au Sexe (Paris: Vincent, 1775).

27. These assumptions guided Pierre Roussel's influential treatise. See Roussel, Système physique et moral de la femme. For discussions of sexual difference and intellectual activity, see the articles by Robert A. Nye, Anne C. Vila, and Kathleen Wellman in "Forum: Biology, Sexuality, and Morality in Eighteenth-Century France," Eighteenth-Century Studies 35, no. 2 (Winter 2002): 235–78; Anne C. Vila, Enlightenment and Pathology: Sensibility in the Literature and Medicine of Eighteenth-Century France (Baltimore: Johns Hopkins University Press, 1998), 84–87, 225–57; and Alexandre Wenger, La fibre littéraire: Le discours médical sur la lecture au XVIIIe siècle (Genève: Librairie Droz, 2007), 137–70. On novel reading, see Lisa Jane Graham, "What Made Reading Dangerous in Eighteenth-Century France?," French Historical Studies 41, no. 3 (August 2018): 449–71.

28. For Enlightenment views of female puberty and moral degeneration, see Mary McAlpin, Female Sexuality and Cultural Degradation in Enlightenment France: Medicine and Literature (Farnham, UK: Ashgate, 2012).

29. G. S. Rousseau, Perilous Enlightenment: Pre- and Post-Modern Discourses; Sexual, Historical (Manchester, UK: Manchester University Press, 1991), 44–64.

30. Elizabeth Colwill, "Women's Empire and the Sovereignty of Man in La Décade philosophique, 1794–1807," Eighteenth-Century Studies 29, no. 3 (Spring 1996): 275–76.

31. Jean-Baptiste Moheau, Recherches et Considérations sur la population de la France (Paris: P. Geuthner, 1912), 259.

32. Peter Brown, *The Body and Society: Men, Women, and Sexual Renunciation in Early Christianity*, twentieth-anniversary ed. (1998; New York: Columbia University Press, 2008); Giulia Sissa, *Sex and Sensuality in the Ancient World* (New Haven CT: Yale University Press, 2008), 167–91.

33. Crawford, *European Sexualities*, 33.

34. Jean-Louis Flandrin, *Le sexe et l'occident: Évolution des attitudes et des comportements* (Paris: Seuil, 1981); Sarah Hanley, "Engendering the State: Family Formation and State Building in Early Modern France," *French Historical Studies* 16, no. 1 (Spring 1989): 4–27; and Sarah Hanley, "'The Jurisprudence of the Arrêts': Marital Union, Civil Society, and State Formation in France, 1550–1650," *Law and History Review* 21, no. 1 (Spring 2003): 1–40.

35. The phrase *le coït thérapeutique* comes from Alain Corbin, who discusses the new science of sexual pleasure that emerged in France between 1760 and 1840. See Corbin, *L'harmonie des plaisirs*, 212–13.

36. Blum, *Strength in Numbers*, 118.

37. Abbé Claude Yvon, François-Vincent Toussaint, and Denis Diderot, "Adultere," in *Encyclopédie* (ARTFL Encyclopédie Project, Autumn 2017), https://artflsrv03 .uchicago.edu/philologic4/encyclopedie0521/navigate/1/930/, accessed April 15, 2022.

38. Leslie Tuttle, *Conceiving the Old Regime: Pronatalism and the Politics of Reproduction in Early Modern France* (Oxford: Oxford University Press, 2010).

39. M. Nicolas Venette, *La génération de l'homme, ou tableau de l'amour conjugal, considéré dans l'état du Mariage* (London: n.p., 1751), 2: 23.

40. Corbin, *L'harmonie des plaisirs*, 72, 90–96, 212–13.

41. Montesquieu, "Letter CXVII," *The Persian Letters*, 196.

42. Blum, *Strength in Numbers*, 61–75; Lynn Salkin Sbiroli, "Generation and Regeneration: Reflections on the Biological and Ideological Role of Women in France (1786–1796)," in *Literature and Medicine during the Eighteenth Century*, ed. Marie Mulvey Roberts and Roy Porter (London: Routledge, 1993), 272.

43. Maurice de Saxe, *Mes rêveries, ouvrage posthume de Maurice, comte de Saxe, . . . augmenté d'une histoire abrégée de sa vie, et de différentes pièces qui y ont rapport, par Monsieur l'abbé Pérau* (Paris: Durand, 1757), 2: 158.

44. Madeleine [d'Arsant] de Puisieux, *Le plaisir et la volupté, conte allégorique* (Paris: n.p., 1752).

45. Abbé Jean Pestre, "Happiness," in Diderot and d'Alembert, *Encyclopédie, ou dictionnaire raisonné des sciences, des arts et des métiers, etc.*, http://encyclopedie .uchicago.edu/.

46. Denis Diderot, *Madame de La Carlière* (1773), in *Contes et romans*, ed. Michel Delon (Paris: Gallimard, 2004), 519–38. This story was part of the trilogy that

included *Supplément au Voyage de Bougainville*. Two lesser-known examples from the 1750s are Louis de Boissy, *Les filles femmes* (1751); and Marie-Antoinette Fagnan, *Kanor* (1750). De Boissy's text was suppressed, and he barely escaped the Bastille.

47. Goodman, "Marriage Choice and Marital Success," 28.

48. Alexandre-Balthazar-Laurent Grimod de La Reynière, *Réflexions philosophiques sur le plaisir; par un célibataire*, second ed. (Neufchâtel, France, 1783).

49. On actresses, see Lenard R. Berlanstein, *Daughters of Eve: A History of French Theater Women from the Old Regime to the Fin de Siècle* (Cambridge MA: Harvard University Press, 2001). On celibacy, see E. Claire Cage, *Unnatural Frenchmen: The Politics of Priestly Celibacy and Marriage, 1720–1815* (Charlottesville: University of Virginia Press, 2015). On luxury, see John Shovlin, *The Political Economy of Virtue: Luxury, Patriotism and the Origins of the French Revolution* (Ithaca NY: Cornell University Press, 2006).

50. See Rebecca Spang, *The Invention of the Restaurant: Paris and Modern Gastronomic Culture* (Cambridge MA: Harvard University Press, 2000), 88–91, 150–69. On his parents and their salon, see Antoine Lilti, *The World of the Salons: Sociability and Worldliness in Eighteenth-Century Paris*, trans. Lydia G. Cochrane (New York: Oxford University Press, 2015), 73–77.

51. Nadine Bérenguier, *Conduct Books for Girls in Enlightenment France* (Farnham, UK: Ashgate, 2011), 102–4; Blum, *Strength in Numbers*, 61–75.

52. For the luxury debates, see Sarah Maza, "Luxury, Morality, and Social Change: Why There Was No Middle-Class Consciousness in Prerevolutionary France," *Journal of Modern History* 69, no. 2 (June 1997): 199–229; and Shovlin, *The Political Economy of Virtue*.

53. The Diamond Necklace Affair was an elaborate hoax in which swindlers used Marie-Antoinette's name to steal a lavish necklace. The ensuing scandal damaged the Queen's reputation even though she had no connections to the scheme. See Sarah Maza, "The Diamond Necklace Affair Revisited (1785–1786): The Case of the Missing Queen," in *Eroticism and the Body Politic*, ed. Lynn Hunt (Baltimore: Johns Hopkins University Press, 1991), 63–89.

54. Blum discusses the central role of celibacy in the population debates that raged in the eighteenth century. See Blum, *Strength in Numbers*, 21–60. Corbin also discusses the campaign against celibacy; see Corbin, *L'harmonie des plaisirs*, 117–32. For a literary example, see Denis Diderot, *La Religieuse*, ed. Florence Lotterie (1796; Paris: Flammarion, 2009). For a medical critique, see François Amédée Doppet, *Traité du fouet et de ses effets sur le physique de l'amour* (Geneva: n.p., 1788).

55. For an analysis of enlightened attacks on celibacy, see Blum, *Strength in Numbers*, 21–60; and Cage, *Unnatural Frenchmen*.

56. See the essays in Dena Goodman, ed., *Marie-Antoinette: Writings on the Body of a Queen* (New York: Routledge, 2003); Chantal Thomas, *The Wicked Queen: The Origins of the Myth of Marie-Antoinette*, trans. Julie Rose (New York: Zone, 1999); Caroline Weber, *Queen of Fashion: What Marie Antoinette Wore to the French Revolution* (New York: Henry Holt, 2006).

57. Maza, "The Diamond Necklace Affair Revisited."

58. Simon Burrows, *Scandal, Blackmail, and Revolution: London's French libellistes, 1758–92* (Manchester, UK: Manchester University Press, 2006).

59. Lynn Hunt, "The Many Bodies of Marie-Antoinette: Political Pornography and the Problem of the Feminine in the French Revolution," in Goodman, *Marie-Antoinette*, 124–26; Jacques Revel, "Marie-Antoinette in Her Fictions: The Staging of Hatred," in *Fictions of the French Revolution*, ed. Bernadette Fort (Evanston IL: Northwestern University Press, 1991).

60. *Essais historiques sur la vie de Marie-Antoinette d'Autriche, Reine de France, pour servir à l'histoire de cette Princesse* (Londres, 1789).

61. *Essais historiques*, part 1, 16.

62. *Essais historiques*, part 1, 19.

63. "The Love Life of Charlie and Toinette," in Thomas, *The Wicked Queen*, 185–86.

64. "The Love Life of Charlie and Toinette," 188.

65. *Le cadran des plaisirs de la cour, ou les aventures du petit page Chérubin, pour server de suite à la vie de Marie-Antoinette, ci-devant Reine de France* (Paris, 179[?]), 43.

66. Jean Marie Goulemot, "The Literature of Intimacy," in *History of Private Life*, ed. Philippe Ariès and Georges Duby, vol. 3, *Passions of the Renaissance*, ed. Roger Chartier, trans. Arthur Goldhammer (Cambridge MA: Harvard University Press, 1989), 327–62.

67. *Essais historiques*, part 2, 72.

68. On the monstrosity of the royal couple, see Michel Foucault, *Abnormal: Lectures at the Collège de France 1974–1975*, ed. Arnold I. Davidson, trans. Graham Burchell (New York: Picador, 2003), 97–101.

69. "The Political Testament of Marie-Antoinette, the Widow Capet" (1793), in Thomas, *The Wicked Queen*, 252. For an analysis of the incest accusation in the queen's trial, see Lynn Hunt, *The Family Romance of the French Revolution* (Berkeley: University of California Press, 1992), 101–3.

70. Clyde Plumauzille, *Prostitution et révolution: Les femmes publiques dans la cité républicaine (1789–1804)* (Ceyzérieu, France: Champ Vallon, 2016), 231–36.

71. The 2021 exhibition at the Cognacq-Jay museum in Paris and accompanying catalog, *L'empire des sens: De Boucher à Greuze*, ed. Annick Lemoine (Paris: Paris Musées, 2020), offers one example of the persisting appeal of this image.

72. Andrew Israel Ross, *Public City/Public Sex. Homosexuality, Prostitution and Urban Culture in Nineteenth-Century Paris* (Philadelphia: Temple University Press, 2019); and Plumauzille, *Prostitution et révolution*.

73. Blum, *Strength in Numbers*, 39. Corbin makes the same argument in *L'harmonie des plaisirs*.

Suggested Reading

Blum, Carol. *Strength in Numbers: Population, Reproduction, and Power in Eighteenth-Century France*. Baltimore: Johns Hopkins University Press, 2002.

Corbin, Alain. *L'harmonie des plaisirs: Les manières de jouir du siècle des Lumières à l'avènement de la sexologie*. Paris: Perrin, 2008.

Daumas, Maurice. *Le mariage amoureux: Histoire du lien conjugal sous l'Ancien Régime*. Paris: Armand Colin, 2004.

Desan, Suzanne, and Jeffrey Merrick, eds. *Family, Gender, and Law in Early Modern France*. University Park: Pennsylvania State University Press, 2009.

Gerber, Matthew. *Bastards: Politics, Family and Law in Early Modern France*. New York: Oxford University Press, 2012.

Goodman, Dena, ed. *Marie-Antoinette: Writings on the Body of a Queen*. New York: Routledge, 2003.

Hunt, Lynn. *The Family Romance of the French Revolution*. Berkeley: University of California Press, 1992.

Kavanagh, Thomas M. *Enlightened Pleasures: Eighteenth-Century France and the New Epicureanism*. New Haven CT: Yale University Press, 2010.

Laqueur, Thomas. *Making Sex: Body and Gender from the Greeks to Freud*. Cambridge MA: Harvard University Press, 1990.

Maza, Sarah. "The Bourgeois Family Revisited: Sentimentalism and Social Class in Pre-Revolutionary French Culture." In *Intimate Encounters: Love and Domesticity in Eighteenth-Century France*, edited by Richard Rand. Princeton NJ: Princeton University Press, 1997.

Plumauzille, Clyde. *Prostitution et révolution: Les femmes publiques dans la cite républicaine (1789–1804)*. Ceyzérieu, France: Champ Vallon, 2016.

Popiel, Jennifer J. *Rousseau's Daughters: Domesticity, Education, and Autonomy in Modern France*. Hanover NH: University Press of New England, 2008.

Quinlan, Sean M. *The Great Nation in Decline: Sex, Modernity, and Health Crises in Revolutionary France, c. 1750–1850*. Aldershot, UK: Ashgate, 2007.

Scott, Joan. *Only Paradoxes to Offer: French Feminists and the Rights of Man*. Cambridge MA: Harvard University Press, 1997.

5

THE QUEER GAZE IN HAUSSMANN'S PARIS, 1850–1900

ANDREW ISRAEL ROSS

In early August of 1860, the Prefecture of Police of Paris received a letter complaining about "a young man between seventeen and eighteen years old with a feminine *fisionomie* [*sic*]" (physiognomy), who appeared "every evening, between 10:00 and midnight . . . on the northern side of the boulevards from the Porte St. Denis toward the Madeleine." The man, from the Grand Duchy of Baden in present-day Germany, nevertheless "speaks French well," and, along with his feminine appearance, his "long blond and bright hair, short height, pretty figure, [and] serious gait make him remarkable"; he "is fairly well dressed, wears a large straw hat, and often carries a roll of paper in his hand." That the author of this missive noticed this young man was not surprising, since he sought "to attract men's attention and have them remark and follow him, which happens to him often, since any attentive walker could not help but notice him." Therefore, the letter concluded, "it will not be hard [for the police] to locate him."[1]

Though the writer acknowledged that he had a personal interest in his target because the young man had taken up with one of his nephews, he framed his complaint through his apparently objective observation. The letter emphasized the visual cues of "pederasty," as sexual relationships between men were often called in the nineteenth century, and argued that anyone in the city could recognize them.[2] Though the writer did not fall victim to these temptations, the sheer detail of the description indicates the apparent regularity of these occurrences and the letter writer's awareness of the signs of same-sex sexual solicitation. It is perhaps for this reason that the writer called on the authorities to intervene. Surely they would be able to clear the streets without the writer having to take action himself.

The encounter between the letter writer and the German led to a cascading set of observations that culminated in the attention of the police. By attracting the looks of passers-by, the young man also fell under the eye of the letter writer (among others, presumably), who in turn told the police what he saw. The police, in response, ordered surveillance of the area in order to find and arrest the German.[3] About a month later, the police reported that although they had managed to arrest "several individuals indulging in acts of pederasty," they had not "met the young man mentioned in the note on these boulevards."[4] Although the specific object of concern therefore evaded capture, his activities had brought the authorities to his preferred cruising ground, which the police then placed under watch. At first targeting a single individual, the police fanned out and found new groups of men supposedly seeking sex with other men as they placed the entire area under sexual surveillance. We are unable to know what those targeted did to attract the attention of the authorities, and we are left only with the police's assertion that they had correctly identified more pederasts. In doing so, this chapter argues, the police themselves participated in the process of creating queer space in nineteenth-century Paris. By entering a city space with the expectation that they would find evidence of queer desire, the police created associations between public behaviors and illicit sexual practices and desires.[5] The creation of queer space in the heart of Paris occurred through a constant dialogue between observed and observer, policed and police.

This chapter addresses queer sex, queer space, and queer desire to indicate a form of sexual possibility that was not necessarily attached to any single identity.[6] Urban space both shaped and was shaped by the various interactions between Parisians and tourists, between men who sought sex with other men and those who did not, and between the authorities and those they accused. Untangling the distinctions between these groups was and remains difficult, as men in various social positions looked upon one another and responded with desire, disgust, disregard, disdain, or some combination of these. These interactions helped produce a queer male urban culture in late nineteenth-century Paris. By queer urban culture, I mean a set of interrelated practices and discourses that inscribed same-sex sexual desire in certain areas of the city, as men recognized the possibility of engaging in same-sex sexual behavior, whether they actually did so or not. As men looked or gazed upon other men in public, they sometimes recognized their own and others' queer desire. This recognition, enabled by urban spaces that brought together people of different classes, nationalities, origins, and purposes, constituted one mode of experiencing late nineteenth-century Paris, available to all men, not just those we would later deem—or who might have deemed themselves to be—homosexual. Accessing this queer culture and understanding the multivalent meanings of male-male observation and interaction in a period prior to the crystallization of the homo-hetero binary thus provides an entry point into greater understanding of modern urban culture more broadly.

In making this claim, this chapter demonstrates that attention to sexuality reshapes histories of urbanism and urban culture, the police, and early mass culture in two primary ways. First, it centers queer life in our understanding of late nineteenth-century Paris. Spaces that provided or facilitated new leisure practices as the Baron Haussmann renovated the city enabled queer appropriation that was not hidden from other Parisians.[7] Further, those other Parisians were not innocent in the process of generating queer space. The police, in particular, participated in the creation of the very forms of disorder they claimed they had an obligation to manage. Second, therefore, attention to sexuality moves us toward a more dynamic understanding of the ways that state authorities intervened in urban life.

These processes were, of course, most meaningful for those who sought out same-sex sexual partners. As this chapter shows, however, they also had broader ramifications, as all Parisians increasingly came to recognize the existence of same-sex sexual activity in public space and to fall under the gaze of police and medical authorities who sought to manage and understand it. This chapter argues that the possibility of queer male desire stood at the heart of Parisians' relations with one another as they interacted in emerging and transforming public spaces, entertainment venues, and public health establishments, and as they encountered those tasked with maintaining urban order. Just as Michelle K. Rhoades elsewhere in this volume demonstrates the centrality of female prostitution to the urban economy of Bordeaux, I show the importance of queer male sexuality to the urban culture of Paris.

Rather than reconstructing the ways in which men who sought sex with men distinguished themselves from other men, this chapter highlights the interrelationship and blurriness between queer and nonqueer desires as men entered and used public spaces and thereby placed themselves not only in the middle of a thriving culture of consumption but also under the watchful eyes of a modern police force.

Queering the Male Gaze

Ever since Walter Benjamin began describing Paris as the "capital of the nineteenth century," urban historians and other scholars have argued that the redevelopment of Paris begun by Baron Haussmann during the Second Empire and continued during the early Third Republic entailed not just the physical reconstruction of a supposedly medieval city but also the emergence of forms of urban life that characterized "modernity."[8] To understand this new form of urban life, historians, art historians, sociologists, and other scholars have often reached for Benjamin's own example of urban wandering, the *flâneur*.[9] The flâneur first emerged in the urban commentary and literature of the postrevolutionary period as a representation of the man at home in public, "the character responsible for the readability of the city, the man occupied with tasting the pleasures of observing the urban milieu."[10] Following Benjamin, scholars have focused on the flâneur of Haussmann's Paris, defined by Gregory Shaya as "a figure of the modern artist-poet, a figure keenly aware of the bustle of modern life, an amateur detective and investigator of the city, but also a sign of the alienation of the city and of capitalism."[11] The fleeting pleasures of the city came to stand in for the experience of modernity writ large, from both the perspective of the outsider (the flâneur was a possible criminal) and the view of the authorities (he was also an urban detective), as Tom McDonough describes the possibilities.[12] In either case the flâneur stands for a particular way of seeing, not a specific and identifiable person on the streets. In the words of Vanessa R. Schwartz, he represents a "positionality of power—one through which the spectator assumes the position of being able to be part of the spectacle and yet command it at the same time."[13] As such, the flâneur has come to represent a detached but still dominating practice. The privileged male gaze looked on others but refused to be implicated in what it saw.

So dominant has the flâneur been to cultural approaches to nineteenth-century Paris that it has become almost impossible to evade his shadow.[14] This chapter thus engages with the figure in turn in order to showcase how attention to same-sex sexuality might reshape our understanding of nineteenth-century urban life. To do so, I draw on two strands of critique vis-à-vis the flâneur. First, feminist approaches have emphasized the flâneur's privileged masculinity; the freedom to move about the city was predicated on the intersection between masculinity and bourgeois status. The exercise of that male privilege rested, moreover, on the sexualization of women who also appeared in public.[15] Some feminist scholars have pointed out that women, too, used public space. Whether as *flâneuse* (female flâneur) or not, female shoppers and walkers used the city in ways that did not simply render them prostitutes.[16] Indeed, as Sharon Marcus argues, even the sexualizing male gaze brought women into the city, requiring them to also participate in public urban life.[17]

These critiques often rest on implicit heterosexist expectations of the relationship between women and men but also between men and between women. Men, after all, also gazed upon other men, just as women often gazed upon other women. A second line of inquiry, therefore, traces the development of a particular kind of gaze endemic to modern gay life back to the gaze of the flâneur. "It is impossible to be homosexual without having a gaze," the Dutch sociologist Henning Bech once declared.[18] The origins of this gaze lay in the same historical moment and in the same spaces as those of the flâneur. For example, Dianne Chisholm locates what she calls the "cruising flâneur" in the same spaces as the traditional flâneur, but the "cruising flâneur," instead of remaining aloof, "loses composure (or decomposes) with exposure to the city's erotic spectacles."[19] I take up this emphasis on the flâneur's queer potential, as men were increasingly encouraged to look upon one another, but argue that the queer gaze was more broadly shared.

A queer mode of looking emerged as Parisians recognized the opportunity to look and be looked upon and depended on some of the characteristics of the flâneur. Some Parisians who wrote to the police evinced a desire to depict themselves as objective, though certainly not disinterested, observers, even as they revealed themselves to have seen something they might not have been supposed to have witnessed. For instance, in an 1875 letter sent to the prefect of police, a resident of Vincennes wrote, "Having the habit of taking a promenade each night in the bois de Vincennes, I have perceived for a long time monstrosities which happen there.... Every day of the week and particularly on Mondays, Thursdays, and Sundays, there are men from Paris and Vincennes (always the same) who come to promenade in the bois and who indulge in pederasty with civilians or soldiers."[20] The author then provided the police with specific directions to the area where these activities were taking place. The letter writer's confidence that he would not implicate himself through his familiarity with these particulars—the days of the week the pederasts appeared, the faces of the men who engaged in pederasty, the precise location where these activities took place—seems wholly unearned. Indeed, though he used the verb "perceived" (*aperçu*) to describe his own activity, it seems more appropriate to describe it as one of constant, fascinated observation. The letter concluded by arguing that without police intervention, "this state of things . . . will prevent us from promenading with our wives and children."[21] The writer thus attempted to situate himself within a series of apparently heterosexual relations, even as the letter itself implied that he has been taking his walks on his own. It may have been his masculinity—referenced through his familial obligations—that gave him the right to move freely about the park and look upon these men, but in doing so he put his own desires into question by revealing his interest in continuing to look.

Letters such as these imply less an opposition between observer and observed than their mutual imbrication. In an 1861 letter an "étranger" (foreigner), as he anonymously signed his missive, described "an innumerable quantity of young men" who entrapped other men. These blackmailers, the writer claimed, worked "above all where the crowd was the most numerous, such as in the Champs-Elisées [*sic*], in the Palais Royal, in the Tuileries." Expressing surprise at their presence on the streets of "the first city of Europe," he contrasted their activities with what he ostensibly expected to see on his visit to the French capital. This visitor thereby situated these "honest young men," as he sarcastically described them, both within and without the urban milieu. They were "innumerable" but identifiable; they were problems, but they lay at the heart of urban life.[22]

These supposed blackmailers hid themselves in the crowd but were easy to spot, if the police only tried: "These young men who by dress, manner, and conversation are easy to recognize; they cannot escape the surveillance of a police so well made as your own." In fact, the police did not seem terribly concerned, writing in the upper left-hand corner that if "the disgruntled [*indigné*] honest man" wanted something to be done, he would "deliver to the police the perpetrator of these kinds of acts."[23] This response may have stemmed from suspicion of anonymous complaints, which, the police believed, were often written by pederasts themselves.[24] That possibility, however, highlights the ultimate effect of the letter. It did not effectively differentiate between the supposed blackmailers and their victims but rather brought them together. The letter writer claimed that even the victims included those "whose morality could not be doubted [*qualifier*], but are no less victimized by these industrials," out of fear of scandal.[25] The letter writer's emphasis on "blackmail"—a common enough conceit of commentators who spoke of male same-sex sexual activity—may have attempted to associate the young men with crime, but it also implicated the letter writer himself as a possible victim.[26] Moreover, his call for the police to surveil the group put himself at risk.

These letters from the 1860s and 1870s relied upon and reflected a growing moral discourse that struggled to distinguish between appropriate and inappropriate ways of looking and being looked at, but ultimately muddled the two. Popular accounts of the Parisian underworld informed and warned men about those who sought to attract their looks.[27] The moral commentator Flévy d'Urville declared in *Les ordures de Paris* (1874), for instance, that pederasts knew "how to recognize one another like freemasons, through certain physiognomic games and some external signs, by, for example, letting one see their handkerchief."[28] D'Urville may have implied here that these signs were known only by members of this freemasonry, but the very act of publishing this description ensured that these signs were more broadly understood. Similarly, the journalist Ali Coffignon, in his *Paris-vivant: La corruption à Paris* (1888), echoed the idea of an "international of vice," and added: "The pederast always has an affected politesse, his gait reveals a certain nonchalance that is almost soft; his look has an entirely unique languor; he generally possesses a passion for jewelry and perfumes; often still he is obsessed with music."[29] Though he concluded with pederasts' apparent favorite hobby, Coffignon, too, emphasized the importance of visual recognition. Recognizable by how he walked, what he wore, and how he looked, a man with an interest in same-sex sexual activity demanded constant attention.

Like d'Urville, Coffignon emphasized that these signs, even if difficult to discern, differentiated those considered to be dishonest from the "honest" (*honnête*). And yet, he concluded by arguing: "One finds the pederast in every society. . . . This common vice effaces all social differences."[30] One only needed to know how and where to look. The male privilege of urban wandering thus intersected with discordant uses of that privilege. It is not, therefore, that the flâneur enabled one kind of gaze and queer solicitation another. Rather, the two relied upon the same practices by the same kinds of individuals. By entering public space, men were encouraged to be on the lookout for evidence that other men might desire them and, potentially, respond in kind.

The Gaze of the State

The legal framework that enabled the Paris police to harass men who sought sex with other men enhanced the importance of visual cues more broadly. Following the French Revolution, France had no antisodomy statute on the books, but it did grant local police forces the right to intervene in moral concerns. In Paris the *brigade des mœurs* (morals police) focused their attention on regulating female prostitution but also on men who sought sex with other men in public.[31] Lacking explicit legal authority to arrest men simply because they had had sex with other men, the police often turned to Article 330 of the penal code, "public offenses against decency."[32] Such an offense constituted any activity that was committed in a public space or in front of a public and crossed implicit moral boundaries.[33] On the one hand, Article 330 allowed the police to keep harassing men who sought sex with other men.[34] On the other hand, it imposed new requirements on police efforts. No longer oriented around the sin of sodomy—one that might or might not occur behind closed doors—the policing of same-sex sexual activity now required public witnesses, as it was a public problem.[35] This transition thus constituted one part of the broader transformation of urban culture during the nineteenth century. The increasing presence of the police in public complemented the other ways in which Parisians were enticed to use public space to consume and view the urban spectacle.[36] The gaze of the police thus shaped how Parisians, tourists, and others experienced the city.

The Paris police did not consistently focus on male same-sex sexual behavior during the nineteenth century, but the conservative turn of the Second Empire encouraged greater attention than before.[37] Men who sought sex with other men were particularly problematic when they solicited sex in busy parts of the city. On November 24, 1864, for example, the head of the morals brigade, Félix Carlier, submitted a long report detailing the circumstances of a series of arrests that had taken place the prior weekend on the boulevards around the rue de la Chaussée d'Antin. This area, not far from the boulevards mentioned in the letter described at the beginning of this chapter, was the center of high-class Parisian consumer culture, a particularly important site of social display and spectacle.[38] Carlier described "different groups of individuals going back and forth along the boulevards, walking with affectation, rubbing shoulders with prowling men around some urinals and, in a word, provoking to debauchery like female prostitutes." According to Carlier, these activities led to regular complaints: "Why don't the police free the boulevard of all these individuals who one encounters every night and whose presence scandalizes everyone."[39] These groups of apparently working-class—Carlier claimed that they almost all wore smocks under their jackets—and effeminate young men knew quite well how to make themselves known, to attract the eyes and touches of those they passed. They may have caused a "scandal," but they did so by situating themselves at the center of the crowd, exciting those they encountered and encouraging a police response.

It was not always so easy to locate men who sought sex with men and distinguish them from other Parisians. Though the police were well aware of the medical discourse that increasingly asserted the ability of experts to identify pederasts through examination, police practice was fairly haphazard, given to chance meetings and reliant on denunciations and assumptions.[40] For instance, in February of 1858, a police officer reported to his superiors that he had attempted to arrest two men he had seen seated next to one another at about three o'clock and again at five o'clock in the morning underneath a flower-shop tent located at the place de la Madeleine. The two men explained that they were sitting under the tent to keep watch because they were trying to prevent someone from moving in before their lease was up.

The documents go into no further detail regarding this excuse, but the story was apparently believable enough to the police that the officer let the two men go after confirming their identities. Nevertheless, the officer concluded his report by arguing that it was "important to know their habits and the nature of their relationship" and made sure to place the report in the dossier under "pederasts."[41] Whatever these two men were really doing that morning, it was the police officer who asserted and defined their relationship in terms of same-sex desire and the possibility of queer sex, not the men themselves.

The police worked within an urban environment that encouraged the intermingling of sexual and nonsexual practices, and distinguishing between the two required knowing how to look. Men seeking sex with men elicited a range of emotions from those who saw them. Sometimes disgust mixed with an awareness of the quotidian nature of same-sex sexual solicitation. As one passerby declared the night of Carlier's police action after witnessing some arrests, "There go three more. . . . It's disgusting, look at their behavior."[42] The offhand "there go three more"; the nonchalant claims that gait, clothing, or gestures revealed the existence and possibility of male-male desire; and the reference to the presence of men displaying these characteristics "every evening" all highlighted the relative familiarity that these men—pederast, police officer, Parisian—had with one another. Even as the reciprocal looks of each member of the public were shaped by the attention of the authorities, these gazes remained locked on one another, perhaps with mutual disgust, but also with mutual fascination. Indeed, one might wonder how men who did not complain reacted to this sight of queer desire in one of the most important commercial spaces of the city. The attention of the police to same-sex sexuality may have simply made an increasing number of people aware of what they were witnessing and made the very thing the authorities claimed to abhor more visible.

Becoming Queer in Public Space

As the police increased their attention to sexual solicitation between men, so too did legal and medical authorities, concerned with diagnosing the danger and causes of same-sex desire.[43] These texts indicate a growing fear that the practices of observation and looking described above could, in essence, create more pederasts.[44] As the French psychiatrist Henri Legrand du Saulle declared in his *Étude médico-légale sur la séparation de corps* (1866), "In the past twenty or twenty-five years pederasty has taken more and more worrying proportions in Paris."[45] In particular, medical, legal, and other experts worried that the increasing presence of same-sex desire could incite similar feelings in the men who witnessed it. The desire for sex with other men was something that any man might find within himself, once such desires were activated by his public encounters. The effect of urban observation, then, was to create more queer Parisians.

To some commentators, same-sex desire remained a vice, a bad habit in which the city allowed men to indulge. Du Saulle, for instance, asked whether a husband could violate his marital obligations—and thus justify legal separation—by abusing his "droit marital," or marital rights, including by engaging in "acts against nature."[46] The apparent increase of male same-sex sexual activity in the capital city involved not only the downtrodden and morally disreputable but also "the highest levels of society." These men, according to du Saulle, "do not fear to frequent certain seductive spaces and to commit with the most abject representatives of vagrancy, vice or crime!"[47] Uninterested in this sodomitical milieu for its own sake, du Saulle quickly turned his attention to any man who "makes his wife submit to the caprices of his debauched imagination" and asked whether the law had anything to say about a man who thereby "abuses his rights and engages in acts against nature on her."[48] Du Saulle thus returned his discussion of "pederasty" to his primary concern of marital sexual relations with little consideration of the shift in sexual object choice.

Du Saulle did not prove his claim that Paris offered greater opportunities—and thus greater risks—for men to find other men for sexual adventures.[49] Nor did he provide evidence for his view that male sexual object choice was essentially fluid, defined by a possibly ill attraction to particular acts rather than to particular people. The city in this depiction encouraged men to frequent other men for sex, encounters that led not necessarily to homosexual desire per se, but rather to sexual behaviors that could be forced upon or welcomed by women as well. The modern city, it seemed, enabled "pederasty," but not necessarily "pederasts." It offered new sexual opportunities to ostensibly good husbands who would otherwise not have been inclined to have sex with other men. The sexual opportunities offered by late nineteenth-century Paris thus crossed and muddied sexual categories defined by sexual orientation or object choice. Instead, these men were but some of the "minor perverts"—those who behaved in ways that deviated from the procreative, marital norm—that proliferated in the medical discourse of the time, as experts groped toward the contemporary idea of homosexuality.[50]

Du Saulle published his pamphlet as more and more commentators, especially doctors, turned their attention to male same-sex desire. Even as talk elsewhere increasingly emphasized the possibly inborn nature of "inversion," French discourse often continued to understand same-sex desire and behavior as a "fall" that remade the individual "victim."[51] In his brief 1881 pamphlet on male prostitution, the doctor Cox-Algit, for instance, focused on the case of one young man "recruited" into pederasty. He warned, "[This] hideous sect ... counts among its members the most disparate people: it is an agglomeration of shameful youth and ignoble old men, who occupy the most humble and the most brilliant jobs in the world."[52] Even before arriving at his story, then, Cox-Algit gave the game away; the society of pederasts was already everywhere. Perhaps because of this fact, Cox-Algit maintained that although he could not bring himself to describe the activities of these men, he still had to describe "the story of a young man thrust onto this path [in order to] put you, the reader, on guard against the debauched old men and sensual young men charged with gaining new recruits."[53] This young man, anonymized as "X," was "a charming serving boy of seventeen years. Fresh and pink like a girl, he had attracted through his grace, elegance, and agreeable manners, numerous clients. An old man, among others, gazed on him fondly." Eventually, this client invited X to go for a walk in the bois de Boulogne. Readily accepting the invitation, X became increasingly disconcerted as they proceeded into the park. Eventually, the old man took X back to "a splendid hotel" where, after champagne, served by a "barely dressed boy of fifteen," X "lost all force of character" and the old man "threw him on the bed." "What happened during this night?" Cox-Algit asked; he did not answer except to emphasize that from that point, X "was a lost man, dishonored in his own eyes," who eventually confided this story "of his first fault" to the good doctor.[54]

This story is many things at once. It is a lurid description of possible sexual abuse, of the seduction of a young man by an older partner, and of the entry of a young man into a milieu oriented around same-sex desire. It tells of a temporary fall into degradation, but also of the first of X's own mistakes. As a new recruit into this society, the young man was both an innocent victim who had made a horrible error and someone who had entered into a permanent state of abjection, evidenced by having "taken with a horrible sickness" that had sent him to Cox-Algit's care.[54] Cox-Algit could not seem to decide, in other words, whether X was ill or whether he had been corrupted. His turn to pederasty may have been overdetermined by his effeminate body, but it was also conditioned by his environment.[56] X may have been susceptible to pederasty, but engaging in pederasty ultimately depended upon outside forces. To borrow phrasing from Simone de Beauvoir, one was not born a pederast; one became a pederast.[57]

Even as French commentators increasingly engaged in debates over whether same-sex desire was innate or acquired, the latter view remained important and was grounded in the experience of urban life. We can witness the continued valence of this threat in the idiosyncratic 1896 sexological text *Uranism and Unisexuality* by the Jewish, Catholic-convert, Russian-born, French-raised expatriate Marc-André Raffalovich. Using terms first coined by the German sexologist Karl Heinrich Ulrichs, Raffalovich claimed that what he called "virile uranists" often did not seek out other "authentic uranists," but rather "heterosexuals." He wrote: "The ideal for many uranists would be a uranist who is apparently heterosexual and whom they would be the first to discover. They would deflower, in a sense, a man who is a virgin vis-à-vis these emotional or sensual experiences, and they would not run the risk of social ostracism. Many uranists would not dare approach men who were the target of gossip but who attracted them; they hope for a chance encounter instead."[58]

The last comment is key. The hoped for "a chance encounter" depended on the anonymity of the city. Raffalovich thus implied the process of cruising. But the quest relied on a fundamental indeterminacy of the targets rather than mutual recognition among them. Grounded in the experience of the street, the uranist sought not a like-minded individual but rather one who could be awakened to the possibility of same-sex sexual pleasure. The apparent heterosexuality of the target was not incidental or an obstacle to the pleasure of same-sex desire but rather its very source. That such meetings were up to chance highlights the ways the unexpected encounter in public space between walkers and observers of different kinds enabled the confusion and construction of queer desire.

Creating Queer Space

To sum up, as men acted the flâneur, they also faced the queer possibilities of the city. The modernizing city ensured the possibility of encountering same-sex sexual activity and desire. Such possibilities, however, were always also conditioned by the eyes of the authorities on the hunt for supposed pederasts. The urban culture of the late nineteenth century thus became queer through moments of triangulation among those explicitly seeking out same-sex sexual opportunities, those who policed them, and other men who encountered both groups. Ultimately, the mutual observations of these three groups created the possibility of queer space throughout late nineteenth-century Paris. The police therefore were not simply the representatives of a state concerned with clearing the streets in the interests of morality and order but instead actively participated in the creation of queer possibilities as well.

The 1876 case of the comte de Germiny, a member of the Paris Municipal Council, illustrates the difficulties in untangling these relationships. Germiny was arrested soliciting sex from a working-class man named Edmond-Pierre Chouard in a public urinal on the Champs-Elysées. In court, as one of the most popular of the Parisian dailies, *Le petit journal*, reported, Germiny excused his presence in the urinal by referring to his position as a member of the city government. After taking a walk with his wife, he explained, he decided to "undertake a kind of inquest" into the "indecent" activities he had heard about. Knowing that the morals police had been increasingly interested in the urinals, Germiny entered one and found himself with his co-conspirator. "His action," he explained, "was brazen, but innocent." While he was there, other people arrived who had "suspect appearance," and Germiny placed himself in the longest compartment, "in order to better observe."[59] His desire to know and witness for himself, as a representative of both state and familial authority, supposedly had led the count into the urinal. Disavowing his sexual desire in favor of the needs of the regulatory state, he had thus found himself not simply observing suspect individuals, but being among them. The flâneur-as-detective had entered the queer crowd, but only because as he had already heard about what went on within it from the authorities.

The arresting officers, of course, offered a different perspective on these events, as they sought to attribute other motivations to Germiny's encounter with Chouard based on what they thought they saw. As the police officers who arrested Germiny laid out their evidence in court, one declared that "the physical placement of the two individuals left no room for doubt" as to their intentions. In addition, the judge asked the final police witness to confirm that Germiny had confessed, saying after his interrogation: "I looked at others' nudity and showed my own; I do not want to resort to denials unworthy of me."[60] The nesting subject positions—Germiny as watcher and watched, the police recording their observations so we in turn can observe them—implicate all involved. I would argue, in fact, that even as Germiny was placed on the docket for his queer observation, the readers of the account, too, were granted their own queer potential, as the newspaper Le petit journal turned their eyes upon the count. "The accused is pale, but calm; a gentle tremble in the hands is the only indication of emotion," the paper reported. Germiny was forced into becoming the object of any Parisian's gaze, even before the newspaper readers witnessed his final humiliation, If, as Vanessa Schwartz argues, newspapers provided Parisians with the means to play the flâneur without wandering the streets, then so too did they provide the opportunity to enjoy the pleasures of queer looking.[61] If the ability to look and be looked upon was based upon the apparently heterosexual privilege that Germiny asserted, then anyone who read the paper found heterosexuality to be a bit queer in the end.

The public urinal may have been the most important space for these kinds of encounters during the Second Empire and early Third Republic, but by the end of the century, a new space was becoming popular as well: the bathhouse. As others have argued, the late nineteenth- and early twentieth-century bathhouse was particularly important for the development of queer subcultures in Paris and in other European and American cities.[62] Indeed, the bathhouse had the potential to serve as a safe space for the development of practices of queer cruising, as Aaron Betsky puts it when he describes its "internal boulevards of flâneurs, where men would cruise by each other as they looked for the wares they wished to consume."[63] The bathhouse, composed of corridors, changing rooms, and steam rooms, provided the interior space for men who sought sex with other men. But the bathhouse was not immune from the interests of the authorities, nor was it used only by men who sought sex with other men. Therefore, it was not just men who sought sex with other men who took on the position of the "queer flâneur." The bathhouse did not simply enable the emergence of a gay community, in other words, safe from prying eyes. It also provided an enclosed space for encounters between the authorities, men who sought sex with other men, and men present for a bath. In doing so, these kinds of spaces highlight how the police themselves participated in a process that produced a queer gaze that incorporated all three groups.

Bathhouses became increasingly popular in French urban centers as part of a broader movement for public hygiene that aligned well with a burgeoning consumer culture. Lise Manin, for instance, notes a common framework of male voyeurism in representations of both *cafés-concerts* (cafés featuring entertainment, usually music) and bathhouses during the second half of the nineteenth century.[64] Like public urinals, bathhouses could provide space for men to enjoy looking upon other men while disavowing their exact desires. According to the police inspector Gustave Macé, there are men who "desire neither women nor have any taste for unnatural pleasures, and yet, they spend entire days in these establishments; they eat, drink, smoke, move about and seem happy to listen to obscene words, to rub shoulders with sodomites and assist in their repugnant acts. This here is an unhealthy curiosity, fairly common, which charms their ears and satisfies their sight."[65] The bathhouse attracted men who wanted nothing more than to participate, by hearing and by sight, in the various desires these spaces enabled. The longing to look on queerly did not, in this sense, make one into a pederast, though it did, perhaps, make one into what would eventually be called a voyeur.

The police participated in constructing this dynamic play of looking without precisely knowing what one was looking at. Police officers occasionally entered bathhouses incognito. As Coffignon explained, in order to "assure themselves" of what was happening inside a bathhouse, "it was necessary to arrange for meticulous surveillance." Coffignon found this somewhat humorous, describing how one pair of officers decided to enter only after the steam had stopped, in order to see better: "They discovered the truth, but finding themselves in their bathing trunks, found it impossible to proceed to an arrest." Further, "the funniest part of the affair, one of the two agents, a solid, strapping guy, well built, had attracted the enthusiasm of one of the habitués who poured out the least equivocal advances toward him." According to Coffignon, this kind of encounter was a large reason why the police "hesitate[d] to act"—because they did not want to be accused of "provocation."[66] Upon entering the bathhouse, in other words, the police were compromised in the very activities they sought to stamp out. Unable to sufficiently separate themselves from the patrons of the bathhouse, having stripped down themselves, they supposedly stayed away.

This hesitation did not prevent the police from continuing to selectively target bathhouses. One of the most famous cases occurred at 30 rue de Penthièvre, which the police surveilled from the 1880s to World War I and raided several times.[67] In 1898 a police officer entered the bathhouse and reported that the clientele seemed familiar with one another and with the attendants and "that it is morally certain that one indulges in this establishment in acts of pederasty." During this particular visit, however, the officer claimed, "As soon as an unknown person enters into the rooms, all those found there already quiet themselves, the laughs and jokes stop, and the stranger is slowly stared at." In the end he argued, "A raid would have no result, because all the doors accessing the communication corridors are glazed and before one could arrive in the steam rooms one would have been signaled by people who are constantly on the lookout."[68] The ability of these men to make their own space by virtue of their careful observation blocked the ability of the police to adequately see.

Two years later, however, another police officer entered and found more than enough evidence to justify a raid of the bathhouse. On August 1, 1900, the officer filed a detailed report narrating his experience in the bathhouse. He apparently gave no impression of disinterest, as he almost immediately found himself under the eyes of some of the clients. The first, "around thirty-five years old, very well built, brown hair, appearing to belong to the elegant world," presented himself to the undercover officer. "Completely naked, he planted himself before me and, taking his erect penis in his hands, remained before me for several seconds," the officer recounted, before returning to a bench opposite the officer in order to continue masturbating on his back while continuing to stare. Ultimately, the officer was with this man for ten minutes and was able to describe, in his report, the man's penis: "Long, thin, and pointed, and continually erect."[69]

The bathhouse thus encapsulated the ways in which the varied gazes of the late nineteenth century were simultaneously deployed against and with that of the state. Even as men felt free to enter the bathhouse, move about within it, and look upon one another, they were often also under watch by the police. At the same time, however, by placing themselves within a space of same-sex sexual activity, the police also became the desired objects of that queer gaze. Both dependent upon and subservient to their own participation in these scenes to regulate space, the police revealed themselves as both participants in and opponents of the creation of a queer milieu within late nineteenth-century Paris. The police did not simply repress queer life. They, despite themselves, participated in it and, in some ways helped create it.

In 1904, an English painter named Ernest Bulton gathered a group of men at his studio at 83 Boulevard Montparnasse. Word of Bulton's party reached the police, who, after observing the event from the rooftop, eventually intervened and arrested the diverse group, nineteen in all. Word reached the press, and the arrests became a minor "affair." The newspaper *Le Journal* described it in its subhead as "the diversions of an English painter. Like in the time of Oscar Wilde." As with Germiny, the newspaper described the ringleader—"thin, elegant, shaven face"—and also published a print of his face.[70] The press, however, did not simply content itself with providing its readers with yet another opportunity to gaze upon the queer subject and, in doing so, become a bit queer themselves. A week after the scandal first hit the papers, *Le Journal* published a cartoon mocking the police as well (figure 1). Subsequently clipped and saved in the police archives, the cartoon lampooned the police's desire to watch. Grinning as he peeks at the party below, the officer, cane half erect, calls to hold off on intervening: "They don't seem to be doing anything wrong."[71] Enjoying a good look, and perhaps truly not seeing anything amiss, the cartoon officer stands in, perhaps, for the reader. The act of policing thus also becomes an acting of

AFFAIRE DE MŒURS   Dessin d'ABEL FAIVRE

— Allons, c'est assez vu. Nous n'avons plus qu'à les arrêter.
— Mais rien ne presse, chef... Ils n'ont pas l'air de se faire du mal.

FIG. 1. The police keep looking at a party of pederasts. "Affaire de moeurs," *Le Journal*, March 28, 1904. Courtesy gallica.bnf.fr/Bibliothèque Nationale de France.

queering, rendering the people looked upon into suspects. But it is reciprocal, shaping a queer look by the police as well. Just as Sarah Horowitz shows in her chapter in this volume the ways that the press deployed sexuality to critique the politicians of the Third Republic, so too did it implicate the instruments of the state in the creation of the very scandals it pursued.

These varied modes of looking reveal at one and the same time the essentially mobile character of the queer gaze, even as they reveal the participation of ostensibly repressive forces in the creation of queer life. Male same-sex desire thus stood at the heart of late nineteenth-century urban life as an ever-present possibility, one both enunciated and disciplined by the police.

Just as female prostitution became central to the economic practices of late nineteenth-century urban neighborhoods, discussed in Michelle K. Rhoades's chapter in this volume, queer male desire shaped how men understood their interactions with one another on the streets, with the authorities, and with the objects of their desires. Predicated on the lack of a clear distinction between homosexual and heterosexual identity, the queer experience of late nineteenth-century Paris was more broadly shared than we have previously recognized. Crossing in public spaces such as the streets, parks, urinals, and even bathhouses, men who sought sex with other men produced a queer gaze that all men could, and sometimes did, enjoy or, in the case of the police, attempt to use to their advantage. Even if such feelings more often remained latent than acted upon, they nonetheless showcase the ways in which displacing the assumption of heterosexuality deepens our understanding not only of sexual identities before homosexuality and heterosexuality, but also of late nineteenth-century Parisian culture more broadly.

Notes

1. Letter to préfet de police, August 2, 1860, DA 230, doc. 280, Archives de la Préfecture de Police de Paris (hereafter APP).

2. The terms "pederasty" and "pederast" do not necessarily refer to age-differentiated relationships between men. Rather, in the nineteenth century they referred to men who had sex with other men more broadly. I use the nineteenth-century term throughout to distinguish the pederast from the modern homosexual. For a history of the term, see Jean-Claude Féray, *Grecques, les mœurs du hanneton? Histoire du mot* pédérastie *et de ses dérivés en langue française* (Paris: Quintes-Feuilles, 2004).

3. Note, "Individu signalé comme pédéraste à surveiller," August 7, 1860, DA 230, doc. 281, APP.

4. Rapport, "Surveillances aux boulevards," September 4, 1860, DA 230, doc. 282, APP.

5. In this regard I follow Romain Jaouen and Anna Lvovsky, who both emphasize the role the police played in the construction of new sexual identities and forms of public knowledge. See Romain Jaouen, *L'inspecteur et "l'inverti": La police face aux sexualités masculines à Paris, 1919–1940* (Rennes, France: Presses universitaires de Rennes, 2018); and Anna Lvovsky, *Vice Patrol: Cops, Courts, and the Struggle over Urban Gay Life before Stonewall* (Chicago: University of Chicago Press, 2021).

6. This form of queer historicism is well summarized in Julio Capó Jr., *Welcome to Fairyland: Queer Miami before 1940* (Chapel Hill: University of North Carolina Press, 2017), 17–18.

7. On the appropriation of urban space by men and women seeking sexual encounters with the same sex in Paris, see, for instance, Leslie Choquette, "Homosexuals in the City: Representations of Lesbian and Gay Space in Nineteenth-Century Paris," *Journal of Homosexuality* 41, nos. 3–4 (2001): 149–67; Michael Sibalis, "The Palais-Royal and the Homosexual Subculture of Nineteenth-Century Paris," *Journal of Homosexuality* 41, nos. 3–4 (2002): 117–29; William A. Peniston, *Pederasts and Others: Urban Culture and Sexual Identity in Nineteenth-Century Paris* (New York: Harrington Park, 2004), esp. chap. 10; Régis Revenin, *Homosexualité et prostitution masculines à Paris, 1870–1918* (Paris: L'Harmattan, 2005), esp. pt. 1; Nicole G. Albert, "De la topographie invisible à l'espace public et littéraire: Les lieux de plaisir lesbien dans le Paris de la Belle Époque," *Revue d'histoire moderne et contemporaine* nos. 53–54 (2006): 87–105; Leslie Choquette, "Gay Paree: The Origins of Lesbian and Gay Commercial Culture in the French Third Republic," *Contemporary French Civilization* 41, no. 1 (2016): 1–24.

8. Walter Benjamin, *The Arcades Project*, ed. Rolf Tiedemann, trans. Howard Eiland and Kevin McLaughlin (Cambridge MA: Belknap, 1999), 3–26. On Paris and modernity, see esp. David Harvey, *Paris, Capital of Modernity* (New York: Routledge, 2003).

9. On the flâneur and urban culture, see, for example, Janet Wolff, "The Invisible Flâneuse: Women and the Literature of Modernity," *Theory, Culture & Society* 2, no. 3 (1985): 37–46; Keith Tester, ed., *The Flâneur* (New York: Routledge, 1994); Priscilla Parkhurst Ferguson, *Paris as Revolution: Writing the Nineteenth-Century City* (Berkeley: University of California Press, 1994), chap. 3; Aruna D'Souza and Tom McDonough, eds., *The Invisible Flâneuse? Gender, Public Space, and Visual Culture in Nineteenth-Century Paris* (Manchester, UK: Manchester University Press, 2006); Catherine Nesci, *Le flâneur et les flâneuses: Les femmes et la ville à l'époque romantique* (Grenoble, France: Ellug, 2007).

10. Nesci, *Le flâneur et les flâneuses*, 55.

11. Gregory Shaya, "The *Flâneur*, the *Badaud*, and the Making of a Mass Public in France, circa 1860–1910," *American Historical Review* 109, no. 1 (February 2004): 47. See also Charles Baudelaire, *The Painter of Modern Life and Other Essays*, trans. Jonathan Mayne, second ed. (London: Phaidon, 1995), chap. 1.

12. Tom McDonough, "The Crimes of the Flâneur," *October* 102 (Autumn 2002): 101.

13. Vanessa R. Schwartz, *Spectacular Realities: Early Mass Culture in Fin-de-Siècle Paris* (Berkeley: University of California Press, 1998), 10.

14. Even recent work that seeks to move beyond the flâneur remains in constant dialogue with the figure. See, for instance, Temma Balducci, *Gender, Space, and the Gaze in Post-Haussmann Visual Culture: Beyond the Flâneur* (London: Routledge, 2017); and Alastair Phillips and Ginette Vincendeau, eds., *Paris in the Cinema: Beyond the* Flâneur (London: Palgrave, 2018).

15. Wolff, "The Invisible *Flâneuse*"; Susan Buck-Morss, "The Flaneur, the Sandwich-man and the Whore: The Politics of Loitering," *New German Critique*, no. 39 (Autumn 1986): 119. See also Christopher Prendergast, *Paris and the Nineteenth Century* (Cambridge MA: Blackwell, 1992), 137.

16. See, for instance, Ruth E. Iskin, "Selling, Seduction, and Soliciting the Eye: Manet's *Bar at the Folies-Bergère*," *Art Bulletin* 77, no. 1 (March 1995): 33–37; Balducci, *Gender, Space, and the Gaze*.

17. Sharon Marcus, *Apartment Stories: City and Home in Nineteenth-Century Paris and London* (Berkeley: University of California Press, 1999), 38–40.

18. Henning Bech, *When Men Meet: Homosexuality and Modernity*, trans. Teresa Mesquit and Tim Davies (Chicago: University of Chicago Press, 1997), 108.

19. Dianne Chisholm, *Queer Constellations: Subcultural Space in the Wake of the City* (Minneapolis: University of Minnesota Press, 2005), 46.

20. E. Mallard to préfet de police, July 19, 1875, "Bois de Vincennes," JC 104, formerly BM2 16, APP.

21. E. Mallard to préfet de police, July 19, 1875, "Bois de Vincennes," JC 104, formerly BM2 16, APP.

22. "Un étranger" to préfet de police, "Renseignements Généraux: Plaintes Générales," October 16, 1861, DA 222, doc. 1, APP.

23. "Un étranger" to préfet de police, "Renseignements Généraux: Plaintes Générales," October 16, 1861, DA 222, doc. 1, APP.

24. Félix Carlier, *Études de pathologie sociale: Les deux prostitutions (1860–1870)* (Paris: E. Dentu, 1887), 287. On anonymous letters, see Andrew Israel Ross, *Public City/Public Sex: Prostitution, Homosexuality, and Urban Culture in Nineteenth-Century Paris* (Philadelphia: Temple University Press, 2019), 166–68.

25. "Un étranger" to préfet de police, "Renseignements Généraux: Plaintes Générales," October 16, 1861, DA 222, doc. 1, APP.

26. Blackmail was a common trope in discussions of male same-sex sexual relations during the nineteenth century. Ross, *Public City/Public Sex*, 88–90. On this theme more generally see Angus McLaren, *Sexual Blackmail: A Modern History* (Cambridge MA: Harvard University Press, 2002), esp. chap. 1.

27. On the underworld, see esp. Dominique Kalifa, *Vice, Crime, and Poverty: How the Western Imagination Invented the Underworld*, trans. Susan Emanuel (New York: Columbia University Press, 2019).

28. Flévy D'Urville, *Les ordures de Paris* (Paris: Librairie Sartorius, 1874), 69. The relatively frequent association of pederasts with freemasons during the nineteenth century draws on a long history. See esp. Kenneth Loiselle, *Brotherly Love: Freemasonry and Male Friendship in Enlightenment France* (Ithaca NY: Cornell University Press, 2014), chap. 3.

29. Ali Coffignon, *Paris-vivant: La corruption à Paris* (Paris: Librairie illustrée, 1888), 329–30.

30. Coffignon, *Paris-vivant*, 330.

31. On the origins of the nineteenth-century morals police, see Jill Harsin, *Policing Prostitution in Nineteenth-Century Paris* (Princeton NJ: Princeton University Press, 1985), pt. 1. On the relationship between policing female prostitution and men who sought sex with other men, see esp. Andrew Israel Ross, "Sex in the Archives: Homosexuality, Prostitution, and the Archives de la Préfecture de Police de Paris," *French Historical Studies* 40, no. 2 (2017): 267–90.

32. On the development of the legal framework used to arrest men who sought sex with other men, see esp. Peniston, *Pederasts and Others*, chap. 1. On the relationship between the formal decriminalization of sodomy and police attention to same-sex sexual activity, see Elwin Hofman, "The End of Sodomy: Law, Prosecution Patterns, and the Evanescent Will to Knowledge in Belgium, France, and the Netherlands, 1770–1830," *Journal of Social History* 54, no. 2 (Winter 2020): 480–502.

33. Marcela Iacub, *Through the Keyhole: A History of Sex, Space and Public Modesty in Modern France*, trans. Vinay Swamy (Manchester, UK: Manchester University Press, 2016), 2.

34. Laure Murat has, in this vein, argued that decriminalization did not mean greater tolerance or acceptance for same-sex sexual behavior by the police. Rather, it was seen as a "juridical hole." Laure Murat, *La loi du genre: Une histoire culturelle du 'troisième sexe'* (Paris: Fayard, 2006), 29–30. On this theme, see also Michael David Sibalis, "The Regulation of Male Homosexuality in Revolutionary and Napoleonic France, 1789–1815," in *Homosexuality in Modern France*, ed. Jeffrey Merrick and Bryant T. Ragan (New York: Oxford University Press, 1996), 80–101.

35. Several historians have described the transition from conceptions of same-sex sexual activity as sin to conceptions of it as public disorder. See esp. Michel Rey, "Police et sodomie à Paris au XVIIIe siècle: Du péché au désordre," *Revue d'histoire moderne et contemporaine* 29, no. 1 (1982): 113–24; Jeffrey Merrick, "Commissioner Foucault, Inspector Noël, and the 'Pederasts' of Paris, 1780–3," *Journal of Social History* 32, no. 2 (Winter 1998): 301; Jeffrey Merrick, "Sodomy, Suicide, and the Limits of Legal Reform in Eighteenth-Century France,"

Studies in Eighteenth-Century Culture 46 (2017): 191. See also Thierry Pastorello, "L'abolition du crime de sodomie en 1791: Un long processus social, répressif et pénal," *Cahiers d'histoire*, nos. 112–113 (2010): 197–208; and Hofman, "The End of Sodomy."

36. On policing and public space during the latter part of the nineteenth century, see Quentin Deluermoz, *Policiers dans la ville: La construction d'un ordre public à Paris, 1854–1914* (Paris: Publications de la Sorbonne, 2012), esp. pt. 1.

37. Vernon A. Rosario, "Pointy Penises, Fashion Crimes, and Hysterical Mollies: The Pederasts' Inversions," in Merrick and Ragan, *Homosexuality in Modern France*, 148; Pierre Hahn, *Nos ancêtres les pervers: La vie des homosexuels sous le second empire* (Béziers, France: H&O, 2006), 82.

38. H. Hazel Hahn, *Scenes of Parisian Modernity: Culture and Consumption in the Nineteenth Century* (New York: Palgrave Macmillan, 2009), 1.

39. [Félix] Carlier, "Extrait d'un rapport du service des mœurs joint au dossier de la 1ère Section," November 24, 1864, DA 230, doc. 308, APP.

40. The most influential text to make this claim was Ambroise Tardieu, *Étude medico-légale sur les attentats aux mœurs* (Paris J. B. Baillière, 1857).

41. "Note pour classer au dossier général de pédérastes," February 4, 1858, DA 230, doc. 274, APP.

42. [Félix] Carlier, "Extrait d'un rapport du service des mœurs joint au dossier de la 1ère Section," November 24, 1864, DA 230, doc. 308, APP.

43. On the growing connection between law and medicine in this period, see esp. Robert A. Nye, *Crime, Madness, and Politics in Modern France: The Medical Concept of National Decline* (Princeton NJ: Princeton University Press, 1984).

44. In this regard, these thinkers recognized the ways that the visibility of same-sex desire created new communities and thus the possibility for self-recognition, as described by John D'Emilio in "Capitalism and Gay Identity," in *Powers of Desire: The Politics of Sexuality*, ed. Ann Snitow, Christine Stansell, and Sharon Thompson (New York: Monthly Review Press, 1983), 109.

45. [Henri] Legrand du Saulle, *Étude médico-légale sur la séparation de corps* (Paris: F. Savy, 1866), 7. The official psychiatrist of the Prefecture of Police during the 1870s and 1880s, du Saulle focused much of his attention on supposedly female disorders such as hysteria and kleptomania. On his work, see esp. Mark S. Micale, "Discourses of Hysteria in Fin-de-Siècle France," in *The Mind of Modernism: Medicine, Psychology, and the Cultural Arts in Europe and America, 1880–1940*, ed. Mark S. Micale (Stanford CA: Stanford University Press, 2004), 82–83. Jessie Hewitt's contribution to this volume showcases medical debates over sexual secrecy, many of which also concerned marital sexual obligations.

46. Du Saulle, *Étude médico-légale sur la séparation de corps*, 35.

47. Du Saulle, *Étude médico-légale sur la séparation de corps*, 7.

48. Du Saulle argued that whereas a wife who willingly engaged in these acts with her husband had no cause for separation, a woman forced to submit to them had grounds for a legal complaint under Article 231 of the civil code. Du Saulle, *Étude médico-légale sur la séparation de corps*, 8.

49. Representations of Paris as a modern-day Sodom and Gomorrah became more prominent in the 1870s. See Michael Sibalis, "Paris-Babylone/Paris-Sodome: Images of Homosexuality in the Nineteenth-Century City," in *Images of the City in Nineteenth-Century France*, ed. John West-Sooby (Moorooka, Australia: Boombana, 1998), 13–22.

50. Benjamin Kahan, *The Book of Minor Perverts: Sexology, Etiology, and the Emergence of Sexuality* (Chicago: Chicago University Press, 2019), 4–5. See also Michel Foucault, *The History of Sexuality*, vol. 1, *An Introduction*, trans. Robert Hurley (New York: Vintage, 1990), 38–49.

51. On some of the unique characteristics of French thinking around homosexuality in the late nineteenth century, see Robert A. Nye, "The History of Sexuality in Context: National Sexological Traditions," *Science in Context* 4, no. 2 (Autumn 1991): 397–99. See also Robert A. Nye, "Sex Difference and Male Homosexuality in French Medical Discourse, 1830–1930," *Bulletin of the History of Medicine* 63, no. 1 (Spring 1989): 32–51.

52. Cox-Algit, *Anthropophilie, ou Étude sur la prostitution masculine à notre époque* (Nantes, France: Morel, 1881), 4.

53. Cox-Algit, *Anthropophilie*, 8–9.

54. Cox-Algit, *Anthropophilie*, 9–10.

55. Cox-Algit, *Anthropophilie*, 10.

56. On debates over the role of environment in the creation of criminality more broadly, see esp. Nye, *Crime, Madness, and Politics in Modern France*, chap. 4.

57. Simone de Beauvoir, *The Second Sex*, trans. Constance Borde and Sheila Malovany-Chevallier (New York: Vintage, 2011), 283.

58. Marc-André Raffalovich, *Uranisme et unisexualité: Étude sur différentes manifestations de l'instinct sexuel* (Lyon, France: A. Storck, 1896), 45. The translation is from Raffalovich, *Marc-André Raffalovich's Uranism and Unisexuality: A Study of Different Manifestations of the Sexual Instinct*, ed. Philip Healy with Frederick S. Roden, trans. Nancy Erber and William A. Peniston (New York: Palgrave Macmillan, 2016), 68–69.

59. "Affaire de Germiny," *Le petit journal*, December 25, 1876. On the Germiny affair, see esp. Peniston, *Pederasts and Others*, chap. 12.

60. "Affaire de Germiny," *Le petite journal*, December 25, 1876.

61. Schwartz, *Spectacular Realities*, chap. 1.

62. See, for example, George Chauncey, *Gay New York: Gender, Urban Culture, and the Makings of the Gay Male World, 1890–1940* (New York: Basic, 1994), chap. 8; Allan Bérubé, "The History of Gay Bathhouses," in *Policing Public Sex: Queer Politics and the Future of AIDS Activism*, ed. Dangerous Bedfellows (Boston: South End, 1996), 187–220; Revenin, *Homosexualité et prostitution masculines*, 60–64; Matt Houlbrook, *Queer London: Perils and Pleasures in the Sexual Metropolis, 1918–1957* (Chicago: University of Chicago Press, 2005), chap. 4.

63. Aaron Betsky, *Queer Space: Architecture and Same-Sex Desire* (New York: William Morrow, 1997), 164.

64. Lise Manin, "Perverses promiscuités? Bains publics et cafés-concerts parisiens au second XIXe siècle," *Genre, sexualité, et société* 10 (Autumn 2013), http://journals.openedition.org/gss/2955.

65. Gustave Macé, *La police parisienne: Mes lundis en prison* (Paris: G. Charpentier, 1889), 168–69.

66. Coffignon, *Paris-vivant*, 344–45.

67. On the surveillance and raids of the Bains de Penthièvre, see Revenin, *Homosexualité et prostitution masculines*, 62–63.

68. "Rapport," December 18, 1898, "30, rue de Penthièvre," JC 53, formerly BM2 65, APP.

69. "Rapport," August 1, 1900, "30, rue de Penthièvre," JC 53, formerly BM2 65, APP. This description echoes that of Ambroise Tardieu from 1857. See Rosario, "Pointy Penises."

70. "Un scandale à Montparnasse," *Le Journal*, March 21, 1904, 3.

71. "Affaire de mœurs," *Le Journal*, March 28, 1904. See also "Descente de Police du 20/3/1904, 83 Bld de Montparnasse, Pédérastes," BA 1690, APP. Thanks to Hannah Frydman for pointing me to this cartoon.

Suggested Reading

Balducci, Temma. *Gender, Space, and the Gaze in Post-Haussmann Visual Culture: Beyond the Flâneur*. London: Routledge, 2017.

Chisholm, Dianne. *Queer Constellations: Subcultural Space in the Wake of the City*. Minneapolis: University of Minnesota Press, 2005.

Deluermoz, Quentin. *Policiers dans la ville: La construction d'un ordre public à Paris (1854–1914)*. Paris: Publications de la Sorbonne, 2012.

Jaouen, Romain. *L'inspecteur et "l'inverti": La police face aux sexualités masculines à Paris, 1919–1940*. Rennes, France: Presses universitaires de Rennes, 2018.

Nesci, Catherine. *Le Flâneur et les flâneuses: Les femmes et la ville à l'époque romantique*. Grenoble, France: Ellug, 2007.

Peniston, William A. *Pederasts and Others: Urban Culture and Sexual Identity in Nineteenth-Century Paris*. New York: Harrington Park, 2004.

Revenin, Régis. *Homosexualité et prostitution masculines à Paris, 1870–1918*. Paris: L'Harmattan, 2005.

Ross, Andrew Israel. *Public City/Public Sex: Homosexuality, Prostitution, and Urban Culture in Nineteenth-Century Paris*. Philadelphia: Temple University Press, 2019.

6

SECRETS, SEX, AND MEDICINE IN LATE NINETEENTH-CENTURY FRANCE

JESSIE HEWITT

The word "secret" comes up time and again in two distinct but related contexts in nineteenth-century medical literature: the *maladie secrète* and the *secret médical*. "Maladie secrète" was a polite term for sexually transmitted infection, and rarely has a euphemism so effectively made a case for its own utility. Books featuring the term in the title—of which there were at least fifty-three published from 1800 to 1914—generally sought to explain to a lay or medical audience the symptoms and possible treatments for an array of illnesses.[1] Sexually transmitted infections like genital warts, herpes, gonorrhea, and syphilis were secret because they were considered shameful, and shameful because of how one contracted them. By continuously referencing secrecy in the very act of calling attention to such ailments, doctors perpetuated this sense of shame and positioned themselves as capable of keeping its source hidden (therefore shielding patients from shame's public consequences, not to mention the anger of their wives). The second term—secret médical—often revolved around the circumstances under which a doctor should or should not reveal a patient's maladie secrète. Most French doctors advocated for complete confidentiality when it came to protecting their male patients' sexual secrets. This consensus slowly began to change with the advent of degeneration theory in the late 1850s, at which point a growing contingent of medical practitioners argued that venereal and, especially, hereditary ailments were too dangerous to the health of the nation to keep them hidden, no matter the cost to individuals.

This chapter examines medical discussions of sexual secrecy from the perspectives of general practitioners, venereal infection specialists, and alienists, some of whom worked within a degenerationist paradigm and many of whom did not. Some of these doctors explicitly concerned themselves with the topic of medical confidentiality, while others referenced it more obliquely through the depiction and even the promotion of their patients' duplicitous behaviors. Nineteenth-century French legal and moral standards of medical confidentiality reflected and upheld a gender system that conceived of sexual behavior and sexual knowledge through the prisms of feminine virtue and masculine honor, in which emergent medical concepts rubbed up against older notions of sexual propriety without supplanting them. Arguments put forth by doctors who hoped to maintain patients' right to confidentiality or who helped patients hide their conditions from their sexual partners often proved complementary to this regulatory framework. These doctors therefore propped up already widespread gender expectations via their professional pronouncements and expanded their own influence by association. In contrast, doctors challenged contemporary notions of respectability when they highlighted the costs rather than the benefits of medical and sexual secrecy. This happened with increasing frequency between approximately 1860 and 1900, in accordance with the rise of degeneration theory and related perceptions of national decline connected to the loss of the Franco-Prussian War, the increased visibility of bourgeois women in the public sphere, and concern over falling birthrates (among other signals of social and cultural transformation).[2]

The practice of medicine revolved around a fundamental tension between the revelation and concealment of sexual secrets. This was a productive tension throughout much of the century in the sense that hiding patients' sexual indiscretions simultaneously augmented medical power and supported the interests of "honorable" bourgeois families.[3] As Michel Foucault notes, doctors strategically exposed the secrets of sexually and medically "abnormal" individuals in ways that served to define them as "deviant" and distinguish them from those considered "normal," aggrandizing the authority of medicine in the process.[4] This was perhaps especially the case during the early Third Republic, by which time doctors held unprecedented influence in the political and legal realms.[5] "What is peculiar to modern societies," Foucault famously explains, "is not that they consigned sex to a shadow existence, but that they dedicate themselves to speaking of it *ad infinitum*, while exploiting it as *the* secret."[6] The writings and the behaviors of doctors constituted sexually transmitted infection as an object of shame, opening the door for medical practitioners to step in as the protectors of their patients' reputations in addition to their health (thereby exploiting sex as "*the* secret"). Hiding their patients' sexual secrets thus contributed to the professional advancement of individual doctors and the glorification of the medical profession. Foucault's insights are fundamental to my assessment of secrets, sex, and medicine because they highlight the ways in which medical power supported that of the French bourgeoisie, and vice versa.

That said, focusing solely on the expansive nature of medical authority in the nineteenth century can obscure how medical pronouncements remained subordinate to other sources of cultural legitimacy. Even before the frenzy over the nation's falling birthrate erupted at the end of the century, bourgeois marriage served to protect and perpetuate family wealth over generations (and a spouse with a sexually debilitating medical condition could certainly throw a wrench in a family's plans). But when keeping a sexual secret merely threatened the prospects of one particular couple, doctors defended confidentiality despite the possible dangers or inconveniences. They did so because hiding sexual secrets served to maintain gender-based notions of respectability that supposedly justified the right of bourgeois men to rule, which trumped the individual interests of any one person or family. Only when some doctors began to concern themselves with the apparent degeneration of the French "race" did the attachment to total confidentiality begin to wane.

Crucially, there is little evidence that the rest of French society shared the concerns of degeneration theorists about the potentially devastating effects of medical confidentiality. Paying attention to the place of sex in doctors' pronouncements on medical secrecy and national regeneration therefore destabilizes straightforward narratives of professionalization and medicalization more broadly. If historians have traditionally argued that medical professionals successfully inserted themselves into national debates by asserting their specialized authority over key biopolitical questions, consideration of the history of sex shows just how attenuated such efforts were. The history of sexual and medical secrets tells us a great deal about the people who hid them and the power they derived from acts of concealment and strategic revelation. But this history also reveals the limits of medical authority when it came into conflict with alternative ways of comprehending the world, indicating that the medicalization of sexuality was both more contested and less thorough than we might imagine.

"Odious, Repugnant, Incurable!": The Doctor as Keeper of Dishonorable Secrets

The Napoleonic Code dictated the legal status of the doctor-patient relationship in postrevolutionary France. The Hippocratic oath—a matter of custom rather than policy—had long advised physicians to keep "things that should never be divulged" to themselves, and the Paris Faculty of Medicine established formal guidelines requiring all affiliated physicians to maintain near-total confidentiality around 1600.[7] The inclusion of medical confidentiality in the Penal Code of 1810, however, considerably upped the stakes when it came to respecting the bonds of secrecy. Article 378 ensured that doctors who breached medical confidentiality could face fines, the revocation of their license to practice, and even imprisonment. Nineteenth-century doctors took what could be interpreted as a check on their authority as an opportunity to enhance their reputations as trusted professionals and to distinguish themselves from lay healers and others not bound by such obligations. The legal principle of doctor-patient confidentiality might have begun "as a sanction," as Robert A. Nye explains, but it soon came to represent the "source of medical authority itself."[8] It is therefore unsurprising that most doctors defended patients' rights to confidentiality even when it came to contagious venereal infections.

Doctors' professional interests aligned nearly seamlessly with those of their most influential clients. The law on medical confidentiality, and the part played by the doctor as a keeper of potentially shameful secrets, served to promote the interests of the French bourgeoisie, a diverse group whose elevated social status depended on marks of cultural distinction rather than noble blood.[9] The exposure of a man's medical secrets could compromise his place in society if those secrets were deemed dishonorable, because they implied a lack of self-control, as in the case of infections acquired through illicit sexual contact or participation in sexual acts that were themselves deemed pathological (such as masturbation and other nonprocreative sexual behaviors). A man's honor signaled his own respectability and that of his family, making its protection and projection vitally important among bourgeois men in particular.[10] A woman's sexual virtue similarly signaled her family's respectability, although the protection of women's virtue was more a byproduct of dominant confidentiality practices than their primary purpose, given that the most jealously guarded secrets were those of male patients. Maintaining secrecy in cases of male sexual indiscretion eventually gave rise to controversy, yet the need to keep these secrets hidden was also the most aggressively defended feature of the law.

The cultural significance of masculine honor was embedded in Article 378. As the legislative reporter noted at the time, the "ravages" caused by an attack on a man's honor "often [did] not stop with the slandered person, but [brought] desolation to all of his family."[11] Revealing secrets that "compromise[d] the reputation of the person whose secret" was "betrayed" should therefore be considered a "grave crime." Furthermore, the betrayal of such a secret would certainly bring future harm by convincing "those who [found] themselves in the same situation" that it was preferable to remain "victims of their silence rather than [victims of] another's indiscretion." Medical confidentiality likewise protected doctors by helping them maintain their positions as "benefactors and true consolers" instead of exposing them as "traitors."[12] Legislators therefore explicitly framed the issue of medical secrecy as a question of honor—that of the physician, whose reputation would be compromised were he seen as an untrustworthy gossip, and that of the patient, whose health and good name would be protected by the assurance that his shameful ailment would remain confidential if he received treatment. As Raymond Villey notes, the law was not applied to people of all social backgrounds equally, with prostitutes, workers, and servants all losing the right to medical privacy to some degree vis-à-vis the state, their employers, or both.[13] Nonetheless, it is possible that the gradual democratization of honor over the course of the nineteenth century contributed to the continued support for Article 378, even when some doctors started to criticize the law.[14]

Similarly, although the wording of the law was gender neutral, in practice it mainly served to protect men by hiding their potentially shameful actions at the expense of their wives and children (although, as Napoleonic legislators implied, the maintenance of a man's honorable reputation served the interests of his family as well as his own). Some doctors did note that medical confidentiality also applied to women. The author of a widely read physicians' guide, for example, urged caution when confronted by a husband whose wife exhibited symptoms of a sexually transmitted infection, advising discretion except when "the virtue of the wife absolutely defies suspicion."[15] Still, most medical commentaries took it for granted that husbands would discuss their wives' medical information with the family doctor, whereas the reverse was not the case.[16] Thus, in addition to safeguarding men's honor, medical confidentiality kept women ignorant of potential threats to their own sexual health. Jill Harsin makes a convincing case that the application of the law on medical secrecy favored the interests of bourgeois men while endangering the health of their wives, noting that Alfred Fournier, the foremost expert on the treatment of syphilis in the late nineteenth and early twentieth centuries, insisted that a doctor could not even tell a man's wife if he had infected her.[17]

In fact, Paul Diday, a contemporary and admirer of Fournier, recommended outright deception when it came to hiding sexually transmitted infections from his patients' wives. The Lyonnais surgeon claimed that a wife's ignorance of her husband's infidelity was in her own best interest, especially when the prognosis for the ailment in question was less serious than that of syphilis.[18] He noted that the group of illnesses "baptized *maladies secrètes*" were appropriately named, considering the persistent hope among patients of all social backgrounds that they might access appropriate medical treatment "as slyly as possible."[19] Yet actually following through with the prescribed regimen without getting caught was rather difficult. Physicians recommended that people undergoing treatment should avoid drinking coffee and alcohol, but most men could not abstain without calling attention to themselves. More pressing was the issue of sexual activity between husband and wife. "Of all our special clients," he explained, "the *vénérien en ménage* [coupled venereal patient] is surely that who has the greatest need of mystery, and it is precisely he who has the most difficulty obtaining it."[20] Pretending to have a kidney stone, heart palpitations, or a recurrent bout of hemorrhoids could apparently do the trick, at least temporarily.

Although doctors and legislators tended to justify medical secrecy in the name of men's honor, the maintenance of confidentiality likewise supported widespread assumptions concerning bourgeois women and their innate sexual innocence, thereby sustaining the power of elite men from another direction. The outspoken and oft-cited Diday serves as a case in point. Addressing the charge that medical confidentiality essentially meant hiding husbands' infidelities, he gave two justifications. First, he admitted that men visited doctors more often than women for the treatment of sexually transmitted infections, which meant quite simply that their secrets were the ones that needed keeping. "But it is equally true," he continued, "although it seems paradoxical, that the discovery of a husband's infidelity compromises the household peace more gravely than that of a wife's, when that discovery of infidelity takes place through the revelation of a venereal illness."[21]

Of course, he continued, a man's pride would be injured if he found out his wife had cheated, and he might even vow to get vengeance. The blow to a woman's pride, however, would be compounded by her ignorance of both medical knowledge and masculine social norms. There was no woman, according to Diday, "who could admit any distinction between an accidental error in conduct . . . and intentional infidelity." Furthermore, no wife was capable of understanding the difference between "this or that venereal disease"—for her, all sexually transmitted ailments were "equally odious, repugnant, incurable!" The discovery of anything from genital warts to herpes to syphilis therefore transformed the husband ("until then, tenderly loved") into an "object of insurmountable disgust!"[22] Women did not know enough about sexual health to be told the truth about sexual health. It was practically coincidental that women's ignorance so clearly benefited the interests of their husbands. Furthermore, the trope of bourgeois women's sexual naivete, though apparently worthy of mockery, served to distinguish bourgeois wives from women of the popular classes, thereby symbolically upholding the real political and economic power of the bourgeoisie as a whole.

Sexual secrecy, therefore, came up in several related contexts in the medical literature on sexually transmitted infections: how a man might hide his condition, when and why a doctor might help him, and the dire consequences if he failed to do so. Yet the theme of secrecy runs through more general discussions of the medical profession as well, particularly as it relates to doctors' protection of their own honor and that of their patients. For example, the influential physicians' guide *Le médecin* by A. Dechambre begins with a section on the ideal qualities of the private doctor by noting, "There is no particular moral code for the physician. The fact is that he is an honest man in the exercise of his profession as in all other circumstances of his life. That's all." However, the medical profession has "a special character" because doctors are charged with "responsibilities so heavy" and initiated into "so many secrets."[23] They therefore have to be especially scrupulous in their conduct.

Dechambre argued that a moral code as much as the penal code required doctors' discretion. The physician's "access to the domestic foyer at all hours of the day and night" and his need to investigate "the intimacies of family life" to ascertain a diagnosis meant that patients had to have absolute trust in their doctor.[24] He advised doctors on all aspects of their background, including parts of their personae that might strike the modern reader as totally irrelevant to the practice of medicine (such as age, weight, marital status, and even literary sensibilities). In particular, he stressed that the doctor should have a wife, because patients and their families believed a married man would best understand their desires for confidentiality.[25] Familial and medical prerogatives thus conveniently aligned when it came to the question of secrecy. Family secrets—"honorable or not"—would stay safely out of public view.[26] In the meantime the ability to keep them hidden secured the doctor's reputation as an "honest man."[27]

Nevertheless, it was not always easy for doctors to balance the tension between revelation and concealment. Although the law on medical secrets was initially proposed as a way to safeguard the honor of doctor and patient alike, medical men soon came to realize that maintaining confidentiality could potentially compromise their honor as well, especially when a syphilitic patient sought to marry or when an infected husband became a father. There were also numerous examples of wet nurses contracting syphilis from babies born with the disease because their parents withheld the child's diagnosis, imperiling the life of the wet nurse in addition to that of her own children and sexual partners.[28] In such cases holding onto a medical secret could injure the doctor's reputation, not to mention his sense of personal decency. Despite Dechambre's claims to the contrary, a doctor's honor as a man came into conflict with his identity as a doctor easily and often—a point that even the most rigid proponents of medical secrecy seemed to acknowledge and one that critics of the confidentiality rules sought to exploit.

All doctors writing about medical confidentiality considered the various situations in which divulging a secret might prove beneficial or even necessary. The professor of legal medicine Paul Brouardel, whose 1887 book *Le secret médical* established him as France's leading authority on the topic, pointed to several exceptions to the rule on total confidentiality, including the revelation of past or future criminal behavior, the results of a physical examination for entrance into the military or for the purposes of health insurance, and the discovery of a contagious illness that might trigger an epidemic. Sexually transmitted infections were notably absent from this list. Brouardel admitted that some doctors disagreed with this omission because of the dire consequences of syphilis, in particular, for a would-be wife and her future children. Syphilis was not only painful, resulting in the outbreak of lesions all over the patient's body, but advanced cases could also result in facial disfigurement and neurological damage. Furthermore, a pregnant woman who experienced an outbreak could pass syphilis on to the fetus. Still, Brouardel did not see why the revelation of a patient's sexual health status should be up to a doctor's personal discretion. He had little sympathy for doctors who wanted to breach medical confidentiality, noting, "This secret that weighs you down, you have received it because it was confided to you . . . you would have remained unaware of it had you not been a doctor."[29] For Brouardel, keeping a secret he might personally find distasteful was a sign of a doctor's strength of character and his commitment to his professional obligations.

At the same time, Brouardel and other medical writers encouraged their colleagues to obstruct engagements between syphilitic men and the "innocent" women they sought to marry (although doctors expressed fewer qualms about keeping the secrets of men diagnosed with less grave sexually transmitted conditions). Most of these attempts hinged on the doctor's ability to encourage men to do the right thing and refrain from marriage until after the syphilis had been in remission for about six months, which supposedly indicated that it was no longer contagious. Diday, for example, warned that the parents of young men seeking to delay marriage should accept their sons' apprehensions and avoid getting into too many specific details about why someone in the prime of life would want to stay single, implying that family pressures constituted one reason why a man with syphilis might marry despite the dangers.[30]

Experts in sexually transmitted infections, most notably Fournier and his followers, believed men with syphilis could safely marry if they caught the illness early and treated it aggressively with mercury. The option to merely delay marriage rather than to forbid it gave doctors some leverage when trying to convince men to postpone their plans when the danger of transmission to their wives and unborn children was believed to be most acute.

This tactic only worked when the patient considered the health of his future family a greater priority than marrying immediately for financial gain, which could not be taken for granted, as evidenced by doctors' handwringing over the issue. Diday made note of the so-called "matriomania" of those diagnosed with syphilis, whose desire for marriage supposedly intensified when they could not satisfy it immediately.[31] This was especially likely when a man had the lucky opportunity to marry above his station, as in the case of a clerk who became engaged to his boss's daughter. Diday reported this story as evidence that even a patient with syphilis could achieve the bliss of matrimony, explaining that the man finally married his beloved after going several months without symptoms.[32] Things were far more complicated when a doctor could not convince a patient to wait a safe amount of time on his own accord. Diday gave another example in which a woman's father asked him the health status of his future son-in-law. He refused, but had the man return with the fiancé, who, under pressure, agreed to allow the doctor to reveal the details of his medical condition in the presence of his would-be father-in-law.[33] The secrecy expert Brouardel would have likely looked askance at his colleague's behavior in this case because it came too close to compromising medical ethics. Yet even he sympathized with would-be fathers-in-law, encouraging one such individual to take out an insurance policy on his daughter's fiancé in a none-too-subtle reference to the inevitability of his declining health.[34] Few doctors openly embraced their role as a syphilitic's accomplice, even when they defended sexual and medical secrecy. It was only a matter of time before some would begin to criticize longstanding confidentiality practices and even call for the elimination of Article 378.

In Defense of Indiscretion

Voices rallying against absolute medical confidentiality started to coalesce in the last several decades of the nineteenth century, usually making their case by contrasting the individual patient's desire for secrecy against the common good. Pierre-Charles Favreau's 1888 doctoral thesis *Contribution à l'étude du secret professionnel en médicine mentale* focused on the harm caused by people diagnosed with mental illness when doctors insisted on keeping medical information confidential at all costs. Favreau called out Brouardel, who had recently published *Le secret médical*, in particular. Whereas Brouardel viewed the doctor's duties in terms of healing the individual patient, Favreau insisted that he must also consider whether the patient posed a danger to the "milieu social."[35] If a doctor discovered a railroad worker was going blind, would he keep that information to himself? Favreau claimed that Brouardel would merely try to convince him to switch jobs, similar to the case of a syphilitic looking to marry.

A wide array of situations called for the breaching of medical confidentiality, according to Favreau, although, as in the case of other doctors writing on the topic, many of his examples involved sex. One of the forms of mental illness considered most destabilizing to married life was *folie lucide*. "Lucid madness" involved individuals who seemed sane on the surface but were in fact afflicted by various forms of alienation, often of an erotic nature. Such afflictions were dangerous, Favreau said, because they were so difficult to uncover without input from a medical professional. Favreau listed a number of examples of people with lucid madness, including an adulterous nymphomaniac wife, an "erotomaniac" fiancé, and a mendacious alcoholic who tried to convince people that his wife had given him syphilis. Much distress might have been avoided if the partners of such individuals had access to their mental health histories before getting married, warned Favreau. The consequences of keeping one partner in the dark were especially dire when that individual was a "jeune fille" (young girl), someone whose sexual innocence presumably proved her virtues as a wife but also left her unprepared to cope with unexpected developments in the bedroom. This was apparently the case for one woman described by Favreau whose wedding night ended with her husband sneaking away, seeming to arrange for some sort of romantic surprise, only to be discovered in the foyer smearing feces on the fireplace.[36] Favreau's medicalization of sexual behavior often complemented gendered notions of respectability, in that he justified doctors' revelations of medical and sexual secrets in the early phases of courtship to avoid more shocking revelations later on. At the same time, his attitudes persistently challenged both the letter and the intent of the 1810 law, whose principal aim was the protection of men's honor, not women's virtue.

The advent of degeneration theory truly exposed the ways in which an attack on medical confidentiality also constituted a threat to predominant sex-gender norms. Complaints among doctors regarding Article 378 became much more common following the 1857 publication of the asylum doctor Benedict Morel's *Traité des dégénérescences physiques, intellectuelles et morales de l'espèce humaine*, and, indeed, few doctors had felt the need to defend confidentiality regulations before the popularization of Morel's treatise. Morel did not concern himself with sexually transmitted ailments but rather with hereditary ones. He therefore focused on the potential offspring of so-called degenerates and what their propagation meant for French society. Morel identified mental illness as the most obvious proof of a person's degenerate nature but claimed that a wide variety of so-called abnormalities—from hysteria to "idiocy" to epilepsy—likewise signaled an individual's susceptibility to mental and physical breakdown. Furthermore, he claimed that these traits would inevitably be passed down from one generation to the next, creating a "sick" society full of sick people. Morel's resolution to this paranoid vision of France's future was the final stage of hereditary degeneration: sterility (which supposedly afflicted individual members of a "degenerate" family's fourth generation). "Degenerates" would eventually die off on their own—unequipped with traits that would allow them to flourish in the evolutionary struggle of all against all—but this would take generations. What would happen to France in the meantime? Not surprisingly, degeneration theory inspired eugenic schemes in the late 1800s and beyond, providing "scientific" justification for selective human breeding and the occasional call for forced sterilization.[37]

Morel's belief that hereditary afflictions signaled the downfall of the French "race" influenced everything from the practice of medicine to *fin-de-siècle* art and politics.[38] France had become a society obsessed with its own decline following its defeat in the Franco-Prussian War and the subsequent slaughter of approximately twenty-five thousand Parisian revolutionaries by French national troops during the Paris Commune.[39] The first decades of the Third Republic, founded after the capture of Napoleon III by Prussian forces in 1870, were defined by a distinct sense of class conflict that heavily influenced trends within the medical sciences. Such theories likewise gained popularity amid increasing pushback from French women against the supposedly natural gender norms associated with the middle-class family.[40] Growing numbers of women professionals, the legalization of divorce, and the drive for women's suffrage all indicated disruptions to the status quo that the many proponents of degeneration theory took as evidence of national decline. Furthermore, birth rates fell in the last decades of the century, a particularly worrisome trend for those preoccupied with regaining the French territories lost in the Franco-Prussian War.[41] Doctors began to focus increasing attention on constraining the sexual behaviors of so-called degenerates when the right kinds of people failed in their duty to reproduce. In so doing, these doctors pitted efforts to maintain the respectability of the bourgeois family by hiding their sexual secrets against this new preoccupation with keeping society safe from the effects of hereditary degeneration.

Members of the Société Médico-Psychologique, the preeminent professional organization for French doctors of mental medicine, began discussing the advisability of revealing medical secrets to patients' potential spouses in 1863. It is possible that alienists were willing to critique confidentiality regulations earlier than their generalist colleagues because the management of mental illness had been considered a family matter long before the rise of degeneration theory. Although, as mentioned above, the Napoleonic Code stated a doctor could be fined or even imprisoned for revealing a patient's medical history, the records of asylum inmates were never truly private because doctors regularly discussed them with their patients' families (in fact, many institutionalized people in the nineteenth century were in asylums because their parents or spouses chose to commit them).[42] Asylum doctors, like specialists in sexually transmitted infections, were still not supposed to discuss past or current patients with anyone outside the family unit, and there is little indication that they wanted to do so, at least at the start of the century.

Some alienists in the 1860s started to wonder if discretion regarding a family history of mental illness was still justified if it might lead to a marriage with "deplorable consequences."[43] During meetings at the Société Médico-Psychologique, Casimir Pinel, nephew of the founder of French psychiatry, Philippe Pinel, brought up numerous scenarios in which it might be necessary to inform a potential spouse of a patient's medical history, many of them sexual in nature. Would it be so wrong to inform a mother that her future son-in-law had syphilis?[44] Or that he was impotent, had atrophied testicles, or masturbated obsessively? Should not a potential husband know that his future wife had a history of nymphomania or prostitution, or a fixation on sodomy?[45] He admitted such situations could be delicate; what, for example, was a medical professional's responsibility to a "young girl" whose fiancé had experienced mental alienation years before but had since been cured?[46] Ultimately, Pinel concluded that such "deadly alliances" contributed to the "deterioration of the race" and that it was beyond unfortunate that doctors did not have the legal power to stop them.[47]

Notably, just one of these scenarios concerned a sexually transmitted infection. Instead, Pinel focused on the revelation of conditions or behaviors that he considered pathological and therefore indicative of future threats to the family's health. In some cases, as in the examples of atrophied testicles and impotence, Pinel emphasized a man's inability to have healthy offspring. In others, such as a fiancée's past participation in various nonprocreative sexual activities, he linked specific actions to proof of mental illness and suggested this too would keep a couple from producing healthy children. As another nineteenth-century doctor explained regarding women masturbators, most would never be able to have children at all, and, if they did, those children would be "poor and miserable creatures, veritable caricatures of humanity."[48] Pinel also discussed supposed threats to the family that were not obviously sexual in nature. Yet, according to the logic of degeneration, almost any issue coded as a mental or physical health problem should be revealed to the future spouse. For Morel and his intellectual followers, a parent with one affliction— say, epilepsy—could pass a seemingly distinct condition like hysteria or alcoholism on to the next generation, who might then pass on something else entirely to the generation after that. Within the framework of degenerative reproduction, every medical secret was a sexual one.

This is not to say, however, that degeneration suddenly replaced respectability as the organizing principle through which the French comprehended medical secrecy. In Pinel's telling it was quite possible for these two ways of thinking to overlap and even complement one another. For example, he suggested that the rising influence of degeneration theory exposed a conflict between medical confidentiality and masculine honor that had been present all along, between the family's right to keep secrets that might negatively affect their reputation and the doctor's desire as an honest, bourgeois head of household to uphold his own.[49] Pinel claimed that keeping medical secrets not only undermined the needs of French society but also came into conflict with a doctor's personal honor, noting that a doctor should be allowed to reveal secrets because he "first and foremost" was "an honest man and he" was "often the father of a family."[50] Whereas someone like Dechambre argued that a married doctor would understand a family's desire to keep sexual secrets confidential for honor's sake, Pinel argued the opposite: that a doctor with children of his own could never hide dangerous secrets from other parents. He claimed that keeping certain types of secrets, especially from other honorable men, might be interpreted as a dishonorable act. Pinel thus saw no conflict between exposing medical secrets under certain circumstances and promoting the interests of honorable families.

That said, rhetorical sleights of hand could not hide the radical nature of the degenerationist position. These doctors had begun to thoroughly rework their understanding of professional ethics in light of widespread concerns over national weakness and social instability, as evidenced by their attacks on the longstanding prerogative of medical confidentiality in defense of the French "race." They included men like the alienist Favreau, who was not explicitly a degenerationist, as well as practitioners and theorists of numerous specializations who, like Casimir Pinel, were inspired by Morel in a much more obvious fashion. Rather than owing loyalty to their patients, or even to patients' families or those of their betrothed, such doctors consistently argued that they owed their allegiance to French society itself. This obligation entailed, first and foremost, the revelation of sexual secrets. They therefore aimed for nothing short of the reconfiguration of the duties of the medical profession.

As Dr. J. Dupuy explained in his *Le dogme du secret médical* (1903), the time had come "to purely and simply abrogate Article 378 of the Penal Code."[51] He went on to imply that France already restricted the right to medical confidentiality in the case of military service: "When we occupy ourselves with the material security of the nation, we put aside all arguments that are more or less sentimental."[52] So too should these rules be put aside in the case of marriage, he argued. For Dupuy and his allies in the medical profession, the link between the health of the nation and the health of the family could not be clearer. Like soldiers vital to the anticipated *revanche* (revenge) against Germany, the future husband and wife were called upon to sacrifice their right to privacy for the good of the nation. Although "seeing his shame become public" could injure a male patient's "amour propre," this price must be paid in the name of "public utility."[53]

Dupuy did not argue that all medical secrets should be revealed, just those concerning illnesses that might be transmitted to a couple's offspring. Syphilis ranked highest among the threats discussed by Dupuy for obvious reasons. He recounted multiple examples of men with syphilis who sought to marry despite doctors' objections. A representative case involved a young man who had contracted syphilis while sowing his wild oats ("enterre sa vie de garçon") whose doctor sent him to the countryside for treatment. The man's future mother-in-law visited the doctor and asked the purpose of the trip. The doctor responded evasively and, when asked if she should allow her daughter to marry her betrothed, he merely replied, "Don't ask me." The wedding took place. The young wife subsequently suffered two miscarriages and "succumbed in her second year of marriage to malignant syphilis."[54] The best way to avoid such circumstances in the future, according to Dupuy, was for all couples to visit a mutually agreed upon "marriage doctor" before the wedding.[55] The doctor would interrogate each partner about their health history and that of their family. Then, if everything checked out, he would issue a certificate vouching for the good health and untainted family line of each partner. At this point the doctor's transition from the keeper to the revealer of secrets was complete.

Health certificates proved popular with doctors concerned about the effects of hereditary and contagious disease on France's future.[56] One of the most explicitly degenerationist takes on medical confidentiality came from the doctor Henry Cazalis in a wide-ranging medical treatise entitled *La science et le mariage*, published in 1900. Not only did the author suggest that all couples be required to submit to a medical exam before marriage, but he also argued that people with certain hereditary conditions should not be allowed to marry at all. Science forced society to adopt a "new morality" that must reflect new obligations to the species in light of the dangers of degeneration, he said. The point of marriage was to "continue the race," whereas sex outside of marriage represented egotism pure and simple.[57] Love, he claimed, was always about the conflict between passion and duty, but the new science—evolutionary science—introduced novel conflicts and questions. In this new scientific and moral universe, the doctor was like a general, sometimes forced to sacrifice the few in the name of the many.[58] Like Dupuy, who noted that the military already required proof of "the health and vigor of citizens," Cazalis likened the married couple to soldiers in battle.[59] He went on to argue that people afflicted with any of a number of illnesses (including syphilis, tuberculosis, and certain forms of mental alienation) should be forbidden to marry, that no one should marry without seeing documentation of their partner's clean bill of health, and that those who attempted to deceive their partners should face legal punishment. Cazalis admitted that it might appear counterproductive to limit births during a depopulation crisis, but he thought there was little point in increasing the birth rate only to have the resultant children end up in prisons and asylums.[60]

This sort of thinking subtly but persistently challenged cultural associations between health, virtue, and bourgeois class distinction that had been established earlier in the century. Although problems like vagrancy and crime were often cited as evidence of both social decline and individual pathology, French degeneration theorists considered the middle and upper classes just as susceptible to hereditary conditions as their less well-off counterparts. In fact, Cazalis advised wealthy families who exhibited degenerate traits to seek out poor, healthy spouses as a way to reinvigorate their declining stock.[61] He also criticized dowries, the necessity for which kept many a "healthy, charming, and beautiful young girl" from reproducing.[62] These attitudes clearly implied that the medical and sexual secrets of the upper classes were no more precious than those of the rest of French society, as Cazalis himself recognized.

He therefore proclaimed the arrival of a new morality and tried to position this bold stance within prevailing class-based notions of respectability—noting, at one point, that a health certificate was really not so different from a marriage agreement based on the word of two honorable men (the fiancé and his father-in-law to be).[63] But of course the health certificate was practically the opposite. Marriage decisions had long been made on the basis of trust between men, certainly among the upper and middle classes to which Cazalis and others writing about medical secrecy most often referred. To require a premarriage health certificate implied that a man's word was no longer enough when the fate of French society rested in the balance. Yet, despite expressing anxieties over the nation's future, French legislators never took up Cazalis's suggestion. Ultimately, degenerationists and their allies failed to change prevailing attitudes toward confidentiality within or outside the medical profession, indicating that many French were not yet prepared to sacrifice masculine honor in the name of national regeneration.

Considering the persistence with which degeneration theorists beat the drum of civilizational decline in the decades preceding the World War I, it should come as some surprise that their calls to change medical secrecy practices gained little traction. Significantly, even Cazalis, the most stridently degenerationist of the medical writers to address the topic of medical secrecy, insisted that the letter of the confidentiality law should remain unchanged. He argued that medical certificates should vouch for a person's personal and family health rather than list specific ailments. Furthermore, as noted above, the most prominent experts on medical secrecy remained dedicated to almost complete confidentiality long after the publication of Morel's treatise on degeneration, and lawmakers did not overturn Article 378.[64] Despite the deservedly central place of degeneration theory in the historiography of the early Third Republic, the late nineteenth-century history of medical secrecy suggests that its influence was both limited and contested. It is easy to perceive medical power as all-encompassing when it accommodated and buttressed the already pervasive cultural authority of bourgeois respectability. Medical power appears much more fragile when doctors' pronouncements came into conflict with this rival, time-worn arbiter of sexual morality.

Historian Laura Doan reminds us that medical conceptions of sexuality and sexual behavior have not always been embraced by the wider culture from which they emerged. Her readings of court cases from interwar Britain suggest instead that multiple frameworks structured how people thought and talked about sex, emphasizing the ways in which sexual and medical naivete (what she calls "unknowing" or "tactical silences") operated as a form of social protection for women whom we might now identify as lesbians but who did not self-identify as such at the time.[65] That juries tended to accept their own interpretations of events over those of expert medical witnesses suggests that historians cannot take the influence of medical ideology for granted outside of medical circles, and that the normal/deviant dichotomy is just one possible way of understanding past conceptions of sex and sexuality. As Doan explains, "On view in these provocative exchanges concerning female friendship, courtship, marriage, chastity, and perversion is a sexual landscape of rival regulatory systems otherwise known as 'norms,' each with the authority to police and arbitrate according to its own rules, and subject to any number of intersecting configurations of power, such as gender, class, and national identity."[66] Medicine constituted an important, but certainly not the only, such regulatory mechanism in both interwar Britain and late nineteenth-century France.

The culture of respectability and the law on medical confidentiality were mutually reinforcing regulatory frameworks throughout the nineteenth century, both of which primarily served the interests of elite married men. Advocates for medical confidentiality (not to mention proponents of active deception) took the sexual double standard for granted, allowing men to face few repercussions for infidelity because the medico-legal system shielded them from the public consequences of private indiscretions. In the medical literature on sexually transmitted infections, in particular, men's cheating comes across as both ubiquitous and almost completely free of social repercussions. Women, on the other hand, suffered the physical, emotional, and material effects of men's duplicity and discretion, contracting illnesses that caused great personal harm and marked them as damaged goods in the process (because of the possibility of contagion, but also because contracting such an ailment compromised a woman's sexual virtue).[67] The French bourgeoisie, as a class, kept up the appearance of respectability despite the obvious hypocrisy of it all. The collaboration of the medical profession proved indispensable to maintaining this class distinction, and doctors were rewarded with social influence, financial success, and public accolades for their efforts. To support the law on medical confidentiality was to preserve the status quo.

Conversely, to question the law on confidentiality was to threaten the entire edifice. As Sarah Horowitz shows in the following chapter, revealing secrets could prove hugely disruptive to the political and social hierarchies they supported. This is not to say that degeneration theorists were necessarily sexually progressive or feminist, given that they maintained an understanding of sexual activity that inextricably tied it to reproduction. Degenerationist thinking regularly expressed itself alongside natalism and exhibited a tendency to pathologize various "aberrant" sexual behaviors. These included sexual couplings that might lead to the reproduction of so-called degenerates or the transmission of disease; they also included the performance of particular sex acts (such as anything nonprocreative, but also sadism and masochism, which many Europeans in the late nineteenth century viewed as atavistic sexual throwbacks).[68] These writers nonetheless put themselves at odds with one of the most basic tenets of French medicine when they insisted that doctors stop covering up dirty little secrets and expose them instead, convinced that the threat posed by hereditary degeneration was so dire that halting its spread was worth biting the respectable, bourgeois hands that fed them. In so doing, they let their actions bring to the surface something that had been implicit since France's implementation of confidentiality regulations at the start of the nineteenth century. Sex did not merely influence debates within the medical profession but was central to the establishment of medicine's place in French society at every level: individual, family, class, and nation.

Notes

1. According to a title search of the catalog of the Bibliothèque Nationale de France, August 8, 2018.
2. On the many ways in which medicine reflected the sense of national emergency, see Robert A. Nye, *Crime, Madness, and Politics in Modern France: The Medical Concept of National Decline* (Princeton NJ: Princeton University Press, 1984).
3. On secrecy and the bourgeoisie, see Alain Corbin, "Backstage," in *A History of Private Life: From the Fires of Revolution to the Great War*, ed. Michelle Perot, trans. Arthur Goldhammer (Cambridge MA: Belknap, 1990), 451–668. Discussion of medical secrecy appears on 558–61.

4. See especially Foucault's brief discussion of the taboo placed on childhood masturbation and how it pertained to the expansion of medical authority in which doctors used "these tenuous pleasures as a prop, constituting them as secrets (that is, forcing them into hiding so as to make possible their discovery)." Michel Foucault, *The History of Sexuality*, vol. 1, *An Introduction*, trans. Robert Hurley (New York: Vintage, 1990), 38–42.

5. Jack D. Ellis, *The Physician-Legislators of France: Medicine and Politics in the Early Third Republic, 1870–1914* (Cambridge: Cambridge University Press, 1990).

6. Foucault, *The History of Sexuality*, 35. Emphasis in the original.

7. Raymond Villey, *Histoire du secret médical* (Paris: Seghers, 1986), 18, 42.

8. Robert A. Nye, "Médecins, éthique médicale et État en France 1789–1947," *Le mouvement social* 1, no. 214 (January–March 2006): 23.

9. For an overview of the extensive literature on bourgeois class distinction, see Sarah Maza, *The Myth of the French Bourgeoisie: An Essay on the Social Imaginary* (Cambridge MA: Harvard University Press, 2003).

10. Robert A. Nye, *Masculinity and Male Codes of Honor in Modern France* (Berkeley: University of California Press, 1993).

11. Jean-Guillaume Locré, *La législation civile, commercial, et criminelle de la France*, vol. 30 (Paris: Treuttel et Würtz, 1832), 491.

12. Locré, *La législation civile*, 494–95.

13. Villey, *Histoire du secret médical*, 65. On sex workers in particular, see Jill Harsin, *Policing Prostitution in Nineteenth-Century Paris* (Princeton NJ: Princeton University Press, 1985).

14. On the democratization of honor see Nye, *Masculinity and Male Codes of Honor*; and Andrea Mansker, *Sex, Honor, and Citizenship in Early Third Republic France* (Houndmills, UK: Palgrave Macmillan, 2011).

15. Amédée Dechambre, *Le médecin, devoirs privés et publics, leurs rapports avec la jurisprudence et l'organisation médicales* (Paris: G. Masson, 1883), 183.

16. Dechambre suggests this himself when discussing a woman with curvature of the spine. He did not want to alarm the patient, so he discussed the diagnosis and treatment with her husband instead. Dechambre, *Le médecin*, 179.

17. Jill Harsin, "Syphilis, Wives, and Physicians: Medical Ethics and the Family in Late Nineteenth-Century France," *French Historical Studies* 16, no. 1 (Spring 1989): 80. Harsin perceptively notes that this injunction allowed doctors to sidestep messy family situations without discouraging men from seeking treatment.

18. Paul Diday, *Le péril vénérien dans les familles* (Paris: Asselin et Cie., Libraires de la Faculté de Médecine, 1881), 35.

19. Diday, *Le péril vénérien*, ix. Emphasis in the original.

20. Diday, *Le péril vénérien*, ix.

21. Diday, *Le péril vénérien*, 35.

22. Diday, *Le péril vénérien*, 36.

23. Dechambre, *Le médecin*, 52.

24. Dechambre, *Le médecin*, 164.

25. Dechambre, *Le médecin*, 62.

26. Dechambre, *Le médecin*, 164.

27. Dechambre, *Le médecin*, 52.

28. See Joan Sherwood, *Infection of the Innocents: Wet Nurses, Infants, and Syphilis in France, 1780–1900* (Montreal: McGill-Queen's University Press, 2010).

29. P. Brouardel, *Le secret médical* (Paris: J.-B. Baillière, 1887), 47.

30. Diday, *Le péril vénérien*, 153.

31. Diday, *Le péril vénérien*, 213.

32. Diday, *Le péril vénérien*, 265–68.

33. Diday, *Le péril vénérien*, 277–78.

34. Brouardel, *Le secret médical*, 50.

35. Pierre-Charles-Egide Favreau, *Contribution à l'étude du secret professionnel en médicine mentale* (Paris: A. Delahaye et Lecrosnier, 1888), 10.

36. Favreau, *Du secret professionnel*, 32.

37. The French generally subscribed to a more positive approach to eugenics than their counterparts in England, Germany, and the United States. As Robert A. Nye argues, however, degeneration theory heavily influenced French plans for social and hygienic reform. See Nye, *Crime, Madness, and Politics in Modern France*, esp. chap. 5. For an example of a doctor who considered the sterilization of mental patients, see Casimir Pinel's discussion of medical secrets discussed later in this chapter: Pinel, "Du secret médical dans ses rapports avec l'aliénation, notamment au sujet du mariage," *Annales Médico-Psychologiques*, no. 2 (1863): 216–238.

38. Daniel Pick, *Faces of Degeneration: A European Disorder, c. 1848–c. 1918* (Cambridge: Cambridge University Press, 1989), 50–51.

39. In addition to Nye, see Elinor Accampo, Rachel Ginnis Fuchs, and Mary Lynn Stewart, eds., *Gender and the Politics of Social Reform in France, 1870–1914* (Baltimore: Johns Hopkins University Press, 1995), esp. chap. 1.

40. See Karen Offen, "Depopulation, Nationalism, and Feminism in Fin-de-Siècle France," *American Historical Review* 89, no. 3 (June 1984): 648–76. Joshua Cole makes a similar point: Cole, *The Power of Large Numbers: Population, Politics, and Gender in Nineteenth-Century France* (Ithaca NY: Cornell University Press, 2000), 4.

41. Cole, *The Power of Large Numbers*, esp. introduction and chap. 6.

42. Robert Castel notes that approximately 20 percent of patients in 1853 were placed in asylums "voluntarily" (i.e., by relatives), whereas 80 percent were

institutionalized by the state. That said, relatives and doctors often brought such cases to the attention of the prefect in order to have the state subsidize the cost of institutionalization. Castel, *The Regulation of Madness: The Origins of Incarceration in France*, trans. W. D. Halls (Berkeley: University of California Press, 1988), 196–97.

43. C. Pinel, "Du secret médical," 221.
44. C. Pinel, "Du secret médical," 222.
45. C. Pinel, "Du secret médical," 233.
46. C. Pinel, "Du secret médical," 223.
47. C. Pinel, "Du secret médical," 224.
48. Dr. Harris [G. Harris], *Nouveau guide médicale du mariage*, eleventh ed. (Paris: Office de librairie, 1886), 41.
49. On masculine honor and the professions, see William M. Reddy, *The Invisible Code: Honor and Sentiment in Postrevolutionary France, 1814–1848* (Berkeley: University of California Press, 1997), esp. intro.
50. C. Pinel, "Du secret médical," 222.
51. J. Th. Dupuy, *Le dogme du secret médical (essai de réfutation), étude de médicine légale d'hygiène sociale et de morale professionnelle* (Paris: Société d'éditions scientifiques et littéraires, 1903), 123.
52. Dupuy, *Le dogme du secret médical*, 124.
53. Dupuy, *Le dogme du secret médical*, 126.
54. Dupuy, *Le dogme du secret médical*, 81.
55. Dupuy, *Le dogme du secret médical*, 88.
56. In a different context, neoregulationist reforms in late nineteenth-century Paris involved implementing a health certificate system for sex workers. See Harsin, *Policing Prostitution*, 343.
57. Henry Cazalis, *La science et le mariage, étude médicale* (Paris: Octave Doin, 1900), 3–4.
58. Cazalis, *La science et le mariage*, 6.
59. Dupuy, *Le dogme du secret médical*, 124.
60. Cazalis, *La science et le mariage*, 137.
61. Cazalis, *La science et le mariage*, 146.
62. Cazalis, *La science et le mariage*, 169.
63. Cazalis, *La science et le mariage*, 177.
64. Only in 1892 were epidemic diseases added to the list of ailments that a doctor must legally reveal to the public. In 1902 tuberculosis was added as well, but sexually transmitted infections and hereditary diseases were not. Doctors and lawyers were still debating the issue, particularly the issuance of health certificates to warn against marrying a partner with a sexually transmitted infection,

in the 1920s and 1930s. See Georges Jacomet, *Le secret médical* (Paris: G. Doin & Cie., 1933).

65. Laura Doan, *Disturbing Practices: History, Sexuality, and Women's Experience of Modern War* (Chicago: University of Chicago Press, 2013), 188.

66. Doan, *Disturbing Practices*, 166.

67. Marriage was supposedly a "desperate hope" among unmarried or widowed women with syphilis. Diday, *Le péril vénérien*, 346.

68. See Alison M. Moore, *Sexual Myths of Modernity: Sadism, Masochism, and Historical Teleology* (London: Lexington, 2015).

Suggested Reading

Cole, Joshua. *The Power of Large Numbers: Population, Politics, and Gender in Nineteenth-Century France*. Ithaca NY: Cornell University Press, 2000.

Corbin, Alain. "Backstage." In *A History of Private Life: From the Fires of Revolution to the Great War*, edited by Michelle Perot, translated by Arthur Goldhammer, 451–668. Cambridge MA: Belknap, 1990.

Doan, Laura. *Disturbing Practices: History, Sexuality, and Women's Experience of Modern War*. Chicago: University of Chicago Press, 2013.

Harsin, Jill. "Syphilis, Wives, and Physicians: Medical Ethics and the Family in Late Nineteenth-Century France." *French Historical Studies* 16, no. 1 (Spring 1989): 72–95.

Hewitt, Jessie. *Institutionalizing Gender: Madness, the Family, and Psychiatric Power in Nineteenth-Century France*. Ithaca NY: Cornell University Press, 2020.

Maza, Sarah. *The Myth of the French Bourgeoisie: An Essay on the Social Imaginary*. Cambridge MA: Harvard University Press, 2003.

Moore, Alison M. *Sexual Myths of Modernity: Sadism, Masochism, and Historical Teleology*. London: Lexington, 2015.

Nye, Robert A. *Crime, Madness, and Politics in Modern France: The Medical Concept of National Decline*. Princeton NJ: Princeton University Press, 1984.

———. *Masculinity and Male Codes of Honor in Modern France*. Berkeley: University of California Press, 1993.

Sherwood, Joan. *Infection of the Innocents: Wet Nurses, Infants, and Syphilis in France, 1780–1900*. Montreal: McGill-Queen's University Press, 2010.

Villey, Raymond. *Histoire du secret médical*. Paris: Seghers, 1986.

7

SEX, SCANDAL, AND POWER IN THE STEINHEIL AFFAIR OF 1908–1909

SARAH HOROWITZ

The French often claim not to regard politicians' sex lives as a matter for public consumption as Americans do. As a result, French politicians have typically had considerable latitude to explore extramarital relations without much scrutiny, at least compared to their counterparts in the United States. This has not always been the case, however. In the 1780s and 1840s scandals revolving around monarchical and aristocratic sexual license discredited the ruling elite and fueled revolutions.[1] During the Third Republic (1870–1940) extramarital relationships of political figures could also provoke outrage. Indeed, in 1899 President Félix Faure had a stroke during an assignation with his mistress in the Élysée Palace, the French equivalent of the White House, and died a few hours later. Though initially kept under wraps, this moment in French sexual history became public almost ten years later when Faure's mistress, Marguerite Steinheil, was accused of double murder. This scandal revealed a whole host of misdeeds at the highest level of the French government, including state-funded prostitution and financial and judicial corruption, and led to extensive debates about the failings of the Third Republic and the men in charge of it.

This case became a full-blown *affair* when the press started using it to critique the self-representation of government officials and their elite social milieu as being fit for power on the basis of their restraint, including in sexual matters. For many, the Steinheil affair proved that the Third Republic replicated the worst excesses of the Old Regime. In the eighteenth century pamphlets attacking the monarchy suggested that sex allowed women to have power over men and collapsed the hierarchies of status that were necessary to good governance.[2] Similar concerns were also present in the Third Republic. In particular, journalists used the Steinheil affair to decry the fact that the men governing France valued their sex lives more than their commitments to the republic's fundamental principles of democracy, transparency, and equality under the law.

The Steinheil affair represents a rare moment in the history of the Third Republic, because it was a sex scandal that was also a political one. Other sex scandals monopolized headlines for a period, including the Caillaux affair and the Pranzini affair. Yet, these scandals often reaffirmed ideas about gender and race—and therefore who should have power in France.[3] At the same time, the government was beset by near-constant political scandals, including ones centering on allegations that officials and politicians engaged in espionage or financial corruption.[4] Like other sex scandals, the Steinheil affair offered a lurid spectacle of sexual misbehavior, but it unfolded more like the political scandals of the era by unsettling power relations as opposed to shoring them up. In particular, observers used the Steinheil affair to paint powerful officials and the Parisian elite more generally as immoral, corrupt, and hypocritical—and therefore undeserving of political authority. Because the Steinheil affair was a moment when concerns about sex came together with ones about politics, it can help us understand the political meanings of extramarital sex and how anxieties present in the latter half of the eighteenth century resonated in the Belle Époque.

One of the central differences between the Old Regime and the Third Republic was the role of publicity. There was nothing secret about the fact that kings took mistresses in the eighteenth century. The problem was not sex but that the king and many aristocrats were thought to put sexual pleasure above duty. That a monarch could openly take mistresses allowed him to occlude his government's lack of transparency. In theory, the Third Republic solved both of these problems, as the government was supposed to be accessible, transparent, and responsive to the needs of the people, as opposed to the whims of politicians and their mistresses. The men governing France were also supposed to be committed to duty, reason, and the principles of liberty and equality, not pleasure.[5] Moreover, women were not supposed to have any official role in political life, as they were excluded from voting or holding office. One guardrail was publicity; in the

Belle Époque, the press saw itself as having a duty to hold the powerful accountable for their actions.[6]

Under the glare of the press, politicians and officials were at pains to show that they were self-disciplined and adhered to the codes of respectability. In theory, this meant that they exclusively engaged in heterosexual, procreative, and marital sex, and acted with a sense of decorum and restraint, in both public and private. These codes were in many ways class based. Powerful officials and politicians tended to come from wealth and the bourgeoisie defined itself in part through a commitment to propriety.[7]

In practice, though, things were more complicated. The Belle Époque was also an era when Parisian high society—the world to which many politicians and high officials belonged—increasingly tolerated heterosexual affairs among both men and women, as long as these individuals kept them private.[8] The extramarital liaisons of powerful men thus often had the status of open secrets, guarded by journalists and the politicians themselves. As a result, only insiders had access to the truth about the elite's sexual behavior. Many also assumed that politicians' mistresses had considerable political influence behind the scenes.[9]

In the Steinheil affair, this world of open secrets spilled out into public view. It revealed the dirty laundry of both politicians and officials and gave newspaper readers the sense that they were getting a peek into a realm that was otherwise off limits to them, one held together by power, sex, and lies. In this context sexual misbehavior was thought to be central to the operation of political power. The Steinheil affair shows how a sex scandal could democratize knowledge and create the transparency that was supposed to be the foundation of the republic.

Centering sex in the political history of the early Third Republic highlights how illicit sexuality was not a private matter but was fundamental to political debate. Moreover, it reveals how the state was more like the Old Regime than it claimed to be. Women still had sway over governmental decisions and sex shored up social inequality by providing supposedly immoral and manipulative women with access to the halls of power. As in an earlier era, the presumed sexual power women held over men was thought to introduce political corruption into a realm that was supposed to be rational and transparent. Further, the scandal revealed a seam of sexual license within Parisian high society that contrasted with elites' claims to respectability. Thus, for critics of the government on the left and the right, the Steinheil affair proved that politicians and officials could not be trusted to tell the truth. Sex revealed that the Third Republic was not living up to its promises and that the seemingly respectable men in power could not be relied on to govern in the people's interests or respect the regime's egalitarian principles. And yet, this scandal seemed to bring the republic closer to its values by democratizing forms of sexual knowledge that were typically held by elites. This tension at the heart of the political history of the Third Republic only becomes clear through attention to the role of sex in the emergence of—and the weaknesses within—democratic governance.

Status and Scandal in the Life of Mme Steinheil

The woman at the center of the Steinheil affair was the wife of the mediocre Parisian painter Adolphe Steinheil.[10] Their marriage had always been unhappy and the two often considered divorcing. They stayed married, however, partly because divorce was seen as scandalous at the time. It would have required airing the household's secrets, something that bourgeois families sought to avoid at all costs.[11] From its inception their marriage was devoted to the preservation of the family's reputation.

Beginning in the mid-1890s, Mme Steinheil began a series of extramarital liaisons with wealthy men who gave her money and helped her enter into their milieu. Her clients included politicians, high state officials (particularly among the judiciary), and industrialists. As Mme Steinheil rose in high society, she entered a world of deep contradictions. Although France was a republic based on universal manhood suffrage, vestiges of an older, hierarchical order remained intact. Politicians and the men who occupied the upper reaches of France's powerful civil service tended to come from wealth. Ties of family, friendship, and education knit them to prominent industrialists, and the Parisian social and political elite were closely interlinked.[12]

This elite had complicated attitudes toward sex. The bourgeoisie regarded themselves as moral and the poor as sexually profligate.[13] Publicly demonstrating a commitment to duty and sobriety allowed the rich to justify holding so much power in a regime that was nominally democratic. But the wealthy gave themselves increasing freedom to pursue sex outside of marriage in the Belle Époque as long as they did so with a modicum of discretion. Not being too flagrant about flouting the rules was a sign of courtesy to one's family and one's station.[14] Publicity divided the respectable from the disreputable and elites had the press's assistance in maintaining this code of silence.[15] Journalists were often hesitant to reveal information about the personal lives of politicians and high state officials.[16]

These norms of discretion structured Mme Steinheil's sex work. To explain her absences from her house during her assignations and her earnings, she first told her family that she was visiting a mysterious "Aunt Lily."[17] Once her husband realized the truth, he agreed to facilitate her transactional sexual affairs. Clients bought paintings from her husband, after which she made herself available for sex. By having her clients pay for art, as opposed to sex, she could claim that she did not engage in sex work, but merely had affairs with some of her friends who happened to buy her husband's art.[18] She also used gossip to market herself, a practice that kept knowledge of her sex work within the bounds of high society.[19] Mme Steinheil thus relied on the broad agreement among her class that breaking the rules of sexual decorum, at least privately, was less of a problem than doing so openly. In this atmosphere knowing the truth about extramarital affairs was a sign of status. It meant you had access to the circuits of society gossip that provided a more accurate depiction of reality than the façade of bourgeois propriety.[20]

In 1897 Mme Steinheil began an affair with Faure. The affair revealed how she used sex to maintain her position and how sex could corrupt the principles of good governance. Mme Steinheil benefited financially from the liaison when Faure arranged to have the government pay a vast sum for one of Adolphe Steinheil's paintings.[21] The president also helped her family members who were in the civil service. Her husband's brother-in-law went from being an obscure judge to chief of staff to the minister of justice.[22] Faure helped her brother, an employee of the Ministry of Finances, to get an advantageous transfer.[23] Other civil servants found that approaching Mme Steinheil sped their promotions.[24] It was a system built on insider access. To get a promotion, a civil servant would have to be well connected enough to know that Mme Steinheil was having an affair with Faure and that appealing to her was the easiest way to preferment. He would also need to be able to obtain an invitation to call on her.

Their relationship ended on February 16, 1899, when, according to legend, Faure had a fatal stroke while Mme Steinheil was fellating him.[25] Faure's death had a profound impact on French politics. The nation was in the midst of the Dreyfus Affair, an espionage scandal that centered on Alfred Dreyfus, a Jewish army officer wrongly convicted of spying. The affair polarized the nation. Dreyfus's partisans included republicans and socialists, whereas the ranks of anti-Dreyfusards, as they came to be known, were made up of antisemitic nationalists and monarchists. Faure was aligned with anti-Dreyfusards and refused to reopen Dreyfus's legal case.[26] Faure's successor reversed this decision and eventually pardoned Dreyfus. The president's death was thus a major blow to anti-Dreyfusards, some of whom were convinced that their opponents had assassinated Faure.[27]

Although Mme Steinheil's role in Faure's death circulated as gossip within elite circles, few newspapers reported on it. The official narrative contained no mention of Mme Steinheil. Rather, Faure "suddenly found himself feeling ill" and then died "after three hours of suffering," "after having made the most touching goodbyes to his wife, two children, and those around him."[28] This account promoted Faure's image as a devoted head of household, avoided embarrassing his family or compromising the dignity of the presidency, and protected Mme Steinheil's reputation.

Significantly, an anarchist newspaper, *Le Journal du Peuple*, came closest to revealing how Faure had actually died. As a journal for and by those who supported dismantling France's political and social structure, it had no investment in maintaining a system that protected the powerful. It also used the conservative Faure's death to score political points against the regime and the bourgeoisie the president was seen to represent. Thus, a journalist wrote that Faure "died because he sacrificed too much to Venus" and that "the young person who enjoyed [*jouissait*] . . . presidential favors" was a "Mme. S." "Jouissait" meant both "enjoyed" and "orgasmed," and the ellipses, which were present in the original, made sure that no one missed the pun. In this journalist's mind, Faure embodied the hypocrisy of the bourgeoisie, who preached the value of a sexual restraint they did not practice: "Bourgeois . . . admit that your principles do not conform to your practice . . . that Love . . . must be free, liberated, unfettered from your Ethics of Slavery and Lies." The author urged readers to "scrutinize the life of the . . . highest magistrate in France. And judge!"[29] In an atmosphere where secrecy about sex helped the rich maintain power, revealing secrets could call into question both the elites' values and their claims to be moral exemplars.

On May 31, 1908, Mme Steinheil returned to the limelight when her husband and mother were found dead of apparent strangulation in their house in Paris. Mme Steinheil, who had been tied to the bed, was the sole survivor. Over the next six months, she told a series of shifting and outlandish tales about what she had seen on the night of the crime. She first blamed four strangers who had broken into the house with the intention of robbing it. They had killed her husband and mother but spared her, thinking she was the couple's adolescent daughter. Her story never made any sense; there were no signs struggle on her body or her mother's corpse, and only the faintest on her husband's. There were valuables left in plain sight and many rooms in the house were untouched. The details of the crime scene led many journalists and members of the public to believe that the murderer was either Mme Steinheil or one of her powerful clients.[30]

Despite the cloud of suspicion that hung over Mme Steinheil, journalists showed a great deal of reticence in discussing her liaisons. In the initial press coverage of the double murders, she was often described as a hostess who received many prominent officials and politicians. Newspapers listed the powerful men who posed for a portrait by her husband, but a reader would have to have been aware of the rumors that flowed through Parisian society to know that this was also a list of Mme Steinheil's clients.[31] Journalists were typically silent about her relationship with Faure. For instance, in its first article on the double murder, *Le Figaro* noted that Adolphe Steinheil and Faure had been friends and that "M. Steinheil became well-known at the Élysée Palace, where his wife was also received," as if Mme Steinheil had barely known Faure.[32] The press was happy to drop hints for those who were already in the know, but it was not going to reveal her transgressions, lest anyone outside the circles of gossip acquire this knowledge.

The authorities also sought to protect Mme Steinheil's reputation and insisted that she was innocent and had nothing to do with the crime. It helped that the lead investigator into the affair, an examining magistrate named Joseph Leydet, was an admirer and possibly a client. In addition, Octave Hamard, the chief of the Parisian detective brigade, was rumored to be close to another one of Mme Steinheil's wealthy long-term clients.[33] Leydet and Hamard repeatedly told journalists that the murder was most certainly the work of common criminals.[34] After a few weeks in the headlines, the case faded from view.

Nevertheless, Mme Steinheil still felt the need to clear her name. Rumors of her involvement in the crime threatened her standing in the elite. One of her clients told her that he would not resume their relationship until the perpetrators had been found. Her high-society friends shunned her after the murders because of her disrepute.[35] In November 1908 she planted evidence on her valet and had him arrested. After her deception was discovered, she then blamed her cook's son. He, too, was arrested, despite his rock-solid alibi. Mme Steinheil, in blaming a series of working-class and poor individuals, attempted to shift scrutiny away from herself and shore up a vision of society where crime and violence came from outside of bourgeois society.[36]

On November 26, 1908, after a series of dramatic courthouse confrontations covered by reporters, Leydet decided he had no choice but to arrest Mme Steinheil and send her to Saint-Lazare, the Paris women's prison. Having placed her in a prison that housed common prostitutes, he then resigned his position as the chief investigator of the murders. Mme Steinheil's faith that her class would protect her floundered in the face of the publicity she generated. Ultimately, she lost her class privilege not necessarily because she was involved in the murders, but because she had attracted so much attention with her blatant lies that she dissolved the privacy on which her status depended.

At this point, the case was monopolizing the headlines. Many members of the public were furious that the police and the judiciary—two realms of officialdom from which she was rumored to have drawn many of her clients and which were charged with upholding moral order—had gone to such great lengths to shield Mme Steinheil's reputation and indulge her lies.[37] To manage this crisis, the judiciary appointed an examining magistrate, who was far more hostile to Mme Steinheil than previous officials had been and who presumed she was the murderer. One year later, in November 1909, Mme Steinheil was tried for the murders of her husband and mother. She was acquitted and then moved to London to escape the press attention.

In 1917 she married a British lord. She died in 1954 without ever having revealed who had killed her mother and husband.

Mme Steinheil's life from her marriage to her arrest provides significant insight into the relationship between status, misbehavior, and privacy in the Belle Époque. Elites worked hard to maintain their reputations for moral rectitude, but the appearance was more important than the reality. After all, Mme Steinheil had been accepted into high society, despite the fact that many knew full well that she was having sex for money.[38] Her case also shows the many resources—from journalistic norms to personal connections—that elites could call on to keep their secrets. Mme Steinheil's ability to stay under the radar unraveled after the murders. Her increasingly reckless actions to clear her name backfired and resulted in her arrest. Evidently, she was willing to go to great lengths to salvage her reputation in order to resume her life of discreet rule-breaking in high society.

The unraveling of the affair illuminates the weakness of democracy in the Third Republic. Mme Steinheil's patronage power is one instance of how the government relied on secrecy and insider access, as it had during the Old Regime. The press was supposed to ensure that the state acted with transparency but, when it came to sexual matters at least, it failed to do so and protected the powerful rather than hold them accountable.

Seeing the Reality of Sex

Once Mme Steinheil was arrested and thrown into prison, she lost her status as a member of an elite. The Parisian women's prison of Saint-Lazare was a place for criminals and prostitutes, both seen as outside bourgeois society.[39] In this environment she was no longer accorded the privileges of privacy. For example, *Le Matin* wrote that Mme Steinheil was a "fallen socialite, thrown into the dreadful jail of thieves and prostitutes" and recounted that it must have been humiliating for "a woman with such pride and who used to have great power" to have been strip searched, as were all inmates of Saint-Lazare.[40]

Now that the state was treating her as a woman of the working class, the press could too, and thus could spill her secrets. In the wake of her arrest, the case became a full-blown "scandal"—that is, a moment when an individual or an institution's transgressions become public.[41] The affair was front-page news in many of the major Parisian dailies for weeks. This case was almost tailor-made for the era's mass press, which thrived on tales of crime, celebrity, extraordinary true events, and beautiful, if morally dubious, women.[42] It was a highly competitive media environment, with seventy-nine dailies in Paris, including four mass-circulation newspapers (*Le Journal, Le Matin, Le Petit Journal,* and *Le Petit Parisien*), all of which claimed to be politically neutral. Others had distinct ideological bents; there were newspapers for socialists, centrists, conservatives, and right-wing nationalists.[43] Undoubtedly, coverage of the latest twists in the Steinheil affair helped many a newspaper's bottom line, and the scandal was a moment when the press's moral imperative to tell the truth about the state and its capitalist imperative to make money converged.[44]

Journalists could now write about what they had known for years, and they published detailed information about Mme Steinheil's sexual affairs. As they did so, some papers, especially those in the right-wing press, explicitly questioned prevailing journalistic norms that not only protected certain people but, by implication, the government as a whole. These papers were quite ready to point out the hypocrisy of the leaders of the Third Republic by puncturing the privacy of elites. The right-wing paper *L'Action française* even explicitly appealed to readers with a headline that screamed, "No more initials: names!" It was a way to indicate that the newspaper was no longer engaging in the journalistic practice of referring to elites by their initials when discussing their private lives. As promised, the newspaper then listed some of Mme Steinheil's clients, including judges, a senator, a member of the Chamber of Deputies, industrialists, and a man in the upper reaches of the Parisian police.[45]

Other newspapers returned to Mme Steinheil's relationship with Faure. They stated that she had accompanied him to his hometown of Le Havre for his summer vacation, that the two had planned to visit her family's home in eastern France together, and that the president had used "certain medicines" (i.e., aphrodisiacs) in the course of their affair.[46] Mme Steinheil's political influence during her relationship with Faure also came to light in both the right-wing, antirepublican press and the mass-circulation dailies that claimed to be politically neutral. One right-wing newspaper recounted that during their liaison, Mme Steinheil became "the great distributor of presidential favors … officials in every part of the government and of every rank assiduously paid her court."[47] Sex was no long a private indiscretion but a question of public corruption.

Some of this coverage was so detailed as to be graphic. The nationalist daily *L'Intransigeant* reported that after Faure had a stroke, Mme Steinheil was "wrapped in a guard's coat, her chest bare under her open corset" by Faure's aides, who then ushered her into a car outside the Élysée Palace. Once she got into the car, she gave the coat back. In other words, she was driven through the streets of Paris in a state of undress. Back at the Élysée, no one could "finish re-dressing the president" because "cantharidin continued its effects even in his death throes." Faure was thought to have been taking this substance, also known as Spanish fly, as an aphrodisiac, and the newspaper intimated that his erection endured after his last sexual encounter. *L'Intransigeant* also reported, "*The president had strands of a woman's hair in his hand. . . . It is certain that, in the first spasm of the congestion* [i.e., the stroke], *the presidential hand contracted in Mme Steinheil's hair.*"[48] Although the author avoided explicitly saying that Mme Steinheil had been fellating Faure, this description made it clear to all but the most unimaginative reader what the two had been doing.

All this reporting on Mme Steinheil's life gave rise to a rich culture of jokes, songs, and illustrations, which often revolved around the difference between the official, respectable version of events and the true, sexual one. Breaking the taboo against revealing private indiscretions in the press thus gave rise to a popular culture of the affair in which anyone could participate and helped democratize political knowledge. Many jokes played with homonyms of the word *pomper* (to fellate). One politician quipped of Faure, "Voulait être César, il ne fut que Pompée" (He wanted to be Caesar, but was only Pompey). The superficial meaning was that Faure wanted to be a Julius Caesar–like figure but was more like Caesar's rival Pompey, who failed in his quest for power. But the other reading was that Faure wanted to be Caesar but was only fellated.[49] The ability to unpack this joke would have required a knowledge of Roman history and its appeal might have been limited to those who were relatively well educated.

Other works capable of reaching a broader audience also revolved around the gap between the elite's claims about their morality and the reality of their lives. For instance, the song "Les Mémoires de Madame Steinheil," which might have been sung in a dive bar or on the streets of Paris and which, as an oral means of communication, would have been accessible to those who were not literate, uses its structure to convey the difference between the respectable myth and the salacious truth. The former lies in the verses and the latter in the nonrepeating refrains, which are filled with references to sex. In one refrain the subject, who is supposedly Mme Steinheil, describes her salon: "I even frequently received / Very influential members"—members here meaning "individuals" (such as members of the Chamber of Deputies) but also, in the slang of the time, "penises." In the next verse, Mme Steinheil claims she was so innocent that she did not even know of what she had been accused. Yet in the refrain, she sings, "I was acquitted, it is logical / I don't need to explain it to you." The suggestion is that the influential members were responsible for her acquittal.[50] The entire song was a way to show the gap between the official narrative and the underlying truth. It also suggested that all elites were oversexed; the reference to "influential members" indicates that lust defined all powerful men.

Jokes about Mme Steinheil having sex with prominent officials could be found in newspapers across the political spectrum. The right-wing press published puns on fellatio that suggested Mme Steinheil had been having sex with Leydet, the first examining magistrate of the case.[51] In January 1909 the anarchist satirical magazine L'Assiette au beurre devoted an entire issue to the figure of "Tante Lily" (or "Aunt Lily"), suggesting that desire and deception pervaded high society. "Aunt Lily" was the generous relative whom Mme Steinheil had invented to shield her family from learning about her assignations. The images in the issue all depict figures with an "Aunt Lily," such as a husband asking his wife if her "Aunt Lily" left the bite marks on her shoulder. As a whole, they imply that lies about sex and exchanges of sex for money are common among the elite. In one image set in a courtroom (see figure 2), the witness at a trial (who is obviously a man of wealth), the prosecutor (the man on the left), and the presiding judge (the bald man in the center) all realize that they know each other from "Aunt Lily's place." Each of the three has a bemused smile on his face, and the judge and prosecutor slouch toward the witness, indicating an attitude of informality and even warmth toward him. As these men realized that they share a mistress and are in on the same secret, what should have been a formal procedure takes on a distinct air of clubbiness. This issue of the magazine implied that Mme Steinheil and her clients were just one of the many nodes of elite life drawn together by exchanges of money for sex, and that in this milieu, being an insider meant knowing the seamy truth. Ironically, in making this argument, the anarchist journal found itself in agreement with the right-wing press.

None of the journalists who covered the Steinheil affair expressed astonishment that politicians were having affairs and only mild surprise that elite women were engaging in sex work.[52] Indeed, this scandal had many literary precedents in shedding light on the elite's underbelly. For example, Émile Zola's *Nana* (1880) centered on the sexualized atmosphere of Parisian elite life and Octave Mirbeau's *Diary of a Chambermaid* (1900) described the many moral failings of the bourgeoisie. Yet, unlike these literary depictions, the Steinheil affair was rooted in specificity and revealed the transgressions of real individuals. Ultimately, there was a difference between knowing in general that elites were oversexed and knowing precisely which politicians and officials were. In this respect, the scandal gave the public a sense that they were getting unmediated access to the truth. Far more than any novel, the Steinheil affair democratized knowledge by letting the public in on secrets that had previously been only accessible to insiders.

The popular culture of the affair thus took sex as the hidden reality of power, the force that drove politicians' and officials' actions and bound high society together. And although there was plenty of comedy in pointing out the gap between the façade of propriety and the truth that it concealed, there was a critique of the government and the elite within it. If the truth was rarely visible, this meant that politicians and officials could not be trusted and that ordinary citizens were fundamentally alienated from the regime because they were denied knowledge about the real stuff of politics—that is to say, sex. Moreover, bourgeois codes of privacy became a political problem in the Steinheil affair. Because the social elite was so closely linked to the political elite, sexual secrets were also political secrets and they blocked the public from knowing the truth. Politicians and officials, it would seem, were more committed to pursuing sex and maintaining their reputations than to acting with honesty and transparency.

Le procureur. — Premier témoin, Monsieur Dupont... Mais nous nous sommes déjà rencontrés...
Le témoin. — En effet... il me semble...
Le président. — Chez tante Lily !

FIG. 2. A courtroom scene where all participants realize they know each other from "Aunt Lily's." *L'Assiette au beurre*, January 23, 1909, 696. Courtesy gallica.bnf.fr /Bibliothèque Nationale de France.

In this atmosphere a scandal was democratizing. It broadened knowledge of how decisions were made and what politicians and officials were like behind closed doors, promising the public access to the truth that was usually off-limits to them. A scandal could ensure that the state's actions were transparent when the government would not.

The Scandal of Politics

The Steinheil affair also became bound up in struggles over the legitimacy of the regime. On the left and the right, journalists and politicians expressed a populist outrage that the government and the elite were hypocritical and self-dealing. Sex weakened democratic norms as Mme Steinheil's life exposed the degree to which the Third Republic was mired in patterns of financial and sexual corruption that recalled the monarchy of the Old Regime.

The Steinheil affair gained particular traction among right-wing nationalists. For almost a decade they had maintained that Dreyfusards had assassinated Faure. In 1908 and 1909 they were convinced that Mme Steinheil had been involved in Faure's death and that the murders of her husband and mother were somehow connected to this earlier crime.[53] Day after day, they crafted increasingly elaborate versions of this narrative and claimed that the ghastly truth would soon be revealed.[54] Alongside spewing baseless conspiracy theories, nationalists also expressed horror at the sexual license of the men running France. The antisemitic journalist Édouard Drumont decried "this Bourgeoisie which took power by endlessly speaking about establishing probity and virtue in politics" but that "stunned France by the cynicism and enormity of its scandals." He took Mme Steinheil for "the incarnation, the personification of this Republic" because the government, like her, was "vicious, venal and greedy, wearing elegant clothes and exhaling . . . the odor of debauchery and deprivation."[55] This explicit political critique relied on notions prevalent in the popular culture about the Steinheil affair in which Mme Steinheil became a synecdoche for the regime and a way to suggest that the elite's efforts to project an appearance of propriety concealed a profound immorality. For Drumont, the Third Republic was illegitimate in part because of the sexual hypocrisy of those who ran it. Better, perhaps, to return to monarchy, in which leaders were more honest.

Similar claims could be heard on the left. The author of an opinion piece in the socialist newspaper *Le Radical* described the house in the Parisian suburbs where Mme Steinheil entertained her clients as a place where "only the people of high society, official defenders of family, religion, morality and property, could enter."[56] This article echoed Drumont's claim that Mme Steinheil and her milieu were representative of a licentious elite and proof of the bourgeoisie's hypocrisy and sexual debauchery. Likewise, a union for domestic servants sought to use the Steinheil affair to start an inquiry into the "life of corruption and crime among the bourgeoisie in general."[57] As working-class individuals laboring among the rich, servants knew the details of the reality that could hide behind the façade of bourgeois respectability. Because so many people were paying attention to the misconduct of elites in the context of the Steinheil affair, members of the union saw a chance to use their knowledge in order to bring down the entire social hierarchy. Unlike Drumont's critique, that of the left implied the need for a new social and political order altogether. The bourgeoisie had used the supposedly immoral lifestyle of the poor to justify their monopoly on power, but in fact they were the ones who needed to behave better.

This was the flip side of a system in which the wealthy kept their behavior hidden in order to maintain their status; revelations could call their power into question. Nationalists and socialists were united in their populism, which led them to attack the hypocrisy of the bourgeoisie for preaching the importance of a sexual restraint it did not necessarily practice. Yet the critiques on the left and the right differed in key ways. Drumont was appalled at what he saw as the loose sexual morals of the Belle Époque.[58] In contrast, many socialists were more bothered by the lies and wanted sex to be unconstrained by norms of bourgeois propriety.[59]

Left and right also attacked the judiciary's unwillingness to consider Mme Steinheil a suspect in the months after the murders, a refusal that they understood as a failure of democratic values. For instance, the conservative politician Georges Berry held that Mme Steinheil's treatment was a violation of the principle that "for the judge in a Republic, there [was] no rich or poor, no powerful or lowly."[60] On the left, Raymond Figeac wrote, "'The . . . edifying death of a famous man protects her,' they say. 'She gets along well, too well with the judges they say again. . . . And it seems that this is true. It follows from this that, once again, the law is not equal for all. Hard on the little people and the weak, it has only kindness for those gentlemen and especially for the ladies 'of society.'" As evidence, he cited the fact that "Rémy Couillard [the valet] and Wolf [the cook's son] were arrested on simple suspicion, and the judiciary spent six months *not* arresting Mme Steinheil!"[61] In many respects, historians concur with Couillard's judgments. The justice system was often harsh toward the poor.[62] At the same time, many women were acquitted of violent crimes on the grounds of insanity. This legal defense was based on the idea that women were inherently psychologically unstable.[63] Yet for Figeac, the reason for the justice system's indulgence toward elite women was not the sexism of those deciding Mme Steinheil's fate, but rather their sexuality. The desire that powerful men had for her and other elite women distorted the egalitarian principles of the republic.

Mme Steinheil's power to direct government resources was understood as another indication of the regime's commitment to maintaining inequality. During the Steinheil affair it came out that some of her clients routed state funds to her in what were essentially instances of government-sponsored prostitution. After her arrest newspapers reported that the undersecretary of fine arts, Étienne Dujardin-Beaumetz, had arranged for the state to purchase one of Adolphe Steinheil's paintings for 600 francs after his death. A journalist for *L'Humanité* described this work as "fairly bad" and then asked, "Why did M. Dujardin-Beaumetz, representative of the State, think it necessary to buy this painting which is less than mediocre with our money and pay Mme Steinheil for it?"[64] The answer was easy: sex. The day before, Dujardin-Beaumetz had been revealed as one of Mme Steinheil's clients.[65] This sum was, however, a drop in the bucket compared to the patronage that Faure directed toward the Steinheil household, as he arranged for the state to commission a painting from her husband for 30,000 francs. This was an astronomical sum at the time, especially for a work by an artist who was not seen as particularly talented.[66] A song from the time of her trial that directly spoke to Mme Steinheil stated: "What's clearest in this story / ... Those who are the real suckers / Are surely still us / Since in order to do you justice and a favor / It cost us thirty thousand francs!"[67] As in the article in *L'Humanité*, those who footed the bill for a politician to have sex with Mme Steinheil were invoked in the first person plural. It was the French public who paid, while only Mme Steinheil and her clients benefited. This was financial corruption and a diversion of public funds for private purposes. It was also an abandonment of the egalitarian principle of merit, as politicians directed the state to buy bad paintings when it should have patronized only the most meritorious art.[68]

For critics of the government, the Steinheil affair offered proof that the Third Republic was just like the Old Regime, which was regarded as financially and sexually corrupt. Access to elite circles, not talent, determined who got state patronage. Desire, not reason, drove government officials' decisions. In particular, Mme Steinheil was frequently compared to the royal mistresses of Versailles, women who had played a central role in the patronage economy of the Old Regime, and to Louis XV's mistress Mme de Pompadour in particular.[69] In fact, the two women were quite different. Mme de Pompadour was much more powerful than Mme Steinheil ever was. The former was often seen as essentially governing France during her tenure as the king's mistress. In contrast, Mme Steinheil's role was confined to distributing patronage within the civil service.

Nevertheless, the two women were seen as essentially the same. For instance, an image from a February 1909 issue of *L'Assiette au beurre* features a parade of contemporary political figures in which Mme Steinheil appears as the Mme de Pompadour of the Third Republic (figure 3). She is carried around in a sedan chair, an outmoded means of transportation for an aristocratic elite, onto which the emblems of republican France— the Phrygian cap and "RF" for "République française"—have been affixed. She is shown wearing little except a pearl necklace, a reference to the fact that after Faure's stroke, she was allegedly driven back to her house in a state of undress. The image suggested that the fundamental structure of the government was still monarchical and only superficially republican.

This was also an explicit theme of a number of opinion pieces in the nationalist daily *L'Intransigeant*. An editorial from December 1908 used the Steinheil affair to discuss what the author saw as the many crimes of the state. The author stated, "Politicians and pedagogues rail against the Old Regime. . . . But we see with our own eyes the filthy immorality, the atrocious crimes, the buffoonery, and the infamy of the current regime.

Mme STEINHEIL
en marquise de Pompadour de la 3ᵉ République

M. BORDEREL
en fermier génér...eux

FIG. 3. Madame Steinheil as the marquise de Pompadour of the Third Republic. *L'Assiette au beurre*, February 20, 1909, 764. Courtesy gallica.bnf.fr/Bibliothèque Nationale de France.

We see with our own eyes the feudalism of the politicians ... parasites on the nation, fleecing France to enrich their creatures, their mistresses, their offspring."[70] Although the men governing France maintained that the Third Republic was more egalitarian and less debauched than the monarchy had been, their pursuit of sex and patronage belied any commitment to equality.

In many respects, the Steinheil affair represented the coming together of long-standing fears about the political perils of sex with newer ones about the weakness of democracy. Many in the Belle Époque felt that elites, including those in the government, were not willing to live up to the demands of equality and that they wanted a state that would continue to give them preferential treatment.[71] The Steinheil affair seemed to validate these concerns and the sense that behind the façade of democracy, the government had not truly reformed its monarchical ways. In other scandals in this era, the public regarded money and the greed of politicians and officials as the problem.[72] What was unusual about concerns voiced in the Steinheil affair was that sex was the source of corruption, desire the danger to democracy.

This reaction constituted a revival of eighteenth-century attacks on the political influence of seductive women who sapped the king of his rightful power. The Steinheil affair gave many the sense that lust was once again overwhelming the men governing France. Yet there were significant differences between this scandal and those of the eighteenth century. For one, under the monarchy the problem was that sex flattened hierarchies, as the king ceded power to individuals of lesser status.[73] In the Steinheil affair sex magnified hierarchies by giving elite women preferential treatment. Additionally, Mme Steinheil was regarded in a far more positive light than were the women of the eighteenth-century pamphlet literature. The latter were often described as disgusting, whereas Mme Steinheil was frequently presented as an exceptionally talented lover with universal sex appeal.[74] Indeed, the anger in the Steinheil affair was often directed less at Mme Steinheil than at the prominent men around her. This is a sign that women whose beauty and charm gave them sway over men were often more generously assessed in the Belle Époque than in earlier eras.[75]

There was also a difference in emphasis between the Steinheil affair and the scandals of the eighteenth century in terms of how observers saw them as revealing hidden transgressions. In the prerevolutionary and revolutionary eras, the focus was on the many sins of the women around Louis XV and Louis XVI. In contrast, the heart of the Steinheil affair was the revelation of what was hidden and the gap between the appearance of good behavior and the reality that it concealed. This reflected a view of sex as more private than it had been in the eighteenth century as well as the intricate ways that privacy was a sign of power in the Belle Époque.[76]

Last but certainly not least, the fallout from the Steinheil affair was relatively mild. The pamphlet literature of the eighteenth century helped to fuel a revolution, but this scandal resulted only in embarrassing a few officials. The Third Republic would survive, and its resilience is attested to by the fact that it held up under the stress of World War I, just a few years later. Nevertheless, the Steinheil affair opened up an opportunity for those on the left and the right to attack the regime and describe it as undemocratic and corrupt, its elite as hypocritical. Sex was a particular danger because it could undermine the fundamental principles of the Third Republic.

The Steinheil affair provides a fascinating narrative of a woman whose efforts to salvage her reputation ended up causing an outcry about the misbehavior of the rich and powerful. The story of Mme Steinheil's life also complements Jennifer Anne Boittin's argument in this volume that sex and sex work, and in particular women's abilities to use these categories to their own ends, could provide avenues for disrupting assumptions about women's place in the political world. It also echoes Nina Kushner's argument showing the enduring social and legal power of iterations of categories of unchaste woman.

Overall, the affair illuminates the relationship between sex, knowledge, and power in the Belle Époque. In an environment in which elites justified their prestige through propriety, these men and women needed to keep their sex lives private to maintain their status. As a result, only insiders had access to the truth about the lives of the powerful. As the Steinheil affair opened up knowledge of elite transgressions to the public, critics of the government decried the bourgeoisie's hypocrisy and its outsized power within the state. The publicity around what was supposed to remain private—sex—proved disruptive to a political world that depended on sex remaining in its proper place. Historians have frequently highlighted the degree to which knowledge about sex shored up the state's power over both citizens and imperial subjects in the Third Republic.[77] During the Steinheil affair, however, the shoe was on the other foot. As ordinary individuals came to learn about the sexual behavior of the ruling elite, they used their knowledge to call into question the social and political order.

Looking at sexuality in this context thus leads to a richer understanding of France's democratic tradition. Sex was an avenue for corruption. It opened up routes to favoritism and led politicians and officials to violate the republican principles of equality. The codes of respectability and privacy also weakened democracy, as they led powerful individuals to betray their commitment to transparency. Moreover, though the press was supposed to serve as a watchdog for the government's actions, it could be complicit in hiding the truth from the citizenry. The Steinheil affair thus reveals that many in France felt estranged from the state and that the true nature of power was almost always hidden. Sex scandals, though, could be democratizing, as the exposure of politicians' and officials' secrets gave the public the sense that the truth was finally visible.

Notes

1. Sarah Maza, "The Diamond Necklace Affair Revisited: The Case of the Missing Queen," in *Eroticism and the Body Politic*, ed. Lynn Hunt (Baltimore: Johns Hopkins University Press, 1991), 63–89; and Sarah Horowitz, "The End of Love: Politics, Emotions and Domestic Violence in the Choiseul-Praslin Affair," *Journal of Family History* 42, no. 4 (October 2017): 381–400.

2. Maza, "Diamond Necklace Affair"; Lynn Hunt, "The Many Bodies of Marie Antoinette," in Hunt, *Eroticism and the Body Politic*, 108–30.

3. Edward Berenson, *The Trial of Madame Caillaux* (Berkeley: University of California Press, 1992), 50; and Aaron Freundschuh, *The Courtesan and the Gigolo: The Murders in the Rue Montaigne and the Dark Side of Empire in Nineteenth-Century Paris* (Stanford CA: Stanford University Press, 2017).

4. Examples of these scandals include the Panama affair, the Dreyfus affair, and the Humbert affair.

5. On the values of the Third Republic, see Paul Jankowski, *Stavisky: A Confidence Man in the Republic of Virtue* (Ithaca NY: Cornell University Press, 2002), 5.

6. Hannah Frydman, "Capitalism's Back Pages: 'Immoral' Advertising and Invisible Markets in Paris's Mass Press, 1880–1940," in *Capitalism's Hidden Worlds*, ed. Kenneth Lipartito and Lisa Jacobson (Philadelphia: University of Pennsylvania

Press, 2019), 126–29; Christophe Charle, *Birth of the Intellectuals, 1880–1900*, trans. David Fernbach and G. M. Goshgarian (Cambridge: Polity, 2015).

7. Discussions of bourgeois codes of respectability include Berenson, *Trial of Madame Caillaux*, 128, 130; Anne-Marie Sohn, *Du premier baiser à l'alcôve: La sexualité des Français au quotidien, 1850–1950* (Paris: Aubier, 1996), 12–15; Lela F. Kerley, *Uncovering Paris: Scandals and Nude Spectacles in the Belle Époque* (Baton Rouge: Louisiana State University Press, 2017), 7; Theodore Zeldin, *France, 1848–1945*, 2 vols. (Oxford: Clarendon, 1988), 15–16. See Ann Laura Stoler, *Race and the Education of Desire: Foucault's History of Sexuality and the Colonial Order of Things* (Durham NC: Duke University Press, 1995) for a detailed treatment outside of the French context.

8. Anne-Marie Sohn, "The Golden Age of Male Adultery: The Third Republic." *Journal of Social History* 28, no. 3 (Spring 1995): 480; and Michele Plott, "The Rules of the Game: Respectability, Sexuality, and the Femme Mondaine in Late-Nineteenth-Century Paris," *French Historical Studies* 25, no. 3 (Spring 2002): 531–56.

9. Marie Colombier, *Mémoires: Fin de siècle* (Paris: Ernest Flammarion, 1898–1900), 122–23; and Madeleine Pelletier, *La femme vierge* (Paris: ⊠Indigo and Coté-femmes éditions, 1996), 65.

10. Except where otherwise noted, the account of Mme Steinheil's life and the double murder comes from Armand Lanoux, *Madame Steinheil: Ou la connaissance du président* (Paris: Bernard Grasset, 1983); Benjamin Martin, *The Hypocrisy of Justice in the Belle Epoque* (Baton Rouge: Louisiana State University Press, 1984), chap. 1; and Pierre Darmon, *Marguerite Steinheil, ingénue criminelle?* (Paris: Perrin, 1996).

11. Marguerite Japy Steinheil, *My Memoirs* (New York: Sturgis and Walton, 1912), 34; "L'interrogatoire de Mme Steinheil," *Le Radical*, December 2, 1908, 1; Plott, "Rules of the Game," 553; Andrea Mansker, *Sex, Honor and Citizenship in Early Third Republic France* (Houndmills, UK: Palgrave Macmillan, 2011), 95.

12. Christophe Charle, *Les élites de la République* (Paris: Fayard, 2006); Christophe Charle, *La crise des sociétés impériales* (Paris: Seuil, 2001), 112.

13. Zeldin, *France*, 1: 15–16; Dominique Kalifa, *Les bas-fonds: Histoire d'un imaginaire* (Paris: Seuil, 2013), 113–14.

14. Plott, "Rules of the Game," 533.

15. Mansker, *Sex, Honor and Citizenship*, 95–99.

16. Luc Boltanski, *Mysteries and Conspiracies: Detective Stories, Spy Novels and the Making of Modern Societies*, trans. Catherine Porter (Cambridge: Polity, 2014), 111.

17. "Interrogatoire de Mme Steinheil," *Le Journal*, November 4, 1909, 5.

18. "Interrogatoire de Mme Steinheil," *Le Journal*, November 4, 1909, 5.

19. "Mme Steinheil est bien une criminelle," *Le Petit Journal*, November 29, 1908, 1.

20. Ari Adut, *On Scandal: Moral Disturbances in Society, Politics, and Art* (Cambridge: Cambridge University Press, 2008), 19–20, 44–45.

21. Martin, *Hypocrisy of Justice*, 19.

22. Employment dossier of Georges Leloir, BB 6 II 1008, Archives Nationales (hereafter AN), Pierrefitte-sur-Seine.

23. "L'Affaire Steinheil," *La Libre Parole*, December 6, 1908, 2.

24. "Nos Échos," *L'Intransigeant*, December 4, 1908, 2; and Steinheil, *Memoirs*, 77.

25. Martin, *Hypocrisy of Justice*, 19.

26. Jean-Denis Bredin, *The Affair: The Case of Alfred Dreyfus*, trans. Jeffrey Mehlman (New York: G. Braziller, 1986), 395.

27. Ernest Dudley, *The Scarlett Widow* (London: F. Muller, 1960), 28.

28. "Mort de Félix Faure," *Le Petit Journal. Supplément du dimanche*, February 26, 1899, 7.

29. E. Janvoin, "La vérité sur la mort de Félix Faure," *Le Journal du Peuple*, February 23, 1898, 2.

30. Memo to the prefect of police, December 12, 1908, BA 1584, Archives de la préfecture de police (hereafter APP), Le Pré Saint-Gervais; "Pour retrouver les assassins," *Le Petit Parisien*, April 11, 1909, 118; and "Mme Steinheil est bien une criminelle," 1.

31. "Mystérieuse tragédie à Vaugirard," *Le Journal*, June 1, 1908, 2.

32. "Assassinat du peintre Steinheil et de sa belle-mère Mme veuve Japy," *Le Figaro*, June 1, 1908, 2.

33. Memo to the prefect of police, November 24, 1909, BA 1584, APP; memo to the prefect of police, December 2, 1908, BA 1584, APP; "L'Affaire de l'impasse Ronsin," *Le Matin*, November 6, 1908, 1; Edouard Bernaert, "L'Affaire Steinheil," *L'Action française*, January 13, 1909, 2. "Après l'arrestation de Mme Steinheil," *L'Humanité*, November 28, 1908, 1.

34. "Mme Steinheil parle: Les détails du drame," *L'Intransigeant*, June 2, 1908, 1.

35. Attorney-General of the Parisian Court of Appeals to the Keeper of the Seals, Minister of Justice, Paris, November 30, 1908, BB 18 2369, AN; and Steinheil, *Memoirs*, 207.

36. Kalifa, *Bas-Fonds*.

37. Memo to the prefect of police, December 2, 1908 BA 1584, APP. On the police's role in enforcing codes of sexual morality, see Jill Harsin, *Policing Prostitution in Nineteenth-Century Paris* (Princeton NJ: Princeton University Press, 1985); Jean-Marc Berlière, *La police des mœurs sous la IIIe République* (Paris: Seuil,

1992); William A. Peniston, *Pederasts and Others: Urban Culture and Sexual Identity in Nineteenth-Century Paris* (New York: Harrington Park, 2004).

38. See also Caroline Weber, *Proust's Duchess: How Three Women Captured the Imagination of Fin-de-Siècle Paris* (New York: Alfred A. Knopf, 2018), 118–86, 203–41.

39. Kalifa, *Bas-fonds*.

40. "Mme Steinheil à Saint-Lazare," *Le Matin*, January 2, 1908, 5.

41. Adut, *On Scandal*, 11–21. On uses of the term "scandal" to describe this case after Mme Steinheil's arrest, see "Le Drame de l'impasse Ronsin," *Le Figaro*, November 29, 1908, 1.

42. Dominique Kalifa, *L'encre et le sang: Récit de crimes et société à la Belle Époque* (Paris: Fayard, 1995); Vanessa R. Schwartz, *Spectacular Realities: Early Mass Culture in Fin-de-Siècle Paris* (Berkeley: University of California Press, 1998); and Dominique Kalifa, "L'envers fantasmé du quotidien," in Dominique Kalifa et al., *La civilisation du journal: Histoire culturelle et littéraire de la presse française au XIXe siècle* (Paris: Nouveau monde, 2011), 1330–31.

43. Vincent Robert, "Périodiser: Paysages politiques, cohérences médiatiques," in Kalifa et al., *Civilisation du journal*, 264; Christophe Charle, *Le siècle de la presse, 1830–1939* (Paris: Seuil, 2004), 160–61.

44. Frydman, "Capitalism's Back Pages," 126–29.

45. "Plus d'initiales: des noms!," *L'Action française*, November 29, 1908, 2.

46. "L'Affaire Steinheil," *Le Petit Journal*, December 4, 1908, 1; "L'affaire Steinheil," *Le Petit Journal*, December 5, 1908, 3; "Félix Faure et Mme Steinheil," *La Libre Parole*, December 1, 1908.

47. "Nos Échos." Instances of information about Mme Steinheil's affairs circulating in the mass press include "Mme Steinehil est bien une criminelle"; "Quelques clartés dans les ténèbres," *Le Journal*, November 29, 1908, 1; "L'affaire Steinheil," *Le Petit Journal*, December 5, 1908, 3; "L'affaire Félix Faure," *Le Matin*, November 30, 1908, 1; "On exhume les corps de M. Steinheil & Mme Japy," *Le Journal*, November 30, 1908, 2. On the supposed neutrality of the mass press, see Berenson, *Trial of Madame Caillaux*, 211.

48. "Les minutes tragiques," *L'Intransigeant*, December 6, 1908, 1. Emphasis in original.

49. Urbain Gohier, "La Haute Pègre," *L'Intransigeant*, December 5, 1908, 1.

50. Serpieri, Plébus, and Danerty, "Les Mémoires de Madame Steinheil," Paris: Pèle-Mèle Édition, 1914.

51. "Nouvelles à la main," *L'Écho de Paris*, December 3, 1908, 1.

52. "Le mystère Steinheil," *L'Humanité*, November 30, 1908, 2.

53. "L'autre nuit tragique," *L'Intransigeant*, December 7, 1908, 1.

54. Henri Vaugeois, "Trop de zèle!," *L'Action française*, November 30, 1908, 1.

55. Édouard Drumont, "La menteuse," *La Libre Parole*, December 1, 1908, 1.

56. "Tante Lily," *Le Radical*, December 3, 1908, 1.

57. "L'interrogatoire de Mme Steinheil," *Le Radical*, December 2, 1908, 2.

58. Grégoire Kauffmann, *Édouard Drumont* (Paris: Perrin, 2008), 205–6.

59. Thomas Bouchet, *Les fruits défendus: Socialismes et sensualité du XIXe siècle à nos jours* (Paris: Stock, 2014), 107–9.

60. Georges Berry, "La justice et la politique," *L'Intransigeant*, December 6, 1908, 1.

61. Raymond Figeac, "Mme Steinheil à Saint-Lazare," *L'Humanité*, November 27, 1908, 1. Emphasis in original.

62. Benjamin Martin, *Crime and Criminal Justice under the Third Republic: The Shame of Marianne* (Baton Rouge: Louisiana State University Press, 1990).

63. Ruth Harris, *Murders and Madness: Medicine, Law, and Society in the Fin de Siècle* (Oxford: Oxford University Press, 1989), 214; Berenson, *Trial of Madame Caillaux*.

64. "Autour de l'affaire," *L'Humanité*, November 30, 1908, 2.

65. "Toute la lyre!," *L'Intransigeant*, November 29, 1908, second ed., 1.

66. Darmon, *Marguerite Steinheil*, 8–9.

67. Jean Péheu, "Elle acquittée . . . Saint-Lazare?," JA 13, APP.

68. See also William Reddy, *The Invisible Code: Honor and Sentiment in Postrevolutionary France, 1814–1848* (Berkeley: University of California Press, 1997), 114–83.

69. "Propos d'un parisien," *Le Matin*, December 13, 1908, 1.

70. Gohier, "La Haute Pègre," 1.

71. Zeldin, *France*, 1: 570; Robert de Jouvenel, *La république des camarades* (Paris: B. Grasset, 1914); Pierre Birnbaum, *Le peuple et les gros: Histoire d'un mythe* (Paris: B. Grasset, 1979).

72. Birnbaum, *Peuple et les gros*; and Jankowski, *Stavisky*.

73. Maza, "Diamond Necklace Affair."

74. Hunt, "Many Bodies of Marie Antoinette"; "Le Revenant l'assassin: Interview de M. Félix Faure de M. Steinheil & Madame Japy" (n.p.: Imprimerie Edgard Klotz, n.d); and "Mme Steinheil rêve encore," *Le Matin*, November 17, 1909, 2.

75. Lenard Berlanstein, *Daughters of Eve: A Cultural History of French Theater Women from the Old Regime to the Fin de Siècle* (Cambridge MA: Harvard University Press, 2001).

76. See also Marcela Iacub, *Through the Keyhole: A History of Sex, Space and Public Modesty in Modern France*, trans. Vinay Swamy (Manchester: Manchester University Press, 2016).

77. Michel Foucault, *The History of Sexuality*, trans. Robert Hurley, vol. 1 (New York: Vintage, 1988); Harsin, *Policing Prostitution*; Alain Corbin, *Les filles de*

noce: *Misère sexuelle et prostitution: 19e et 20e siècles* (Paris: Aubier Montaigne, 1978); Sander Gilman, *Difference and Pathology: Stereotypes of Sexuality, Race, and Madness* (Ithaca NY: Cornell University Press, 1985); Ann Laura Stoler, *Carnal Knowledge and Imperial Power: Race and the Intimate in Colonial Rule* (Berkeley: University of California Press, 2010).

Suggested Reading

Adut, Ari. *On Scandal: Moral Disturbances in Society, Politics, and Art.* Cambridge: Cambridge University Press, 2008.

Ben-Amos, Avner. *Funerals, Politics, and Memory in Modern France, 1789–1996.* Oxford: Oxford University Press, 2005.

Berenson, Edward. *The Trial of Madame Caillaux.* Berkeley: University of California Press, 1992.

Charle, Christophe. *Le siècle de la presse, 1830–1939.* Paris: Seuil, 2004.

Clayson, Hollis. *Painted Love: Prostitution in French Art of the Impressionist Era.* New Haven CT: Yale University Press, 1991.

Freundschuh, Aaron. *The Courtesan and the Gigolo: The Murders in the Rue Montaigne and the Dark Side of Empire in Nineteenth-Century Paris.* Stanford CA: Stanford University Press, 2017.

Horowitz, Sarah. *The Red Widow: The Scandal that Shook Paris—and the Woman behind It All.* Naperville IL: Sourcebooks, 2022.

Kalifa, Dominique. *Vice, Crime, and Poverty: How the Western Imagination Invented the Underworld.* Translated by Susan Emanuel. New York: Columbia University Press, 2019.

Martin, Benjamin. *The Hypocrisy of Justice in the Belle Epoque.* Baton Rouge: Louisiana State University Press, 1984.

Maza, Sarah. *Violette Nozière: A Story of Murder in 1930s Paris.* Berkeley: University of California Press, 2011.

Plott, Michele. "The Rules of the Game: Respectability, Sexuality, and the *Femme Mondaine* in Late-Nineteenth-Century Paris." *French Historical Studies* 25, no. 3 (Spring 2002): 531–56.

8

MÉRIADECK, SEXUAL COMMERCE, AND THE URBAN MILIEU

MICHELLE K. RHOADES

In January 1914 sixteen-year-old Léon Lafleur took seven hundred and twenty francs from his mother's safe, spending the entire amount in several Bordelais brothels over the course of three days. The police report on the incident carefully tracked the amounts spent and the locations Lafleur visited. First, "on the payment of the sum of twenty francs, [Lafleur] spent part of the night with Raymonde." The following night (a Sunday), he visited another brothel, where he "spent forty francs on two bottles of champagne." He then gave brothel keeper Sophie Despeyroux one hundred francs "to find for him a young girl who would consent to going out with him in an automobile and give him favors." Encouraging his fantasies of freedom and sexual adventure, Despeyroux introduced him to Violette Blanchet. Blanchet accompanied him to a hotel, where he spent another hundred francs for her favors. On Monday, Lafleur visited a prominent brothel in the Mériadeck *quartier* (neighborhood) of Bordeaux, "where he offered two bottles of champagne to two *pensionnaires* (women living in brothels), the sisters Jeanne and Louise André." Bordeaux's police reported that "for the two bottles and his entry into the brothel he paid one hundred and forty francs and gave one hundred francs to each of the André sisters to compensate them for their favors." During his last visit alone, Lafleur spent three hundred francs more than the most expensive brothel fees recorded for the period.[1] Clearly the Bordelais brothel keepers and pensionnaires saw the opportunity present in Lafleur's visits, and he knew where to go among the dozens of brothels that existed on the few streets that made up Mériadeck's red-light district.

Understanding the influence of sexual commerce as a driving force in urban development requires an analysis of residents' interpretation of prostitution in their surroundings. Urban historians have considered a multitude of factors that influenced growth, work patterns, spending, and socialization. But researchers have tended to overlook the acceptance of sex work as a factor in residents' social relations and the economic influence that brothel spending had on local economies. Like other residents, brothel keepers needed common goods such as coal and furnishings, but Mériadeck's brothel keepers also influenced immigration and employment. Hiring immigrant Italian musicians as brothel entertainers changed Bordeaux's demographics and introduced new wages into the local economy; wages paid to immigrants had the knock-on effect of supporting landlords through rents and local businesses as the immigrants purchased goods and services. Finally, pensionnaires who required personal-care items made purchases that supported notions shops and pharmacies. Interrogating the influence of sexual commerce on Mériadeck's urban environment reveals a complex web of social and economic factors that left the area dependent upon and the residents loyal to the sexual commerce on its streets. Moving studies of prostitution to smaller French cities such as Bordeaux allows researchers to explore the impact of sexual commerce in different contexts and in the urban environment.

For historians interested in the history of sexuality or urban history, Lafleur's adventures provoke many questions. For example, did the madams of Mériadeck use their earnings to recruit pensionnaires or purchase supplies? Did they renovate or add new services and entertainments like music? The answer to both questions, in this case, is yes. But more importantly, historians should ask how France's nineteenth-century system of regulated prostitution influenced Mériadeck's urban geography, affected sociability in cities, and altered purchasing, spending, and employment patterns. Sexual commerce in Mériadeck changed the urban environment. It influenced and created new social ties among residents, it supported local businesses economically, and the nearly forty brothels that existed on the cramped avenues shaped the neighborhood's local urban geography.

Past approaches to the study of urban history have addressed a number of different topics, many related to national interests or public health. For example, researchers have studied the history of urban development as a product of national and socioeconomic changes. In this approach the study of smaller urban areas identifies residents' classes or professional affiliations as a reflection of national growth. And national patterns of socioeconomic change discovered at the local level have demonstrated the influence of national events on communities and commercial developments.[2] Researchers using "thick description" to understand the growth of a single city street have identified how changes in consumer demands influenced purchasing choices or work patterns that then affected urban expansion, housing growth, or the appearance of new commercial enterprises.[3] Other historians have shown that concern for sanitation and public health transformed the urban landscape by prompting the eradication of slums, alteration of city streets, improvement of water supplies, and fabrication of sewer systems. In nineteenth-century France the appearance of typhoid fever in large cities drew significant attention to public health. William B. Cohen argues that "fears of infested slums" in Paris and other cities encouraged local governments "to regulate housing quality," ultimately destroying slums and re-creating the urban landscape.[4] Renovations created substantial social change as well. Philip G. Nord argues that renovating the *halles* food market in central Paris (to make it safer and more hygienic) left the capital in the hands of the middle class, so that it "underwent a definite embourgeoisement."[5] Social historians have demonstrated an interest in the results of commonalities among residents. Historians have argued that issues such as corporate affiliation, class, immigrant status, and gender created ties among residents that influenced housing and consumption patterns and emboldened them to make demands on municipal leadership.[6]

Understanding the impact of sexual commerce on a community enriches our understanding of urban development in Mériadeck and, more broadly, Belle Époque France. For example, the existence of prostitution in this area fostered political solidarity among residents and increased support for sex work. This situation in turn generated social and geographic stability that was recognized by brothel keepers, police, landowners, and commercial enterprises. In Mériadeck prostitution proved to be a powerful economic engine that shaped Bordelais assumptions about the urban environment and drove a local commitment to defend social and economic relationships. Sex work did not disrupt urban harmony in Mériadeck. Instead, it became a mechanism through which residents bound themselves to each other in their community. Attention to residents' interpretation of sex work in urban histories of France reorders our assumptions about the relationship between supposedly marginal and disruptive activities—prostitution—and the economic and social stability of an urban community.

Urban Geography and Sexual Commerce

Policies to regulate Bordeaux's sexual commerce developed slowly during the nineteenth century, as city officials augmented Old Regime ordinances to control prostitution. France's system of state-regulated prostitution came to be considered a first line of defense—one that protected the bourgeoisie, the family, and the social body from disease. Of those who supported regulation, hygienist Alexandre Jean-Baptiste Parent-Duchâtelet was the most prominent. Concerned with health in large urban areas, Parent-Duchâtelet maintained that unless regulated, prostitutes would spread disease through communities. But if their behavior and health were supervised through medical exams, treatment for illness, registration with the police, and a system of enclosed brothels, prostitutes would be "an indispensable excremental phenomenon that protect[ed] the social body from disease."[7] In other words, sex workers would drain disease away from respectable individuals and families, promoting the good health of the state. By 1887 an impressive list of ordinances regulated prostitution in Bordeaux; they addressed the day-to-day functioning of Mériadeck's brothels (e.g., rent, fees, sale of alcohol, and hours of operation), brothel keepers' responsibilities (how to control their charges, run the houses, or report to police), and the circulation of prostitutes on urban streets.[8] In Bordeaux Mériadeck's nineteenth-century urban geography grew from the city's early efforts to rebuild neighborhood streets and the area's general acceptance of sexual commerce.

The nineteenth-century design of Mériadeck's streets derived from eighteenth-century city-renewal projects that left their mark on the urban geography. According to Cohen, Bordeaux's "provincial intendant, Louis Tourny, tore down much of the old city" as he "constructed wide avenues and the grand Place Royale; and imposed stately standard classical facades on the new, sumptuous residences that were built."[9] After Tourny's work was completed, the city council enlarged streets, built the well-visited Place des

Quinconces, and removed from the center of the city undesirable elements such as slaughterhouses, housing for impoverished residents, and cemeteries.[10] But the 1811 addition of a tobacco manufacturer altered circulation patterns in Mériadeck, and poor street construction slowed commercial development. These issues ended the early promise of the centrally located Place Mériadeck as the heart of the neighborhood's community life. Circulation patterns shifted and businesses failed to develop. In addition, the large La Chartreuse cemetery at the edge of the quartier was never relocated, encouraging affluent residents to flee the miasmas commonly thought to emanate from the dead. Manufacturing changes and urban renewal projects exacerbated economic stagnation in the neighborhood until Mériadeck earned the reputation of being unhygienic and lugubrious. As the area's overall prosperity dwindled, sexual commerce grew until it became an important part of the quartier and a critical factor in the urban environment.[11] But not all communities would develop such a pattern of acceptance.

Unlike the Mériadeck inhabitants who accepted prostitution, residents of other communities near Bordeaux rejected sexual commerce and limited its influence on the urban geography. In the commune of La Bastide, located across the Garonne River from Bordeaux, citizens complained about the cafés that hired prostitutes as servers and the rivalries that developed among prostitutes to attract the most clients with their "charms and eccentric attire."[12] The small community of Libourne's two brothels stood close to each other but remained situated far from the center of town. This appealed to police, as the *maisons* (brothels) did not disturb the town's residents and their proximity to each other facilitated supervision.[13] In the commune of Cantenac residents and small *commerçants* (shopkeepers) complained about the clandestine prostitution that kept residents awake all night and brought scandal to the community.[14] In these cases residents supported state approaches to urban control and development, asking state representatives to enforce ordinances that would limit the extent to which prostitution could alter the urban environment and social milieu. Built primarily around brothels, prostitution in Mériadeck developed differently.

As part of a neighborhood in Bordeaux, Mériadeck's brothels remained simple enterprises; their police classifications differed from those in larger cities like Paris. For example, the brothels classified as *maisons de tolérance* in Bordeaux would have been classified as no more than popular *maisons de rendez-vous* in Paris, where rooms could be rented cheaply but where the *filles* (prostitutes) often did not take up residence. In the larger city police reserved the category of maisons de tolérance primarily for upscale brothels, where anonymity and luxury remained key.[15] In the provinces and areas like Mériadeck, any popular brothel that had community salons and separate areas for women to work could be classified as a maison de tolérance. In Bordeaux's system of regulation, the keepers of the maisons de tolérance offered women from whom clients could choose, a community salon, alcohol of some kind, and music for entertainment. In Paris this type of brothel might only achieve the categorization of *maison de passe*, a less refined, ordinary, or working-class brothel with fewer amenities, or *maison à estaminet*, a series of rooms attached to a bar or café.[16] Smaller, unrefined, and with no extravagant amenities, Mériadeck's brothels might have had minimal impact—except that there were so many of them, enough to have a significant effect on the social, economic, and physical structure of the community.

In 1870 thirty-eight brothels existed in Mériadeck, concentrated on a few streets of the neighborhood. These included the rue Lambert, rue de Gasc (later Dalon), and rue Latterade. During the *fin-de-siècle*, rue de Gasc (Dalon) and rue Lambert housed 71 percent of Bordeaux's brothels.[17] In 1886 twenty-five brothels existed on rue Lambert alone, including three *première classe* (first class or deluxe) brothels, which offered premium amenities such as pianos for entertainment.[18] Clients visiting Mériadeck's brothels paid for the services they received and for the champagne and food they consumed. Spending by brothel visitors translated into revenue that individual women used to purchase goods and services at local shops. A petition to the mayor signed by local commerçants reveals that the purchase of dress materials, notions, food items, and services (such as visits to the hairdresser) were common among prostitutes, even if their frequency remains difficult to determine.[19] As Nathan Roth and Jill Grant show, large-scale government policies and infrastructure change can have a dramatic effect on urban streets and communities. But, arguing that cities remain "dynamic," they also note that "retail districts prove especially fluid, responding to changing population patterns, consumer tastes, transportation patterns,

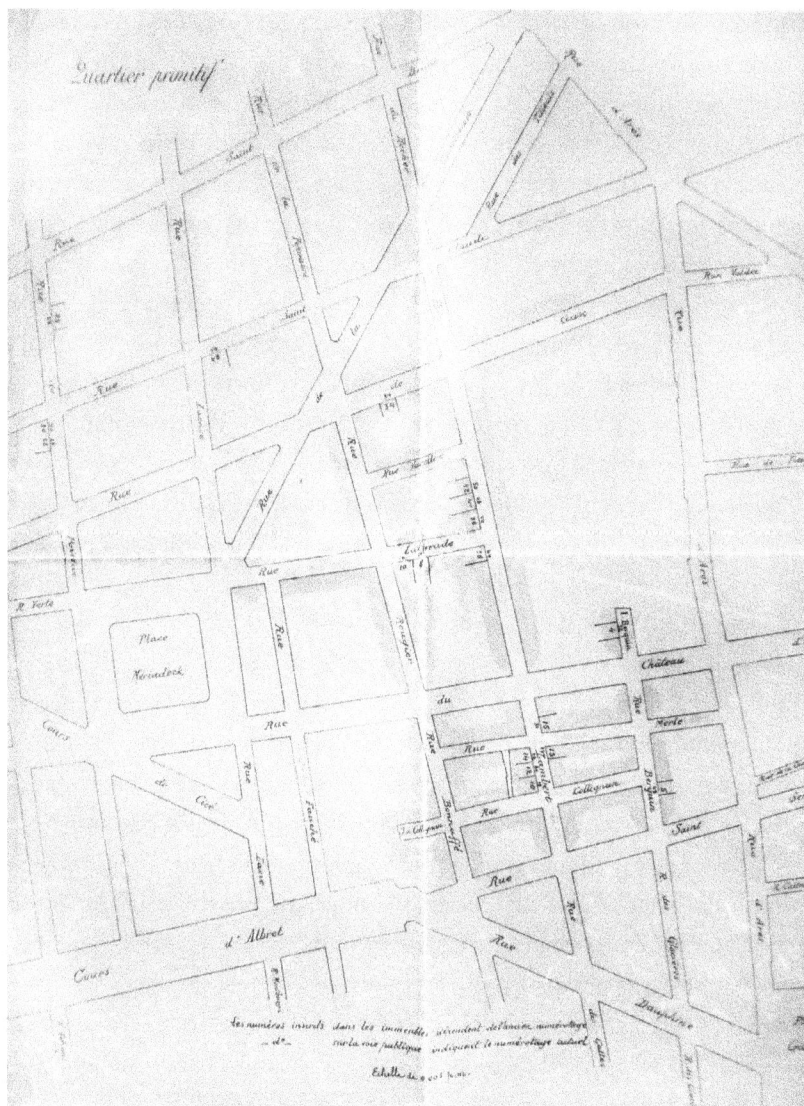

FIG. 4. Place Mériadeck is at the base of the map. Shaded areas indicate the location of brothels from 1883 to 1905. Map of Mériadeck before changes to street names. 1211-I-16, Archives Municipales de Bordeaux. Author collection.

and economic conditions."[20] Mériadeck's brothel keepers used revenues to purchase furnishings and consumables and to pay rent. Even their small supply of coal still had to be paid for and came from the revenue produced in the brothels.[21] This spending, multiplied dozens of times over in the neighborhood, changed and shaped the urban landscape. The commercial composition of the neighborhood's streets, particularly its notions shops and dressmakers, reflected the interests of sex workers and the influence of the sexual commerce in the area.[22] Women in brothels required dresses and sewing-related items to repair their clothes as needed in order to attract customers; Mériadeck's prostitution encouraged growth among those businesses that most catered to brothel needs. Because of the sheer number of brothels concentrated on a few streets in Mériadeck, the brothels and their residents represented significant purchasing power recognized by the local commerçants, the mayor's office, immigrants, and landlords.

Immigrants, Music, and Employment in Mériadeck

Researchers have shown that employment practices and guild affiliations influenced the structure of urban spaces by encouraging growth in specific industries or promoting change in local employment practices. In Mériadeck immigrant musicians performing outside of France's traditional venues (e.g., bars, cabarets, and music halls) contributed to a trade that impacted the quarter's growth and immigration patterns. Brothel keepers' interest in including music in their brothel offerings required the employment of musicians and established new employment opportunities for immigrants. Italian immigrant musicians, especially, played a key role in the social structure of the urban environment. David Garrioch and Mark Peel argue that neighborhoods accepted migrants based on their industriousness and how they showed their new neighbors who they were. Neighborhoods acted as a key element in the integration of migrants into the larger national community.[23] Inclusion could come quickly as well. Garrioch argues elsewhere that "a sense of belonging and of community did not depend on long residence or on life-long familiarity with every aspect of the lives of friends and neighbors."[24] Catharina Lis and Hugo Soly note that through reciprocity, doing for others, and accepting the tight-knit neighborhood that included brothels and sexual commerce, migrants found a place to live and to work.

The strength of a community relied on how residents gave support to and received it from others, including immigrants; altruism did not exist in this environment, but an exchange of meaningful support did.[25] Because of the existing sexual commerce around them, immigrants discovered a path to acceptance by working in brothels and supporting an urban sociability in Mériadeck, one deeply influenced by prostitution.

Mériadeck's brothel keepers identified music as an important amenity for their clients that augmented their offerings and stabilized businesses; even the police recognized the positive influence of music on the community. Because the musicians provided a valuable service, brothel keepers defended their right to hire musicians and supported them in the face of a tedious French bureaucracy. In October 1881 six Mériadeck brothel keepers wrote to the mayor to maintain their right to employ Italian musicians. They emphasized the critical role that musicians played in their brothels and in the municipal economy and urban environment. The women argued that they paid "a professional tax to run [their] brothels" and "took on [the musicians] as monthly, salaried employees, based on their merits and talents." They required the services of musicians to compete with "establishments similar to" theirs that were "more richly organized and endowed, possessing pianos that entertain[ed] their personnel as well as those" who went "there to pass time."[26]

In 1883 a series of brawls among laborers broke out on Mériadeck's streets. In an effort to control the neighborhood, the mayor's office revoked authorization for musicians to work in brothels, reasoning that music contributed to a festive atmosphere that could disrupt the peace in public spaces.[27] This effort provoked petitions from brothel keepers and musicians emphasizing the economic importance of the brothel to the stability of Mériadeck and its social environment. Fourteen brothel keepers and the musicians Prosper Messina, Giuseppe Rossi, and Giovanni Conti submitted a petition to the mayor in 1883. In it they argued that employing musicians provided the community an extraordinary benefit because of the stability that musicians and music provided. "Paid directly by the brothel keepers," the musicians "distracted and entertained the pensionnaires, keeping them inside the maisons, something that guaranteed tranquility for everyone," the group wrote.[28] The employment of musicians altered the urban geography of the area, making it safer (or at least more pleasant) for the community by removing prostitutes and their customers from the city streets. Police who directly supervised Mériadeck's brothels also supported the musicians' work and the brothel keepers' petition. They recognized that well-run brothels often provided unique or unrecognized benefits to a community.

Bordeaux's police made a case for the social and physical benefits to the urban environment that brothel entertainment provided. In a lengthy report to the mayor, they recognized the delicate balance between state authority over prostitution and the important role sexual commerce played in Mériadeck. But in spite of that, police remained unwilling to regulate sexual commerce too strictly. Richard Evans demonstrates that in Germany, police also resisted enforcing regulations too harshly, as they did not want prostitutes to relocate or avoid the regulationist system.[29] Bordeaux's police had other objectives, though they remained careful to point out that "like many questions associated with prostitution, this [issue had] many sides."[30] According to police, recent changes in Bordeaux's prostitution ordinances that limited the employment of musicians in brothels had undesirable economic and social effects on the urban environment. "Many [maisons de tolérance] have closed, many others have reduced the women available by a significant number" the police reported. "As vice does not disappear, it is the *garnis* [hotels] of the sixth *arrondissement* and sometimes other quartiers that have received the collected inheritance of these establishments—to the great detriment of public health and security." The police report replicated the regulationist trope that brothels served the public good by limiting disease and providing stability. But this report also identified the centrality of prostitution to the entire urban area. Police argued that they were "driven not to protect the brothels . . . but to avoid depriving them of those elements essential to their existence" and those that benefited the public spaces that surrounded brothels.[31] Brothel keepers argued that they expected mayoral decisions to be fair to their businesses and expected the mayor to acknowledge the importance of music to their community.[32] Music augmented the environment for sex work inside brothels and enhanced the economic stability of Mériadeck, but as the police recognized, keeping brothel inmates happy and contained in Mériadeck benefited other areas of Bordeaux. Prostitution remained in a single neighborhood.

As much as brothel keepers and police saw the value in ensuring that live music remained available to brothels, controlling the employment of musicians can be seen as an extension of municipal efforts to control migration in Bordeaux. During the late nineteenth century, family members seeking to immigrate to France applied for authorization to play music in Mériadeck's cafés and area brothels. For example, in 1881 Michel Mancini and his cousin Louis Caponsachi wrote to Mayor Albert Brandenburg for permission "to earn [their] living by working" and playing "violin and harp music" in the Café de l'Amitie on rue Rougier. Living on nearby rue Lambert, the two emphasized that if they had the mayor's approval to work, "the café . . . [would] hire [us] as salaried musicians and employees."[33] In October 1881 Ange Conti and Gaétano Conti, brothers in their late twenties, requested permission to work in a brothel on rue Rougier. Gaétano Conti, who had lived in Bordeaux for eight years, explained that as the "oldest of [his] family," he had multiple duties, which required moonlighting as a musician. During the day he worked "buying and selling objects of use." But he explained, "[I need] to combine this profession with music because I have my two aging parents with me. As the eldest of the family, I am the only one who can furnish their daily needs."[34]

Kathleen Lord argues that by controlling certain aspects of spatial relations, such as by restricting an individual's ability to move freely on city thoroughfares, allowing certain types of vendors, issuing tavern licenses, or permitting musicians to perform in brothels, the government expressed political control that molded urban landscapes to suit elite impressions of acceptability.[35] Allowing immigrants to play music in area taverns or brothels altered the urban geography by creating a more pleasant space, one that encouraged sex workers and their clients to remain indoors. Controlling special relations influenced employment practices and encouraged other urban businesses to prosper.[36]

Family or personal situations figured in almost all requests to work, and many requests emphasized that the money earned would go directly to supporting others. In 1881 Giuseppe Christofano (who later appears in the records as "Joseph") requested permission to play the accordion in Madame Claverie's brothel at 12 rue Lambert. He wrote that he had few resources and that he needed the work because he had "just left the hospital."[37]

François Fioril lived at 7 rue Latterade, an address adjacent to two brothels. He requested authorization to work at 37 rue Lambert, a brothel around the corner from his residence. He submitted his request to "play freely in Bordeaux's establishments" because as "the father of two young children," he had a family that depended on his wages.[38] Requests from Pierre Fleure, Vincent Messina, Prosper Messina, Pascal Messina, and other Italian musicians contained similar personal details. Almost all of the musicians who sought consent to play in Bordeaux had lived there for seven years or more, had family troubles, and needed to earn a living by playing music. Some emphasized that any wages earned from moonlighting as musicians would supplement income from respectable daytime occupations; in these cases, police investigation confirmed the claims. In Fioril's case, for example, the morals police verified that he had "lived as man and wife with twenty-four-year-old L. Toulouse for six years" and that they had two children, ages six months and two years.[39] Any extra income would help Fioril's young family, but it held the potential to support local businesses as well.

The wages musicians earned remained modest but provided enough for them to survive with some left over. For example, in November 1881 Joseph Christofano played the accordion in Madame Chevalier's brothel at 43 rue Lambert. There, he earned twenty francs per month plus meals.[40] With an eight-franc monthly rent for a flat on nearby rue Rougier, Christofano used almost half of his income for housing.[41] For his work, François Fioril earned meals and thirty francs a month to support his wife and two children.[42] Prosper Messina and his son earned fifty francs per month (combined) and received meals as well.[43] Pascal Messina received twenty francs per month and meals for his work playing the violin (the lowest wages in the area, along with Christofano's).[44] Other area musicians playing the accordion, harp, or violin received similar wages, somewhere between twenty and forty francs per month.[45]

Most musicians in Mériadeck paid between eight and ten francs a month for housing costs, leaving a small amount for other expenditures.[46] Bordeaux's growing economy provided a number of popular amusements for that portion of musicians' salaries that did not fund daily needs. The least expensive tickets in Bordeaux's new Grand Théâtre cost two francs, expensive for the laboring classes but still within the musicians' reach. The city's busy Théâtre des Arts offered performances that cost as little as half a franc for a ticket and attending as a family group became a prevalent pastime among the popular classes. The annual forty francs needed to join Bordeaux's rowing club remained well out of reach for brothel musicians, but their salaries could probably cover the annual ten-franc fee at Bordeaux's popular athletic club.[47] Identifying how money flows through a community is a daunting task, and musicians' exact expenditures are difficult to trace. But it is reasonable to assume that as the availability of popular entertainments such as penny arcades, circuses, and freak shows increased during the Belle Époque, immigrant musicians would have sought them out, just like other residents.[48]

Despite the economic reliance on sex work in the quartier, in 1883 tensions developed in Mériadeck and support from residents for sexual labor seemed to be declining. Renewed interpretations of the area as a *quartier louche* (shady neighborhood) drew some attention from the city's politicians, but they remained more committed to other areas of Bordeaux.[49] For example, Mayor Albert Brandenburg focused much of his attention on urban development on Bordeaux's river ports. A high level of maritime commerce existed during the fin-de-siècle, but the quantity and types of goods that moved through Bordeaux's port after 1880 remained volatile; wine exports, especially, fluctuated. Wine exports to the United States, one of Bordeaux's largest markets, declined from 14,000 hectoliters in 1883 to fewer than 4,000 in 1905. At one point, wine exports to the United States accounted for 9 percent of the commercial traffic in the port.[50] In the same period, wine exports to Latin America accounted for more than 15 percent of the wine exports through the port and remained constant. Other port traffic shifted as well. Imports of British coal rose dramatically during the fin-de-siècle, from 200,000 tons in 1870 to more than 1.8 million tons by 1906.[51]

The growing port activity led many in Bordeaux—especially the members of the Chamber of Commerce—to question the ability of the port to acquire or maintain new business. In 1884 discussions held during Chamber of Commerce meetings addressed the port's conditions and their relation to steady growth. Armand Lalande, president of the Chamber of Commerce, argued, "All you have to do is walk along the *quais* [docks] . . . to see [their inferior condition]. The means to load and unload ships are insufficient and the docks are so short that ships must often dock three deep to slowly and carefully manually load and unload their cargoes." Things did not improve once the merchandise reached the shore: "The shores of the docks are overcrowded with merchandise that is then exposed to all possible weather and theft."[52] Arguments about the cost of modernizing Bordeaux's docks and maritime areas would continue well into the 1890s, especially between the members of the Chamber of Commerce and the *négociants* (wine merchants).[53]

In addition to addressing whether to develop the docks, Brandenburg faced public works projects that included adding twenty new elementary schools, building the Grand Marché Couvert des Capucins (a covered market), developing new public parks, and constructing the colleges of medicine and pharmacy and of science and letters.[54] In other words, Bordeaux was a rapidly developing fin-de-siècle city where official attention to infrastructure, building, and commerce remained critical for the city's growth. Any difficulties in Mériadeck remained just that: neighborhood difficulties. Responding to a police report about disturbances that occurred in the neighborhood in 1883, the mayor simply noted that brawls, skirmishes, and other public incidents in Mériadeck "were not unprecedented" and cast his attention elsewhere, focusing instead on the more pressing maritime matters and the development of Bordeaux.[55] In spite of the mayor's disinterest, however, Mériadeck could not be ignored forever. The neighborhood remained an important part of Bordeaux's larger urban landscape because of its proximity to the city's cathedral, municipal buildings, commercial districts, and residential neighborhoods. As social interests changed and Bordeaux's politics shifted, residents and officials would pay more attention to prostitution in Mériadeck.

Movement, Community, and Tensions

In the last decade of the nineteenth century, Mériadeck's sexual commerce came under increasing scrutiny. Letters concerning prostitution or brothels appeared regularly in the mayor's office, revealing a growing tension between property owners, residents, sexual commerce, and municipal toleration. According to one police report, the number of *filles soumises isolées* (registered prostitutes not working in brothels) increased yearly after 1888, when police identified 332 such women on the city's avenues. By 1898 Bordeaux's police reported 475 filles soumises isolées on the city's streets. In the same period the number of filles soumises (registered prostitutes) in maisons de tolérance declined from 209 to 135, with an exceptionally low number (67) of identified brothel prostitutes in 1894. In other words, the number of women who sought clients on Mériadeck's streets from 1888 to 1898 far exceeded those working in brothels.[56] These women needed locations to conduct their work and often rented rooms from local property owners. This in turn influenced the social and economic structures of the urban environment, drastically altering toleration for prostitution and the alliance that had formed among residents.

As prostitutes moved onto the streets of Mériadeck, competition for clients escalated, and local property owners, residents, and businesses appeared to view prostitution in a new light. In 1889 more than a dozen residents wrote to the *commissaire central* (police commissioner) to complain about prostitution. "[The] proprietors, businessmen, fathers, who live on the rue Rougier and the neighboring [streets]," they wrote, "ask for your immediate intervention to stop the scandalous activities in their neighborhoods." The writers painted an unsavory picture of degeneration in Mériadeck, caused primarily by filles soumises or *insoumises*, those registered or unregistered prostitutes who rented building spaces in which to conduct their work. The women, the petitioners wrote, were "constantly on their thresholds," where they caused a public nuisance. "These women . . . are not content to stop passersby, [they also] sprinkle their conversations and their quarrels with expressions and gestures that make it impossible to pass them or to remain near them."[57] Ultimately, the petitioners wanted the women removed from the streets for causing public disturbances.

Property owners who had little objection to prostitution itself identified "unfair" business practices among landlords who rented to sex workers. They argued that "in order to better rent the first-floor rooms of their buildings," other landlords "had converted" those rooms "and put up prostitutes." Rentals to prostitutes did not cause concern, as "the work of [the] renters was not bothersome," but the prosperity derived from the new rentals did. The petitioners wrote that "these proprietors" had "benefited from excessive [and] lax toleration" to earn more than others in the area. With greater reliance on the profits derived from sex work, the petitioners claimed, "many others" had "followed their example" making "it impossible for honest people or commerçants . . . to live in the quartier. It is a genuine expropriation; the street belongs to sex workers."[58] The economic structure of the entire community had transformed, and friction had developed between landlords because Mériadeck's sexual commerce had changed.

Support for sexual labor in the area did not disappear completely, however, especially among long-standing residents. For example, in the summer of 1896, when a restaurateur on the rue des Glacières asked police to remove prostitutes from the streets near his establishment, he received significant scrutiny from those who knew him and had deep-seated connections to the quartier.[59] Police did not act immediately on M. Fontanier's request even though it came with a petition supposedly signed by others in the area; in the interim, eleven other landlords and residents of Mériadeck wrote to the police. They opposed any action to remove the filles soumises from the streets. Revealing knowledge of Fontanier's complaint and request, their letter complained about Fontanier in turn: "Most of the signatories [of the earlier petition] are neither established in the neighborhood nor proprietors. This removes all moral and material value [from their petition]." They attacked Fontanier specifically, writing that "for personal reasons, he wanted the women removed," as he had given a "large part of his fortune to the filles in question."[60]

The leader of this new petition, B. Baradou, emphasized the importance of belonging to the neighborhood and the solidarity that existed among the long-term residents and commerçants of Mériadeck. Baradou noted that most of the signatories on Fontanier's letter were "neither taxed [in the area] nor landlords" and pressed the central issue, namely that retaining the prostitutes mattered a great deal to the storekeepers and landlords of the community. "If the action is taken [to remove the women], we would be obligated to close our buildings and cease all commerce. We are weighed down with overhead [expenses] and it would be impossible to meet our expenses [without the filles soumises]; the quartier is absolutely worthless for any other type of business. Because of the ill repute of the quartier, few people would come and stay with us."[61]

As the community grappled with potential changes in the urban landscape, more petitions arrived at the mayor's office and police headquarters, each overwhelmingly supporting the sexual commerce in Mériadeck in the hope of maintaining the prosperity it brought to the area. In 1902 nearly thirty residents argued in a petition that "for half a century" prostitutes had existed in the neighborhood and that they remained an important source of revenue for those who lived there because "the livelihood of business owners depend[ed] on [these women's] clients."[62] It is clear from the many letters and petitions the residents of Mériadeck sent to officials that they saw value in the area's entire system of sexual commerce, value that contributed to their livelihoods and supported the social structure of the community.

Neil Shumsky argues that in areas of sexual commerce where prostitutes were forced to "shop locally," community merchants who supplied goods and services profited from the women like "parasites who attached themselves to prostitutes and took advantage of their activities."[63] In Mériadeck nothing could be further from the truth. Business owners and residents alike recognized the economic benefits they received from the area's sexual commerce, but they also recognized the humanity of the women themselves. As in other French cities, Bordeaux's city ordinances controlled where and how sex workers conducted their business and required all sex workers to pass the despised *visite sanitaire* (health exam). Such restrictions, according to Baradou and the other petitioners, made for an unpleasant existence for the women: "The existing, very severe police regulations already render the lives of the *filles* in question difficult and tiresome because they cannot even appear on the sidewalks without [receiving] a contravention. They are even very embarrassed to do their household shopping."[64]

Finally, the petitioners added that if the police really wished to remove the women from the rue des Glacières and nearby streets to improve the neighborhood, they "would need to also remove the women from the rue Lambert and rue Rougier. . . . It would also be indispensable to change all of the names of all the streets in the quartier: in a word, to re-create the quartier from scratch."[65] The citizens of Bordeaux's Mériadeck neighborhood had reached a tacit agreement. The *fille soumise* and efficiently run *maisons de tolérance* encouraged an economy on which many residents and businesses depended. But this situation also relied on the state to regulate and control prostitution.

As one complaint later noted: "We know that this quartier, however central and *common*, has been sacrificed to prostitution. But we know also that prostitution must be strictly regulated."[66] Janet Oswald argues that "the importance of 'place' in the study of prostitution cannot be overestimated: no two places are identical."[67] Within the confines of Mériadeck, sexual commerce found a home, and the women who worked in the industry found sympathy from the other residents. As the participants and writers of these last letters and petitions have shown, sexual commerce in Mériadeck directly shaped the social structure of the community and influenced the urban landscape.

Near the turn of the century, as sex workers took their commerce past the boundaries of Mériadeck, area newspapers wrote about prostitution in the city, attacking it as a civic and municipal problem. In May 1898 the paper *Le Nouvelliste* reported on Bordeaux's street life by reprinting a letter received from "a reader" in hopes of "attracting the mayor's attention" to civic problems engendered by sex work in Bordeaux: "Monsieur the Director: It is not only on the rue d'Aviu, or in the walkways of the Jardin-Public at ten o'clock at night that these hideous specimens of solicitation [appear]. It is also in the middle of the day and on [the major thoroughfare of] Intendance and the allées de Tourny. Three or four of these hagglers actively comment on you or try to solicit you . . . in addition, there is a resurgence of mendacity. On these two points, will the new municipal administration make us wish for the previous one?"[68]

Prostitution outside of Mériadeck's boundaries did not suit Bordeaux's wider population or the city's administrators. The new mayor faced increased public scrutiny on the issue, and some residents claimed that the city needed firmer control over the regulation of prostitution than the police or the mayor were displaying. In May 1898 the weekly journal *La Vie joyeuse*, questioned conditions in Mériadeck: "In spite of the *arrêtés* [ordinances] forbidding women from the vulgar quartiers from appearing outside their domicile, these women take up residence in the middle of the street, wash themselves in public, sleep on the pavement, and soon start . . . their commerce." The journal continued, "What a delightful sight for those who pass the Place Mériadeck and the streets Chartreuse, d'Arès, St-Sernin and Dauphine!"[69] These conditions needed attention: "We demand that the municipal arrêtés that are violated each day in the quartier be respected, it is because of this promiscuity in the center of town that the regulations must be maintained, strictly and rigorously observed."[70] This journalistic interest reinforced external, negative impressions of Mériadeck and prostitution. A later conference on public morality and pornography that studied the detrimental social effects of prostitution also made public the case for its elimination. Combined, these events forced Bordeaux's officials to reevaluate the implications of supporting a *quartier réservé* (red-light district) in the midst of a cosmopolitan and prosperous fin-de-siècle city.[71]

The Moral Challenge, Political Change, and Mériadeck

The 1904 reelection of Alfred Daney to serve as mayor for a third term set the stage for new, vigorous attacks on prostitution in Bordeaux; it also meant disaster for Mériadeck's urban geography. Interested in arts, letters, and the cultural life of the city, Daney had originally replaced the one-term mayor Paul-Louis Lande.[72] In contrast to Lande, Daney had long served in Bordeaux's municipal government and had numerous connections to the city's political and economic affairs. He had worked as a member of the *conseil municipal* (municipal council) for thirty years before his first term as mayor. Daney's extensive municipal government experience had included working as adjunct to Bordeaux's first elected mayor (Brandenburg), supervising public works projects, and running city finances. A fixture in the public life of the city, Daney would eventually become one of its most influential and decorated citizens.[73]

Perhaps recognizing that the political landscape had changed with Daney's election, residents in Mériadeck wrote to the new mayor to request changes to prostitution ordinances. As with their previous attempts to enact changes to public ordinances, residents emphasized their interest in benefiting from the sexual commerce; they did not want to eradicate it completely. Daney's office received a series of complaints about the negative influence brothels had on the community and about the influence the increased numbers of sex workers had on local landlords' abilities to rent properties in the area.[74] Although the emphasis on the economic importance of prostitution remained, a new argument emerged framing prostitution as being central to the well-being of Daney's new administration and of Bordeaux more generally; the tax burden of Mériadeck's property owners supported the city.

After 1900 the appearance of more sex workers on Mériadeck's streets provided an opportunity for landlords to approach the mayor about changing city ordinances on property rentals and taxes. In 1904 Mesdames St. Blaugual and Desmortier requested that the new mayor issue city ordinances that would authorize building rentals to sex workers and avoid the necessity of identifying the buildings as brothels or punishing landlords for renting clandestinely. The increasing numbers of prostitutes on the streets of Mériadeck simply impeded rentals to average citizens, they said.[75] No progress was made, and the landlords received little by way of official response. Mme St. Blaugual wrote again: "[Our meeting] with your representative left us hopeful but alas, nothing has changed. These women still live around us [and] it is truly unfortunate that the brave citizens in the prostitution quartier cannot mine the advantages produced on this street [by sex work]." Madame St. Blaugual emphasized that her situation was "the same [as that of] all the landlords on half of the street." Permitting landlords to rent openly to sex workers would augment incomes. This increased income would then continue to support city taxes.[76] Letters about rentals and prostitution arrived in the mayor's office well into the summer of 1905. One property owner emphasized the "devoted [political] support" that her family had given Daney in the last elections and asked for changes in regulation. The prostitutes "[took] up the entire street, up to the Place Mériadeck" and made it "impossible to rent rooms," she complained. Emphasizing the common problem of rentals, she also underscored the importance of paying taxes: "[Municipal] taxes will soon be due and they are fairly high. If you do not give me the means [to rent], how will I be able to pay my taxes?"[77] Property owners hoping to take greater advantage of the tradition of cohabitation that had existed in Mériadeck experienced disappointment. Mayor Daney's attention was focused instead on developing the city and supporting large public events.[78]

For politicians, developing the city also meant responding to changes in prostitution and recognizing its influence on the city. Given increasing public interest in the subject, Mayor Daney issued a new arrêté in 1905 directed at the "expulsion of prostitutes from the rue Dalon." Issued on May 31, it barred brothels and prostitutes from one of the longest streets of Mériadeck. A busy, important thoroughfare, rue Dalon hosted a number of brothels and traversed the quartier, covering at least five city blocks; police identified it as a hot area of Mériadeck, one where brothel prostitution had long existed. In the geography of Mériadeck, rue Dalon allowed visitors to move quickly from one brothel to another or later to roam freely through the quartier in search of independent prostitutes.[79] We may never fully know Daney's motive for issuing the 1905 ordinance, but the results are clear. Rather than improving conditions in the quartier by removing women from the streets or rejuvenating businesses, the new ordinance had the opposite effect. A wave of complaints and pleas arrived in the mayor's office from local businesses and residents asking him to rescind the arrêté.

The inhabitants of Mériadeck recognized that the ordinance of May 31 had permanently changed the structure of the neighborhood's streets, in the process damaging a local economy that had grown dependent on the sex trade. The ordinance ordered brothels on Mériadeck's rue Dalon to relocate and eliminated traffic to the area. More importantly, removing the brothels eliminated their need for goods and services and the sales upon which local merchants depended.[80] Area shopkeepers and property owners joined brothel keepers to petition the mayor about the economic damage the new ordinance was inflicting on Mériadeck's inhabitants.[81] On July 19, only a few weeks after the mayor issued his arrêté, twenty-four business owners wrote to him complaining about the new policy and demanding that the mayor "revisit his decision." They argued, "The application of this arrêté will be very detrimental, from considering the buildings that as a result will not be rented, to the serious decline in sales suffered by small businesses and boutiques."[82] Of the petitioners, only four owned and rented properties. The remaining signatories represented the businesses that supported daily life on rue Dalon. These included a pastry shop, a butcher, a baker, a haberdasher, a sausage shop, three different groceries, three bars, a coal supplier, a hair salon, a loom worker, and a cobbler.[83] Along with the property owners, these merchants remained dependent on the commercial sex work of the neighborhood. They understood the importance of prostitution and brothels in terms of their own economic livelihoods. The brothels of the Mériadeck neighborhood offered more than entertainment and sexual services to clients and visitors. The income generated by brothels on rue Dalon flowed outward into the community, where it supported local merchants and contributed to the economic vitality of the neighborhood.

Mayor Daney did not revoke his arrêté, and the loss of brothel business reshaped Mériadeck's urban geography, frustrating local inhabitants. Five years later, the effects of Daney's actions had taken a toll on the street. In 1910 a group of inhabitants and proprietors on Bordeaux's rue Dalon again petitioned the mayor to allow brothels and prostitution to return to rue Dalon and reinvent the limited vitality that sexual commerce had provided the area. Writing to the mayor, they emphasized the economic and social benefits that sex work provided in Mériadeck, disregarding any negative public discourse about prostitution. "The women who used to live on the street . . . are now spread throughout the city," the group intoned. "Before, when the women were here, rue Dalon thrived. Now, it's squalor and destitution; the neighborhood is inhabited by people with badly kept houses who are preyed on by illnesses, including tuberculosis." The writers pleaded with the mayor to the alter his recent ordinances on brothels "in the interest of the morale of the city, even more because the [nearby] rue de la Galles maintained its privileges, allowing the women to live and work there."[84] In other words, the writers complained that rue Dalon suffered physically and economically; in the process, they specifically recognized how sexual commerce added to the vitality of the community and contributed to a positive urban experience.

In Bordeaux brothels and prostitution supported the economic vitality of a small portion of the city, exerting substantial influence on residents' lives and the urban landscape. Just as the police and queer men moved about the city of Paris in a tense but reciprocal relationship, as Andrew Israel Ross shows earlier in this volume, female prostitutes and other urban residents relied on one another in complicated ways. In Mériadeck brothel keepers employed musicians, who then provided support for immigrant families. Those who attended to the sex workers' daily needs, such as the hairdresser who provided services at 16 rue Dalon, saw a stream of women in their shops. Service providers, especially, recognized the importance of sex workers' personal expenditures. In spite of the area's social reciprocity, however, public concern for morality and sex workers who could reportedly "stroll half-naked from morning to night" generated negative interest in Mériadeck that was stronger than the neighborhood's ties; intervention by the mayor was perhaps inevitable.[85] Ultimately, the local economic benefits of female prostitution could not outweigh the perception in some circles that allowing sexual commerce to exist in this small neighborhood of Bordeaux hampered the development of the populous city more generally.

Sharon Wood writes that "great questions can be asked in small places."[86] Mériadeck is one such place. As expressed in petitions and letters to municipal officials, Mériadeck's stability and residents' support for prostitution reveal that urban sociability and social cohesion existed in the quartier, due almost exclusively to the brothels and prostitutes on its streets. When no one else would have them, Italian immigrants to Bordeaux flocked to Mériadeck to become part of the area's café culture, work in its brothels, and join a system of firmly established neighborliness and reciprocity. Reliant on rent paid by sex workers, property owners organized and petitioned the government to retain sexual commerce in the area; the urban environment remained safer and more sanitary with brothels and prostitution on its streets. Prostitutes of all types spent what they earned in local shops, in such amounts that local business owners recognized the degree to which they needed them to survive. Mériadeck's residents argued that they lived in a stable urban environment as a result of the sexual commerce on their streets. They derived significant economic and social benefit from it, not in spite of it. In short, sexual commerce in Mériadeck added wealth to the area's economy and shaped the city's urban environment throughout the nineteenth century.

Notes

1. "Police Register" entry 21, January 1914, 1501 I 8, Archives Municipales de Bordeaux (hereafter AMB). One French franc from 1914 was closer to four euros in 2022. For conversions, see the website of the National Institute of Statistics and Economic Studies, http://www.insee.fr/en/themes/indicateur.asp?id=29&type=1&page=achatfranc.htm, accessed July 20, 2012; for additional information, including inflation, FxTop offers historic rates and tables. See https://fxtop.com/en/inflation-calculator.php?A=1&c1=fra&indice=frcpi1998&dd1=31&mm1=01&yyyy1=1914&dd2=16&mm2=03&yyyy2=2022&btnok=Compute+actual+value, accessed March 16, 2022.

2. Nicholas Lombardo, "White-Collar Workers and Neighborhood Change: Jarvis Street in Toronto, 1880–1920," *Urban History Review/Revue d'histoire urbaine* 43, no. 1 (Fall 2014): 6, 8.

3. Nathan Roth and Jill L. Grant, "The Story of a Commercial Street: Growth, Decline, and Gentrification on Gottingen Street, Halifax," *Urban History Review/Revue d'historie urbaine* 43, no. 2 (Spring 2015): 39.

4. William B. Cohen, *Urban Government and the Rise of the French City: Five Municipalities in the Nineteenth Century* (New York: St. Martin's, 1998), 150, 173.

5. Philip G. Nord, *Paris Shopkeepers and the Politics of Resentment* (Princeton NJ: Princeton University Press, 1986), 100. See also Victoria E. Thompson, "Urban Renovation, Moral Regeneration: Domesticating the *Halles* in Second-Empire Paris," *French Historical Studies* 20, no. 1 (Winter 1997): 88.

6. See, for example, David Garrioch, "The Everyday Lives of Parisian Women and the October Days of 1789," *Social History* 24, no. 3 (October 1999): 231–49; Catharina Lis and Hugo Soly, "Neighborhood Social Change in West European Cities: Sixteenth to Nineteenth Centuries," *International Review of Social History* 38, no. 1 (April 1993): 1–30.

7. Alain Corbin, *Women for Hire: Prostitution and Sexuality in France after 1850,* trans. Alan Sheridan (Cambridge MA: Harvard University Press, 1990), 4.

8. "Règlement général sur la Police des Mœurs," July 12, 1887, 1211 I 19, AMB.

9. Cohen, *Urban Government,* 212.

10. Cohen, *Urban Government,* 213. See also Sean M. Quinlan, *The Great Nation in Decline: Sex, Modernity and Health Crises in Revolutionary France c.1750–1850* (Burlington VT: Ashgate, 2007), 76, 83, 84; David S. Barnes, *The Making of a Social Disease: Tuberculosis in Nineteenth-Century France* (Berkeley: University of California Press, 1995), 206.

11. Laurence Amiel, *La prostitution et les prostituées à Bordeaux: Du début du XIXe siècle au début du XXe* (Bordeaux, France: IAES, 1994), 49–50.

12. Letter to the prefect of the Gironde, June 17, 1881, 4M 337, Archives Départementales de la Gironde, Bordeaux (hereafter ADG).

13. Report to the mayor of Libourne, January 23, 1893, 4M 337, ADG.

14. Report from agents of the Gendarmerie Nationale, January 5, 1885, 4M 337, ADG.

15. Corbin, *Women for Hire,* 122.

16. Corbin, *Women for Hire,* 58–59.

17. Map of Mériadeck before changes to street names, 1211 I 16, AMB; see also Amiel, *La prostitution,* 51.

18. "État des Maîtresses de maisons de tolérance," June 11, 1886, 1250 I 4, AMB.

19. Letter to the mayor, June 20, 1910, 1211 I 10, AMB; and letter to the mayor, August 26, 1912, 1211 I 10, AMB. Furnishings for rooms and brothels have been well documented. For a discussion of women's interest in furnishing their own space, see Diane Yvonne Ghirardo, "The Topography of Prostitution in Renaissance

Ferrara," *Journal of the Society of Architectural Historians* 60, no. 4 (December 2001): 421.

20. Roth and Grant, "The Story of a Commercial Street," 39.

21. Letter to the mayor, July 19, 1905, 1211 I 16, AMB.

22. For a discussion of the spatial and commercial changes that neighborhood demographics can provoke, see Lombardo, "White-Collar Workers," 5–19.

23. David Garrioch and Mark Peel, "Introduction: The Social History of Urban Neighborhoods," *Journal of Urban History* 32, no. 5 (July 2006): 663. See also Lis and Soly, "Neighborhood Social Change," 14.

24. David Garrioch, *Neighborhood and Community in Paris, 1740–1790* (Cambridge: Cambridge University Press, 1986), 227–28.

25. Lis and Soly, "Neighborhood Social Change," 9, 13.

26. Letter to the mayor, October 1881, 1262 I 3, AMB.

27. Police report on a series of disturbances located on rue Lambert, May 21, 1883, 1211 10, AMB.

28. Letter to the police, June 9, 1883, and letter to the police from M. Antonio, August 18, 1883, 1262 I 3, AMB.

29. Richard J. Evans, "Prostitution, State and Society in Imperial Germany," *Past and Present* 70, no. 1 (February 1976): 113.

30. Police report, June 14, 1883, 1262 I 3, AMB.

31. Police report, June 14, 1883, 1262 I 3, AMB.

32. Letter to the mayor, October 1, 1881, and August 13, 1898, 1262 I 3, AMB.

33. Louis Desgraves and Georges Dupeux, eds., *Bordeaux au XIXe siècle* (Bordeaux, France: Fédération historique du Sud-Ouest, 1969), 562; Michel Mancini to Albert Brandenburg, November 1881, 1262 I 3, AMB.

34. Ange Conti to Albert Brandenburg, October 27, 1881, 1262 I 3, AMB.

35. Kathleen Lord, "Permeable Boundaries: Negotiation, Resistance, and Transgression of Street Space in Saint-Henri, Québec, 1875–1905," *Urban History Review/Revue d'histoire urbaine* 33 no. 2 (Spring 2005): 18–19.

36. Roth and Grant, "The Story of a Commercial Street," 39.

37. Giuseppe Christofano to Albert Brandenburg, October 28, 1881, 1262 I 3, AMB.

38. François Fioril to Albert Brandenburg, October 1, 1881, 1262 I 3, AMB.

39. Fioril to Brandenburg, October 1, 1881; police report on François Fioril, October 8, 1881, 1262 I 3, AMB.

40. Police report on "Joseph" Christofano, November 16, 1881, 1262 I 3, AMB. Christofano earned 20 francs plus meals. In their files, the French police changed his name from Giuseppe to Joseph.

41. Police report on Christofano, October 30, 1881, 1262 I 3, AMB.

42. Police report on Fioril, October 8, 1881, 1262 I 3, AMB.

43. Police report on Prosper Messina, November 9, 1881, 1262 I 3, AMB.

44. Police report on Pascal Messina, November 16, 1881, 1262 I 3, AMB.

45. Letter to the police, July 19, 1883, 1262 I 3, AMB. A brothel on rue de Gasc paid the highest salary in the area at forty francs plus meals.

46. Police report on M. Régis, October 30, 1881, 1262 I 3, AMB. Régis rented a room for ten francs per month and received a salary of thirty francs plus meals to work in a brothel run by Mme Guénand, 37 rue Lambert.

47. Desgraves and Dupeaux, *Bordeaux au XIXe siècle*, 439–40, 445, 448.

48. For a discussion on changes in mass culture during the fin-de-siècle, see Leo Charney and Vanessa R. Schwartz, eds., *Cinema and the Invention of Modern Life* (Berkeley: University of California Press, 1995); Vanessa R. Schwartz, *Spectacular Realities: Early Mass Culture in Fin-de-Siècle Paris* (Berkeley: University of California Press, 1998); Thomas Richards, *The Commodity Culture of Victorian England: Advertising and Spectacle, 1851–1914* (Stanford CA: Stanford University Press, 1990); Brenda Assael, *The Circus and Victorian Society* (Charlottesville: University of Virginia Press, 2005); and Nadja Durbach, *Spectacle of Deformity: Freak Shows and Modern British Culture* (Berkeley: University of California Press, 2010).

49. Letter from the mayor, May 25, 1883, 1211 I 10, AMB.

50. Desgraves and Dupeaux, *Bordeaux au XIXe siècle*, 384n6.

51. Desgraves and Dupeaux, *Bordeaux au XIXe siècle*, 384, 389.

52. Desgraves and Dupeaux, *Bordeaux au XIXe siècle*, 384.

53. Desgraves and Dupeaux, *Bordeaux au XIXe siècle*, 384, 389.

54. *Histoire des maires de Bordeaux* (Bordeaux, France: Les Dossiers d'Aquitaine, 2008), 345.

55. Letter from the mayor, May 25, 1883, 1211 I 10, AMB; Desgraves and Dupeaux, *Bordeaux au XIXe siècle*, 562.

56. "Statistiques," 1888 to 1912, 1211 I 8, AMB.

57. Letter to the *commissaire central*, October 12, 1889, 1250 I 4, AMB.

58. Letter to the *commissaire central*, October 12, 1889, 1250 I 4, AMB.

59. Letter to the police, July 14, 1896, 1211 I 10, AMB.

60. Letter to the mayor, July 14, 1896, 1211 I 10, AMB.

61. Letter to the mayor, July 14, 1896, 1211 I 10, AMB.

62. Petition to the mayor, May 21, 1902, 1250 I 4, AMB.

63. Neil Larry Shumsky, "Tacit Acceptance: Respectable Americans and Segregated Prostitution, 1870–1910," *Journal of Social History* 19, no. 4 (1986): 666.

64. Letter to the mayor, July 14, 1896, 1250 I 4, AMB.

65 . Letter to the mayor, July 14, 1889, 1211 I 10, AMB.

66. Letter to the *commissaire central*, October 12, 1889, 1250 I 4, AMB.

67. Janet Oswald, "The Spinning House Girls: Cambridge University's Distinctive Policing of Prostitution, 1823–1894," *Urban History* 39, no. 3 (August 2012): 469.

68. "Extrait du journal," *Le Nouvelliste*, May 23, 1898, 1211 I 10, AMB.

69. "Extrait du journal," *La Vie joyeuse*, May 7, 1898, 1211 I 10, AMB.

70. "Extrait du journal," *La Vie joyeuse*, May 7, 1898, 1211 I 10, AMB.

71. In March, the Ligue pour le relèvement de la moralité publique and the Société de protestation contre la licence des rues met in Bordeaux for the first time at the Congrès National contre la Pornographie. See "Rapports, discussions, vœux et conférences, 14–15 mars 1905" (Bordeaux, France: 1er Congrès national contre la pornographie, 1905). On the fight against pornography and the resulting legislation, see Fédération des sociétés contre la pornographie, "Manual pratique pour la lutte contre la pornographie" (Paris: Fédération des sociétés contre la pornographie, 1909). On public morality and public campaigns, see Steven C. Hause, "Social Control in Late Nineteenth-Century France: Protestant Campaigns for Strict Public Morality," in Christopher E. Forth and Elinor Accampo, eds., *Confronting Modernity in Fin-de-Siècle France: Bodies, Minds and Gender* (New York: Palgrave, 2010), 135–49.

72. Alfred Daney was elected on May 15, 1904. See Desgraves and Dupeaux, *Bordeaux au XIXe siècle*, 344–45, 562.

73. *Histoire des maires de Bordeaux*, 347.

74. Letter to the mayor, April 17, 1904, 1211 I 16, AMB.

75. Letter to the mayor, November 22, 1904, 1211 I 16, AMB.

76. Letter to the mayor, January 20, 1905, 1211 I 16, AMB.

77. Letter to the mayor, May 28, 1905, 1211 I 16, AMB.

78. Bordeaux hosted a colonial exposition in 1895 and a maritime colonial exposition in 1907. See *Histoire des maires de Bordeaux*, 359, 370, 371.

79. "Quartier Primitive," n.d., 1211 I 16, AMB.

80. Letter to the mayor, July 19, 1905, 1211 I 16, AMB.

81. Notice regarding prostitution, May 31, 1905, 1211 I 16, AMB. Daney ordered the police to give written notice to all registered women, lodging houses, and brothels on the street to ensure "the strict execution" of the ordinance.

82. Letter to the mayor, July 19, 1905, 1211 I 16, AMB.

83. Letter to the mayor, July 19, 1905, 1211 I 16, AMB.

84. Letter to the mayor from residents of rue Dalon, June 20, 1910, 1211 I 16, AMB.

85. Letter to the mayor, August 26, 1912, 1211 I 10, AMB.

86. Sharon E. Wood, *The Freedom of the Streets: Work, Citizenship, and Sexuality in a Gilded Age City* (Chapel Hill: University of North Carolina Press, 2005), 13.

Suggested Reading

Accampo, Elinor, and Christopher E. Forth, eds., *Confronting Modernity in Fin-de Siècle France.* Houndmills: Palgrave Macmillan, 2010.

Berlière, Jean-Marc, Catherine Denys, Dominique Kalifa, and Vincent Milliot, eds., *Métiers de police: Être policier en Europe, XVIIIe–XXe siècle.* Rennes, France: Presses universitaires de Rennes, 2008.

Charney, Leo, and Vanessa R. Schwartz, eds., *Cinema and the Invention of Modern Life.* Berkeley: University of California Press, 1995.

Cohen, William B. *Urban Government and the Rise of the French City: Five Municipalities in the Nineteenth Century.* New York: St. Martin's, 1998.

Corbin, Alain. *Women for Hire: Prostitution and Sexuality in France after 1850.* Translated by Alan Sheridan. Cambridge MA: Harvard University Press, 1990.

Durbach, Nadja. *Spectacle of Deformity: Freak Shows and Modern British Culture.* Berkeley: University of California Press, 2010.

Ferguson, Eliza Earle. *Gender and Justice: Violence, Intimacy, and Community in Fin-de-Siècle Paris.* Baltimore: Johns Hopkins University Press, 2010.

Fuchs, Rachel G. *New Approaches to European History: Gender and Poverty in Nineteenth-Century Europe.* Cambridge: Cambridge University Press, 2005.

Harsin, Jill. *Policing Prostitution in Nineteenth-Century Paris.* Princeton NJ: Princeton University Press, 1985.

Hershatter, Gail. *Dangerous Pleasures: Prostitution and Modernity in Twentieth-Century Shanghai.* Berkeley: University of California Press, 1999.

Nord, Philip G. *Paris Shopkeepers and the Politics of Resentment.* Princeton NJ: Princeton University Press, 1986.

Quinlan, Sean M. *The Great Nation in Decline: Sex, Modernity and Health Crises in Revolutionary France c.1750–1850.* Burlington VT: Ashgate, 2007.

Schwartz, Vanessa R. *Spectacular Realities: Early Mass Culture in Fin-de-Siècle Paris.* Berkeley: University of California Press, 1998.

Wood, Sharon E. *The Freedom of the Streets: Work, Citizenship, and Sexuality in a Gilded Age City.* Chapel Hill: University of North Carolina Press, 2005.

9

TWO READINGS OF GABRIELLE, OR PASSION, MOBILITY, AND THE GOVERNANCE OF WHITE PRESTIGE IN COLONIAL SENEGAL

JENNIFER ANNE BOITTIN

In 1927 Gabrielle D., a white French woman originally from Lille, traveled from Paris, where she worked as a milliner, to French West Africa (hereafter AOF, short for l'Afrique occidentale française).[1] She was thirty-nine years old, but her brother-in-law back in Pantin (in the Paris suburbs), François Mugnier, felt that he urgently needed to intervene on her behalf with the governor-general of AOF, whose administration was in Senegal, because he believed her to be in grave danger. François explained that although she was well educated, she had allowed her "pathological, romantic temperament" to engulf her in dreams of overseas passion.[2] She had started to read *Le chasseur français*. The publication, which, according to François, was well regarded, had included personal ads to which Gabrielle had responded. Soon afterward, she had built what she referred to as an "epistolary relationship" with Doctor Abel Adolphe André Mazohyié. Born in 1876 in Rouen, the son of a lawyer, he was the tenant of either a hotel or a restaurant in Thiès, Senegal. He had sent her family proof of his business license and a reproduction of his passport, complete with photo, which revealed that he had arrived in Dakar on June 17, 1918, having traveled there from Brazil via Buenos Aires, Argentina.

With a firm promise of marriage, Gabrielle embarked on a ship departing from Marseille. Upon arriving in Dakar, she sent a joyous letter via airmail to confirm her safe arrival; this letter was accompanied by a shorter one from Mazohyié. The couple traveled on to Thiès, and her family heard nothing more for a month, at which time the postman simultaneously delivered three missives: a somewhat inane letter from Gabrielle filled with insignificant details, which seemed stylistically out of character for her; a bland letter from Mazohyié, in which he affectionately called her family members "brother-in-law" and "sister-in-law"; and finally, from Louis Peverelly, an employee of the Thiès-Niger railway line, a letter dated August 28, 1927, in which he claimed that Gabrielle was "morally suffering in promiscuity with a man who was a human decrepitude," with *décrépitude* perhaps meant to signal moral degeneration.[3]

Peverelly's letter begged Gabrielle's sister back in Pantin to initiate a formal request for Gabrielle's repatriation, or paid return to metropolitan France, by contacting the Ministry of Colonies. He specified that her family members should first note in their letter to the ministry that Doctor Mazohyié had previously been legally sanctioned, given that he was "interdit de séjour" (banned from entering) a place or places Peverelly left unnamed. Had her family been colonial administrators, Peverelly wrote, they would have noticed the problem before she ever left the metropole—via Mazohyié's passport's references to Brazil and Argentina. Peverelly signaled these references as the second and far more urgent reason for initiating Gabrielle's repatriation. Doctor Mazohyié had had many professions and traveled to numerous places, including French Guiana, but he was mostly known for having practiced, in Dakar, the "white slave trade." Buenos Aires and Dakar were common ports of call along one of the itineraries for European sex workers moving between Europe, Africa, and South America. The doctor planned to open a brothel in Thiès, and Gabrielle was to serve as its "cornerstone" prostitute. Peverelly, who may have slipped up briefly when he mentioned that, like most locals, he habitually frequented the establishment that was becoming a brothel, went on to describe the doctor as "under cover of a sweet appearance . . . mentally and morally defective." He finally recommended that before requesting repatriation, Gabrielle's sister should head to the Place Vendôme in Paris, where the Ministry of Justice would help her to unearth the doctor's criminal record. Peverelly explained that he felt it was his duty to interfere because Gabrielle had asked for his help and hers was an appalling situation. While Gabrielle waited for her family to act, Peverelly had persuaded her to continue to "play her role," without letting the doctor suspect that she was trying to escape his clutches. In the meantime, her family could write to her by sliding their letters into an envelope and then placing that first envelope into a second one addressed to Peverelly. All these precautions were necessary, he wrote, because they should "fear reprisals" against Gabrielle. After all, he added, "What's one more pistol shot for [Mazohyié]?"[4]

This missive was alarming to receive, and although it had been addressed to Gabrielle's sister, Gabrielle's brother-in-law promptly wrote to the governor-general of AOF to inquire about Gabrielle's safety and to initiate her rapid repatriation. He included a transcript of Peverelly's letter, highlighting in his own missive words such as "white slave trade" to give the governor-general's office a sense of urgency. He also underscored how duplicitous the doctor had been to use marriage as the lure for his seedy enterprise and questioned how the bureaucracy could have failed to secure its territories from such abhorrent predators.

Based on these facts, Gabrielle's repatriation was hastily granted. And we twenty-first-century readers of the archival files about her are left with the sense that we have just read a tale with vaudevillian resonances: a villainous doctor and righteous champions in the form of Gabrielle's concerned brother-in-law, local men, and civil servants, all prepared to rush in and save her; and, of course, the naive white woman who fell into the debauched clutches of a profiteering colonist, the sort of immoral man who might invite not only European but also African men to pay for her services. There was only one critical twist to this moral tale. After her repatriation was granted, Gabrielle roundly rejected it and then asked that the decision be formally overturned. She acted the part of victim very poorly indeed.

In Gabrielle's story, the word "sex" was never used. The word that came closest to directly invoking sex was "promiscuity." Prostitution generally involves sex acts as part of a paid transaction, but none of these texts spoke of prostitution as sex; they instead defined it as slavery. The absence of sex in Gabrielle's file matters because examining the history of sexuality can often require reading around such glaring absences, looking for silences and the unsaid. For example, Peverelly wrote that Gabrielle was forced to live in "promiscuity" with a man he described as a "human decrepitude," a combination of coded phrases that let readers know that sex acts were occurring, while implying that they were not to her taste. Yet archives rarely reveal the specifics of what happened between lovers, let alone what people felt about their intimate acts. The absence of the word "sex" in Gabrielle's file also matters because sex is very rarely just about sex. Gabrielle's story garnered its readers' attention because of both concrete and imagined sex acts. Yet even before we see Gabrielle's own version of her story, we already know that sex in her case worked in tandem with danger, confinement, and financial hopes, because someone (but not Gabrielle) had positioned himself to profit from her sexual labor. We see loneliness, adventure, escape, travel, discovery, kindness, humanity, and finally comradeship, because Gabrielle confided in a man who in turn felt compelled to assist her.

Even without the word "sex," Gabrielle's story was about sex, because most of the men involved saw it as about the potential for prostitution while she saw it as about passion. To account for these two angles, this chapter analyzes Gabrielle's story twice. First, I read her story via the lens of sexuality as it related to colonial governance. Colonial civil servants integrated the tracking of sex into their civilizing mission, a mission that this chapter shows did not just focus upon people indigenous to West Africa but also extended to European colonists, particularly women whom officials perceived as lower class.[5] Sex was tightly linked to colonial governance when it came to white women, because if they behaved in any way less than appropriately bourgeois, in the European sense of the term, administrators feared that white prestige overseas, and hence French control over the region, would be upended.

Second, using the lens of sexuality, I show that, despite all the men involved, this was Gabrielle's story, and sex meant passion and mobility to her. She was far more present in her own narrative than the early flurry of official reports in her file suggests. Moreover, her responses to bureaucrats revealed her to be a woman with a strong voice who displayed none of the romantic fantasies that her brother-in-law saw in her. She had a precise reason for refusing to return to the metropole, and she was practical and grounded in her knowledge of her colonial situation when she explained herself to authorities.

Moving from a superstructural to a micro, human lens reveals that for all the systems, ideologies, and rhetoric in place to guide, aid, and ultimately attempt to control white women's bodies and imperial mobility, the colonial bureaucracy had no clothes. It could not force a woman who was mentally sound and no longer a minor to do something that she did not wish to do. This chapter also argues that what imperial administrators and Gabrielle's brother-in-law overlooked was that the sex at the heart of her story was really passion. As a concept, passion carries within it both sex and sentiment, both desires and emotions, and hence functions as a motivator and tactic for mobility. The desires were not only erotic but also included the pursuit of financial independence, comfort, and companionship. Because women were assumed to be controlled by them, emotions were both what led women to be stereotyped as passive and therefore in need of help, and that from which women drew strength. As Sara Ahmed explains, on the surface, "to be emotional is to have one's judgement affected: it is to be reactive instead of active, dependent rather than autonomous."[6] Thinking about mobility via passion is thus useful for two reasons: first, passion underscores the gendered stigma of unreason, of passivity rather than autonomy.[7] Women were suspect and unwanted as independent migrants because they were assumed to be passive and therefore vulnerable. Second, sex in Africa has often been studied via prostitution (including sexually transmitted infections, or STIS) or as a transactional act. Hence it has been viewed through a prism of unequal power relations more generally, and thus as separate from sentiment.[8] Yet passion allowed migrants to assert themselves in ways that belied the passive assumptions made about them. Passion, therefore, marks this chapter's intervention into the history of sexuality.

When we focus on case studies of individual lives, it becomes clear that women perceived as victims of trafficking were often instead willing migrants who chose to root their labor and income in sex, as Elisa Camiscioli shows.[9] Women's sex labor was central to imperial governance in part because constructions of nations and empires centered women in domestic roles (mother-wife-daughter), and men as protectors and defenders.[10] Simultaneously, myths of coercion and white slavery obfuscated the decision-making process behind women's migrations and practices of sex work.[11] Moreover, as Caroline Séquin shows, the regulation of sex workers helped to reinforce all racial hierarchies around sex in the colonies.[12] The European owners of regulated brothels kept African men from entering those highly segregated spaces and enticed European men to seek out European rather than African women. The deliberate segregation of brothels slushed over and mixed with administrative attempts to regulate and segregate the sexual and social practices of all independent female migrants traveling from Europe to Africa.

Studies of independent women who migrated to French colonies have tended to focus upon sex workers or missionaries, who were regulated by state or religious authorities, which is not to say these travelers did not find autonomy.[13] Other work has focused on women who migrated with the explicit goal of inhabiting a domestic sphere, as spouses, fiancées, mothers, or daughters, all of whom were expected to be surveilled by the men in their lives.[14] This chapter concentrates instead upon an independent migrant perceived as both a potential prostitute and a potential wife, but who claimed to be neither a sex worker nor a domestic figure, leaving open the question of who could claim authority over her and thus giving her an opening to claim authority over herself. This chapter complements Séquin's emphasis on the ways in which sex was used to reinforce racial hierarchies in French colonies by showing how independent women could use colonial assumptions about sex for their own ends. In doing so this chapter contributes to the history of women by demonstrating that passion provided a tactic for navigating colonial society or establishing a life in the colonies not despite but through the various sexual and racial assumptions placed on women by colonial and familial authorities.

Thus, this chapter argues that by focusing on an individual case involving sex in the context of a woman's intimate (rather than professional) life, considering the willingness of migrants to travel, and injecting the sentimental back into our readings of sex—in other words, by thinking about passion—we can better understand how women functioned as independent migrants overseas in part by using the supposed reactivity and passivity of their sentiments as tools. Women's independence was defined as passion, which was coded as out of control like their emotions in general, which in turn were perceived as a threat by male regulators and trackers. The paradox contained within the concept of passion is that not only did women like Gabrielle use their supposed passivity to actively gain support from the administration, but their passion made them less controllable. Therefore, this chapter intervenes in the field of colonial history by showing how the disarray of imperial systems of domination was not only brought about by Wolof, Fula, Serer, and other peoples indigenous to West Africa and the difficulty administrators had in attempting to control them and their large swaths of land. Nor was that disarray only caused by the tenuous foundations of segregationist regulations around sex and the challenges raised by population intermingling more generally—foundations that in part depended upon European women self-regulating interracial sex. Ultimately, Gabrielle's story reveals how such efforts floundered because these systems failed to fully account for the motivations of individuals within those systems.

Considering the ways in which women were autonomous and willingly mobile reveals sex as not only physical, but also as emotional, financial, and practical. Centering sex while accepting the messiness of the sentiments and practicalities surrounding it, then, allows us to better understand the disorderliness of colonial governance. Administrators controlled surprisingly little when it came to the individuals in overseas France, even when those individuals were white Europeans whom the administration formally tracked from port to port and city to city. Scholarship on the policing of suspects and governance in the French empire has shown that even as people were closely tracked, they found creative ways to escape scrutiny.[15] This chapter adds to that scholarship by focusing on sex beyond sex trafficking and labor. Centering passion's role in the stories that make up the experiences of everyday life allows us to continue to break apart monolithic readings of independent women overseas as victims (for example "white slaves" and "indigents") and instead think about how their capacity to refuse imperial structures and categories was a crucial component of their colonial mobility. That refusal was present first and foremost among indigenous West Africans, but also among colonists. Overseas, passion was more inspiring than sex as a driving force of mobility, labor, and defiance.

Reading Gabrielle, Part I: Governance and White Prestige

Scholars of empire have previously shown how sometimes unspoken but often explicit hierarchies of gender, race, and class guided governance, especially in the colonies, but also in metropolitan France.[16] Female migrants posed problems within those hierarchies, especially when sex played a role within their trajectories. From that perspective, Gabrielle's story can be read as a story of white male colonists with various degrees of power who sought to shape her trajectory. Depending on where they were situated and their status within the administration, they could initiate a request to help her from afar (like Peverelly) or make the decision to pay for her trip to France (like Léonce Jore, the governor of Senegal with whom she communicated and who answered to the governor-general of AOF, Jules Carde). The promptness with which her repatriation was granted was possible because an entire system was in place to deal with situations such as Gabrielle's. The very existence of that system shows how her story was both unique and common. It was unique because no two stories interacting with that system were alike, because her voice was particularly dynamic, and because we do not often hear women's perspectives regarding their repatriation. Gabrielle's story was common because there was a protocol for initiating repatriation, as hard luck was a common feature of colonial mobility.

Most often, requests for repatriation or financial aid because of indigence were personally generated by the people who needed help. Gabrielle's case initially fell into a different category, because her brother-in-law's letter was classified as a "search in the interest of families," or a search for someone considered missing. To put his request into perspective, data from 1935 and 1936 show that there were 31 such official files filtered by the *Sûreté*, which was in charge of intelligence and policing in AOF. During this same period the Sûreté recorded 10,803 arrivals in Dakar and 7,056 departures, in the process creating 1,729 new dossiers.[17] Thus there were relatively few missing persons requests, but administrators took them seriously. Concern for a relative's safety was a less common motivation for the Sûreté to create a case than spouses trying to locate their partners, especially women seeking men who owed child support. To track such cases, relevant ministries and governors' offices used logs and records generated at ports of entry and sent letters (or, more rarely, telegrams) from the Ministry of Colonies in Paris to the offices of the governors-general, which in turn forwarded these requests for information to the circles of administration within AOF or beyond. If administrators located the individual, there was a caveat; the tracked person was under no obligation to reveal their location.[18]

In Gabrielle's case Peverelly had signaled her exact location and need for support after she had used long-standing assumptions regarding women's emotions and passivity to secure assistance. That he contacted her family rather than someone in Thiès or Dakar was consistent with his paranoia regarding the doctor's violent tendencies. If Peverelly even knew that she could initiate her own repatriation request, he either suspected she might refuse to do so, felt a patriarchal imperative to help her personally, or feared the repercussions from Mazohyié should she be seen marching into the local police station to request help. Regardless, in Gabrielle's case the problem was not finding her but returning her to the metropole. Once a white woman showed signs that she was indigent or was in a potentially improper, morally ambiguous relationship, men such as Jules Carde, who was governor-general of AOF from 1923 to 1930 and personally followed Gabrielle's case, feared that her next step would be to have sex with men of color, either under duress from men such as Mazohyié or, worse, consensually.[19] Repeatedly, documents related to white women in AOF focused on behavior considered to be problematic: alleged madness, drunkenness, and most regularly, the threat of having sex across the color line. All these acts were public behavioral slippages and therefore capable of tarnishing French prestige.[20] Thus, throughout the empire, administrators tracked white women and explicitly linked their cases with French prestige, which some in AOF also termed "white prestige."[21]

Where did administrators observe the public performance of bad white womanhood in Gabrielle's case? Where was the threat to white prestige? First, Gabrielle independently pursued her long-distance passion for a man she had never met, threatening the ways migration worked and the controls put in place to regulate movement; her mobility revealed the system's dangerous permeability. Second, she had left behind the structure of her metropolitan family and rejected the stand-in patriarchy provided by the administration in Senegal. Third, as the potential inceptive prostitute in a volatile man's illegal brothel, she was operating outside of the imperial systems that tracked female sex laborers, including those that did so via regular doctor's examinations for STIs. She had not arrived as a registered prostitute but rather as a potential victim of so-called "white slavery." Globally, in the early twentieth century, various movements that sought to eliminate prostitution used that term irrespective of whether women believed themselves to be victims of trafficking. Brian Donovan emphasizes the importance of paying attention to the specificity of the term "white" in conjunction with "slavery" because "the creation and maintenance of racial categories depends upon characterizations of people as sexual actors."[22] "White" was explicitly underscored as the racial category driving associations and movements to track and push back against women's sexually driven migrations. "White slavery" was not a term specific to France or to colonial settings. It was used across Europe and the United States. Paradoxically, whereas Gabrielle's passion-driven mobile independence was perceived as threatening overseas, campaigns against "white slavery," by their very use of the term "slave," focused on white women's lack of independence, suggesting they were at risk of being as subjugated as were, campaigners assumed, women of color, whom they perceived as having fewer rights and freedoms than white women. The broader contradiction here was that France was both a strong advocate for regulating prostitution via registration and other measures that curtailed women's independence and an important participant in efforts to abolish "white slavery" ostensibly to reinstate that independence.

As a result of regulation, registered white sex workers in Dakar, for example, often traveled from the French metropole to service white men exclusively. In the 1920s there were approximately twenty-five to thirty such women working in four and later five brothels gathered along the rue Raffenel, numbers deemed insufficient by authorities, who assumed a dearth of white women was the reason that sailors were turning to African prostitutes. The latter were unregulated and therefore assumed to be the source of the sexually transmitted infections that some of these men contracted, despite later reports suggesting that men were more likely to use prophylactics with women they knew were not regularly tested.[23] Yet despite the risks to all sex workers from crime, pimps, and violence, African sex workers were also in principle freer than European ones. They were free to live where they liked, to set their own work hours, to move about the city, to choose and refuse clients if they had the economic means to do so, and to operate free from medical surveillance. His realization that African sex workers potentially had more freedom informed administrator Ponzio's 1936 plea for the deregulation of prostitution in Dakar, in which he noted that it was "prohibited for any [European] woman registered in a brothel to go into town unaccompanied or to show herself in a public space: café, restaurant, dancehall, etc."[24] Instead, white prostitutes should be able to move freely around the city like Africans. Gabrielle's role in Thiès as the unregistered building block for the entire local enterprise, ironically, gave her more freedom than a registered white prostitute in Dakar.

Yet she risked—from the point of view of most administrators reading her case—becoming isolated as a black-market prostitute. In Senegal the fear was that such women would sleep with anyone—meaning with African men—which was a moral concern that directly affected white prestige. During and after World War I and World War II, both the military and civilian colonial authorities tried to break apart Franco-African couples in the metropole and to prevent white women from following African men to their overseas homes. They were only partially successful, given that there were constant examples of African soldiers having sex with, marrying, impregnating, or falling in love with white French women, and some women did follow their partners to Africa. Nevertheless, the authorities kept trying.[25]

Thiès was a military town, had an air base dating from the 1920s, and served as an anchoring town for the railroad. European and African soldiers and workers, including French-educated Africans, were based there.[26] Some local men certainly thought they needed a brothel. When the military air base expanded during World War II to more than 900 men, including 450 Europeans, European military personnel complained about the lack of formalized sex labor: "The long hours of inactivity imposed by this climate during the hot periods of the day naturally favor daydreaming—which is normal for any young individual—of an erotic nature. . . . The spectacle of privileged comrades, whose wives are in the Colony, is a constant reminder of the legitimate and habitual satisfactions of which they are deprived, and a temptation to succumb to illegitimate loves." According to the Air Force officer who authored the quoted text, the three options left were: sex with African prostitutes; "homosexual relations, the morally inconvenient nature of which it is pointless to insist upon"; and finally "relations with married European women, which are a source of scandal, especially when they are the wives of army pals."[27] Acknowledging that sex was already happening in all the ways that troubled white prestige, the report concluded that the solution was to recruit sex workers to Thiès and centralize their services in a brothel. Similar issues vexed men in Thiès between the wars, inspiring Mazohyié's business model.

Yet even though few unmarried white women lived in Thiès, Gabrielle was unevenly welcomed there, because administrators handling Gabrielle's case faced a paradox. She was not a prostitute, but she was also not a paradigm of white bourgeois respectability, because she had asked that her repatriation be overturned and had moved into a house with two men. Gabrielle, by arriving because of a false promise of marriage, bypassed the entry controls, and then used her emotions and assumed passivity as a tool to influence some men, refused help from others, and found her own solutions. In so doing she slipped from the somewhat respectable status of human-trafficking victim seeking help into the murkier status of unmarried woman who chose to live with two men. The AOF's regulatory system shuddered. Gabrielle's story, when analyzed at the metalevel of the state, reveals not only how sex was tracked overseas via careful documentation, profuse communication, and personal contact, but also why these vested attempts to control white female sexuality existed in the first place. As this first reading of Gabrielle has shown, studying sex in colonial history through the conceptual lens of passion reshapes our understanding of the effectiveness of the colonial apparatus. Men used women's supposed passivity and incapacity to control their own emotions to justify regulating them. In their discussions, officials hinted that Gabrielle used that same alleged lack of control to persuade men of her choosing to help her and thus to secure a place for herself overseas, a tactic that begs a second reading of Gabrielle.

Reading Gabrielle, Part II: Passion and Mobility

A portrait of Gabrielle shows her looking slightly to her right, with strong yet elegant features: a refined nose; full, relaxed, but unsmiling lips; dark, carefully styled eyebrows, and short wavy hair worn cut to barely cover her ears and to highlight her cheekbones. A necklace catches the light in a structured vee around her slender neck, and her shoulders and décolleté appear entirely bare, with just the hint of a low-cut gown in the photograph. When she finally penned two letters to the governor of Senegal, Léonce Jore, and thereby inserted her voice into this story, Gabrielle did something that might appear unexpected given the references to the white slave trade.

In her first letter, she asked for a job with the local postal service so that she could stay in Thiès. She had a shrewd understanding of precisely which language would pull at the strings of administrators' hearts. First, she paid particular attention to defending her reputation, explaining that only with the promise of marriage, and after verifying that Mazohyié's metropolitan family were honorable, had she agreed to the engagement and to travel to Senegal, arriving on August 11, 1927. She concurred with everyone regarding Mazohyié's bad character, adding to their analysis when she labeled him "taré" (degenerate) and a "misérable" (wretch).[28] Then she explained how she had fended for herself (rather than awaiting rescue) by moving out of his home on September 3. When asking for official permission to work for the local postal service, she added, "I have always lived from my work," by which she meant not from sex. She used the word "charity" to explain why two men invited her to live with them. With this term she again underscored her respectability because, as she openly acknowledged, in the tight-knit colonist community of Thiès she risked what she termed "public reprobation" if she lived with two men: "So as not to incur public reprobation, I cannot continue to profit from the hospitality offered me, I do not know whence to go." This led her to follow her interlocutors' own logic that if all else failed, she would need repatriation to the metropole, although her strong preference would be the job at the post office that someone had promised her if the governor of Senegal's office supported her application. With its hint of anguish, "I do not know whence to go" exemplified how Gabrielle instrumentalized women's supposed emotional reactivity and passivity to position herself as in need of help. Yet overall, her letter was a cogent defense of her actions that indicated precisely how the administration could help her without infantilizing her by forcing her return to the metropole. In response Governor Jore turned down her request for employment, even though local administrators in Thiès had encouraged her to apply for the position. Jore worked under Governor-General Carde, who was uncomfortable with allowing this sort of independent mobility to succeed, and in AOF administrative positions were rarely given to single white women. Jore opted instead to repatriate her.

Then Gabrielle started refusing, in the process deploying more emotion, desire, and resistance. In a second letter to Governor Jore two months later, on November 17, Gabrielle wrote that the repatriation decision was "made for me."[29] She meant that Jore had forced it upon her. She wanted to remain and work at the post office. The handwriting on her September 12, 1927, repatriation application was consistent with that of her letters, so she certainly had filled out and submitted her own request. She felt, however, that she had been pressured to believe that she had no other choice but to fill it out. She went on to state that she had been ill, or she would have written sooner, but that now that she was well again, she wanted her repatriation annulled, for she had "found a situation permitting me to return to France by my own means." His curiosity piqued, Governor-General Carde wrote to Governor Jore and tasked him with requesting more information from local administrators. By December Jore had received an answer via two interlocutors: the chief of police and the commander of the administrative unit, or *cercle*, of Thiès. Jore wrote back to inform Carde that Gabrielle was living maritally with Lucien Marville, who was a *chef ouvrier d'art* (chief artisan) employed by the Thiès-Niger railroad line and one of the two men who had housed her "charitably" after she moved out of the doctor's place. A widower of one year, he was deemed honorable and had every intention of "making his family situation official."[30] Indeed, on January 29, 1928, Gabrielle wrote yet again to Carde's office, this time to ask for the return of her papers, which she needed to finalize her marriage dossier.[31] The administration seemed content with this normalization of Gabrielle's situation through this second promise of marriage.

So if we shift from a suprastructural to a micro, human focus, with both approaches situating sex at the heart of Gabrielle's case, how does such a move realign our readings of French colonial history? During a period of close to five months, Gabrielle resisted all attempts to force her compliance with local norms. She engaged in colonial mobility based on an exchange of vows via mail; she lived with her fiancé for almost a month in what was either already, or on its way to becoming, a brothel. She then moved in with two other men, one of whom eventually became first her lover and then most likely her husband. Various administrators at the colonial government's headquarters in Dakar and Peverelly in Thiès, even while recognizing that her conduct was beyond reproach, tried to wear her down and persuade her to return to France.[32] We have already seen how colonial governance was anchored in conceptions of patriarchy and white prestige that would have drawn these men's attention to the case of a woman who appeared on paper to be a victim of the white slave trade and whose bourgeois family cared about her and had not been conscious that she was being conscripted into sex work. In contrast, most women who went overseas knew when they were being recruited as sex workers. They had already worked in the sex industry and might have had their papers and belongings, and even their wages and more respectable dresses, held by brothel owners, who thus ensured that their employees did not move about town unchaperoned or leave before reimbursing the price of their passage overseas. Using such techniques, brothel owners controlled sex workers' movements, just like the police did when they registered women to keep track of their whereabouts and to ensure (like the military) that designated doctors regularly inspected the women for STIS.

Mazohyié had a bad reputation, but arguably the most formidable force in the world of sex work in Senegal was Lily Cadilhac (born Marie Pique-mal), better known as Lily Cernay.[33] She had contacts with known pimps in Casablanca, Bordeaux, and Marseille who sent her women (when she did not go get them in the metropole herself). She also had ties to the Corsican mafia. A shrewd woman, she lobbied the Dakarois and central colonial administration on numerous occasions to defend her business, including after the 1946 Loi Marthe Richard, the law that abolished broth-els in France and in several regions of the empire, including AOF. Not all the women who worked for Lily enjoyed doing so. When "Mireille" and "Monique" (their professional names) decided to leave Dakar on the Ker-guelen steamer, Lily had numerous "stormy" fights with her two employees because she was not satisfied that they had reimbursed her for the price of passage to Dakar. Eventually Lily ceded, but she refused to turn over the women's earnings and bags, which contained clothes she had bought them in France. Outraged, Monique threatened to reach out to her *amant de coeur*—a phrase used by prostitutes to signal the man they considered to be an affair of the heart—Guérini. Known in Marseille as "the terror," Guérini was considered to have strong connections to the *milieu*, meaning the mafia. He had lent Monique to Lily, but Monique returned to him in a state of near indigence, with only the clothes on her back.[34] Although

I have yet to find records of them, similar sentiments to those that kept Gabrielle in Thiès may have impelled Monique back to her amant de coeur in Marseille. Yet the administration regarded Gabrielle's sexuality as different from Monique's. Gabrielle's threatened prostitution had mostly bypassed that exploitative and occasionally violent milieu and hence did not threaten to start a turf war in Senegal. Moreover, Gabrielle's sexuality was a more explicit example of how powerful sentiment combined with sex could be, powerful enough for her to brave a pistol-wielding man like Mazohyié in choosing to stay in Senegal.

Gabrielle's letters, along with her brother-in-law's description of her character as romantic, suggest that her motivations in connecting with both her first and second partners in Thiès were not merely material, but also about passion. Her stubborn refusal to return to the metropole even in her first letter, in which she requested work first and repatriation only as a last recourse, reinforces the idea that Gabrielle had been actively seeking to escape her life in the metropole. Moreover, in describing the letters she had exchanged with Mazohyié as an "epistolary relationship," she was bolstering her description of him as duplicitous but also acknowledging that the doctor had written in ways that had sparked or met her desires: for love, adventure, travel, and sex. When Gabrielle arrived in Senegal, she found someone so entirely different that she felt the need to label him a "taré," although everyone acknowledged his dangerous skills as a perverse manipulator. Thus she meant to insult him via another sense of the term, one closer to "unhinged degenerate." His tastes and attitudes aligned so little with her own that she could only describe him as being of base character, defective in his Frenchness and his manliness.

By terming her romanticism "sickly," her brother-in-law's language was in line with interwar uses of the term "romantic" that designated a person as a daydreamer, metaphysically anxious, unrealistic, and sentimental rather than practical.[35] Passion similarly signaled, at the time, a lack of control and pragmatism, but Gabrielle showed that it was also a source of strength. She did not write administrators in the style of a naive woman. There is a distinct possibility that she reserved her romantic letters for men who sparked her passions and thus that Gabrielle knew how to control her registers. If we combine her letters with her brother-in-law's comment regarding her sickly romanticism, the overlap between these two perspectives reveals a complex woman who was seeking more than romance. Doctor Mazohyié's sexuality and her own were not aligned, but that does not mean sex did not motivate her. Rather, she found him to be incompatible with the totality of her desires.

Her second attempt at colonial domesticity opened with her moving into a house with two men. Her file does not reveal whether she shared their home before becoming close to Marville, the man who promised to marry her, or after. Certainly, his promise to make their family situation official suggested that they were living as lovers rather than merely housemates at that point in time. There were other cases of unmarried couples in AOF who lived as single-home families with children and were respected and supported. For example, Irène Azelart wrote in 1922 from Tambacounda, Senegal, to ask for her repatriation to France. She explained that her health was poor and that she had already lost her first child in Africa. Her second baby was six months old and born disabled. She wished to return to the metropole both to care for him and to "deal with some affairs that, until now, have kept me from marrying warrant officer Peloix," the child's father. Those who researched her case were so firmly on her side that although she was not married to her partner (and likely married to someone else, given her desire to handle some affairs back in the metropole), they confirmed her "bonne vie et mœurs," or good life and morals. Some reports even gave her the inaccurate title of "wife," both as a reflection of the couple's love and devotion and because Peloix was a much-admired "noncommissioned officer" and she "a valiant partner."[36] Madame Joachim was similarly convincing in her explanation of why, even though she was still married to Monsieur Dodelande back in France, her intent to marry the man she had followed to the colony, a "noncommissioned officer of the colonial infantry," was virtuous. She was waiting for her divorce to be formalized while in an advanced state of pregnancy by her newer partner. She sought repatriation because she did not think she had the strength to give birth a second time in the colony. (Her first child, also by her lover, was nineteen months old.) Here, too, rumors and neighbors worked in her favor. The couple had lived "in a very dignified fashion"; he had worked as a portraitist and she as a seamstress to supplement his military income, and "all the neighbors are unanimous . . . the Guesnon household is of a morality beyond criticism."[37]

Thus, the fact that Gabrielle was living with a man outside of marriage should not have troubled local administrators. In her case the greater issues made up a triptych. First, she had entered the colony as a potential sex worker, and the time she had spent living with her aspiring pimp and appearing in his establishment cast a shadow over her every choice, even though she had refused to pursue that line of work. Second, she was from a family willing to cause some scandal. And third, though she and her newest partner presented themselves as domestic—so that while in an extramarital relationship they otherwise adhered to sex and gender norms—her living situation carried a whiff of polyamory.

Like the administrators who tracked her case, Gabrielle never used the word "sex" to discuss her situation. Instead, she alluded to its presence in her story via the ways that she went to great lengths to accentuate her respectability. She did so because she was aware of being scrutinized for potential abnormalities in her sexual behavior. She used ingenuity to contend that she be allowed to remain in Senegal after her administrative repatriation had been granted, at first because her interlocutors feared that any woman left alone overseas was at risk of sliding toward a most problematic form of prostitution.[38] Beyond the racist, sexist, and classist assumption that a white woman would only have sex with a Black man for money, the existence of such cases reinforced the pressure upon Gabrielle to repeatedly prove her respectability. Thus, when she wrote of her impending marriage as one by which she had "found a situation permitting me to return to France by my own means"—*situation* being a French term that was regularly used to denote employment—her focus upon the material aspects of her new setup was intentional.[39] She was explaining in prosaic terms that she had something transactional to gain from her impending marriage, namely the freedom to remain in Senegal or to return to France. In fact, her terms were so prosaic that Carde wrote back to Jore in Thiès to ask what Gabrielle meant by "situation," assuming she had found work.

Gabrielle was clearly aware that even after she tried to reassure the colonial administration that she had found a proper domestic structure within which to function, those tracking her case would still fear that she was in danger of becoming a sex laborer working outside of official networks—or as they assumed of such laborers, an indigent white woman who might have sex with Africans. She may have known that, alternatively, they could fear that she was a serial monogamist who might have sex with one man after another, driven by love, lust, friendship, and other forms of connectivity as well as by the need to secure material resources allowing her to survive. There were many cases of such women overseas, living in a gray zone between prostitution and domesticity, mistresses and concubines. Such cases also distressed local administrators, because when their serial partners offered them a combination of emotional and material support, such women also often cohabited with men of any origin. But the money exchanged in these relationships was too subtle to track, so these women were not registered sex workers. The second part of this chapter has shown how critical it is to our understanding of imperial migration to think about the history of sexuality and women via a concept of passion that comprises desires, and how emotions perceived as womanly weakness could be instrumentalized in support of independence by someone like Gabrielle.

Gabrielle's dossier contains at least thirty-seven pages tracing exchanges among bureaucrats, policemen, and male family members. But it contains only two letters—two and five pages in length, respectively—written by the woman at the heart of it all. The dossier's heft and detail might suggest that the security system overseas was highly functional. But when we look at Gabrielle's story closely, we realize that in her two penned letters, she alluded to two elements that were absent from official reports and comments on her case. First, sex was the driving force behind her mobility, but not in the way it was for sex workers whose independent female migration was made possible by or in anticipation of paid sexual acts. Hers was the domestic flipside of sex labor. Her mobility was made possible by the fact that she was able to find "situations" via her engagements to marry men with whom she would be or was having sex; in this, she in some ways resembled Mme Steinheil, described by Sarah Horowitz in this volume. Second, archival files about Gabrielle that brim with the term "white slavery" elide the facts that she did not see herself as a victim and she was motivated by a complex set of passions, which stirred her to thwart repeated attempts from her family and officials in Thiès and Dakar to send her back to the metropole. Third, she used logos, self-advocacy, and assumptions regarding the reactivity and passivity of her sentiments as tools. She knew that speaking about Mazohyié as dangerous would help her gain support because other men would perceive her as a victim. She knew that her family spoke of her as "sickly" and "romantic." While such reactive emotions might not persuade the central administration—although her references to her potential homelessness and passing illness were no doubt aimed to ignite protective instincts—her passionate "romantic" nature could convince local administrators who witnessed her in the act of feeling to help and protect her. She played with assumptions around women via such emotional registers.

Gabrielle's story of sex as mobility and sex as passion echoes many other such stories of women in which sex occurred in ways that distressed officials, in part because it was practically impossible to prevent. Gabrielle's story, in this sense, foreshadows the disruptive possibilities of sex described in the following chapter by Sarah Fishman, who shows how women in the metropole strove to construct modern sexual lives within the framework of traditional French society. The sheer volume of files such as Gabrielle's in colonial archives and the force of policing involved in collecting that data would appear to signal that the colonial administration and police forces were effective apparatuses, capable of finding and controlling suspicious elements.[40] Looking at volume alone, however, could lead us to overlook mobility, in which not only Africans but also white colonists engaged, as a form of collective refusal of colonial governance.[41] If, instead of perceiving the approximately one hundred thousand records tracking people in AOF as examples of functional state control, we start to think about the very heft of these dossiers as examples of what Tina Campt calls "registers of fugitivity," for those who elided state surveillance, or "practices of refusal," for those caught in its web, then our reading of the effectiveness of colonial governance shifts.[41] European and African women's cases were often tracked via the lens of sex and regularly featured women resisting the tracking system to pursue their personal politics of free migration and the right to labor. Perhaps more than anything, then, what we learn about France's overseas colonies by considering Gabrielle's story via her elucidations of her own sexuality is that for all the controls in place, savvy women found uninhibited ways to use passion to move through the empire.

That mobility was made possible because women's sexuality was far more complex than hierarchies of race, gender, and class, or fears of declining white prestige, might suggest. Their sexuality was not made up only of labor, unpaid pleasure, or domesticity, but also of material comforts, sentiments, and ingenuity. Gabrielle's was a story of powerful motivation, maintained by her passions, elements of which she controlled and deployed to move about the empire outside of the structures defined by white male prestige. To her, sex was a mélange of sensuality and sentiment, a consequential intertwining that is not often studied as a twin inspiration for colonial mobility and yet is central to how many women told their colonial stories. Gabrielle's initial pleas played into tropes of the emotional, passive woman, as did passing references to illness. Domesticity and marriage became Gabrielle's final, winning arguments after administrators disdained her capacity for hard work and her resourcefulness; they were also rhetorical arguments, revealing that she had learned more about her audience. After all, she was so committed to her independent mobility within the colony that she wrote not just to inform officials that she would not be taking the train and ship home to the metropole, but to ask that her repatriation be revoked by the administration four months before she was married, in Thiès on June 11, 1928.[43] Central to her story was a stubborn drive to travel overseas and remain there, which is why even her carefully crafted, logos-filled letters let slip in the most delicate way that she had chosen not only to live with but to have sex with not one but two men prior to marrying one of them. That was passion, and although men coded it as out of control, in the end it gave her the control she needed to fuel and defend her mobility.

Notes

1. My warm thanks to Nina Kushner, Andrew Ross, Jessie Hewitt, Jens-Uwe Güttel, and its anonymous reviewers for careful readings of this article. Thanks also to the Paris Institute for Advanced Study, with the financial support of the French State, program Investissements d'avenir, managed by the Agence nationale de la recherche (ANR-11-LABX-0027–01 Labex RFIEA+).

2. François Mugnier to gouverneur général in Dakar, Senegal, Pantin, September 27, 1927, H/S/148, Archives nationales du Sénégal, Dakar, Senegal (hereafter ANS), copy of letter in report by Jules Carde, direction des affaires politiques et administratives (hereafter APA), Saint-Louis, Senegal, October 5, 1927, no.

781. Mazohyié's name is inconsistently spelled within archives. I am using the predominant spelling. I use only Gabrielle's first name because she was suspected of being a sex worker but not formally registered as such.

3. Louis Peverelly in Thiès to Madame Mugnier in Pantin, September 27, 1927, H/s/148, ANS, copy of letter in report by Carde, Saint-Louis, October 5, 1927, no. 781, APA.

4. Peverelly to Madame Mugnier, September 27, 1927, H/s/148, ANS.

5. Alice L. Conklin, *A Mission to Civilize: The Republican Idea of Empire in France and West Africa, 1895–1930* (Stanford CA: Stanford University Press, 1997).

6. Sara Ahmed, *The Cultural Politics of Emotion* (New York: Routledge, 2004), 3. On passion as a driver of mobility, see Jennifer Anne Boittin, *Undesirable: Passionate Mobility and Women's Defiance of French Colonial Policing, 1919–1952* (Chicago: University of Chicago Press, 2022).

7. On passion, see also Julia Clancy-Smith, "The 'Passionate Nomad' Reconsidered: A European Woman in *L'Algérie Française* (Isabelle Eberhardt, 1877–1904)," in *Western Women and Imperialism: Complicity and Resistance*, ed. Nupur Chaudhuri and Margaret Strobel (Bloomington: Indiana University Press, 1992): 61–78.

8. On love and sex in Africa, see Carina E. Ray, *Crossing the Color Line: Race, Sex, and the Contested Politics of Colonialism in Ghana* (Athens: Ohio University Press, 2015); Rachel Jean-Baptiste, *Conjugal Rights: Marriage, Sexuality, and Urban Life in Colonial Libreville, Gabon* (Athens: Ohio University Press, 2014). On intimacy and empire, see Matt K. Matsuda, *Empire of Love: Histories of France and the Pacific* (Oxford: Oxford University Press, 2005).

9. Elisa Camiscioli, "Trafficking Histories: Women's Migration and Sexual Labor in the Early Twentieth Century," *Deportate, esuli, profughi*, no. 40 (July 2019): 1–13.

10. Stephanie A. Limoncelli, *The Politics of Trafficking: The First International Movement to Combat the Sexual Exploitation of Women* (Stanford CA: Stanford University Press, 2010), 5.

11. Keely Stauter-Halsted, *The Devil's Chain: Prostitution and Social Control in Partitioned Poland* (Ithaca NY: Cornell University Press, 2015). Similar patterns exist in the metropole, albeit most often without the assumed threat that white women would be exploited by men of color.

12. Caroline Séquin, "The Shifting Contours of Colonial Prostitution (Fort-de-France, Martinique, 1940–1947)," *Clio. Femmes, Genre, Histoire* 50, no. 2 (November 2019): 19–36.

13. On prostitution overseas, see Christina Firpo, *Black Market Business: Selling Sex in Northern Vietnam, 1920–1945* (Ithaca NY: Cornell University Press, 2020);

Christelle Taraud, *La prostitution coloniale: Algérie, Tunisie, Maroc (1830–1962)* (Paris: Payot, 2003). On nuns, see Sarah A. Curtis, *Civilizing Habits: Women Missionaries and the Revival of the French Empire* (Oxford: Oxford University Press, 2010); Elizabeth Ann Foster, *Faith in the Empire: Religion, Politics, and Colonial Rule in French Senegal, 1880–1940* (Stanford CA: Stanford University Press, 2013).

14. Margaret Cook Andersen, *Regeneration through Empire: French Pronatalists and Colonial Settlement in the Third Republic* (Lincoln: University of Nebraska Press, 2015); Julia Clancy-Smith and Frances Gouda, *Domesticating the Empire: Race, Gender, and Family Life in French and Dutch Colonialism* (Charlottesville: University of Virginia Press, 1998); Ann Laura Stoler, *Carnal Knowledge and Imperial Power: Race and the Intimate in Colonial Rule* (Berkeley: University of California Press, 2002).

15. On suspects' agency, see Kathleen Keller, *Colonial Suspects: Suspicion, Imperial Rule, and Colonial Society in Interwar French West Africa* (Lincoln: University of Nebraska Press, 2018). On policing and empire, see Patrice Morlat, *La répression coloniale au Vietnam (1908–1940)* (Paris: L'Harmattan, 1990); Martin Thomas, *Violence and Colonial Order: Police, Workers and Protest in the European Colonial Empires, 1918–1940* (Cambridge: Cambridge University Press, 2012).

16. Ann Laura Stoler, *Race and the Education of Desire: Foucault's "History of Sexuality" and the Colonial Order of Things* (Durham NC: Duke University Press, 1995); Tyler Edward Stovall, "Love, Labor, and Race: Colonial Men and White Women in France during the Great War," in *French Civilization and Its Discontents: Nationalism, Colonialism, Race*, ed. Tyler Edward Stovall and Georges Van Den Abbeele (Lanham MD: Lexington, 2003); Jennifer Anne Boittin, Christina Firpo, and Emily Musil Church, "Hierarchies of Race and Gender in the French Colonial Empire, 1914–1946," *Historical Reflections/Réflexions historiques* 37, no. 1 (March 2011): 60–90.

17. Dakar, direction de la sûreté générale, rapport sur l'activité du service général de sûreté et de renseignements généraux au cours des années 1935–1936, October 31, 1936, Dakar, 200M13075, Archives nationales, Paris, France (hereafter AN).

18. "Rapport de police," Dakar, May 8, 1924, 200M13061, AN. The "recherche dans l'intérêt des familles" was created in the wake of World War I. The right to refuse to be found also existed in the metropole, although it was harder to disappear there than by crossing a large body of water.

19. On Carde's distress regarding interracial relationships, see Carde, procureur général chef du service judiciaire de l'AOF, October 4, 1923, APA, 4D61/89, ANS. On Carde's philosophy of policing dissidence and social relations, see Boittin, *Undesirable*, chap. 1; Keller, *Colonial Suspects*, 39–40.

20. For example, le secrétaire général au gouvernement général de l'Indochine to ministre des Colonies (CAI), Hanoi, March 1, 1920, 9SLOTFOM10, Centre des Archives d'Outre-Mer, Aix-en-Provence, France (hereafter CAOM).

21. For example, lieutenant-gouverneur de la Côte d'Ivoire to gouverneur général de l'AOF, bureau politique, no. 409GC, Bingerville, September 12, 1923, 4D61/89, ANS. Signature unreadable, but the governor of Côte d'Ivoire in 1923 was Raphaël Antonetti. On the paradox of France not seeing race, see Sue Peabody and Tyler Stovall, eds., *The Color of Liberty: Histories of Race in France* (Durham NC: Duke University Press, 2003); Gary Wilder, *The French Imperial Nation-State: Negritude and Colonial Humanism between the Two World Wars* (Chicago: University of Chicago Press, 2005); Pierre H. Boulle, *Race et esclavage dans la France de l'Ancien Régime* (Paris: Perrin, 2007).

22. Brian Donovan, *White Slave Crusades: Race, Gender, and Anti-Vice Activism, 1887–1917* (Urbana: University of Illinois Press, 2006), 3.

23. Note du médecin général inspecteur, no. 1263/1, Dakar, April 16, 1948, 21G/100, ANS.

24. "Réglementation de la prostitution," Ponzio to gouverneur général, direction de la sûreté générale, November 17, 1936, Guernut51, CAOM.

25. Lieutenant-gouverneur de la Côte d'Ivoire to gouverneur général de l'AOF, bureau politique, no. 409GC, Bingerville, September 12, 1923, 4D61/89, ANS.

26. On the army and women who traveled with it, see Ruth Ginio, *The French Army and Its African Soldiers: The Years of Decolonization* (Lincoln: University of Nebraska Press, 2017); Eric T. Jennings, *Free French African in World War II: The African Resistance* (Cambridge: Cambridge University Press, 2015); Sarah J. Zimmerman, *Militarizing Marriage: West African Soldiers' Conjugal Traditions in Modern French Empire* (Athens: Ohio University Press, 2020).

27. Le général de brigade aérienne to le général de corps d'armée, 1941 [partially illegible date], M13071, AN.

28. Gabrielle D. to gouverneur du Sénégal, September 7, 1927, H/S/148, ANS.

29. Gabrielle D. to gouverneur du Sénégal, November 17, 1927, H/S/148, ANS.

30. Jore, 1er bureau administration générale et communale Thiès to APA Dakar, no. 1842 GA, December 30, 1927, H/S/148, ANS.

31. Gabrielle D. to gouverneur du Sénégal, January 29, 1928, H/S/148, ANS.

32. Extrait de rapport concernant Gabrielle Henriette Adrienne D., commissariat de police de Thiès, no. 472, September 7, 1927, H/S/148, ANS.

33. I am using the name she favored in Dakar. On sex workers in Dakar and Lily, see Caroline Séquin, "Marie Piquemal, the 'Colonial Madam': Brothel Prostitution, Migration, and the Making of Whiteness in Interwar Dakar," *Journal of Women's History* 33, no. 4 (Winter 2021): 118–41.

34. Numerous reports mention Lily Cadilhac *dite* Lily Cernay. For example, Renseignements confidentiels, May and November 1938, 200M13071, AN; and Renseignements confidentiels, May 30, 1938, and September 3, 1938, 300M13075, AN. Authorities in Dakar worried that "la terreur" might bring violence to Dakar because of Monique's treatment by Lily.

35. See historical definitions compiled by the Centre national de ressources textuelles et lexicales, https://www.cnrtl.fr/, accessed December 6, 2019.

36. Irène Azelart, Tamba-Counda, March 14, 1922, H/S/257, ANS; and Administrateur commandant le cercle de Tambacounda to gouverneur du Sénégal in St Louis, April 2, 1922, H/S/257, ANS.

37. Jeanne Marie Dodelande, April 18, 1922, H/S/257, ANS; and commissariat central de Dakar, April 25, 1922, H/S/257, ANS. Other cases in which nonmarital domesticity was accepted include Françoise Oliveri and Sebastiani Nesto, Dakar, commissariat spécial du port, renseignements, March 14, 1938, 200M13074, AN; Louise Pons and an unnamed schoolteacher, commissariat spécial du port, Dakar, January 25, 1938, 200M13074, AN; and Madame Cribère and Monsieur Calac, renseignements, January 4, 1939, 200M13075, AN.

38. For example, Dakar to Saint-Louis, A/S rapatriement des passagers clandestins, no. 3137, December 10, 1923, H/S/148, ANS.

39. Gabrielle D. to gouverneur du Sénégal, November 17, 1927, H/S/148, ANS.

40. Conklin, *Mission to Civilize*, 163; Keller, *Colonial Suspects*, 14.

41. As suggested by Michel-Rolph Trouillot, *Silencing the Past: Power and the Production of History* (1995; repr., Boston: Beacon, 2015), 83.

42. Kevin Coleman, "Practices of Refusal in Images: An Interview with Tina M. Campt," *Radical History Review* 132 (October 2018): 209–18.

43. I have been working on Gabrielle's story for some time but could not find documents confirming her marriage's date. When rereading her file to verify this article's notes, I discovered it hidden in plain sight: eight words scribbled on the folder's cover.

Suggested Reading

Boittin, Jennifer Anne. *Undesirable: Passionate Mobility and Women's Defiance of French Colonial Policing, 1919–1952.* Chicago: University of Chicago Press, 2022.

Camiscioli, Elisa. "Trafficking Histories: Women's Migration and Sexual Labor in the Early Twentieth Century." *Deportate, esuli, profughi*, no. 40 (July 2019): 1–13.

Conklin, Alice L. *A Mission to Civilize: The Republican Idea of Empire in France and West Africa, 1895–1930.* Stanford CA: Stanford University Press, 1997.

Firpo, Christina Elizabeth. *Black Market Business: Selling Sex in Northern Vietnam, 1920–1945.* Ithaca NY: Cornell University Press, 2020.

Jean-Baptiste, Rachel. *Conjugal Rights: Marriage, Sexuality, and Urban Life in Colonial Libreville, Gabon*. Athens: Ohio University Press, 2014.

Johnson, Jessica Marie. *Wicked Flesh: Black Women, Intimacy, and Freedom in the Atlantic World*. Philadelphia: University of Pennsylvania Press, 2020.

Peabody, Sue, and Tyler Stovall, eds. *The Color of Liberty: Histories of Race in France*. Durham NC: Duke University Press, 2003.

Ray, Carina E. *Crossing the Color Line: Race, Sex, and the Contested Politics of Colonialism in Ghana*. Athens: Ohio University Press, 2015.

Séquin, Caroline. "White French Women, Colonial Migration, and Sexual Labor between Metropole and Colony." In *The Routledge Companion to Sexuality and Colonialism*, edited by Chelsea Schields and Dagmar Herzog, 243–63. London: Routledge, 2021.

Stovall, Tyler. *White Freedom: The Racial History of an Idea*. Princeton NJ: Princeton University Press, 2021.

White, Luise. *The Comforts of Home: Prostitution in Colonial Nairobi*. Chicago: University of Chicago Press, 1990.

Zimmerman, Sarah J. *Militarizing Marriage: West African Soldiers' Conjugal Traditions in Modern French Empire*. Athens: Ohio University Press, 2020.

IO

SEX BEFORE 1968

Adolescence and the Presse Féminine

SARAH FISHMAN

As the fiftieth anniversary of the May '68 uprisings in Paris approached, journalist Anne Chemin reexamined its status as "Year I of the Sexual Revolution" in France. Chemin reviewed the years after 1968 to point out that deep changes in law, attitudes, and behaviors had not immediately followed 1968 but had taken place gradually over the next two, even three, decades.[1] But Chemin was too quick to assume that 1968 had marked the beginning of a revolution in the first place. In fact, supposedly traditional beliefs were no longer a Bastille to be stormed in 1968. By the turn of the 1950s, both young men and young women were already starting to grapple with competing social expectations about their sexual lives. On the one hand, they wrestled with the continuing power of older beliefs that linked sex to the family and procreation while sustaining a sexual double standard that allowed men, but not women, to explore and enjoy independent sexual lives. On the other hand, changing religious attitudes toward sexuality, particularly among Progressive Catholics in the wake of Vichy, new scientific studies showcasing the diversity of human desire, and the development of new media forums in which women and men could speak openly to one another about their erotic needs pulled toward a more egalitarian, independent sexual ethos. During the 1950s and early 1960s, conversations about sex and sexuality took place both within and between these two poles.

The push and pull of contradictory ideas about sex mirrored broader political and economic processes underway in the postwar decades, often associated with forces of modernization. Indeed, taking sex and sexuality into account clarifies how these larger historical changes intersected with people's intimate lives. On the personal and the political levels, the apparent modernization of these years occurred via a renegotiation of traditional social forms and mores. Ultraconservative family values were questioned after the fall of the collaborationist Vichy regime. As France was liberated in August 1944, resistance groups had high hopes for the new world that they hoped to build. Rejecting the antidemocratic, racist, and reactionary program Vichy leaders had espoused, France's Provisional Government aimed in 1944 not just to restore democracy, but to create a republic that would avoid the infighting and instability of the Third Republic, ensure social justice, and reflect the humanistic and democratic values that had motivated the Resistance. This vision included questioning the Vichy regime's ultraconservative family values. Examining attitudes toward and the practice of sex, therefore, tells us a great deal about the ways that French society sought to reconstruct itself after the war.

The Fourth Republic that emerged in 1946, however, replicated many of the Third Republic's problems. The Fourth Republic's backward-looking political shortcomings, and in particular its unwillingness to accept the end of empire, gave it a short life; it was overthrown and replaced by the Gaullist Fifth Republic in 1958. Still, despite its political failings, the Fourth Republic successfully laid the foundation for the rapid and massive economic, social, and cultural modernization of the three decades after the war, an era often referred to as the Thirty Glorious Years.[2] At the time, however, the glory was less than apparent to most ordinary people struggling to recover from the trauma of war while also coping with rapid structural changes. French society's breathtakingly rapid modernization and urbanization unmoored longstanding assumptions about how life should unfold, leaving people to sort out every aspect of their lives, from where to live to how to earn a living, organize their families, and create intimate relationships. Nowhere was this shift more pronounced than in the popular culture of the era, which portrayed sexual desire more explicitly than ever before. Popular films of the 1950s, for instance, depicted women openly expressing sexual desire for men and even for other women. This was an era when sex became a thing. Historian Judith Coffin uses the term "mid-century sex" to refer to what today we distinguish as "gender, gender roles, sexuality, sexual identity and subjectivity, desires or drives."[3] The inconsistent and even contradictory ideas about sex and sexuality, the greater but still limited freedoms, and the more open conversations about many previously taboo topics could be both exhilarating and frightening. Women's magazines of the era engaged in dialogue with readers about sex and sexuality, allowing us to hear the voices of ordinary women and men navigating the various and contradictory impulses of the postwar decades.

Starting with the half decade after France's Liberation, this chapter explores how the postwar rejection of ultraconservative Vichy-linked Catholicism opened the door for progressive Catholic voices to take the lead in proposing new approaches to love, sex, and marriage. Unexpectedly, progressive Catholics, willing to go beyond older moral teachings, opened up public discourse on these topics. They argued for confining sexual pleasure to marriage, but rather than portraying sexual desire as sinful they described it as natural and healthy.[4] As the 1950s began, discussions of sex expanded to include secular, scientific, medical, and psychological voices that eventually took over from Catholic progressives.

These new ideas reached broader audiences in the 1950s in part via women's magazines, then at their zenith in circulation and readership. Women's magazines regularly featured articles popularizing the work of experts like Sigmund Freud and Alfred Kinsey. Importantly, via the advice columns that appeared in them regularly, women's magazines engaged their readers in an ongoing dialogue. Letters sent to the magazines provided a space in which ordinary people could query contradictory and changing assumptions about private life. In the dance between tradition and modernity, readers and columnists alike expressed a strong sense that the ground was shifting. Young women found themselves at the center of these contradictory trends.

By examining discussions around sex and sexuality in popular media sources—particularly in women's magazines of the era—this chapter uncovers how broader changes, especially the rapid economic modernization and urbanization from the start of France's Thirty Glorious Years, impacted people, young women in particular, on a personal, intimate level. It shows how the tension between tradition and modernization that characterized the Fourth Republic was experienced as much in the realm of sexual attitudes and practices as in any other. In this context attention to sex reorients our understanding of how not only experts but also ordinary people wrestled with a rapidly changing world that nonetheless seemed to remain rooted in the past. Knowledge of sexual practices and attitudes is thus essential to fully understanding how modernization shaped everyday life.

The Politics of Sexual Knowledge after World War II

Empowered during the Vichy regime, far-right conservatives used France's defeat in 1940 to try to return France to an earlier, prerepublican era. They aimed to shore up traditional values regarding marriage and family life in general and sex in particular.[5] Vichy imposed new restrictions on divorce, defined abortion as a crime against the state punishable by death, and criminalized homosexuality when it involved a person under age twenty-one, six years above the age of consent for heterosexual relations. Even as it urged families to have more children, Vichy could not escape the ever-increasing demands of the German occupiers, which intensified the hardships of daily survival. Over time the public grew increasingly cynical about Vichy moralizing. In the end, collaboration with the Nazi occupiers badly tarnished Vichy and its ultraconservative supporters. The Provisional Government established at the Liberation reversed most Vichy policies as it worked to restore a democratic republic.

Consideration of sexual politics exposes both the extent and the limits of the postwar rejection of Vichy. In August 1944 a Provisional Government ordinance declared null and void all of Vichy's "constitutional acts, legislative or regulatory." But the ordinance then backtracked, specifying that Vichy laws not expressly nullified would remain provisionally in effect.[6] The Provisional Government rescinded Vichy laws on marriage and divorce but not the law criminalizing sex with a minor of the same sex. Instead the Provisional Government moved it, without public notice or discussion, to the section of the Penal Code on the protection of minors, linking homosexuality to pederasty.[7]

The public's postwar censure of Vichy also touched the Catholic Church, given that most prominent Catholic leaders in France had enthusiastically supported Vichy. Catholic voices that had used the language of morality and sin to define sexual desire, tainted by collaboration, went silent just after the war, opening up opportunities for other voices within Catholic circles. After the war a different kind Catholicism, linked to prewar progressive social

Catholic movements, reemerged and explored what a post-Vichy sexual politics might look like. Progressive Catholics, quiet during the war, began enunciating novel ideas about sex and sexuality that validated desire and pleasure, although within the bounds of heterosexual marriage. At that time young priests, anxious about the growing distance between the Church and a working class that was abandoning Catholicism at a rapid rate, searched for ways the Church could speak to and address the needs and concerns of working people. In 1927 the priest Georges Guérin established the Young Christian Workers (Jeunesses ouvrières chrétiennes, or JOC) to re-Christianize workers not through sermons but by asking young male workers to study the social, economic, and political conditions they faced; discuss those issues among themselves; and mobilize to take action.[8] The movement rapidly expanded to include a group for young women workers. The Young Female Christian Workers (Jeunesses ouvrières chrétiennes féminines, or JOCF) remained separate from the male workers' JOC to ensure that young women felt empowered to take leadership roles. The JOC and JOCF spun off a number of similar groups aimed at young people from a variety of backgrounds.

Officially, the groups kept a low profile during the Occupation to focus on helping workers deal with the ever-worsening hardships of low wages, food shortages, rationing, the black market, requisitions, forced labor, air raids, destruction, and displacement. Unofficially, many members of these groups engaged in resistance activities. Just after the Liberation, with the Catholic hierarchy lying low, social Catholic leaders reemerged and spoke openly against Vichy's moralizing. Distancing their ideas about women and family life from association with collaborationist Catholic polemicists, they published the first post-Vichy books about sex and marriage. Although not abandoning traditional prohibitions on extramarital and same-sex sexual activity, these works nevertheless began to assert the value of sexual pleasure within marriage. Validating the importance of the sex in marriage opened the topic for broader discussions among social Catholics but also reached a broader audience. Progressive Catholics positioned their advocacy for sexual propriety as a contrast to Vichy-era religious portrayals of sexual desire as tainted by original sin. Rather than the sinfulness of premarital sex, progressive Catholics emphasized the personal, psychological benefits of premarital chastity.

In 1947 the Young Christian Student Movement (Jeunesse étudiante chrétienne, or JEC) published *"Love" and Marriage*. The book reassured its readers that the authors' "Christian attitude [would] not limit itself to a useless puritanism," a clear jab at Vichy. Similarly, André Merlaud's *Splendor of Conjugal Love* advocated for a return to the riches of "true love and commitment" rather than advising husbands to dominate and wives to submit. Claire Souvenance stressed the "magnificent grandeur of human love sanctified by the sacrament of marriage."[9] All the books suggested the centrality of a positive sexual relationship in marriage. Citing Thomas Aquinas—"grace does not destroy nature but perfects it"—one author explained that because sex was part of nature, it could not be evil in itself.[10]

At the turn of the 1950s, social Catholics began to adapt and apply new forms of secular expertise to bolster their positions on sexual behavior. For example, in 1951 the Catholic-run Institute of Familial Sexology, a name evoking Alfred Kinsey, published a series of books addressing premarital sex and conjugal love, which, in keeping with Catholic teachings, was assumed to be heterosexual love. Many of these books were aimed at women. Authors like Paul Chanson did not frame their arguments in favor of premarital abstinence in moral terms or by referring to Catholic doctrine or teachings. Instead, Chanson referred to literary and philosophical sources, including Madame de Staël, Stendhal, George Sand, and Friedrich Nietzsche to highlight the importance of a healthy sex-life to women's happiness within marriage.[11] To clinch his case, Chanson cited a psychiatry professor: "Female psychological equilibrium requires a durable, binding sentimental attachment that only truly flourishes in marriage. Multiple liaisons . . . have an unhappy impact on the female personality."[12] Chanson highlighted practical over moral reasons, citing a professor who warned, "These unhappy young women who have sex not only expose themselves to venereal diseases . . . they could end up with a pregnancy whose consequences are equally painful for their families as for themselves."[13]

Reformist Catholics, while maintaining the positive personal impact of premarital abstinence, presented a new vision of sex within marriage. Rather than something to endure in order to make babies, heterosexual sex in marriage was a good thing and should be pleasurable. Dr. Bernard Senencourt's book *Conjugal Life and Reflex Control* (1952), published by the Catholic Institute of Family Sexology, explicitly recommended good sex in marriage, focused on the physiology of sex, and instructed married men and women on how to improve their sexual relations.[14] In response to the fear of pregnancy that, they admitted, often hindered women's sexual pleasure, Senencourt and Chanson both recommended that rather than putting artificial "devices" into their bodies, couples enjoy sex without fear of pregnancy by focusing not on intercourse but on mutual pleasuring. Within the boundaries of heterosexual love, these books, published from 1947 to 1957, proposed a kinder, gentler Christian vision of sex and marriage, still set in a religious framework but minus the hectoring, judgmental tone of Vichy-era pronouncements.

Progressive Catholic writers made the case for premarital chastity and sacramental marriage in the hope of reestablishing Catholicism's relevance to a new generation and possibly staving off emancipatory changes already apparent by the 1950s. In doing so, they reflected and contributed to a broader movement that, on the one hand, accepted the importance of the family, marriage, and traditional gender roles and, on the other hand, reassessed the contours of those ideals. Although Catholic thinkers objected to sex outside of marriage, they nonetheless helped to bring discussions of sex and sexual activity into everyday life. By emphasizing the importance of good sex to a happy marriage, religious thinkers validated the topic of heterosexual sexual satisfaction, in particular for women, in new ways. As much as they tried, however, they could not control the public discussion of sex.[15] Social Catholics struggled to remain relevant in the 1960s postcolonial era, when, according to historian Todd Shepard, they shifted their focus to the struggle against prostitution, leading them to highlight stereotypes of the "sexual deviance" of Arab and North African men.[16]

Thus, by the end of the 1950s the progressive Catholic discourse on sex gave way to the popularization of secular, psychological understandings of sexuality and sexological knowledge of the varieties of sexual identity and behavior. If Catholic theorizing represented an attempt at bringing tradition into the modern era, the discourse of psychology informed a secular reconsideration of traditional thinking about sex. Psychologist Jean Dublineau, president of the Medico-Psychological Society, for example, addressed a 1948 conference on childhood at the Paris Medical School. Citing Freud,

Dublineau's talk, "La vie sexuelle et sociale élémentaire" (Elementary sexual and social life), explained young children's oral, anal, and genital phases and recommended avoiding tickling and otherwise prematurely arousing sexual excitement.[17] Freud's emphasis on the importance of the libido and of sexual instinct wound its way into popular consciousness through medical debates, popular accounts such as Françoise Dolto's *Problèmes de petite enfance* (Problems of early childhood), wide-distribution periodicals, and an important new institution, the Parents' School (École des parents), which "worked to teach parents and educators 'the main principles of emotional development.'"[18]

Other sources of scientific expertise re-started discussions that had begun long before the war. Popular books on sexology, such as Dr. Caufeynon's (the pseudonym of Jean Fauconney, a doctor who published several pseudoscientific medical tracts for a popular audience) *La sexualité des filles et des garçons* (The sexuality of girls and boys), began appearing early in the twentieth century.[19] During the Occupation, however, Vichy censored open discussion about sex, a silence that heightened the postwar novelty of such discussions. Alfred Kinsey's studies on male and female sexuality caused a sensation in France. His first book on male sexuality, published in 1948, appeared in French that same year. His 1953 book on female sexuality appeared in French in 1954. These volumes quickly became bestsellers and enabled new discussions of sex and sexuality, showcasing the wide variety of behaviors, attractions, and positions practiced by his American research subjects. Kinsey's research led him to reject a binary understanding of hetero/homosexuality in favor of the notion of a sexual continuum. No longer, thanks to Kinsey, could one simply assume one normal kind of desire.[20]

By the 1950s, then, both moral and scientific authorities had shifted the grounds for understanding sexuality. Their ideas expanded beyond intellectual and scientific communities, gradually gaining wide currency via the dizzying expansion of consumer culture. Rapid economic growth dramatically increased the scope of access to inexpensive, mass-market publications. Thus, as "mid-century sex" emerged in the 1950s, women's magazines played a crucial role in broadly disseminating ideas, research, and theories about sex and sexuality. If the sexual sciences and gender politics of Freud and Kinsey represented the new, postwar sexual modernity, women's magazines took it upon themselves to introduce their readers to the times, without necessarily giving up on the structures that had traditionally constrained men and women's understandings of their sexual roles and identities before and after marriage. Although both sexes were implicated, because of women's magazines assumed female audience the focus narrowed to concentrate primarily on women's sexuality, or heterosexuality, to be precise. The postwar baby boom drew special attention to the growing population of teen girls and young women, who took center stage in these discussions.

The Postwar Golden Age of Women's Magazines

The willingness of the most important defender of traditional values, the Catholic Church, to engage with new ideas around sex and sexuality helped open space for a broader discussion in the popular press, especially in women's magazines. The reemergence of women's magazines after the war provided the opportunity for young women to engage in an active dialogue both between traditional and modern ideas, and between experts and themselves as they worked out what it meant to be female in an era of rapid change. These magazines successfully popularized new ideas—especially those of Freud, Kinsey, and even Simone de Beauvoir—as they also perpetuated older assumptions about sexuality and marriage. This tension between the modern and the traditional proved both productive and problematic, especially for young women struggling to understand gendered expectations in light of their own desires.

An especially rich source for uncovering what ordinary people thought, women's magazines included frequent articles and essays about love, dating, sex, and marriage, primarily aimed at young women. Although directed at women, the magazines also attracted a small but significant number of male readers. In 1952 one columnist noted that one in fifteen of the four hundred letters she received daily were from men.[21] The magazines all encouraged their readers to send in letters and respond to polls, making interactions between magazines and their readers a dialogue.

In France the modern woman's magazine (*la presse féminine*) started with the appearance of *Marie-Claire* in 1937. According to Marcelle Auclair, one of its creators, *Marie-Claire* combined the beauty and fashion of older luxury magazines with modern features on contemporary culture, opinion pieces about important issues of the day, practical information, recipes, sewing patterns, and serialized stories. Its format constituted, to media expert Michel Phelizon, a revolution in women's magazines.[22] Because the magazine had published throughout the Vichy regime, the postwar Provisional Government closed it down. Nonetheless, *Marie-Claire* had shown the way, and its absence after the Liberation created an opening.

Just after the war, Hélène Gordon-Lazareff, with her husband Pierre Lazareff, seized the opportunity by launching *Elle*. They had worked in the press group that included *Marie-Claire* prior to the war. Both Jewish, they had left France in the chaos of June 1940, spending the war years in the United States, where magazines such as *Life* and *Harper's Bazaar* provided inspiration for when they returned. Celebrating modernity, its pages filled with color photographs rather than drawn illustrations, *Elle* included timely coverage of culture and touched on politics and global affairs while primarily focusing on romance, love and marriage, celebrities, food, fashion, and homemaking. Françoise Giroud, who became the director, explained that after the war, "women missed their prewar lives. They just wanted to be pretty, elegant and lighthearted again."[23] *Elle* appealed to urban, middle-class women who aspired to be modern and sophisticated, and it quickly took off. By 1955 about one in six French women read *Elle*.[24]

Elle was not alone. A variety of women's magazines appeared or reappeared after the war. Rather than competing for *Elle's* urban readership, most postwar women's magazines aimed for different audiences. *Confidences* and *Constellation* targeted rural and rising middle-class families. France's largest labor union, the General Confederation of Labor (Confédération general du travail or CGT), published *Antoinette* for working-class women, and a communist women's group published *Heures claires des femmes françaises* (Bright times for French women). *Nous Deux* (The two of us) featured visual storytelling both in drawn panels and, starting in 1950, in photographs, a form called the "photo-novel" (*roman-photo*). After a ten-year hiatus *Marie-Claire* reappeared as a monthly in 1954, appealing to a middle-class urban readership similar to that of *Elle*. Its first print run of three hundred thousand sold out in three days. During the 1950s and early 1960s, the golden age for women's magazines, circulation and readership numbers achieved all-time highs. The top three, *Elle*, *Marie-Claire*, and *Nous Deux*, reached as many as three million readers.[25]

In addition to articles on fashion, romance, and family life, advice columns took prime real estate in women's magazines. An extremely rich vein of material, advice columns provided the space for ongoing debates about family and love relationships. People of both sexes and from varied backgrounds wrote to French advice columnists, who then mined the material for their own articles.[26] Only a small selection of letters from readers received a published response in the pages of the magazines. Advice columnists and magazine editors selected, cut, and edited readers' letters, working to appeal broadly to their readers and thereby sell magazines. Thus, these letters hardly represented a random sampling of public opinion. The advice was prescriptive. Still, in surveying these columns over time, common themes indicate frequently posed questions and topics that columnists and editors considered of wide enough interest to merit inclusion.

The constant inflow of letters from readers underscores the ways in which magazines depended on those who bought and consumed them. In fact, that relationship became the basis of an explicit strategy at *Elle*. Early on, seeking to expand *Elle*'s audience, Gordon-Lazareff insisted to the editors, "Our magazine will win by establishing personal contacts with its readers, by means of correspondence."[27] In a process of give and take, advice columnists provided readers with expert wisdom as the readers, too, guided the form of the magazine. Evidence confirms that these exchanges rested on real letters sent by actual people.[28]

Marcelle Ségal, who unexpectedly found herself thrust into the role of advice columnist for *Elle*, published a book in 1952 about her experiences, *My Profession: Advice Columnist* (*Mon métier: Le courrier du coeur*). In the book Ségal summarized her correspondents' anxieties, hopes, and personalities. In addition to the few responses to letters she published weekly, Ségal asked readers to "imagine that for the last six years" she had "responded directly to thousands of letters." Although she understood that letter writers often posed their questions on behalf of "a friend," she warned writers who sent phony letters that she could spot a fake one a mile away.[29] In 1961 *Confidences* notified readers that, owing to the abundance of mail its staff received daily, it was "no longer possible for" them "to respond directly to" their "correspondents." From then on, they would only respond in the pages of the magazine. Before this point, *Confidences'* advice columnists had responded to some letter writers in the magazine and to the rest directly and privately.[30] *Marie-Claire* reappeared in 1954 without its prewar journalist and advice columnist Marcelle Auclair. Immediately, readers inundated the editor-in-chief, Marcel Haedrich, with letters demanding her return.[31] Early in 1955 Auclair agreed to return and resumed her dialogue with her readers. When, in 1961, *Marie-Claire* instructed its readers on how to submit questions to specific columnists, it included Auclair's home address with instructions to write to her directly.

The flurry of letters sent them by the early 1960s highlights how successfully these female columnists had inscribed themselves into the lives of their readers. During Auclair's time at *Marie-Claire*, her personal trajectory moved from Catholic spiritualism to advocacy of birth control, reflecting, by her own admission, the two-way nature of her conversation with her correspondents. Eventually the letters she received led her, in 1963, to publish *Le livre noir de l'avortement* (The black book of abortion), filled with readers' painful accounts of circumstances that had led them to seek abortions.[32]

Tradition and Modernization

From our contemporary perspective, all postwar women's magazines reinforced the dominant vision of heterosexual love, marriage, and children as central to women's lives. Even *Nous Deux*—which some French parents viewed as too racy because of its sexualized, if modestly attired, images of women—focused not on sex but on stories of love and romance. Although women's magazines varied in production quality, number of ads, and illustration styles, they all featured short stories centering on women searching for love; articles and features on clothing and fashion; and advice on homemaking, raising children, and managing husbands.[33]

Women's magazines therefore couched their depictions of sexuality in light of continued negotiations of sexual morality, knowledge, and desire, shaped by both religious authorities and secular, professional experts. Few of the magazines addressed female sexual desire on its own terms. Nor did they explore same-sex desire, in spite of its appearance in books and films of the time. The tension between traditional moral knowledge resting on Christian values and the modern, scientific knowledge of psychologists and sexologists was replicated in the voices of young women and even men.

Although the magazines provided a space for women to speak to other women about their attempts to navigate their sexual lives, the conversations were ultimately shaped by a tension—one that, as we shall see, was largely produced by an assumed male judgment—between traditional morality and modern (hetero)sexuality. Put differently, though they allowed women and some men to speak to other readers about their experiences and needs, these magazines, by rarely questioning male judgment, validated men's power as the ultimate arbiter of acceptable sexual behavior for women.

The modern image of the magazines often rested on their willingness to deploy new sexual knowledge. More and more often, women's magazines deployed psychological language, referring to Freudian ideas in discussions of personal relations. In *Marie-Claire* a 1957 article warned of a new danger for boys: "The Dominating Mother" (*La mère dominatrice*).[34] By 1965 *Marie-Claire* offered its readers a "psycho-technical service." That same year it published "The Oedipus Complex" by Laurence Pernoud, the well-known female author of the bestselling book on pregnancy and child rearing *J'attends un enfant* (I'm expecting a baby).[35]

Women's magazines also disseminated Kinsey's ideas about heterosexual sex. In recognition of *Sexual Behavior in the Human Male*'s big splash in France, *Elle* quickly published a two-page spread on Kinsey in 1948. Eve Brown responded to the 1953 publication of Kinsey's *Sexual Behavior in the Human Female* with an article explaining why she had refused to take part in Kinsey's survey. Her article articulated a common French reaction, critical of the Kinsey reports' deromanticization of sex and silence regarding its emotional aspects.[36] Guy Robin, in *Constellation*, reassured parents worried by Kinsey's reports that the real lives of female adolescents did not necessarily reflect Kinsey's conclusions.[37] At the same time, he cited Kinsey to warn that girls no longer possessed the "natural modesty" that protected them from engaging in sexual activity. According to Robin, Kinsey's research revealed how rapid economic and social changes combined with early puberty to promote girls' rebellion.[38]

Freud and Kinsey, representing new, modern sexual knowledge, became familiar names and, together, eroded traditional beliefs about and ways of understanding human sexuality. Their influence on women's magazines also highlights how men's voices often shaped the debate between tradition and modernization. Even as women's magazines occasionally referred to Simone de Beauvoir's ideas about women's autonomy, they usually, though perhaps ironically, based their view of women's sexuality on the opinions of men who were not ready to accept young women having independent sexual desires and needs. One of the few writers critical of young men's attitudes, Marcelle Auclair, met in 1959 with a group of thirty young men, ages eighteen to twenty, to probe their ideas about contemporary young women.[39] To her surprise and chagrin, she reported, the young men believed that their female counterparts used sex to trap them into marriage. "If they let themselves go that easily, it's only so that they can get us to marry them." Given that attitude, Auclair asked them directly if it was important to them that the woman they marry "should be a virgin." Several agreed: "We would really like her to be one." Another young man explained, "If she's not a virgin, we would need to know if having sex was an accident . . . or a regular thing." Auclair asked if the same were true of them. Illuminating the double standard, not one young man responded to that particular question. Even more aggravating to Auclair, the young men rejected taking responsibility should a young woman get pregnant, claiming, "Girls know what they're doing. . . . It's their fault if they end up like that!" Barely covering her indignation, Auclair responded, "All the same! Didn't the boy have something to do with it?" Forlornly she concluded, "It seems the answer is no." In retrospect Auclair admitted that most of this was bravado and immaturity. But to ensure that her message came through to her young women readers, she consulted a friend who worked with young men who warned: "Boys disrespect girls, and it's the girls' fault. Spread the word!"[40]

Young men's jumble of contradictory ideas constituted grounds for caution on the part of young women. Further complicating matters for girls, a new social expectation had entered the picture, creating pressures in the opposite direction. Although girls feared rejection by boys for not being virgins, they knew that if they resisted male overtures, boys might label them old-fashioned or prudes. That idea reflected broader cultural trends that, starting early in the 1950s, presented new, liberated visions of young women's sexuality. Books and films painted a picture of teen girls focused completely on their personal pleasure, rejecting older ideas and expectations about love, sex, and marriage. In 1954 Françoise Sagan, then seventeen, published

Bonjour Tristesse (Hello, sadness), later made into a film, featuring Cécile, a teenaged heroine who expresses her sexuality without guilt.[41] Similarly, the 1959 winner of the Grand Prix du Cinéma Français, *Les Tricheurs* (Young sinners) centered on existential, libertine Parisian youth having meaningless sexual hookups. In her first major film, *Et Dieu créa la femme* (And God Created Woman), Brigitte Bardot played a young woman focused entirely on her personal pleasure, openly expressing sexual desire. Lesbian love also appeared in novels and films, including Jacqueline Audrey's 1951 film *Olivia*, set in a girls' boarding school where Olivia and Julie, another student, end up in a love triangle with one of the female teachers.[42]

The new, open representation of female sexuality in books and films con-veyed a positive vision of women's sexual desires. It also heightened young men's expectations for uninhibited premarital sex, even as they insisted on young women's virginity prior to marriage. P. Chambre's 1960 survey of teen boys suggested that some of them, at least, cashed in on the era's changing ideas. Chambre reported that young men pressed their female partners to have sex by appealing to the young women's desire to get with the times. To them sexual liberation was a "great way to get girls to do what they wanted."[43] The tension between the traditional and the modern therefore constituted, in the end, an old-fashioned trap: that of the sexual double standard. Such contradictory ideas about the sexuality of teen boys and girls, at the time enforced by juvenile courts that, with a parent's request, sent sexually active teen girls to reformatories, left many young women confused.[44]

Navigating Young Women's Sexual Lives

Thus young women faced fluctuating and contradictory representations of sex—the open portrayal of homosexual and heterosexual desire, on the one hand, and abstinence in pursuit of marriage on the other. Women's magazines sought to empower young women to make well-informed sexual decisions. In doing so, they modernized their advice by emphasizing young women's need to make practical rather than purely moral choices about their sexual lives, while nevertheless assuming that young women's ultimate goal was heterosexual marriage. The outcome may have been the same— recommending chastity or, in twenty-first century language, abstinence—but, in abandoning the language of sin, magazines laid the groundwork for a later rethinking of women's desire and pleasure. The weakening of older moral codes left teenagers uncertain. Young men and women expressed a series of contradictory beliefs. Young women felt particularly confused. Under serious and contradictory pressures from parents and boyfriends, while also experiencing the raging hormones of adolescence, they were torn and unsure of how to behave and what the consequences their choices might be. In the end young women attempted to uphold many of the ideas that structured family life, even as they recognized the shifting ground upon which they lived. Attempts to square that circle often led to intense anxiety even as teenaged girls recognized new opportunities to assert their sexual needs, which, for some, included same-sex attraction.

By the early 1960s curiosity about what exactly unmarried teenage girls and young women, *jeunes filles* in French, thought about virginity, love, and marriage became nearly an obsession.[45] Small group sessions interrogating young men in 1959 gave way to vast opinion surveys about the contemporary *jeune fille* (young girl). Articles in *Marie-Claire*, *Elle*, and *Constellation*, and a book, *Verités sur les jeunes filles* (The truth about teenaged girls), published the results of polls of young women in France about their attitudes toward love and marriage. Three surveys explicitly probed attitudes about premarital sex. Unlike Kinsey's sex surveys, these surveys did not ask respondents specific questions about their personal sexual behavior.[46] Given the nonscientific methodologies and sampling mechanisms, the bias toward middle-class and elite young women, and the lack of anonymity in two of the surveys, the surveys do not necessarily provide a full, accurate portrait of what young women thought. They do, however, tell us about adult anxieties concerning young women's sexuality. The surveys also reveal traditional attitudes toward sexual morality giving way to practical thinking about sexual choice, as well as young women's continuing need to respond to the contradictory desires and expectations of young men.[47]

Each survey adopted a different set of tactics and targeted a particular group. In 1960 Jean Barses published in *Constellation* a survey of girls attending elite high schools in Paris. Madeleine Chapsal's *Verités sur les jeunes filles* rested on interviews with five different groups of twenty girls. Finally, *Elle* magazine's Anita Pereire published the results of her study of twenty thousand young women ages fifteen to twenty-three who sent responses to eight questions *Elle* had published in October 1960.[48]

All three surveys avoided direct questions about personal sexual behavior, instead exploring general ideas on topics like premarital sex. Madeleine Chapsal, who met in person with each of her five groups, decided that asking her interviewees directly whether they were virgins would put them on the spot without generating reliable information. Instead, she asked them if they thought a young woman should be a virgin when she married. Out of one hundred responses, forty-nine said no, forty-three said yes, and eight said that it depended, without explaining on what it depended.[49] In other words, the expectation that a woman should be a virgin at marriage may have been weakening, but it had not disappeared. Pereire's survey of young women asked a similar question: "Do you consider it important for a young woman to be pure when she marries?" The term "pure" certainly implied virginity, but less clear is whether it allowed for forms of sexual stimulation without intercourse. Either way, a high percentage of Pereire's respondents, 73 percent, answered yes.[50]

The surveys revealed both fluctuating attitudes and the continuing belief in the value of premarital abstinence. But the magazines underscore how even this longstanding ideal was transforming in light of new knowledge and attitudes. Starting in the 1950s, premarital abstinence was upheld not as central to female morality but as a logical response to the perceived nature of young men. Women's choices were predicated on young men pressing them to have sex while insisting that they expected virginity in their future mates. Young women were warned that young men would promise anything to get what they wanted. With birth control devices and information strictly illegal, columnists also warned young women about one potential and serious consequence of premarital sex: pregnancy. Teen girls and young women expressed anxiety that, as hard pressed as they were by their male romantic interests to have sex before marriage, they might be scorned by those same potential marriage partners for not being virgins if they gave in.

Letters, essays, and surveys clearly indicate the difficult decisions young women faced. Facing conflicting ideas and expectations, many feared appearing old-fashioned among their peers if they resisted sexual overtures and feared the rejection of potential marriage partners, the anger of adults, and the possibility of an unwanted pregnancy if they gave in. Advice columnists mostly emphasized risks and vulnerabilities. *Confidences* responded to Lisette, in love with Mario, torn between her parents' expectations and her boyfriend Mario's attempt to persuade her to spend the night with him when her parents were away. She explained: "[Mario] wanted me to give him proof of my love. What do you think?" *Confidences* urged her to "beware of young men demanding that kind of 'proof.'"[51]

Popular sources articulated the continuing, firmly anchored double standard among young males. On the one hand, teenage boys and young adult men wanted to have sexual experiences without having to marry, but on the other, many young men expressed a firm desire to marry a virgin. Based on his survey, Chambre concluded that young men divided young women into two groups: those with whom they could have sexual experiences without thinking about marriage and those whom they would consider marrying. Chambre himself noted the "completely different demands about conduct before marriage depending on whether it concern[ed] the young woman or the young man." Rather than challenging the double standard, however, Chambre warned young women. Whatever young men might say in the heat of the moment, Chambre advised, they wanted "young women with more dignity."[52]

Thus by the early 1960s, teen and young adult women lived in the churning crosscurrents of contradictory public opinion and private pressures, driving many to write to advice columnists. In their responses advice columnists drew on their own experiences as women. They sought to balance competing prerogatives, helping young women navigate men's expectations and assuring them that their own happiness also mattered. The possibility of young women's own sexual desires, however, only appeared in a few articles that made veiled references to the need not just to resist young men's pressure but to exercise self-control. Notwithstanding the open expression of female sexual pleasure in contemporary fiction and film, these conversations assumed the pressure was entirely external, rarely acknowledging, much less validating, female desire and pleasure.

Women's magazines published a rising tide of letters from young women articulating their concerns, asking what they should do when pressed to have sex by a young man they liked. These letters thus contributed to the view of young men as sexual agents against whom women had to respond, but they also provided young women the opportunity to work out their own ideas. In doing so, these letters shaped the magazines' content. The letters rarely used the word "sex." Instead, the young women and presumably their male friends used three expressions that played on teenage girls' emotions and clearly communicated male dominance. A boy would suggest that he and a girl "give [themselves] to each other," ask her "to belong to him," or, in the most explicit form of emotional blackmail, ask her to give him "proof of her love."[53] Popular author Agnès Chabrier wrote as the advice columnist in Nous Deux under the pen name Daniel Gray, thus enhancing the credibility of her responses about young men's attitudes. Gray responded to fifteen-year-old Christine, whose eighteen-year-old boyfriend "asked [her] to belong to him." Having resisted his entreaties, she had finally ceded and then regretted her actions. She no longer cared for the boy but feared breaking off the relationship because he threatened to tell everyone what she had done. Gray expressed sympathy for her plight and, unusually, referred to Christine's awakening but poorly controlled sensuality that had pushed her into the boy's arms. Gray warned her readers: "Very proud of their nascent virility . . . young boys play at being conquerors and tough. Foolish vanity pushes them to scorn their victims." Instead of issuing a conservative response insisting she marry the boyfriend, Gray recommended ceasing all contact and forgetting her "young rooster."[54]

In a rare admission of female sexual arousal, Auclair similarly advised her readers not to equate physical attraction with true love. In Connaissance de l'amour (Understanding love) Auclair included a chapter, "The Love We Dare Call Physical," reassuring young women not to feel guilty for the sensations they experienced while dancing with an attractive young man at a party, for example. Auclair insisted it was normal for a young man and young woman to feel a strong physical attraction to each other. But, Auclair warned young women, "you could be making a tragic mistake if you read too much into one moment of dizziness."[55]

A few letters indirectly suggested the writers' concerns about their sexuality. One eighteen-year-old woman engaged to her boyfriend wrote for advice, hinting at the troubling possibility of same-sex desire. Fear led her to refuse his entreaties to "give herself" to him, which caused her to worry. She loved her boyfriend, so why had the idea of having sex with him repulsed her? Why, when he kissed her, had she felt coldly removed? Other girls had sex with their fiancés. Was she normal? Gray passed over the young woman's unspoken worry about her sexual inclinations and focused on the superficial, assuring her that regardless of the morality or wisdom about what an engaged couple could do, she was well within her rights to refuse him.[56]

In another letter to Gray, a fifteen-year-old girl whose mother had left the family wrote about a teacher who had served as a substitute maternal figure, providing her with much-needed emotional support. Over time, the writer's affection for her teacher had turned into adoration. Eventually she confessed her feelings to her teacher, who denied any potential implications for her sexuality by deeming the writer's affection a typical "crisis of adolescence." Over the summer break the teacher had stopped responding to her postcards. Gray neither directly addressed the writer's sexuality nor disparaged it. Gray expressed sympathy, acknowledged her suffering in loving someone unable to return the feeling, and reassured the writer that time would ease her pain.[57] Similarly, Ségal responded to a letter from young man worried about his love for one of his friends. "I only think about him. If it were a girl I would understand. I ask myself if I'm normal." Ségal told him not to worry about what she described as his "crush." Passionate friendships were common between adolescents.[58]

Neither Gray nor Ségal addressed the possibility that their correspondents' feelings might be more than a passing phase. The refusal to engage in a conversation about same-sex love took place a decade after a critical moment in the public discussion of homosexual love. In 1954 the Association Arcadie promoted tolerance and the dignity of homosexuals in a new journal, *Arcadie Revue Littéraire et Scientifique*.[59] Yet homophobia remained potent. In 1960 the National Assembly approved the Mirguet amendment to the criminal code's list of "social plagues," adding homosexuality to alcoholism, tuberculosis, drug addiction, pimping, and prostitution. The Mirguet amendment doubled the penalties for public indecency if the violation consisted of "an act against nature with an individual of the same sex."[60]

For Gray and Ségal in the early 1960s, openly addressing same-sex love may have been beyond the limits permissible in mass-market women's magazines.[61] But both Gray and Ségal recognized the letter writers' pain and responded in reassuring, supportive language without condemnation. In the response to the woman resisting her fiancé's pressure to have sex, Gray bypassed the young woman's sexual ambivalence but acknowledged her sexual agency and criticized the young man's conduct.

When it came to problems with boyfriends, advice columnists, rather than trying to convince young men not to demand sex from their girlfriends, buttressed young women's resolve. "Hiding beneath her emancipated ways, her free manners and language, often lurks genuine confusion," wrote a Dr. Masse in *Constellation*. Times were changing, Masse warned: "Our country's mores are oscillating between a rigor that is losing ground every day and a liberalism that has had ambiguous results." Absent the moral censure and threatened social ostracism that had once kept most girls from misbehaving, Masse worried, not all girls were strong enough to avoid taking risks.[62] Once again, the onus rested on girls; boys would be boys.

This era of rapidly changing ideas about sex and sexuality left many teenage girls confused and uncertain. Teen girls faced contradictory pressures in making decisions about sex as they navigated among adult expectations, contradictory male pressures, and their own feelings, needs, and desires. Older expectations about female sexuality retained power in spite of the changes. These tensions mirrored the broader situation of France, torn in the postwar decades between traditionalism and modernization, and thus highlight how attention to sex brings larger narratives into relief. The gradually increasing transition to sexual liberation was fraught with complications for girls and women. The traditional understanding of sex provided a framework within which to understand both one's own and others' desire; it gave shape to social relations as it provided rules for how to explore sexuality. The modern understanding endowed young women with the power of their own decision making, moving sex and sexuality from the realm of religious morality to that of the practical and breaking free from the sexual identity of "unchaste woman" discussed by Nina Kushner in this volume. Young women had to figure out how to navigate their way through the contradictory generalizations in the 1950s and early 1960s as they struggled to understand and work through their sexual needs and desires. Long before 1968 sex and sexuality played a critical role in popular culture and the consumer revolution. In her chapter in this volume, Tamara Chaplin reveals how ongoing modernization in France, in this case the emergent technology of the Minitel, continued to serve as fertile ground for shifts in sexual attitudes and practices.

The upheavals of May 1968 provided an opening for feminist anger to explode at the hypocrisies of men's expectations. As Ellen Willis writes, "Liberation for men meant rebelling against the demands of women, while liberation for women meant the opportunity (read obligation) to shuck their 'hangups' about casual sex."[63] Prior to that opening, however, though not in open rebellion, young women had already begun to discuss what new ideas about sexuality would mean, not only for the men to whom they so often had to respond, but for themselves as well. The women's magazines of the 1950s and early 1960s, by providing the space for elucidating both "traditional" and "modern" views of sex, gave women the means to participate in this project. "The personal is political" became a rallying cry of the 1968 youth movement. Attention to sex and sexuality underscores how people's intimate lives expressed the deeply unsettling circumstances of this transitional era, revealing the extent to which the political was also personal.

Notes

1. Anne Chemin, "Mai-68 marque-t-il l'an I de la Révolution sexuelle?," *Le Monde*, March 16, 2018.
2. Jean Fourastié coined the expression with his book title *Les trente glorieuses ou la révolution invisible de 1946 à 1975* (Paris: Fayard, 1979).
3. Judith Coffin, *Sex, Love, and Letters: Writing Simone de Beauvoir* (Ithaca NY: Cornell University Press, 2020), 15. For letters Blossom Margaret Douthat sent in 1959 to Beauvoir about wanting sex without commitment see Douthat, *Un amour de la route: Lettres à Simone de Beauvoir* (Paris: Mauconduit, 2020).
4. Interestingly, here they echoed early feminists Nelly Roussel, Madeleine Pelletier, and Lydia Martial, who confined sexual happiness to marriage. See Lydie Martial, *Action du féminisme rationnel. Union de pensée féminine. Un vœu important: L'enseignement de paternité à la caserne et dans les écoles de l'État* (Alençon, France: F. Guy, 1909).
5. Vichy's sexual politics rested on return-to-the-past policies inscribed with conservative Christian morality, unlike Nazi Germany's politics of sex, which harnessed sexual libertinage to racial propagation. See Dagmar Herzog, *Sex*

after Fascism: Memory and Morality in Twentieth-Century Germany (Princeton NJ: Princeton University Press, 2005), 6.

6. Abortion remained illegal but was no longer a crime against the state punishable by death.

7. Article 33 of the Penal Code. See Scott Gunther, *The Elastic Closet: A History of Homosexuality in France, 1942-present* (Houndsmills, UK: Palgrave Macmillan, 2009). Fifteen years later, the 1960 Mirguet amendment linked homosexuality to prostitution.

8. Sister organizations developed for students (Jeunesse étudiante chrétienne) and rural youth (Jeunesse agricole chrétienne), with separate groups for young women.

9. Jeunesse étudiante chrétienne, *"Amour" et mariage* (Issoudun, France: Imprimerie de Laboureur, 1947), 4; André Merlaud, *Splendeur de l'amour conjugal* (Paris: SPES, 1949), 22, 135; Claire Souvenance, *Initiation à l'amour conjugal: Le livre de la fiancée* (Le Puy, France: Xavier Mappus, 1951), 7; André Clément, *Information familiale: Initiation et éducation de l'enfant, mariage et célibat proposés à la jeunesse,* self-typed pamphlet sponsored by the Cercles d'études paroissiales, 1952, copy available at the Bibliothèque Nationale de France (BNF).

10. Paul Chanson, *L'éveil féminin: La pureté des jeunes filles* (Paris: Institut de sexologie familiale, 1952), 7. Thomas Aquinas, *Summa Theologica,* trans. Fathers of the English Dominican Province (New York: Benziger Bros., 1947), I.1.8, https://www.ccel.org/a/aquinas/summa/home.html.

11. Chanson, *L'éveil féminin,* 7. The BNF catalog lists fourteen books in the series.

12. Chanson, *L'éveil féminin,* 6.

13. Chanson, *L'éveil féminin,* 17.

14. Bernard Senencourt, *Vie conjugale et contrôle des réflexes* (Paris: Institut de sexologie familiale, 1952). Also in 1956, the Institut de sexologie familiale published Paul Chanson's book *L'accord charnel,* 2nd ed (Paris: Institut de sexologie, 1956).

15. My search found no similar works published after 1957.

16. Todd Shepard, *Sex, France, and Arab Men, 1962–1979* (Chicago: University of Chicago Press, 2018), 134, 139, 151–52.

17. Jean Dublineau, "La vie sexuelle et sociale élémentaire: Conférence prononcée le 22 décembre 1948 à la Faculté de médecine de Paris," *L'école des parents et des éducateurs* 10 (1948–49): 11–21.

18. Sarah Fishman, *From Vichy to the Sexual Revolution: Gender and Family Life in Postwar France* (New York: Oxford University Press, 2017), 45.

19. Docteur Caufeynon (Jean Fauconney) published a series of books in the early 1900s, including *La procréation à volonté des filles et des garçons: Suivie de la fécondation artificielle et de l'ami des jeunes femmes* (Paris: P. Fort, 1903); *La*

ceinture de chasteté; son histoire, son emploi, autrefois et aujourd'hui (Paris: P. De Poorter, 1905); and *Homosexualité chez l'homme et chez la femme: Physiologie et psychologie de l'inversion sexuelle*(Paris: Librairie artistique et médicale, 1909).

20. Alfred C. Kinsey, *Sexual Behavior in the Human Male* (Philadelphia: Saunders, 1948); and Alfred C. Kinsey, *Sexual Behavior in the Human Female* (Philadelphia: Saunders, 1953).

21. Marcelle Ségal, *Mon métier: Le courrier du coeur* (Paris: Horay, 1952), 26.

22. Michel Phelizon, "Du Journal des dames à *Marie-Claire*," *Informations sociales: Bulletin mensual*, January 1973, 6–7.

23. Françoise Giroud and Martine de Rabaudy, *Profession journaliste: Conversations avec Martine de Rabaudy* (Paris: Hachette, 2001), 3.

24. Vincent Soulier, *Presse féminine: La puissance frivole* (Paris: L'Archipel, 2008), 112. Susan Weiner cites the one in six estimate in "Two Modernities: From *Elle* to *Mademoiselle*; Women's Magazines in Postwar France," *Contemporary European History* 8, no. 3 (November 1999): 400.

25. The readership varied between 3.4 and 4.2 million readers. Phelizon, "Du Journal des dames," 9–11.

26. Men constituted between one-fifth and one-third of all readers. Phelizon, "Du Journal des dames," 16–17, 30.

27. Ségal's book on her years as advice columnist included a chapter titled "Oui, les lettres sont authentiques" (Yes, the letters are real). When she first started the column, before anyone knew who she was, however, Ségal admitted writing the letters she responded to. Quickly letters began to pour in, and by the 1950s she received four or five letters every day. Ségal, *Mon métier*, 17, 21–26.

28. Ségal, *Mon métier*, 21–29. In addition, journalist Nicole Vulser described *Marie-Claire* as one of the first magazines to include the voices of ordinary women in "*Marie-Claire*: Une histoire de famille," *Le Monde*, February 14, 2001.

29. Ségal, *Mon métier*, 33.

30. "Nos lecteurs écrivent," *Confidences*, April 23, 1961, 43. This notice reappeared over several months.

31. "She's back. . . . Many of you have asked . . . 'When will she resume her dialogue with us?,'" *Marie-Claire*, February 5, 1955, 1. Haedrich describes the events in *Citizen Prouvost: Le Portrait incontournable d'un grand patron de la presse française* (Paris: Filipacchi,1995), 142–44.

32. Marcelle Auclair, *Le livre noir de l'avortement* (Paris: Fayard, 1963) appeared nearly a decade before the 1971 Manifesto of the 343, often seen as signaling the start of the movement to legalize abortion.

33. Samra-Martine Bonvoisin and Michèle Maignien, *La presse féminine*, second ed. (Paris: Presses universitaires de France, 1996), 8.

34. "Allô docteur! Danger pour les garçons: 'La mère dominatrice,'" *Marie-Claire*, no. 29, March 1957, 62.

35. Laurence Pernoud, "Le complèxe d'Oedipe," *Marie-Claire*, no. 123, February 1965, 56; Laurence Pernoud, *J'attends un enfant* (Paris: Editions Horay, 1957).

36. Dagmar Herzog, "The Reception of the Kinsey Reports in Europe," *Sexuality and Culture* 10, no. 1 (Winter 2006): 42–44; Sylvie Chaperon, "Kinsey en France: Les sexualités féminine et masculine en débat," *Le Mouvement Social*, no. 198 (2002): 91–110.

37. Guy Robin, "L'age difficile de nos filettes," *Constellation*, no. 132, April 1959, 74.

38. Robin, "L'age difficile," 75.

39. Marcelle Auclair, "Ce que les garçons pensent des filles: Confidences recueillis par Marcelle Auclair," *Marie-Claire*, no. 54, April 1959, 54.

40. Auclair, "Ce que les garçons," 55–58.

41. Françoise Sagan, *Bonjour Tristesse* (Paris: Livre de Poche, 1954).

42. Other 1950s representations of lesbian love include Nicole Louvier's *Qui qu'en grogne* (Paris: La Table Ronde, 1955); Colette Mars's popular song "La Garconne," Columbia Records, 1958, vinyl, 45 RPM; and Marise Querlin, *Femmes sans hommes* (Paris: Scorpion, 1953).

43. P. Chambre, "Ce que les jeunes gens pensent des jeunes filles," *Revue de L'École Nouvelle Française*, nos. 75–76 (January–February 1960): 2.

44. Two scholars of postwar juvenile justice, Richard Jobs and Guillaume Périssol, conclude that gender determined where adults located threats to heteronormative goals and the system's response. For teen girls, the danger was in sexual activity; boys' sexual activity only aroused concern if it involved homosexuality. Richard Jobs, *Riding the New Wave: Youth and the Rejuvenation of France after the Second World War* (Stanford CA: Stanford University Press, 2009); and Guillaume Périssol, "La domination hétéro-masculine," in *Le droit chemin: Jeunesses délinquants en France et aux États-Unis au milieu du XXe siècle* (Paris: PUF, 2020).

45. See Susan Weiner, *Enfants Terribles: Youth and Femininity in the Mass Media in France, 1945–1968* (Baltimore: Johns Hopkins University Press, 2001).

46. Unlike in Kinsey's and other sex surveys, there were no questions about specific sexual acts or behaviors. The questions asked what respondents thought about premarital sex, not whether they had engaged in it. On the sex survey from Kinsey (1948) through 1994, see Stuart Michaels and Alain Giami, "The Polls—Review: Sexual Acts and Sexual Relationships, Asking about Sex in Surveys," *Public Opinion Quarterly* 63 (1999): 401–20.

47. The only surveys of young men in the early 1960s, published as one book and one article, asked what youngmen thought about young women; Chambre,

"Ce que les jeunes gens pensent des jeunes filles," 44; Auclair, "Ce que les garçons," 54.

48. Jean Barses, "Les 10 énigmes de la jeune fille 1960," *Constellation*, no. 149, September 1960; Madeleine Chapsal, *Vérités sur les jeunes filles* (Paris: Bernard Grasset, 1960); Anita Pereire, "20,000 jeune filles parlent à coeur ouvert," *Elle*, no. 794, March 10, 1961, 133. Barses's young women were all *lycéennes*. Chapsal asked colleagues and friends for names of young women to interview; thirty percent were petty bourgeois, fifteen percent were working class.

49. Chapsal, *Vérités sur les jeunes filles*, 161.

50. Pereire, "20,000 jeunes filles," 139.

51. "Nos lectrices écrivent," *Confidences*, no. 702, April 16, 1961, 43.

52. Chambre, "Ce que les jeunes gens pensent des jeunes filles," 44, 45.

53. "Nos lectrices écrivent," 43.

54. "Daniel Gray se penche sur vos problèmes sentimentaux," *Nous Deux*, no. 772, March 22, 1962, 52. See also "Daniel Gray se penche," *Nous Deux*, no. 843, March 2, 1963, 54.

55. Marcelle Auclair, *Connaissance de l'amour* (Paris: Plon, 1960), 9.

56. "Daniel Gray se penche sur vos problèmes sentimentales," *Nous deux*, no. 970, 1965, 66.

57. "Daniel Gray se penche sur vos problèmes sentimentales," *Nous deux*, no. 709, 1961, 36.

58. Marcelle Ségal, "Courrier du coeur," *Elle*, November 22, 1963, 7.

59. Three years later Arcadie opened a private club. See Julian Jackson, *Living in Arcadia: Homosexuality, Politics and Morality in France from the Liberation to* AIDS (Chicago: University of Chicago Press, 2009).

60. George Sidéris, "*Folles*, Swells, Effeminites, and Homophiles in Saint-Germain-des-Prés of the 1950s: A New 'Precious' Society?," in Jeffrey Merrick and Michael Sibalis, *Homosexuality in French History and Culture* (New York: Routledge, 2002), 226, 231. The Mirguet amendment was repealed in 1982.

61. "Daniel Gray se penche," *Nous Deux*, no. 970, August 8, 1965, 66; "Nos lectrices écrivent," 43. Letters to *Nous Deux*, *Elle*, and *Confidences* also received sympathetic responses that veered away from the possibility of same-sex love. See Fishman, *From Vichy to the Sexual Revolution*, 162–64.

62. Dr. Masse, "Votre fille doit être avertie," *Constellation*, no. 193, May 1964, 134–37.

63. Ellen Willis, "Toward a Feminist Sexual Revolution," *Social Text*, no. 6 (Autumn 1982): 3–6.

Suggested Reading

Bantigny, Ludivine, *1968: De grands soirs en petits matins* (Paris: Seuil, 2018).

Cano, Christine. "The Kinsey Report in France." *Contemporary French Civilization* 35, no. 1 (January 2011): 33–52.

Chaperon, Sylvie. "Kinsey en France: Les sexualités féminine et masculine en débat." *Le Mouvement Social*, no. 198 (2002): 91–110.

Chaplin, Tamara. "Orgasm without Limits: May '68 and the History of Sex Education in Modern France." In *May 68: Rethinking France's Last Revolution*, edited by Julian Jackson, Anna-Louise Milne, and James S. William, 376–97. London: Palgrave, 2011.

Coffin, Judith G., *Sex, Love, and Letters: Writing Simone de Beauvoir*. Ithaca NY: Cornell University Press, 2020.

Martel, Frederic. *Le rose et le noir: Les homosexuels en France depuis 68*. Paris: Seuil, 2000.

Merrick, Jeffrey, and Michael Sibalis, eds. *Homosexuality in French History and Culture*. New York: Routledge, 2002.

Pavard, Bibia. *Si je veux, quand je veux: Contraception et avortement dans la société française 1956–79*. Rennes, France: Presses universitaires de Rennes, 2012.

Roberts, Mary Louise. *What Soldiers Do: Sex and the American GI in World War II France*. Chicago: University of Chicago Press, 2014.

Shepherd, Todd. "'Something Notably Erotic': Politics, 'Arab Men,' and Sexual Revolution in Post-Decolonization France 1962–74." *Journal of Modern History* 84, no. 1. (March 2012): 80–115.

Virgili, Fabrice. *Shorn Women: Gender and Punishment in Liberation France*. Translated by John Flower. Oxford: Berg, 2002.

II

CREATING LESBIAN COMMUNITY

Sexuality on the French Minitel in the 1980s

TAMARA CHAPLIN

The history of sexuality is also a history of the quest for human connection.[1] In the postmodern era new media technologies have radically transformed the social nature of that quest—especially for those whose erotic interests fall outside dominant norms. Indeed, the emergence of queer communities in the twentieth-century West is inseparable from the history of the communications technologies and alternative media—newsletters, journals, magazines, and online platforms—that have helped to forge queer identities and bring queer communities into existence.[2] The internet in particular offered new possibilities to marginalized individuals seeking to connect sexually and affectively with others like themselves.[3] Perhaps surprisingly, France played a pivotal early role in this process. This chapter tells a small part of that story.

More than thirty years after its appearance, few remember the Minitel—a now defunct French prototype for the internet based on a closed network videotex system that connected a computer to telephone lines via a modem—or the interest it generated among gay and lesbian communities in France. There is nevertheless no doubt that the French Minitel and the internet, which superseded it, revolutionized queer life around the globe. Despite the vital import of the internet for queer communities today, very little research on the early history of this phenomenon has been published.[4] That which exists often risks distorting our understanding of the past because it glosses over marked differences between gay (mostly understood as male) and lesbian engagement with new technology.[5]

Since the 1970s lesbian activists in France have used the tools of the modern mass media to forge identities, create communities, and fight for recognition from a republican nation that refuses to acknowledge the rights of groups. The Minitel and later the internet became indispensable instruments in this work. This chapter is about the first online website and email service for lesbians ever created. It examines the intersection in the 1980s between a group of self-avowed lesbian activists, Les Goudous Télématiques (the GTs), and an innovative networking technology, the Minitel, which promised a new way to form lesbian communities that stretched beyond Paris into provincial towns and villages. With its capacity for email, chat, press reviews, news forums, and online listings, the Minitel enabled instant communication, group dialogue, and information access. Lesbian activists sought to utilize the Minitel as a feminist technology that could advance their shared vision of collectivist, noncapitalist community based on solidarity and affective ties. They laid the groundwork in France for a shift in social and sexual relations whose wide-ranging effects have transformed the nature of human existence in the contemporary world.

The Minitel made possible new forms of French lesbian identity untethered to specific locations, organizations, embodiments, or proximities. It also made possible unique ways of being out of the closet in a virtual space that was at once private (experienced in the intimacy of home or office) and public (accessible to others and premised on representation and communication). The result was dialectical; the Minitel not only put a self-identified group of lesbian individuals into contact but also helped to construct a specific incarnation of the social category—"lesbian"—that it was deployed to support. In so doing, it contributed to the emergence of a French lesbian "imagined community" characterized not just by geographic proximity but also by a level of social cohesion born of personal intimacy, common understanding, shared political vision, and mutual experiences of social exclusion.[6] Examining sexual history thus offers insights into how novel communication technologies have reshaped how we understand both modern subjectivity and community, not just for French lesbians, nor even just for French people, but for all individuals with access to these systems. While the internet has, arguably, atomized contemporary life, isolating us in front of our computers and our phones even as it promises virtual connection, the early history of the Minitel demonstrates the potential of such technologies to bring people together in the physical world. Utopian in conceptualization, this website was ultimately unsuccessful in practice. Given the centrality of the internet to queer life by the twenty-first century, however, both the site's achievements and its failures contribute to the evolving history of the relationship between technology and lesbian identity, community formation, sexuality, and experience in modern France and beyond.

Cyberqueer History and Lesbian Identity

Gay newsgroups and bulletin board systems (BBSS), in which users post plain text messages to a publicly accessible online space, appeared in tandem with mainstream internet services in the 1980s. The first French gay and lesbian Minitel sites were also launched at that time. As the technology improved and became commercialized, queer ventures kept pace, developing first web content and then commercial gay-oriented chat spaces and graphical 3D worlds like the short-lived Pride!Universe. Many of the first queer sites were created by individuals involved in telecommunications and the computer industry. One of the first globally accessible queer online spaces to attract lesbian participation was the American Usenet newsgroup net.motss. Established by gay users in 1983 despite initial resistance from homophobic Usenet authorities, the net.motss acronym, the latter part of which stood for "members of the same sex," was deliberately chosen for its obscurity.[7]

Conservative opposition to early cyberqueer activity was all too common. In France the Confédération nationale des associations familiales catholiques (National Confederation of Catholic Family Associations) not only argued that "homosexuals['] ... natural tendency toward sexual vagrancy" was "given free rein thanks to the Minitel," but also warned that gay use of the Minitel would cause France to be "the country most affected" by the AIDS virus.[8] In 1988 the German service provider Prodigy attempted to obtain a court ban against gay forums.[9] In the United States, America Online (AOL) was found to have outed a client, passing on personal data about the homosexual orientation of a member of the U.S. military.[10] Such reactions give the lie to the utopian rhetoric that often dominated early discussions of queer cyberspace, in which the liberating possibilities of virtual technology were idealized. They also justified the fears of the French women who resisted this new technology on the grounds that it could not adequately protect the privacy of those it served.

But not everyone was worried. In 1983, the same year that net.motss went online, the French gay male community enthusiastically recognized the Minitel as a new way to "hook up" cheaply and anonymously. Within the next year, *Gai pied* (a popular magazine aimed at the French gay male public) set up its Minitel site, GP-Rézo. In record time the site was logging about a thousand use hours per day, and the magazine was raking in profits.[11] In fact, *Gai pied* cofounder and gay rights activist Jean Le Bitoux remarked that the technology provided the magazine with "an inexhaustible source of revenue."[12] Email discussion lists—in which messages were sent via email to members rather than publicly posted to electronic bulletin boards—soon heightened queer interest in computer-mediated communication, because they offered an additional degree of privacy and security. Although queer internet and Minitel sites in North America and Europe quickly provided multiple services (job postings, travel ads, medical information, and so on), gay men adopted the new technology first and foremost as a means of sexual communication. For the most part, early lesbian agendas for the technology, in France and elsewhere, could not have been more different.

Much of the early history of lesbian engagement with computer-mediated communication relies on chronologies written by queer internet activists Amy Goodloe and Eva Isaksson, both of whom appear unaware of the existence of French lesbian initiatives on the Minitel.[13] (Of course, scholarship on the cyberqueer world is hindered by the lack of data that thwarts cyberstudies in general.)[14] Goodloe, the founder of the American website lesbian.org (established in the mid-1990s), reports that the first American lesbian email discussion list, SAPPHO, was launched in May 1987 (almost two years after the GTs went live in France). Most subscribers were American, frequently with links to educational institutions, where email was becoming a regular feature of academic life. Lesbian lists like LIS (Lesbians in Science, established in 1991) and OWLS (Older and Wiser Lesbians, established in the spring of 1991) appeared shortly thereafter.[15]

Eva Isaksson began to set up European lists in the early 1990s, creating the first Finnish list, sapfo, in 1993. Wakeford's claim that this was the same year that lesbian chat spaces first appeared neglects to take into account the presence of chat forums on the French Minitel almost a decade earlier.[16] (Goodloe commits the same oversight, dating the first invitation-only chat room—called *clitchat*, on AOL—to the early 1990s.)[17] The site Euro-Sappho launched in 1994 and the first European World Wide Web page, A Dyke's World, appeared in 1995. In North America niche lists with names like GrrlTalk, SacredSisters, Biker-Dykes, LezCouplesWithKids, and Nice-JewishGirls multiplied. In 1997 Isaksson, again omitting mention of France, counted over sixty lesbian lists, fifty running on U.S. servers and nine on European ones, including LLI in Italy and Sapfo-Norden, a Norwegian list running on a Swedish server. According to Isaksson, more than 90 percent of the lesbian online population hailed from North America, where the largest body of resources (hardware, software, networking services, and facilities) was located.[18] By the end of the 1990s, commercially oriented sites proliferated as providers cued into the financial potential of the lesbian and gay market.

Queer online spaces help to produce specific incarnations of sexual subjectivity. The early history of lesbian online sites is illustrative in this regard. When Eva Isaksson reveals, for example, that SAPPHO's founder (known online as Ambar) was a heterosexual woman who ostensibly wanted to provide lesbians with an online meeting place, she unintentionally raises questions about the relationship between identity and the presentation of online personas that are pertinent to the narrative discussed here. How many of the women who logged on to the GTs did not self-identify as lesbian? How many used the site as a place for exploration, education, or titillation? What did the appellation "lesbian" mean to each of them? Given that, like all identities, lesbian identity is situationally and historically contingent, such questions remind us of the disciplinary effects shaping the category. As we shall see, the GTs ultimately encouraged both the politicization and the de-eroticization of the lesbian identity that they aspired to serve.

Lesbians on the Mainframe: Launching Les Goudous Télématiques

The handful of white French women who came together to create Les Goudous Télématiques, the first lesbian Minitel site, were part of a visible minority of politically out lesbians whose militant identities had been forged through participation in the French women's movement and the fights for gay and lesbian liberation that followed May 1968. Some of this militant energy dissipated once the Socialists swept to political power in France in 1981. With the catastrophe of AIDS a bit beyond the horizon, and lulled by a recent series of political gains—including the 1982 repeal of the 1942 law that had set the age of sexual majority for homosexual acts at twenty-one (as opposed to fifteen for heterosexual ones), the declassification of homosexuality as a mental illness, and the dissolution of the "homosexual brigade" within the French police force (a taskforce charged with stamping out homosexual activity)—many in the gay and lesbian community turned away from politics to pursue more personal pleasures.[19] For others, including over twenty groups of lesbians from throughout France who were buoyed by recent victories but anxious about the battles that remained, new forms of community consciousness generated an unprecedented level of social, cultural, and political activity into the 1990s. Interaction with the media played a key role. Lesbian engagement with the Minitel is part of this story.

Developed in 1977 as a virtual replacement for paper telephone directories, the Minitel went public in France in 1982. By the end of the century, the Minitel had fifteen million French users and hosted twenty-five thousand services. In contrast, as late as 1997, only 0.7 percent of the French were connected to the internet.[20] Although it could initially transmit only text, not images, the Minitel could be used—much as the internet later was—to make purchases, send email, and participate in online chats. Minitel users could also access an array of services and information; online banking, stock market quotes, news and weather reports, travel reservations, and insurance were all available through the new technology. Unlike the internet, which is accessed through the open system of the World Wide Web, the Minitel functioned through a closed system run by the French Télétel network that rendered it impermeable to hackers and safe from viruses—features that contributed to its enduring popularity.[21]

The Minitel had both nonprofit and more costly for-profit servers, and enterprises could choose to subscribe to one or the other.[22] The speedy multiplication of erotic bulletin boards and sex-chat lines (collectively known in France as the Minitel Rose) on the Minitel's for-profit servers quickly became the subject of heated debate. Why? In part because during the period in which the GTS existed (from 1985 to 1988), calls to the erotic bulletin boards of the Minitel Rose accounted for fully half of the time spent online by French consumers.[23] Indeed, these sites were the primary factor behind both the popularity and the condemnation of the new technology. Early critics like the minister of telecommunications, Gérard Longuet, and the minister of the interior, Charles Pasqua (who also attempted to have the magazine *Gai pied* banned on moral grounds in 1987), often linked the sexual services on the Minitel Rose to homosexual promiscuity—not without reason, given that, as discussed above, many gay male businesses enthusiastically embraced both the sexual possibilities and the revenue that these sites provided.[24] As we shall see, the GTS' decisions to function as a nonprofit and to reject the pornographic foci of the Minitel Rose reveals how profoundly lesbian and gay male agendas, politics, and social self-conceptions could differ.[25]

The initial idea for a lesbian Minitel site was the fruit of discussions among three young activists: Catherine Gonnard; her partner, Annie Cariou; and their friend Aline Tashjian. Gonnard and Cariou had moved to Paris in 1979 from Quimper in Brittany, where they had experienced firsthand the oppression and isolation associated with identifying as lesbian in a small town. Once relocated to Paris they became involved in the gay rights movement, participating in the founding of the mixed-gender activist group the Comité d'urgence anti-répression homosexuelle (CUARH, Emergency Committee against Homosexual Repression) and its lesbian spin-off, the Mouvement d'information et d'expression lesbiennes (MIEL, Movement for Lesbian Information and Expression). It was at the MIEL in Paris that Gonnard met Tashjian. While writing for the CUARH's militant monthly magazine, *Homophonies*, both Gonnard and Tashjian observed the frenzy that had erupted over the Minitel Rose in the gay press. "It was crazy," Gonnard reports. "Suddenly there was a way to make money in the movement. *Homophonies* had a Minitel site, and Aline and I understood very quickly what the stakes were. . . . [But] while the guys were much more gifted than we were at making money . . . they only went after the sex. Only that. And we felt like this wasn't the way we should be doing it."[26] The Minitel, they agreed, was an opportunity to build community. In the spring of 1985, they brought their agenda for a lesbian Minitel site to a series of national meetings organized by MIEL and known as the Forum lesbien (Lesbian Forum).[27]

The first meeting of the Lesbian Forum, held on April 27–28, 1985, at the Maison des femmes (Women's Center) in Paris, attracted an audience of mostly militant lesbians from throughout France who were active in the lesbian press, on lesbian radio, and in feminist and gay politics.[28] The Lesbian Forum produced a range of special-interest committees, each addressing different aspects of lesbian existence. The project for the GTs was developed during the meetings of the committee Information et coordination par et pour les lesbiennes (ICPPL, Information and Coordination by and for Lesbians).[29] The ICPPL sought to inform French lesbians about women-centered activities, services, and spaces; to valorize their initiatives (militant or not); and to organize projects on a national level. They identified two vectors of concern. The first dealt with access and reflected their desire to reach all women who were attracted to and loved women, whether closeted or out, alone or in groups, old or young. The second stemmed from their belief that "those who use the media should participate in it." They were particularly interested in helping women who lived in rural locations and smaller cities make contact with one another and with the larger lesbian community in Paris, and vice versa.[30]

This was not the first time that French lesbian activists had tried to address problems associated with community formation, communication, and connection. In May 1985 Parisian lesbians had tried and failed to create a public news forum for lesbians by replicating the example of Les Répondeuses (the Responders), a service developed and staffed by a group of dedicated feminists and lesbians that had lasted for over five years during the 1970s.[31] Les Répondeuses had utilized the telephone network to provide a news and information service for lesbians and feminists. Women would call in and leave messages concerning current events or information on a telephone answering machine. Les Répondeuses collated these incoming messages and rerecorded them weekly as one extended outgoing message. By calling the number associated with the answering machine and listening to this outgoing message, women could listen to all the announcements received that week. This system had proven viable for a restricted locale. The ICPPL concluded, however, that the results were "too Parisian" to meet their current national goals, because the information was often irrelevant to those beyond the immediate calling area. In addition, because early answering machines were linear technologies that could not be used interactively, listening to recordings took considerable time, meaning calling costs could be prohibitive for those accessing the service from outside of Paris.

At a second gathering of the Lesbian Forum on June 23, 1985, also held in Paris, the ICPPL debated the merits of a lesbian telecommunications network. Over thirty women from Rennes, Strasbourg, Rouen, Besançon, and Paris attended the meeting. Those in favor of launching a lesbian Minitel site realized that the project's success depended in part on their ability to convince a female public of the merits of the new technology. To this end, Gonnard, Cariou, and Tashjian drafted a mission statement explaining that a dedicated lesbian Minitel site would accomplish five important goals: first, break lesbian isolation; second, favor regional and national exchange; third, support social, cultural, artistic, and other initiatives; fourth, create a fast news and information service that existed in real time and that was produced by and for lesbians; and fifth, permit communication between two or more lesbians through a private message system that functioned via email and chat rooms.[32] Not only would such a Minitel service, through its "rapidity, interactivity, and conviviality," counter the "double oppression" that lesbians experience as both women and homosexuals, but also, Gonnard, Cariou, and Tashjian argued, "in the case of a tightening of social values or of repression, it [would] be a rapid and discreet means to spread information."[33] The sociopolitical agenda was clear. And unlike with most gay male Minitel sites, sex was not—at least not explicitly—on the program.

The gathering closed with the announcement of a third meeting to be held the following September in Rennes. The choice of location underscored the ICPPL's desire to decenter Paris as the locus of lesbian existence and illustrated a deliberate attempt to fight back against the social and moral constraints characteristic of smaller French cities and towns. The group volunteered to organize lodging for participants to alleviate any financial constraints that might hinder attendance. The Rennes meeting proved pivotal, for there the lesbian Minitel project took on its structure and received its distinctive name.

Legally established as a nonprofit association, the GTS were composed of a governing board of five members assisted by six other women. None were paid. The GTS' bylaws required that three of the group's five acting board members reside outside of Paris. The choice to seat their legal address in Rennes rather than the capital likewise reflected their resolutely anticentrist politics and commitment to geographic diversity. Most of the GTS lacked any training in information technology or telecommunications. All were between the ages of twenty and forty-one. The women chose their moniker—Les Goudous Télématiques—by combining the technologically descriptive adjective *telematic* with the plural of the noun *goudou*. The latter is an affectionate French word for "lesbian" that co-opts the negative epithet *gouine* (dyke) and plays on the French words for taste (*goût*) and sweet (*doux*).

Even if the GTS had been technologically savvy, getting a Minitel site up and running in France required the paid assistance of two entities: a telecommunications company to build it and a company entrusted to oversee the daily functioning of the service, handle repairs, provide statistical feedback on monthly traffic, and analyze fiscal status. The French firm SERTEL Services Télématiques was hired to perform the first service; the Association pour l'Autogestion par des Systèmes Informatiques Éclatés (ASPASIE, Association for the Extension of Self-Managed Computer Systems) was employed to cover the latter. One of ASPASIE's employees, a lesbian who regularly attended soirées thrown by MIEL, had pledged her support for the project—a detail that buttresses Wakeford's claims that early lesbian online activity "tended to be facilitated by women working in the computer industry."[34]

Together, the GTS were determined to make their site—and the access it provided to lesbian businesses, organizations, news, events, and services— available to any woman in France with access to a Minitel terminal. Importantly (and in contrast to the internet, which often entails the purchase of a computer and hence disenfranchises economically disadvantaged populations, who are disproportionately female), this meant that every French woman with a home phone could participate, because the French national phone company provided Minitel terminals (each consisting of a text-based screen, a keyboard, and a modem) free of charge to its clients.

Only women interested in using the GTS' email and chat room features were required to purchase an annual subscription, which entitled them to a password and private mailbox.[35] (In 1985 this cost 35 French francs, or just over US$5.60, per year.) This decision was unwise because it meant that although large numbers of women might freely browse the site to access information, read news articles, or peruse current events, members alone generated income. Unless users wanted email privileges and purchased subscriptions, all charges for time spent online bypassed the association and were billed directly by the phone company; the GTs didn't see a penny.

The GTs' nonprofit business plan (which eschewed advertising) reinforced their dependence on private and public funding sources. Although members of the governing board gave generously of their personal savings and held regular fundraising events, private options were scarce, and those companies they did approach, like IBM and Apple Computer France, declined. To lure public funding, the GTs sent out business dossiers to Danielle Mitterrand (wife of the French president), Françoise Fabius (wife of the French prime minister), Yvette Roudy (then minister for the rights of women and purportedly a closeted lesbian), the minister of culture, the national phone company, and regional and departmental councils across France.[36] Despite their best efforts, support for the project was almost nonexistent. In the absence of both private and public monies, the association was heavily dependent on attracting members who would avail themselves of the paid services that generated income for the GTs directly. For reasons outlined below, this turned out to be difficult.

To gauge interest in this new networking possibility among the lesbian community, the GTs formulated a questionnaire for distribution in the lesbian and gay press. Thirty completed questionnaires exist in the archives.[37] Slightly more than one-third of the respondents lived outside Paris. Although they ranged in age from twenty-one to fifty and practiced diverse professions (including teacher, dancer, nurse, student, typesetter, office worker, researcher, and administrator), only four (a professor, a student, a technician, and a social worker) had access to the Minitel in a work environment. This finding proved significant, because, as subsequent studies have shown, workplace use was a frequent prerequisite to home adoption of the new technology.[38] It also reveals the pertinence of gender difference to the GTs' story. None of the women fit the gender-specific socioeconomic profile—that of a "youngish (thirty-to fifty-year-old) educated male working in senior or middle management"—most often associated with Minitel use.[39]

It was far from remarkable, consequently, that though the majority of the questionnaire's respondents were aware that the Minitel could be procured for free from the phone company, only two women had a Minitel at home. Despite almost unanimous agreement among questionnaire respondents that the exchange of "communication and information between lesbians" was "very important," a series of prejudices against the technology remained. Respondents protested that the terminal was "horrifyingly ugly!" and considered the Minitel "too complicated," untrustworthy ("we don't know who is on the other end"), "too impersonal" or "too expensive" (because, as noted above, time spent online cost money). Only one of the thirty women had heard of the GTs' Minitel service, and now that each had read about it, just one woman in five intended to take advantage of it. The survey boded ill, accurately predicting the GTs' areas of vulnerability. All misgivings aside, the service went live on October 24, 1985, a fact that, the GTs quipped, "filled us with satisfaction."[40]

Organized onscreen under four rubrics—directory, current events, press reviews, and message board (which included email and access to the chat rooms)—the GTs service was primed to become *the* Minitel service by and for lesbians. The site provided the first comprehensive online national directory of businesses, associations, organizations, and services—from bars, restaurants, bookstores, nightclubs, and militant groups to facilities, theater groups, vacation spots, clubs, medical doctors, lawyers, and psychological support services—either run by or catering to a lesbian clientele in France.[41] With approximately three million Minitel terminals in use throughout France by the end of 1986, it seemed probable that thousands of women would find the site compelling. "Accessible, simple, speedy, cheap and convivial," its success appeared assured.[42] Certainly, over the next three years the eleven core members would volunteer herculean amounts of unpaid time and energy in order to keep the lesbian Minitel project alive.

Collating the materials for the online directory, a prerequisite to launching the site, proved a massive undertaking. Regional volunteers from throughout France helped to locate contacts. All groups, individuals, and businesses wanting to be listed were required to fill out a form authorizing the GTs to publish their contact information and "calendar of activities." To ensure national coverage, the form included a space to provide information about others "in your region or sector of activities about whom we might be unaware." Respondents were likewise asked to specify whether their organization or service was "lesbian," "[male] homo[sexual]," "mixed," or "other," as well as whether they were "associative" or "commercial" and whether their activities were national, regional, or local.[43] Although most listings were adamantly women-only—such as *Lesbia* magazine, a sports and leisure activities club called Mytilène, and MIEL (all in Paris), as well as the Strasbourg group La lune noire (Dark Moon)—a considerable number were from mixed-gender or male groups that hoped to reach out to a larger lesbian audience. Thus, the Association des médecins gais (Association of Gay Doctors) admitted that it was 95 percent male but nevertheless requested a spot on the site. Likewise, the national help line SOS Gaie described itself as mixed and noted, "Sadly, we only have men staffing our phones." It nevertheless assured the GTS, "We have had about fifty-two calls from lesbians, and two out of three times the conversations are mutually enriching."[44]

Ideologically nonpartisan, the GTS listed religiously based groups like the SOS permanence lesbienne of the Centre du Christ libérateur (the lesbian help line for the Center of Christ the Liberator) and David et Jonathan (a mixed-gender homosexual Christian movement that is still active) alongside such controversial organizations as the GRED, or Groupe de recherche pour une enfance différente (Research Group for a Different Childhood), a male association promoting sexual liaisons between adults and children.[45] Special interest groups, from a committee dedicated to sending French athletes to the 1990 Gay Games in Vancouver, Canada to a pair of lesbians offering workshops on auto maintenance to the Mouvement adolescence guaie [*sic*] (Gay Adolescent Movement, a club for gay teenagers) all requested inclusion. The GTS' geographic range was also impressive; they posted information from regions including Alsace, Aquitaine, Bourgogne, the Côte d'Azur, the Franche-Comté, Lorraine, the Midi-Pyrénées, the Pays de la Loire, Picardie, Provence, and the Touraine. Organizations and publications from beyond France were also represented. Thus the Quebec journal *Amazones d'hier, Lesbiennes d'aujourd'hui* (Amazons of yesterday, lesbians of today) and the Swiss lesbian magazine *Clit 007* both sought to expand their circulation by appealing to French lesbians online. Lesbians from Mexico also posted a request for "much-needed reviews, posters, and books . . . in French, English, or Spanish" and cordially invited their French counterparts to attend the first meeting of Latin American lesbians, scheduled for 1987.[46] Oddly, for reasons he fails to explain, only Daniel Defert, partner of the late Michel Foucault and president of AIDES (the first AIDS awareness association in France), rejected the GTs' invitation to have his organization listed on their site.[47] Correspondence between the GTs and their "listees" nevertheless reveals that by the time the site went live, virtually every known lesbian or lesbian-friendly contact in France was accounted for.

Once these original contacts were made, the current events and press reviews sections fell into place with relative ease. For the latter, the GTs simply scanned the pages of the lesbian and national presses and posted online summaries of books and articles pertinent to the lesbian community. But it was the rubric of current events that provided one of the strongest justifications for the site's existence. As the ICPPL had unanimously agreed (and most of the questionnaire respondents had concurred), extant lesbian reviews, journals, and radio services—although proliferating rapidly—were unable to keep the French lesbian community informed about breaking news and events. There were two reasons for this failure. On the one hand, although selected magazines were available in newsstands throughout France, it was evident that some women did not feel comfortable either subscribing to or purchasing products clearly aimed at homosexuals. The fact that these magazines were often shelved (regardless of content) in sections reserved for pornography further complicated this issue. On the other hand, monthly (e.g., *Lesbia* and *Homophonies*), biannual, and quarterly publications (including *Vlasta* and *Masques*) and even weekly radio shows were by their nature unable to provide up-to-date information. Private, accessible, and virtually immediate, the Minitel offered a discreet, timely solution. Moreover, the GTs argued that the current events rubric was politically efficacious. The Minitel could be used to garner support for political campaigns and human rights issues, from battles over employment, housing, and immigration discrimination to questions of child custody and sexual harassment. The GTs thus made almost instantaneous mobilization on a national scale possible for the first time.

The message board rubric was also deemed particularly important to the GTs' site, because its email and chat functions allowed women who were socially or geographically isolated to connect. Unfortunately, because of the disappearance of data so characteristic of cyberresearch, few traces remain of what transpired when women accessed these services. From the message board printouts that do survive, it appears that the posted communications were often relatively banal, like many email and text messages sent today. Not surprisingly, the GTs themselves appear to have been among the site's most active users. They sent personal messages ("We tried to reach you tonight at 10:30. Isabelle is taking the train; she doubtless arrives Saturday. . . . Dress warmly, because the heating here is only decorative!") and reported on business ("It's 11:15 pm here; didn't have time to get the latest news posted, but the mail for Chalon is sent and the badges are good"). Other users organized rendezvous, both political and festive ("Party on February 1; disguises required under pain of being undressed by the raging *Goudous* of Lille!"). A scant number attempted to establish new contacts ("I'm from Morbihan and want to have more contact with lesbians from Paris. Here nothing happens"), suggesting that the GTs' instincts that the Minitel could foster community were right. No extant messages are sexually explicit, although there is reason to believe that intimate or salacious exchanges would have been neither preserved nor donated to archives for public view.[48]

Although few, these messages are notable in that most lack pseudonyms—a key feature of the heavily eroticized world of gay male Minitel use at that time. Although it can be argued that the pseudonyms employed by French gay men were intended more as erotic shorthand than as cryptic code, they nevertheless helped to hide a user's identity.[49] In contrast, as illustrated by the text the GTs generated for publicity flyers ("the gathering of all our friends on the Minitel—a great banquet of lesbians where all the masks and pseudonyms fall") the GTs adamantly identified the Minitel as a safe space to be out.[50] The fact that women both posted to the GTs' site using their own first names and employed the technology for quotidian rather than purely pornographic purposes further indicates that the GTs' users understood the Minitel as serving a range of needs. The GTs' nominative transparency also contradicts claims that online anonymity was crucial to the technology's role in promoting the urbanization of gay and lesbian sexuality beyond the confines of the city.[51] Thus, if the French gay male community saw the Minitel primarily as a means for contacting transitory sexual partners, for the GTS, the ultimate goal of virtual technology was the enduring extension of an out lesbian community.

Community formation took place in the message board's forum: the ten chat rooms where from two to five women could communicate in real time. Although the chat rooms were labeled with evocative names like "Sappho's Rocks," "Martina's Court" (a reference to lesbian tennis icon Martina Navratilova), "Sarah's Loge" (a tribute to the legendary bisexual fin-de-siècle actress Sarah Bernhardt), and "Amazon's Breast," none of the interviewees with whom I spoke made any reference to these spaces as collectively imagined geographies.[52] In another context it has been suggested that the successful collective construction of a virtual space within the Lesbian Café (a site for women in the American Midwest furnished with a "fireplace," a "pool table," a "bean bag," and "rocking" chairs) may have helped to bind virtual community together.[53] Perhaps the GTS' failure to fashion the forum into a sufficiently realistic and welcoming virtual environment—with fewer chat rooms or more ambient features—contributed to their difficulty in attracting online activity.

Given how quickly the Minitel seduced both the broader public and the gay male community, it seems surprising that drawing users to the GTS' site appears to have been so difficult. And yet, as the earlier questionnaire had foreseen, the barriers that persistently blocked women from adopting the new technology were multiple. These included unfamiliarity with the lesbian Minitel project; fears about its impersonal nature, security, complexity, or expense; and a combination of ignorance about and uninterest in the possibilities that the Minitel's bulletin boards, email, and chat functions provided. In a series of articles published in the lesbian and gay press, the GTS took up each of these obstacles in turn.[54] They also distributed buttons displaying their newly copyrighted logo, developed publicity slogans, organized parties to advertise their venture, and produced a publicity video, as well as giving computer workshops at the lesbian-run Mytilène club in Paris, at which email use was a central focus.[55]

Such initiatives reveal that one of the GTS' principal challenges was simply getting users online. In an article published in *Lesbia* magazine in February 1986, the GTS tried to coax women to cross this Rubicon. Its lighthearted tone is evocative of the unabashedly utopian spirit that often animated early discussions of the new technology:

"Tell me, Annie, specialist of the Minitel," sighs Charlotte, our imaginary user, "what key should I hit?"

"It is very simple," Annie explains. "You fold down the keyboard, you turn on the screen, you pick up the telephone, and you dial 36 14 91 66. Suddenly, you'll hear a dial tone. Okay? Now press on the key 'Connect' and then hang up the phone."

Amazed, Charlotte gasps: "It worked! Wow! I'm on the Minitel!"

Once Charlotte has reached the GTS' home page, Annie explains how to access the email and chat functions by typing in the code and password ("GOUDOU, of course, that sweet little word") and chides, "Don't forget to hit SEND. . . . You see how easy it is to use the Minitel? It's child's play!" she observes.

"Yes," Charlotte concludes, "but can I find a 'tribade' out there who wants to climb the Himalayas with me?"

"More than one, likely," Annie replies.

"This Minitel is soooo much easier to use than most women think," Charlotte concludes, "and it opens so many possibilities. I'm amazed!"[56]

The GTS repeatedly reassured their public that "membership gives you total security," that the service was affordable, and that they had "nothing to do with the [porn] services that [were] overrun by heteros and gay guys."[57] And yet, in the eyes of potential members, the issue of privacy remained a problem. Although the GTS believed that requiring users to subscribe discouraged intruders (notably men) from prowling on the site, control was patently unenforceable, a fact that was especially worrisome in the chat rooms of the forum. Such concerns aside, because the chat rooms were understood as venues for community contact and interaction, the GTS made extra efforts to encourage their use. Although they did not follow the practice common on commercial sites of hiring "animators" to keep users engaged in online conversation, the GTS were not above using their own unpaid online presence to stimulate participation. Annie Cariou, for example, admits that board members routinely logged on to the chat rooms, sometimes under cover of multiple pseudonyms. In this case, however, pseudonyms were used not to maintain anonymity but, rather, to convey the illusion of activity: "When a girl would show up in our chat room and see multiple conversations taking place, well, it stimulates interest, you know? It gives her the sense that something is happening and makes her want to be involved."[58] The GTs justified any subterfuge by understanding it as central to their site's communitarian mission. My interviewees were eager to prove that these tactics worked by reporting at length about the long-standing friendships and romantic relationships that formed subsequent to meeting online. Comments like "One girl from Marseille and one girl from Rennes met this way and they were together for years!" were common.[59]

Despite their enthusiasm, the GTs never managed to convince their audiences that the Minitel offered women a vital service. Indeed, only seventy-five to ninety lesbians subscribed to the service from 1985 to 1988.[60] Although subscription numbers and online activity did not necessarily correlate (given that, as stated above, not all those who browsed the site were paying members), both were fiscally imperative. Despite warning signs that the project was in trouble because of a lack of online traffic, the GTs were reluctant to raise subscription rates because they were committed to keeping the service affordable. Their anticommercialism was further bolstered by their political antipathy toward the profit-oriented projects developed for the gay male market. "We were suspicious of those who had money," Cariou recalls. "The guys had bars, discos, all that, and for lesbians there was always one café, one bookstore . . . and we bewailed our poverty, but we were really kind of proud of it."[61] She continues, "In the milieu of militants it wasn't proper to speak of money. . . . It wasn't supposed to be part of our values."[62] Despite their fundraising efforts (and although the GTs eventually tripled their yearly subscription rate), it was the GTs' ongoing inability to attract paying users to email, bulletin board, and chat use that ultimately led to the failure of the entire enterprise.

The history of the GTs contributes to the history of sexuality in France while nuancing our understanding of how queer communities and individuals originally used cyberspace, in three ways. First, debates among French lesbian activists during the 1970s and 1980s over the moral politics of pornography, along with their tendency to privilege committed relationships over casual sexual encounters, meant that they conceived of the Minitel's potential differently—more politically and romantically—than did the majority of gay French males. Second, while it is true that the lesbian public targeted by the GTS exhibited a slower uptake of the new technology than did gay men, in part this was because, as women, lesbians were largely outside the male-dominated domains of business, banking, and administration in which the Minitel was first introduced and hence were excluded from the circuits that most encouraged—and provided instruction in—its use. This point reminds us that an exclusive focus on sexual orientation can obscure the effects of gender difference, which in this case were also instrumental in undermining the GTS' chances for success.[63] Third, the problematic relationship between militant lesbian politics and finance, seen by many as a competitive domain of patriarchal, capitalist oppression, further undermined the stability of the GTS' project and thus the achievement of their social and political aims.

The story of the GTS reveals precisely how a matrix of ideological positions (about sex and money) and systemic oppressions (regarding technology and patriarchy) prevented this specifically feminist project from succeeding. Just as the desires of men seeking sex with men (described in Andrew Israel Ross's chapter in this volume) were ultimately circumscribed by the forces of the police and public order, the GTS' project ultimately succumbed to the forces that enabled it in the first place. It was "torn from our loving arms," as its board members solemnly announced, "by the cruelty of the World of Money." (Its memorial service was celebrated "at the foot of the Tour Saint Jacques—metro Châtelet—on 18 June 1988 at 4:00 p.m.") Yet despite the premature death of the first lesbian Minitel site, the GTS' historical trajectory demonstrates their project's potential.[64] Letters mailed to the organization from Belgium, the United Kingdom, California, and Mexico also indicate that the ultimate failure of the GTS' site did not attenuate the extent of its influence.[65] For the three years of the site's existence, the GTS both called forth an expressly national lesbian community and provided an unprecedented tool for the construction of a politically and socially activist form of contemporary lesbian identity.

As should by now be apparent, however, the lesbian identity promoted by the GTS was also exclusionary; although not explicitly antierotic, its structure downplayed lesbian sexuality and implicitly criticized the com-modification of lesbian sexual practices.[66] By the end of the 1980s, a plethora of commercial lesbian Minitel sites premised on sexual entertainment, from 3615 ELSEM to 3615 LESB, jumped in to fill this void. The GTs nev-ertheless served as a vital precursor to the activist lesbian cybernetworks that now dominate queer political life in France. Within a decade of the GTs' demise, for example, the Coordination lesbienne nationale (National Lesbian Coordination, established in 1997) launched its presence on the World Wide Web at www.coordinationlesbienne.org. Through at least 2018 it acted as a national and international clearinghouse for lesbian news and politics, conducting regular video meetings via the internet with more than twenty regional lesbian associations and numerous individual members from throughout France, many of whom host their own web presences.[67] Like the GTs before it, the Coordination lesbienne nationale was committed to utilizing computer-mediated communication to support the creation of national lesbian community, decenter Paris and mobilize all of the regions of France, break lesbian isolation, fight lesbophobia, and celebrate lesbian existence. Like the GTs site, the Coordination nationale lesbienne's site had a structure that implicitly displaced the sexual in favor of political, social, and cultural agendas.

The GTs' passion for their Minitel project—evidenced by the many hours they devoted to developing the site, to community education, to animating the chat rooms, and subsequently to archiving materials—speaks to the French site's significance as one of the earliest incarnations of the modern relationship between technology, information systems, community, and sexual identity. Like the other chapters in this volume, this particular sexual history—the story of the lesbian Minitel—thus sheds crucial light on a series of broader issues in the history of France and beyond. For historians of the media, it underscores the critical role played by communication networks in consolidating the connections through which subcultural communities are formed. For historians of technology, it shows an important yet distinctive precursor to the adoption of the internet, especially by marginalized indi-viduals. For historians of sexuality, it adds much-needed complexity to the story of the Minitel, usually understood purely through the Minitel Rose as connecting female sex workers and straight male clients, or as part of a gay male culture of cruising and pornography. For historians of feminism, it captures a hitherto unknown form of lesbian activism, one that was simultaneously antimetropolitian, anticapitalist, and technologically savvy. For historians of political culture in postwar France, the story of the lesbian Minitel stands as a critical example of how French lesbian activists engaged in the utopian projects that animated the Socialist Left during the sweeping sociocultural changes of the late 1970s and 1980s. Finally, as the explosion of virtual lesbian sites on the internet in the twenty-first century suggests, this history of the first lesbian Minitel inevitably also reveals that, in the end, the GTS' project was a revolutionary idea whose time had not yet come.

Notes

1. This chapter is a revised version of my article "Lesbians Online: Queer Identity and Community Formation on the French Minitel," *Journal of the History of Sexuality* 23, no. 3 (September 2014): 451–72. All translations are my own unless otherwise cited. Special thanks to Annie Cariou, Isabelle Audrey, and especially Catherine Gonnard and Angie Estes; to the Archives recherches cultures lesbiennes (Archives for Lesbian Culture and Research, hereafter ARCL) for granting me extraordinary access to their collections; to Annie Metz and the staff of the Bibliothèque Marguerite Durand (hereafter BMD) in Paris; to Antoinette Burton and Clare Crowston at the University of Illinois Urbana-Champaign; and to the anonymous readers at the *Journal of the History of Sexuality* for their helpful comments.

2. Martin Meeker, for example, argues that communications networks are "a central, perhaps the central, thread that makes queer history a recognizable and unified phenomenon." See Meeker, *Contacts Desired: Gay and Lesbian Communications and Community, 1940s–1970s* (Chicago: University of Chicago Press, 2005), 2.

3. On the history of queer online services, see Nina Wakeford, "New Technologies and 'Cyber-queer' Research," in *Handbook of Lesbian and Gay Studies*, ed. Diane Richardson and Steven Seidman (London: Sage, 2002), 115–44. Her work frames my analysis. See also Larry Gross, foreword to *Queer Online: Media, Technology, and Sexuality*, ed. Kate O'Riordan and David J. Phillips (New York: Peter Lang, 2007), vii–x.

4. The burgeoning field of cyberqueer studies initially focused primarily on the United States, Britain, and Asia. See Nina Wakeford, "Cyberqueer," in *Lesbian and Gay Studies: A Critical Introduction*, ed. Andy Medhurst and Sally R. Munt (London: Cassell, 1997). See also O'Riordan and Phillips, *Queer Online*. On the cyberqueer hegemony of English-speaking countries, see Jillana B. Enteen, *Virtual English: Queer Internets and Digital Creolization* (New York: Routledge, 2010). For

a general history of the Minitel in English, see Julien Mailland and Kevin Drisco, *Minitel: Welcome to the Internet* (Cambridge MA: MIT Press, 2017).

5. On French gay male Minitel use, see Mattias Duyves, "The Minitel: The Glittering Future of a New Invention," in *Gay Studies from the French Cultures: Voices from France, Belgium, Brazil, Canada, and the Netherlands*, ed. Rommel Mendès-Leite and Pierre-Olivier de Busscher (New York: Haworth, 1993), 193–203. See also Anna Livia, "Public and Clandestine: Gay Men's Pseudonyms on the French Minitel," *Sexualities* 5, no. 2 (May 2002): 201–17.

6. The term "imagined community" comes from Benedict Anderson, *Imagined Communities: Reflections on the Origins and Spread of Nationalism*, rev. ed. (London: Verso, 2006).

7. Amy T. Goodloe, "Computer Networks and Services," in *Encyclopedia of Lesbian and Gay Histories and Cultures*, vol. 1, *Lesbian Histories and Cultures: An Encyclopedia*, ed. Bonnie Zimmerman (New York: Garland, 2000), 200.

8. M. Perier, quoted in Frédéric Brunnquell, *Les associations familiales: Combien de divisions, dossier, enquête* (Paris: Dagorno, 1994), 104.

9. Wakeford, "New Technologies," 118.

10. Wakeford, "New Technologies," 118.

11. Duyves, "The Minitel," 197.

12. Jean Le Bitoux, Hervé Chevaux, and Bruno Proth, *Citoyen de seconde zone: Trente ans de lutte pour la reconnaisance de l'homosexualité en France (1971–2002)* (Paris: Hachette, 2003), 316.

13. Nina Wakeford also relies on these sources. See Wakeford, "Cyberqueer"; and Wakeford, "New Technologies." See also Goodloe, "Computer Networks"; and Eva Isaksson, "Living with Lesbian Lists," 1997, http://www.sappho.net/lesbian-lists/lll.html, accessed July 14, 2013. See also the interview with Amy T. Goodloe available online at http://archive.org/details/nc105_women, accessed July 14, 2013. This interview was originally broadcast in 1996 on the U.S. television series, NET CAFÉ, a spin-off of the PBS series *Computer Chronicles*. NET CAFÉ focused on the 1990s internet boom and was hosted by Stewart Cheifet, Jane Wither, and Andrew deVries.

14. Online exchanges were rarely saved, and advances in hardware mean that digital traces were frequently erased or lost. Those whose sexual orientations are marginalized may also be more likely to destroy evidence of online activity, rendering work on cyberqueer history more precarious still. My own work on the lesbian Minitel is only possible because the GTs left a significant paper trail at the BMD and the ARCL in Paris, one that I was able to supplement through oral interviews with many of the group's main actors. If materials were not indexed, they are cited by archive location and digital image number in my personal database.

15. Wakeford, "Cyberqueer," 120.
16. Wakeford, "Cyberqueer," 120.
17. Goodloe, "Computer Networks," 201.
18. For specifics on the data mentioned in this paragraph, see Isaksson, "Living with Lesbian Lists," section 2.
19. On the history of homosexuality in contemporary France, see Julian Jackson, *Living in Arcadia: Homosexuality, Politics, and Morality in France from the Liberation to AIDS* (Chicago: University of Chicago Press, 2009), esp. 20–21, 37–39. See also Scott Gunther, *The Elastic Closet: A History of Homosexuality in France, 1942–Present* (Houndmills, UK: Palgrave Macmillan, 2009); Le Bitoux, Chevaux, and Proth, *Citoyen de seconde zone*; and Ursula Tidd, "Visible Subjects: Lesbians in Contemporary France," in *Women in Contemporary France*, ed. Abigail Gregory and Ursula Tidd (Oxford: Berg, 2000), 171–90, esp. 174–81.
20. By way of comparison, 27 percent of Danes and 5 percent of Germans had internet connectivity in 1997. These figures are from John Tagliabue, "Online Cohabitation: Internet and Minitel; Videotex System in France Proves Unusually Resilient," *New York Times*, June 2, 2001, http://www.nytimes.com/2001/06/02/business/online-cohabitation-internet-minitel-videotex-system-france-proves-unusually.html?pagewanted=all&src=pm, accessed November 16, 2013. See also Jean-Yves Rincé, *Le Minitel* (Paris: Presses universitaires de France, 1990); and André Lemos, "The Labyrinth of Minitel," in *Cultures of the Internet: Virtual Spaces, Real Histories, Living Bodies*, ed. Rob Shields (London: Sage, 1996), 33–48. On the importance of computers to French global status, see Simon Nora and Alain Minc, *L'informatisation de la société* (Paris: La Documentation Française, 1978). On the general French anxiety over American progress in industry, technology, and business, see Jean-Jacques Servan-Schrieber, *Le défi américain* (Paris: Denoël, 1967).
21. Because the Minitel ensured "confidentiality of data," as late as 1998 it remained "more popular than the Internet in France." Organization for Economic Co-operation and Development, Directorate for Science, Technology and Industry, and Committee on Information, Computer and Communications Policy, Working Party on the Information Economy, *France's Experience with the Minitel: Lessons for Electronic Commerce over the Internet* (Paris: OECD, 1998), 11.
22. Nonprofit organizations could be reached at minimal cost by dialing 3614 and were charged uniquely for time spent online. Commercial calls to 3615 were more than twice as expensive as those to 3614 because they billed for both connect time and services rendered. Rincé, *Le Minitel*, 103.
23. For arguments linking the Minitel to homosexuality, see Organization for Economic Co-operation and Development, *France's Experience*, esp. 14–16.

24. Le Bitoux, "Le guêpier"; and Le Bitoux, Chevaux, and Proth, *Citoyen de seconde zone*, 256–57.

25. On gay male engagement with the Minitel, see Duyves, "The Minitel"; and Livia, "Public and Clandestine."

26. Interview with Catherine Gonnard, June 28, 2010, Paris. Gonnard later became an archivist at the French television archives (L'institut national de l'audiovisuel). She also spent almost a decade (1989–98) as editor in chief of France's longest-running lesbian magazine, *Lesbia*.

27. Docs. 1613–52, ARCL.

28. For a list of those present, see Tamara Chaplin, "Lesbians Online: Queer Identity and Community Formation on the French Minitel," *Journal of the History of Sexuality* 23, no. 3 (September 2014): 459.

29. "Information et coordination par et pour les lesbiennes" is not referred to with an acronym in the sources. I have used one here (ICPPL) for clarity.

30. Doc. 1613, ARCL.

31. Doc. 1294, ARCL.

32. These goals were later formalized in the GTs' articles of association. See Article 2, *Objèt*, in "Récépissé de Déclaration d'association," no. 9259. This document was filed at Rennes in the Préfecture d'Ille-et-Vilaine on October 25, 1985. A copy exists at the ARCL.

33. Docs. 1273–93, ARCL.

34. Wakeford, "New Technologies," 119.

35. Given that the average connection time ranged from four to ten minutes, the charges were extremely modest, particularly when compared to the costs associated with calls to the message boards of the Minitel Rose on the for-profit line, 3615. See SERTEL, communication statistics, June 16, 1986, Doc. 1319, ARCL.

36. Docs. 1644–68, 1877, ARCL.

37. Docs. 1631–1754, ARCL.

38. Organization for Economic Co-operation and Development, *France's Experience*, 31.

39. Organization for Economic Co-operation and Development, *France's Experience*, 31.

40. Danièle and Corine of the GTs from Paris, in "Les Goudous Télématiques," *Lesbia*, no. 40, June 1986, 16–17.

41. Doc. 1192, ARCL.

42. Doc. 1192, ARCL.

43. Doc. 1067, ARCL.

44. Doc. 1106, ARCL.

45. While sex between adults and children was (and remains) illegal in France, arguing for the decriminalization of pedophilia was not. On French debates over sex between men and boys, see Julian Bourg, "Boy Trouble: French Pedophiliac

Discourse of the 1970s," in *Between Marx and Coca-Cola: Youth Cultures in Changing European Societies, 1960s–1980*, ed. Axel Schildt and Detlef Siegfried (New York: Berghahn, 2006), 287–312.

46. Doc. 1192, ARCL.

47. Doc. 1093, ARCL.

48. Doc. 5376, ARCL.

49. Livia, "Public and Clandestine."

50. "Les Goudous Télématiques."

51. Duyves, "The Minitel," 202.

52. Doc. 1446, ARCL.

53. Shelley Correll, "The Ethnography of an Electronic Bar: The Lesbian Café," *Journal of Contemporary Ethnography* 24, no. 3 (October 1995): 270–98, esp. 295–96.

54. See "Goudou chez vous par Minitel," *Lesbia*, no. 35, January 1986; "Annie et Charlotte au pays du Minitel," *Lesbia*, no. 36, February 1986; "Coût coût Goudou!," *Lesbia*, no. 37, March 1986; "Mots doux sur Minitel," *Lesbia*, no. 38, April 1986; "Minitelles interactives," *Lesbia*, no. 39, May 1986; and "Les Goudous Télématiques."

55. Doc. 1433, ARCL.

56. "Annie et Charlotte," emphases in the original.

57. "Coût coût Goudou!"; and "Les Goudous Télématiques."

58. Interview with Annie Cariou, April 30, 2011, Paris.

59. Gonnard, interview.

60. Docs. 1754–1815, ARCL.

61. Cariou, interview.

62. Cariou, interview; Gonnard, interview.

63. As Mary Bryson observes, cyberstudies often commit this fault in reverse: comparing male and female subjects to identify gender difference and forgetting about the effects of sexual orientation, race, class, or age. See Bryson, "When Jill Jacks In: Queer Women and the Net," *Feminist Media Studies* 4, no. 3 (2004): 239.

64. Doc. 1234, ARCL.

65. Docs. 1685, 1691, 1693, ARCL.

66. It is worth noting that sexuality was hotly debated throughout lesbian and feminist communities in both North America and Europe at this time. For a general overview of the American context, see Lisa Duggan and Nan D. Hunter, *Sex Wars: Sexual Dissent and Political Culture*, tenth anniversary ed. (London: Routledge, 2006).

67. The Coordination lesbienne nationale was renamed Coordination lesbienne en France (CLF) in 2002. The CLF's website remains accessible, but the organization

was dissolved on November 4, 2017. Other examples of French lesbian cybernetworks include the website of Bagdam Espace Lesbien run by Brigitte Boucheron at www.bagdam.org in Toulouse, and the Centre Evolutif Lilith at http://celmrs .free.fr/ in Marseille.

Suggested Readings

Chaplin, Tamara. "Lesbians Online: Queer Identity and Community Formation on the French Minitel," *Journal of the History of Sexuality* 23, no. 3 (September 2014): 451–72.

Duyves, Mattias. "The Minitel: The Glittering Future of a New Invention." In *Gay Studies from the French Cultures: Voices from France, Belgium, Brazil, Canada, and the Netherlands*, edited by Rommel Mendès-Leite and Pierre-Olivier de Busscher, 193–203. New York: Haworth, 1993.

Gunther, Scott. *The Elastic Closet: A History of Homosexuality in France, 1942–Present.* Houndmills, UK: Palgrave Macmillan, 2009.

Jackson, Julian. *Living in Arcadia: Homosexuality, Politics, and Morality in France from the Liberation to AIDS*. Chicago: University of Chicago Press, 2009.

Le Bitoux, Jean, Hervé Chevaux, and Bruno Proth. *Citoyen de seconde zone: Trente ans de lutte pour la reconnaisance de l'homosexualité en France (1971–2002)*. Paris: Hachette, 2003.

Livia, Anna. "Public and Clandestine: Gay Men's Pseudonyms on the French Minitel." *Sexualities* 5, no. 2 (May 2002): 201–17.

Mailland, Julien, and Kevin Drisco. *Minitel: Welcome to the Internet*. Cambridge MA: MIT Press, 2017.

Martel, Frédéric. *The Pink and the Black: Homosexuals in France since 1968*. Translated by Jane Marie Todd. Stanford CA: Stanford University Press, 2000.

Meeker, Martin. *Contacts Desired: Gay and Lesbian Communications and Community, 1940s–1970s*. Chicago: University of Chicago Press, 2005.

O'Riordan, Kate, and David J. Phillips, eds. *Queer Online: Media, Technology, and Sexuality*. New York: Peter Lang, 2007.

Prearo, Massimo. *Le moment politique de l'homosexualité: Mouvements, identités et communautés en France*. Lyon, France: Presses universitaires de Lyon, 2014.

Tidd, Ursula. "Visible Subjects: Lesbians in Contemporary France." In *Women in Contemporary France*, edited by Abigail Gregory and Ursula Tidd, 171–90. Oxford: Berg, 2000.

Wakeford, Nina. "New Technologies and 'Cyber-Queer' Research." In *Handbook of Lesbian and Gay Studies*, edited by Diane Richardson and Steven Seidman, 115–44. London: Sage, 2002.

AFTERWORD

ROBERT A. NYE

This collection of new essays on the history of sexuality in France is a welcome addition to the growing and increasingly sophisticated research in this field by both French and non-French historians. Though global and comparative histories of sexuality have become more common in recent years, national histories remain an important staple of the subject, particularly when coupled with nations' colonial and imperial experiences. The new nations that have replaced former colonies have been stamped with the imprint of their colonizers' laws and sexual practices and are now navigating their sexual futures as sovereign, autonomous entities; as they do this, these nations are gradually becoming the objects of their own national histories. These essays reveal that in a nation as old as France, rich benefits flow from studying the history of sexuality in its myriad interactions with politics, society, culture, and religion.

In his recent summary of the state of the field, *What Is Sexual History?*, British historian Jeffrey Weeks makes ample space for the history of global and postcolonial sexualities, but he makes it clear that though historians tend to favor narratives that are shaped by the most urgent questions of the present, they do so under the influence of identities and traditions formed by social and cultural structures of long historical standing. Thus, he warns, paraphrasing Karl Marx, "We make our own histories, but rarely in circumstances of our own choosing."[1] For the historian of national sexualities, this means understanding the unique legal, religious, cultural, political, and institutional history of a nation, as well as the human and material foundations of population, kinship, and families that have passed legacies down the generations through marriage, births, and inheritance. It follows that debates on contemporary sexual issues take place within historic discourses shaped in part by these long-standing developments. No national culture is impervious to new ideas or influences, but the weight of the past is often decisive in influencing the language, the concepts, and the stakes of these urgent questions.

In their introduction Nina Kushner and Andrew Israel Ross stress the relative tardiness of histories of sexuality by French historians, and, relative to Anglo-Saxon and other European historians, a dearth of mainstream academic support for the subject. They argue that this tardiness extends even to Anglo-American scholars of sexuality in France, notwithstanding the pioneering role they have played in setting the agenda for the field in their universities. There is now good evidence that the gap between French contributions and those of scholars elsewhere is narrowing, but when we examine more deeply the historical lineaments of French scholarship, particularly in the matter of sexuality, we can better account for both the slower embrace of the field in France and the unique way that debates about contemporary sexual issues have unfolded there. This in turn will permit us to better understand the nature and importance of this collection of essays by U.S. scholars.

In his brilliant study of the concept and history of the family in France, Rémi Lenoir asks, "How is it that the family appears so natural that the question of its construction and perpetuation as a unified cognitive and social category is hardly ever posed?"[2] Well before the family provisions of the *code civil*, and throughout the modern era, he writes, "the conception of the family as entirely harmonious, homogeneous and indivisible was linked to the obsession with permanence, continuity, and perpetuation of the group and that which guaranteed it . . . , and which in ordinary language associated the family with the words héritage, hérédité, succession, souche et de racine, de lignée et de postérité, d'ascendance et de descendance (heritage, heredity, succession, descent, roots, lineage, posterity, ascendance, and descendance)."[3] The specter of depopulation that arose in the mid-nineteenth century intensified these concerns and provoked private and public efforts to increase the birth rate, the decline of which seemed to threaten the very existence of the nation, provoking fears of biological degeneration.[4] Government demographers and statisticians constructed a "state-sanctioned vision of the family" through the classification of age, marriages, births, and mortality that "eternalized what they sought to apprehend and measure," thereby "endowing the things they measured with the illusion of the natural."[5] By the end of the century, an official definition of the normal family emerged that was expressed as a duty: "This duty is accomplished when a family raises three children [because it requires two to replace the parents and a third to add to the population or at least sustain it]."[6]

The other putatively natural aspect of family life was the notion of male and female sex presented in the medicine and physiology of late eighteenth-century French science and enshrined in the *code civil* as the foundation of the postrevolutionary society of rights and responsibilities. The property and inheritance rights of the reproductive couple were subsumed in the blood lineage linking them with their genitors and their own offspring, a kind of biological mystique that made adoption inconceivable until a law in 1923 allowed adoption by childless parents over forty.[7] The mutual attraction of the sexes was the engine of this mystique, propelling lineage property down the generations. Jann Matlock reminds us that the first use of the word *sexualité* in French was in 1838 by the doctor J. J. Virey, who wrote, "Sexuality appears in the higher animals endowed with ardent blood, . . . in which the antagonism of the sexes generates the passion of love."[8] As a reflection of the extraordinary investment in procreation, normative sexuality in France was built on solidly heterosexual foundations. Camille Robcis explains how "familialism" has been both a political culture and an ideology in modern France, "as a system of representations in which the family operated as the enactor of the social contract, as the purest expression of the general will, as a structure essential for both the social and the individual."[9]

These enduring principles were directly challenged during the debates that raged over *parité*, the PACS (*pacte civil de solidarité*) law on civil unions, and a new bioethics law in the 1990s, as well as during the campaign for *mariage pour tous* (marriage for all) in 2013. All these laws eventually passed, but only after delays, amendments, and fierce resistance by opponents on the left and right. The anthropologists Irène Théry and Françoise Héritier wrote learned tracts arguing against unmarried or gay couples using medically assisted reproduction or surrogate pregnancy in a PACS contract; they also argued against gender affirmation surgery. The symbolic or "anthropological" function of the law, they held, must reinforce the "natural" biological order, even if we have the means to create alternatives to it. Héritier wrote, "[That means] if filiation is cut from, or at least does not stem from engendering, it is nonetheless linked to the idea of a bisexuated reproduction, which is to say that it necessarily refers to the paternal and maternal status as the supports of the affiliation of the group."[10] If in Héritier's version the laws of kinship were not, in essence, biological, they were nonetheless based on a symbolic social order modeled on nature. Sylviane Agacinski, wife of the Socialist Premier Lionel Jospin, made it clear that she considered the social variations of *genre* [gender] to be subsidiary to *sexe* [sex], which was primordial: "The sexual condition of humanity made up of males and females . . . , has no other basic definition than the one referring back to procreation, no matter how many forms this dichotomy can give rise to."[11]

The bioethics law passed in 1994 finally regulated medically assisted reproduction, but it specified that these methods could only be used in cases of infertility in a man or a woman "of an age to procreate" who could provide evidence of a "common life"—meaning they had been in a relationship—for two years.[12] The pacs law, finally passed after years of discussion in 1999, aimed at providing legal protections in contracts between nonmarried couples, whether gay or heterosexual. But pacs couples did not have the same rights as married couples. Neither could inherit from the other; their lineage families had priority. They could not adopt, and if either had a child from a previous union, the other could not adopt the child, nor could either use reproductive technologies or surrogacy to have a child in the union.[13] Conceptually paired with adoption, surrogacy, or medically assisted reproduction, homosexual marriage, already unnatural in this discursive system, was doubly unnatural, and thus doubly inconceivable.[14] In the course of the pacs debate, Didier Eribon explained in his *Réflexions sur la question gay* (1999) that a legal regime more or less equivalent to marriage was far more threatening to the heterosexist order than were any proclamations for gay and lesbian freedom. Indeed, during the huge public manifestations against *mariage pour tous* in 2013, protesters handed out leaflets denouncing homophobic violence as a distraction from their central aim of preserving the family. The law was passed, adoption was allowed, and ivf procedures for single women and married lesbians were realized in 2021, but surrogacy is still banned. By a ruling of the Cour de cassation in 1992, a person could change the sex of their *état civil* (civil registry) following gender affirmation surgery, but though transgender identity is no longer classified as a mental illness, the Cour de cassation ruled in 2017 that no French citizen could be of a "neutral" sex.[15]

The symbolic order based on bisexuated nature readily bleeds over into other social imaginaries. Apropos the controversy raging over the veil, the feminist professor of literature Claude Habib wrote in *Le Figaro* on October 24, 2019, that the veil is so shocking because it opposes "our [French] culture of gallantry," which is defined by its "playful, light, eroticized nature, which is inconceivable in the Islamic World."[16] On the other hand, as Christine Bard writes, race in postcolonial France has a "double face." Offsetting the "arabophilia" of sexual progressives, there is a xenophobic current in which Arab men are portrayed as sexual predators and Arab women appear in pornography as sexually submissive "beurettes."[17]

The defense of familialism, the procreative couple, and the legal order based upon it has been a project of the secular, universalist republic for over two hundred years, but on these matters at least, it has had the Roman Catholic Church as an ally on every point. Though diminished now in power, the Church laid down the foundations of this system of kinship and sexual norms and has punished deviations from them. Excluded from the charmed circle of the family have been voluntary and involuntary *célibataires* (single people), the infertile, those who do not identify as heterosexual, and those whose sexual lives have not conformed to standard procreative relations. Until recently, the embrace of gender analysis has also been tentative in France—along with several other European countries—for many of the same reasons that have slowed the development of the field of the history of sexuality.[18] The editors of the multiauthor, three-volume *Histoire de la virilité* published in 2011 decided that "masculinity" was not sufficiently "historical" and opted for "virility" instead.[19] On the other hand, *Une histoire des sexualités* (2018), under the direction of Sophie Steinberg, draws widely on gender theory and analysis in its account of sexualities from ancient Greece to the present, with splendid effect.[20] The authors give full credit to the path-blazing work of Anglo-American scholars inspired in the 1970s and 1980s by Michel Foucault, whose work in the domain of sexuality was embraced first and most completely outside of France.

The essays in this volume cover a wide range of topics in the field using sophisticated theories and methods and an imaginative range of printed and archival sources. They illustrate how deeply embedded historical conceptions of sex, gender, and sexuality are in French institutions, law, and politics, and in the myriad practices governing sexual relations, cohabitation, bodies, and pleasures. Several authors explore the regulation and policing of bodies that might produce unsuitable racial or hygienic alliances: in the colonial domain in the essays by Jennifer J. Davis and Jennifer Anne Boittin, or, as Jessie Hewitt illustrates, through the violation of the *maladie secrète* by doctors convinced of the dangers of disease and heritable disorders to the family and the nation. In Cathy McClive's treatment of the Cadière-Girard affair, the symbolism and materiality of blood and the reproductive cycle deeply influenced the judgments made about both the spiritual and legal aspects of the affair. In her essay Nina Kushner suggests the possibility that in the eighteenth century, a *femme de mauvaise vie* carried a socially imposed identity that made her both a doubtful marriage partner and undeserving of the legal protections afforded well-behaved and well-dressed women. The policing and administration of homosexual activity and prostitution in urban spaces in the nineteenth century produced zones of legal and visual separation from respectable society predicated on sexual distinctions, but the lines between these zones were constantly blurred by economic and demographic change and an unacknowledged fascination with sexual "others." Andrew Israel Ross and Michelle K. Rhoades both demonstrate in their essays the legal and human complexities of tolerance.

There is a political dimension to practically all these essays, expressed as the administration or enforcement of the law or the regulation of space, but sexuality has also influenced state politics and has been shaped in turn by state power throughout French history. Lisa Jane Graham demonstrates how the transition from the conception of nonprocreative sex as sin to a more secularized and medical notion of pathology and norm accelerated in the era of the French Revolution in the legal and moral projects of the civil code and family law. The debauched sexuality of the Old Regime was contrasted with the sexual and moral self-discipline of a newly liberated people. Sarah Horowitz's essay reveals how the sexual politics of the Steinheil scandal exposed the limits of sexual self-discipline within the republican political elite. Although it was condemned by commentators on the left, the scandal may have demonstrated the bonds of sexual hypocrisy that united public and private men convinced of the inevitability of male extramarital liaisons.

Sarah Fishman's and Tamara Chaplin's essays show how, on the cusp of our own times, sexuality and gender dynamics both changed and did not change. Chaplin's study of gay and lesbian exploitation of the Minitel reveals the divergent interests of the men and women who used it: the men to pursue anonymous sex, the women to build lesbian political communities. Fishman's advice columnists in postwar women's magazines also acknowledged the gender differences in sex and courtship, in which women exercised a measure of responsibility for defending their virginity as a practical, if no longer a moral, desideratum. All these essays illustrate the weight and power of the past, even as they explore the changes that historical events have wrought on sexuality, identity, marriage, and the family.

Notes

1. Jeffrey Weeks, *What Is Sexual History?* (Cambridge: Polity, 2016), 5.
2. Rémi Lenoir, *Généalogie de la morale familiale* (Paris: Seuil, 2003), 17.
3. Lenoir, *Généalogie de la morale familiale*, 46.
4. The literature on this subject is voluminous. See Robert A. Nye, *Crime, Madness and Politics in Modern France: The Medical Concept of National Decline* (Princeton NJ: Princeton University Press, 1984); Joshua Cole, *The Power of Large Numbers: Population, Politics, and Gender in Nineteenth-Century France* (Ithaca NY: Cornell University Press, 2000); Hervé LeBras, *Marianne et les lapins: L'obsession démographique* (Paris: Olivier Orban, 1991).
5. Lenoir, *Généalogie de la morale familiale*, 85.
6. Lenoir, *Généalogie de la morale familiale*, 227.
7. In general on this point, see Geneviève Fraisse, *La muse de la raison: La démocratie exclusive and la différence des sexes* (Aix-en-Provence: Alinéa, 1989).
8. Jann Matlock, "Et si la sexualité n'avait pas d'avenir?," in *La Sexualité a-t-elle un avenir?*, ed. Pierre Fédida (Paris: Presses universitaires de France, 1999), 16.
9. Camille Robcis, *The Law of Kinship: Anthropology, Psychoanalysis, and the Family in France* (Ithaca NY: Cornell University Press, 2013), 19. On paternity and the legal evolution of the civil code, see also Rachel G. Fuchs, *Contested Paternity:*

Constructing Families in Modern France (Baltimore: Johns Hopkins University Press, 2008).

10. Françoise Héritier, *Masculin/féminine: Le pensée de la différence* (Paris: Odile Jacob, 1996), 280; Irène Théry, *Couple, filiation et parenté aujourd'hui: Le droit face aux mutations de la famille et de la vie privée* (Paris: Odile Jacob, 1998).

11. Sylviane Agacinski, *Politique des sexes* (Paris: Seuil, 2003), 40–1, 49.

12. Robcis, *The Law of Kinship*, 238. See her discussion of the bioethics debate, 216–38.

13. On these debates, see Robert A. Nye's "The Pacte Civil de Solidarité and The History of Sexuality," *French Politics, Culture & Society* 21, no. 1 (Spring 2003): 87–100; Joan W. Scott, "Comment on Robert Nye's 'Le Pacte de Solidarité and the History of Sexuality,'" *French Politics, Culture & Society* 21, no. 1 (Spring 2003): 101–5; Robcis, *The Law of Kinship*, 239–61.

14. On the unique national trajectory of French sexology, see Robert A. Nye, "The History of Sexuality in Context: National Sexological Traditions," *Science in Context*, 4, no. 2 (1991): 387–406.

15. Christine Bard, "Cinquième partie: XXe–XXIe siècle," in *Une histoire des sexualités*, ed. Sylvie Steinberg (Paris: Presses universitaires de France, 2018), 429, 434.

16. As quoted in Musab Younis, "Autumn in Paris," *London Review of Books* 41, no. 23 (December 5, 2019): 10.

17. Bard, "Cinquième partie," 461–63.

18. Roman Kuhar and David Paternotte, eds., *Anti-Gender Campaigns in Europe: Mobilizing against Equality* (London: Rowman and Littlefield, 2017).

19. Alain Corbin, Jean-Jacques Courtine, and George Vigarello, eds., *Histoire de la virilité*, 3 vols. (Paris: Seuil, 2011).

20. Steinberg, *Une histoire des sexualités*.

CONTRIBUTORS

JENNIFER ANNE BOITTIN is associate professor of French, francophone studies, and history at the Pennsylvania State University. She has authored two books: *Colonial Metropolis: The Urban Grounds of Anti-Imperialism and Feminism in Interwar Paris* (University of Nebraska Press, 2010) and *Undesirable: Passionate Mobility and Women's Defiance of French Colonial Policing, 1919–1952* (University of Chicago Press, 2022).

TAMARA CHAPLIN is associate professor of modern Europe at the University of Illinois Urbana-Champaign. She is the author of *Turning On the Mind: French Philosophers on Television* (University of Chicago Press, 2007) and coeditor of *The Global Sixties* (Routledge, 2017). Her new book, *Becoming Lesbian: A Queer History of Modern France*, is forthcoming from the University of Chicago Press.

JENNIFER J. DAVIS is associate professor of history at the University of Oklahoma and coeditor of the *Journal of Women's History*. Professor Davis published *Defining Culinary Authority: The Transformation of Cooking in France, 1650–1830* (Louisiana State University Press, 2013). Her next book reconsiders the significance of libertines in the French Atlantic world, 1619–1814 (University of Nebraska Press, forthcoming).

SARAH FISHMAN is professor of history at the University of Houston. Her research has focused on war and social change, adolescence and juvenile justice, and gender and family life in twentieth-century France. She is the author of many books and articles including, most recently, *From Vichy to the Sexual Revolution: Gender and Family Life in Postwar France* (Oxford University Press, 2017).

LISA JANE GRAHAM is Frank A. Kafker Professor and professor of history at Haverford College. She is the author of *If the King Only Knew: Seditious Speech in the Reign of Louis XV* (University of Virginia Press, 2000), as well as numerous articles and one coedited volume. She is completing a study of debauchery in the French Enlightenment from which this chapter is drawn.

JESSIE HEWITT is associate professor of history at the University of Redlands, where she teaches classes on European history, disability history, and the history of gender and sexuality. She is the author of *Institutionalizing Gender: Madness, the Family, and Psychiatric Power in Nineteenth-Century France* (Cornell University Press, 2020).

SARAH HOROWITZ is professor of history at Washington and Lee University. She has a PhD in history from the University of California, Berkeley, and is the author of *The Red Widow: The Scandal That Shook Paris—and the Woman Behind It All* (Sourcebooks, 2022) and *Friendship and Politics in Post-Revolutionary France* (Pennsylvania State University Press, 2013).

NINA KUSHNER is associate professor of history at Clark University. She is author of *Erotic Exchanges: Elite Prostitution in Eighteenth-Century France* (Cornell University Press, 2013) and coeditor of *Women and Work in Eighteenth-Century France* (Louisiana State University Press, 2014). She is coediting Bloomsbury's *Cultural History of Prostitution* and is working on a monograph on adultery and sexual culture in eighteenth-century France.

CATHY MCCLIVE is Ben Weider Associate Professor of French Revolutionary Studies at Florida State University. She is the author and editor of numerous works, including *Menstruation and Procreation in Early Modern France* (Routledge, 2015) and Marie Baudoin, *The Art of Childbirth: A Seventeenth-Century Midwife's Epistolary Text to Dr Vallant (1671)* (University of Chicago Press, 2022).

ROBERT A. NYE is Horning Professor of the Humanities and professor of history emeritus at Oregon State University, where he taught European history and the history of sexuality. He was a Harry Frank Guggenheim Fellow and a Resident Fellow at Churchill College, Cambridge University, and the Australian National University.

MICHELLE K. RHOADES is associate professor of history at Wabash College, where she teaches European history and the history of gender and sexuality. She is working on a manuscript examining sexual commerce in Bordeaux. Her previous work has appeared in *French Historical Studies* and the *Journal of Women's History*.

ANDREW ISRAEL ROSS is associate professor of history at Loyola University Maryland. He is the author of *Public City/Public Sex: Prostitution, Homosexuality, and Urban Culture in Nineteenth-Century Paris* (Temple University Press, 2019). He is currently working on a second monograph, on the campaign to abolish morals policing in fin-de-siècle Paris.

INDEX

Page numbers in italics indicate illustrations.

class. *See* elites' sexual behavior

Clit 007 (magazine), 307

Code Noir (1685), 27–28

Code Noir (1724), 29

Coffignon, Ali: *Paris-vivant*, 139–40, 148–49

Coffin, Judith, 268

Cohen, William B., 215, 216

colonies: and assimilationist ideal, 19–21, 26, 27; colonial liberties, as political term, 36n5; demographics, 37n6; legal status of slaves in, 27–29; literary idealization of sexual liberties in, 30, 31–33; repatriation regulation, 248–49, 253–54; territorial loss and death of empire, 34, 43–44n91; threats to social order in, 24–27; threats to white prestige in, 25–26, 249–52, 254–55, 258–59. *See also specific colonies*

Colwill, Elizabeth, 109

Combe, Rousseau de la: *Traité des matières criminelles*, 87

Comité d'urgence anti-répression homosexuelle (CUARH), 301

commerce. *See* sexual commerce

community formation. *See* GTS (Les Goudous Télématiques); Minitel; queer space

concubinage, 26, 27, 28, 29, 35

Confédération general du travail (CGT), 276

Confédération nationale des associations familiales catholiques, 297

Confidences (magazine), 276, 277–78, 284

confidentiality. *See* medical confidentiality

Constellation (magazine), 276, 279, 282, 287

consumer culture. *See* sexual commerce

Conti, Ange and Gaétano, 223

Conti, Giovanni, 221

Coordination lesbienne nationale, 314

Corbin, Alain, 6, 14n14, 127n24

Council of Trent (1545–63), 110

coureurs de bois, 24–25

Cox-Algit (doctor), 144–45

Crawford, Katherine, 77

crimes. *See* law and legal discourse

cruising, 137, 145, 147–48

CUARH (Comité d'urgence anti-répression homosexuelle), 301

cyberqueer history, 297–99. *See also* GTS (Les Goudous Télématiques)

Dabhoiwala, Faramerz, 38n16

Daney, Alfred, 231–34, 239n81

David et Jonathan (homosexual Christian movement), 307

Davis, Jennifer J., 124

debauchery: in political sex scandals, 199, 204; and reproduction, 110, 111; from sexual repression, 108; sodomy, 50, 77, 140; as stigmatizing label for sexual desire, 104–5, 110, 114, 117, 120–23. *See also* pederasts and pederasty; prostitutes and prostitution

Dechambre, A.: *Le médecin*, 167–68, 175, 181n16

Defert, Daniel, 308

degeneration, hereditary, 172–75, 176–78, 180

Delamarre, Marguerite, 108

D'Emilio, John, 15n16

Denis, Vincent, 79

desire. *See* sexual desire and pleasure

Desmahis, Joseph-François-Édouard de Corsembleu de, 84–85

Despeyroux, Sophie, 213

Diamond Necklace Affair, 117, 120, 129n53

Dictionnaire de l'Académie française, 85

Diday, Paul, 166, 167, 169, 170

Diderot, Denis, 83; *Encyclopédie*, 84, 85, 91, 104, 107, 111, 117; *The Nun*, 108

divorce, 111–12, 143, 157n48, 270

Doan, Laura, 178–79

doctor-patient confidentiality. *See* medical confidentiality

Dolto, Françoise: *Problèmes de petite enfance*, 274

domesticity. *See* marriage

Donovan, Brian, 249–50

Douglas, Mary, 51

menstruation: cultural anxieties about, 54–55, 56, 59, 61, 62, 63; in medical discourse, 54, 56, 57, 58, 59, 60–63; and pregnancy, 57–59, 60–61; sex during, 56–57; vs. stigmata, 51–53, 55–57, 58, 59, 60–61

mental illness: hereditary degeneration, 172–74; insanity as legal defense, 201; and institutionalization, 173, 182–83n42; lucid madness, 171; from sexual repression, 82, 108

Menuret de Chambaud, Jean-Joseph, 107–8

Merlaud, André: *Splendor of Conjugal Love*, 272

Messina, Pascal, 224

Messina, Prosper, 221, 224

Messina, Vincent, 224

métis, as term, 26

MIEL (Mouvement d'information et d'expression lesbiennes), 301–3

Minitel: and early cyberqueer history, 297–99; impact of, 295–96; launch and popularity of, 300–301; research initiative for establishing lesbian site on, 302–3. *See also* GTS

Minitel Rose, 300–301, 314

minoritizing *vs.* universalizing histories of sexuality, 4, 7, 8, 78

Mirbeau, Octave: *Diary of a Chambermaid*, 197

Mississippi colony, 24–25

Mitterrand, Danielle, 305

mixed-race relationships. *See* interracial relationships

Moheau, Jean-Baptiste, 110

Montesquieu, Charles-Louis: *The Persian Letters*, 108, 111; *The Spirit of the Laws*, 43n77

Morel, Benedict: *Traité des dégénérescences physiques*, 172, 174, 175

Mouvement adolescence guaie, 307

Mouvement d'information et d'expression lesbiennes (MIEL), 301–3

mulatto, as term, 26

Murat, Laure, 155n34

musicians, in brothels, 220–25

newspapers. *See* press

Nietzsche, Friedrich, 272

Nord, Philip G., 215

Nous Deux (magazine), 276, 278, 285

Nye, Robert A., 164, 182n37

nymphomania, 82, 109, 171

Olivia (film), 281

online community formation. *See* GTS (Les Goudous Télématiques); Minitel

orgasms, 109

Oswald, Janet, 230

OWLS (Older and Wiser Lesbians), 298

PACS (*pacte civil de solidarité*) law (1999), 323–24

Padgug, Robert A., 15n16

Parent-Duchâtelet, Alexandre Jean-Baptiste, 216

Pasqua, Charles, 301

patronage politics, 188, 189–90, 201–2

Peabody, Sue, 38n15

Peace, Mary, 82

pederasts and pederasty: as label, 133, 152n2; in legal discourse, 143, 157n48, 270, 307, 318n45; as legal grounds for divorce, 143, 157n48; in medical discourse, 142–45; surveillance of, 133–34, 137–39, 140–42, 146–50; visual recognition of, 139–40, 142

Peel, Mark, 220

Pelletier, Madeleine, 288

Penal Code: Article 330, 140; Article 378, 164, 165, 175

Pereire, Anita, 282–83

Périssol, Guillaume, 291n44

Pernoud, Laurence, 279

Pestre, Abbé Jean, 104, 112

Peverelly, Louis, 242–43, 248–49

Phelizon, Michel, 276

Pinel, Casimir, 175

Pinel, Philippe, 174–75

women's sexuality: confused and naive stereotype, 59–61, 62–63, 167; deceitful stereotype, 60, 62, 63; domesticated role in marriage, 81, 82, 83–84, 109, 114–15, 116–19, 123, 257–59; double standard of, 33, 179, 267, 280, 281, 283–84; emotional stereotype, 256–59, 261; good/bad binary in legal discourse, 86–90; independent mobility as threat to patriarchy, 246, 249–51, 252, 254–55, 258–59, 260–61; judicial weaponization of, 53–54, 61–63; lustful stereotype, 81–83, 120–23; luxury and extravagance stereotype of, 116–17; and male gaze, 137; and medical confidentiality practices, 165, 166–67, 171–72, 179; medical discourse on sexual desire of, 81–83, 108–9, 120; men as arbiters of acceptable, 279–80, 283–85; open representation of, in postwar popular culture, 280–81; passivity stereotype, 245, 246, 252, 253. See also homosexuality; lesbians and lesbianism; marriage; menstruation; prostitutes and prostitution; reproduction; unchaste women

Wood, Sharon, 235

Young Christian Student Movement (Jeunesse étudiante chrétienne, JEC), 272
Young Christian Workers (Jeunesses ouvrières chrétiennes, JOC), 271
Young Female Christian Workers (Jeunesses ouvrières chrétiennes féminines, JOCF), 271

Zola, Émile: *Nana*, 197

www.ingramcontent.com/pod-product-compliance
Lightning Source LLC
Chambersburg PA
CBHW021111270326
41929CB00009B/825